Exchange Rate Management under Uncertai

edited by Jagdeep S. Bhandari

The MIT Press
Cambridge, Massachusetts
London, England

First MIT Press paperback edition, 1987

This book was set in Times New Roman by Asco Trade Typesetting Ltd., Hong Kong and printed and bound by The Murray Printing Company in the United States of America.

Library of Congress Cataloging in Publication Data
Main entry under title:

Exchange rate management under uncertainty.

  Bibliography: p.
  Includes index.
  1. Foreign exchange—Mathematical models—Addresses, essays, lectures.   2. Foreign exchange administration—Mathematical models—Addresses, essays, lectures.
3. Uncertainty—Mathematical models—Addresses, essays, lectures.   4. Rational expectations (Economic theory)—Addresses, essays, lectures.   I. Bhandari, Jagdeep S.
HG3823.E9   1985   332.4'5'0724   84-21822
ISBN 0-262-02210-9 hard
ISBN 0-262-52122-9 paper

Contents

Foreword

The world shift to floating exchange rates in 1973 has revolutionized academic thinking with respect to both exchange rate determination and the management of open economies operating with flexible exchange rates. It is fair to say that most professional economists welcomed the introduction of flexible exchange rates, and a number of them had been prominent in urging the change, against the instincts of many businessmen and officials then in office. But as the subsequent outpouring of academic work has demonstrated, this professional support hardly rested on a thorough examination of the workings of a system of flexible exchange rates. It was much more a case of declaring a second performer the winner in a singing contest after hearing the first performer sing. The weaknesses of the Bretton Woods system of quasi-fixed exchange rates had become manifest, especially in the presence of the possibility of large movements of capital across national boundaries. That system was clearly doomed. To this realization were added certain simple—now generally recognized to be simplistic—and appealing analytical propositions concerning the workings of a system of flexible exchange rates. But in retrospect it is clear that the economics profession treated the then-hypothetical system of flexible exchange rates all too casually.

Economists have long been uneasy about the absence of forward-looking expectations in their models of national economies. Indeed, half a century ago Keynes offered an extensive discussion of forward-looking behavior in his *General Theory*, but it was used to justify some of the functional relationships in his theory rather than being formally incorporated into the theory. Forward-looking behavior is clearly important when it comes to expectations about future price levels, and it could not be avoided when it came to free market determination of an exchange rate between currencies in which capital movements play an important role. It is no accident, then, that what is now called rational expectations was introduced first (by Stanley Black in 1973) into the macroeconomic literature via the exchange rate. Since then it has been applied much less appropriately, in my view, to many other economic variables as well.

Economic analysis of exchange rates has moved from a partial equilibrium approach to exchange markets through the simple monetarist focus on long-run equilibrium rates (too often with the implication or assertion that that also represents short-run equilibrium as well) to the more sophisticated approach represented in this volume, treating the exchange rate as one of several endogenous variables in a necessarily simple general equilibrium system with dynamic properties that permit tracing its value from the time of initial disturbance to the time that it settles down to a new long-run equilibrium. This more sophisticated approach has been made possible by the increasing mathematical sophistication of economists, particularly in dealing with differential equations. This greater mathematical sophistication regrettably also widens the communications gap between those on the frontiers of analytical work and the many others who are interested in the subject of exchange rate determination but are not equipped with the appropriate mathematical skills.

These dynamic general equilibrium models substantiate the view, long recognized by practitioners, that exchange rates can overshoot their long-term equilibrium values in response to some new disturbance. It is yet another illustration in economics of Le Chatelier's principle, that when flexibility is constrained in some part of an interdependent system, for example, wages or prices are slow in adjusting to new circumstances, those variables that are flexible will respond at first to an even greater extent than they would if the constrained variables were also freely flexible.

Virtually all of the papers assembled here adopt the assumption of rational expectations, which might more accurately be labeled stochastic perfect foresight. The analytical attractions of this assumption are obvious. If we quite reasonably want to allow expectations to affect current decisions but have no independent model of how expectations are formed, why should we not simply assume that expectations are always statistically accurate, so that observations for any period $t + 1$ can be substituted for the expectation of that variable in period t? The formulae are greatly simplified by this assumption. Moreover, it has the happy implication that that is precisely what people would expect if they had full information on the workings of the economic system in question.

The difficulty with this assumption is that it may be fundamentally wrong without our being aware of it. It is not refutable. Some set of expectations can always be found which, when applied to the information available at time t, can "explain" the values of all endogenous variables actually observed at time $t + 1$. So far the search by economists for underlying models that accomplish this feat has proved consistently unsuccessful. But it is easier to reject the proffered model than to reject the analytically convenient and attractive assumption of stochastically perfect foresight. The inability of to find appropriate models should cast considerable doubt on the validity of the assumption as applied to firms and households making economic decisions. At a minimum, it places extraordinary faith in the inarticulate intuition of these ordinary economic agents. Economists should be wary of falling into convenient habits of thought and analysis that, while rich in analytical results, offer such little real explanatory power for the economic events they are supposedly studying.

It is a considerable merit of the papers assembled in this volume that they go beyond the perfect foresight aspect of rational expectations and focus on its stochastic aspects. The analysis explores the variability of the entities in which we are interested (for example, output and prices) in relation to the variability of various external disturbances to the system under examination. Focus on these stochastic attributes greatly complicates the analysis, and preserving analytical tractability often dictates great simplification of the real side of the economy. As a result, most of the papers treat economic output rather perfunctorily—either by assuming it is constant or by assuming that it varies endogenously only in response to violations of price expectations. In short, the so-called Lucas supply function is frequently used to characterize real output, even though it excludes by assumption most of what has been of concern to students of the business cycle. The real side of the economy clearly needs to be developed further if we are to gain full understanding of exchange rate determination and the implications of alternative exchange rate policies.

Even in this simplified world, few if any simple generalizations survive all model formulations. This world is full of what would once have been considered perverse cases. It offers much greater complexity and richness of results. Anything can happen, depending most intimately not only on the nature of exogenous disturbances, long known, but also on the assumed rigidities in the system (for example, the exact nature of wage contracts) and on the exact distribution of timely information among the decision-making agents.

The normal recourse of an empirical science in the presence of a plethora of conflicting theoretical results is to look for empirical verification or rejection, to limit the field of possible outcomes. But that is difficult in the case of these models, where diverse results are due not so much to values of the structural coefficients (although they of course play a role) as to the nature of the exogenous disturbances, which are often not directly observable, and to the assumed importance of forward-looking expectations, which are also not directly observable. As noted, the assumption of perfect stochastic foresight, which is crucial for the results of the models, is surely an inaccurate description of reality but is not directly testable in these models. We need direct theorizing about, information on, and testing of models on the formation of expectations, an effort that would take economics into the realm of social and even individual psychology.

This volume offers essays that explore the frontiers of exchange rate determination and open economy macroeconomics. It is a sign of the fluidity and unsettledness of these fields that these essays produce quite different intervention rules for monetary authorities, depending on the precise objectives they are pursuing, on the precise assumptions with respect to the model structure, and on the nature of the disturbances. All agree on one point, however: freely floating exchange rates are almost never optimal. Optimal policy involves some kind of exchange market intervention by the monetary authorities, and under some circumstances even a commitment to fixed exchange rates proves to be optimal policy.

It is not possible in a brief foreword to summarize all of the contributions, particularly since their conclusions depend in a crucial way on the particular assumptions made by the authors. But these papers do foreshadow two developments that are likely to receive much more attention in future work. The first is the focus on the stochastic properties, and particularly the variances, of the exogenous disturbances impacting on the economic system, and the influence of these variances in turn on such economic objectives as output variation or price forecasting error under alternative policy regimes—in this volume, mainly alternative foreign exchange intervention rules.

The second is the attention drawn to the crucial importance for economic performance, at least in stochastic perfect foresight models, of who has exactly what information when. If some parties have better contemporaneous information than others, that will influence the overall performance of the economy because the poorly informed are left to infer what is happening from the behavior of the better informed. A practical question arises from this observation: is it always better to provide to economic agents additional information even when full information is not available? Second best theory suggests that it may not always be preferable to add additional information. Additional information may improve the results, but under some circumstances it may lead to inferences that worsen results, when the structure of disturbances and their relations to one another are unknown. Additional but still incomplete information could lead to one of the numerous rational expectations equilibrium paths that is farther from the optimal path than would be true without the additional information. The paper by the editor of this volume offers an example where more information does not bring the economy closer to the full information outcome. This important topic deserves to be developed much further.

All in all, the volume offers a stimulating collection of original current work on economic management under flexible exchange rates in the presence of uncertainty, and it can fruitfully be mined by professionals and graduate students alike.

Richard N. Cooper
Harvard University

Acknowledgments

This project has been a long undertaking for me, and in the process I have run up substantial intellectual deficits against several persons. I am of course grateful to all the contributors to this volume for their patience and cooperation. In particular, I wish to mention Jon Eaton, Richard Marston, Stanley Black, Michael Mussa, and Jerome Stein. I also wish to thank Richard Cooper, who made time from an extremely busy schedule to write the foreword. Jacob Frenkel has always been unfailingly generous with his support, and this instance is no exception, despite the fact that the vagaries of a complicated production schedule made it impossible for me to include his paper in this particular volume.

To Stephen Turnovsky I owe a special debt. Indeed, without his help the volume might never have been possible.

This is the second occasion on which I have dealt with the MIT Press. And, if I were not certain earlier, I am now convinced that I could not have had a better publisher. Every author should be so fortunate as to work with Robert Bolick, Economics Editor *extraordinaire*.

Exchange Rate Management under Uncertainty

1 Official Intervention and Exchange Rate Dynamics

Michael L. Mussa

1. Introduction and Summary

This chapter investigates the effects of policies of official intervention designed to moderate movements of nominal and real exchange rates in the context of a dynamic model of price level and exchange rate determination. The policies considered are policies of nonsterilized intervention under which the foreign exchange reserve component of the money supply is adjusted up or down in response to changes in the nominal or real exchange rate in accord with a well-defined intervention rule. In analyzing the effects of these policies, it is assumed that economic agents have rational expectations about the future behavior of prices and exchange rate, in the sense that their expectations take account of the true structure of the dynamic system determining the behavior of prices and the exchange rate and of the intervention rule followed by the government authorities.

The model of price and exchange rate dynamics that provides the basis for this investigation is described and analyzed in section 2. It is a modified version of Dornbusch's (1976) familiar model of exchange rate dynamics in which the nominal exchange rate is a freely flexible variable whose value at each instant of time must be consistent with money market equilibrium, interest rate parity, and rationality of expectations concerning the future rate of change of the exchange rate, and in which the domestic price level is a slowly adjusting variable that responds gradually to the extent of disequilibrium as measured by the existing deviation from purchasing power parity, as well as to the expected rate of change of its own equilibrium value. This model is solved in its general form for arbitrarily specified paths of the exogenous forcing variables, which include the world interest rate, the world price level, the domestic credit and foreign exchange components of the domestic money supply, and a shift parameter in the demand for domestic money. This general solution reveals that the equilibrium values of the logarithms of the domestic price level and the exchange rate depend on a discounted sum of expected future differences between the logarithms of the supply of domestic money and the exogenous component of the demand to hold domestic money. It also reveals that the existing state of disequilibrium, as measured by the current deviation from purchasing power parity, depends on a backward-looking discounted sum of past disturbances resulting from unexpected changes in the equilibrium value of the domestic price level that are induced by changes in expectations concerning the behavior of the exogenous forcing variables that determine the equilibrium value of the domestic price level.[1]

This model of price and exchange rate dynamics is used in section 3 to investigate a policy of leaning against the wind under which the authorities intervene through variations in the foreign exchange reserve component of the money supply to resist changes in the nominal exchange rate.[2] It is shown that this intervention policy is likely to reduce the volatility of the nominal exchange rate but that it may either increase or reduce the volatility of the domestic price level and the extent of disequilibrium, as measured by the deviation from purchasing power parity. These results reflect the effects of the intervention policy on the sensitivity of the exchange rate and the domestic price level to internal disturbances resulting from changes in expectations about the exogenous factors affecting the demand and supply of domestic money and to external disturbances associated with unexpected changes in the world price level. In general the intervention rule reduces the sensitivity of the exchange rate to both types of disturbances but reduces the sensitivity of the domestic price level to internal disturbances while increasing its sensitivity to external disturbances. The overall effect of the intervention policy on the stability of the economic system, as measured by the average extent of disequilibrium, depends on the relative importance of internal and external disturbances as sources of instability.

In section 4, it is shown that an intervention policy that resists movements of the real exchange rate, in contrast to movements of the nominal exchange rate, will always reduce the average extent of disequilibrium. The implicit assumption under which this result is derived is that the equilibrium value of the real exchange rate is constant at the level defined by the requirement of purchasing power parity. When allowance is made for a varying equilibrium value of the real exchange rate, the possibility arises that an intervention rule that resists movements of the real exchange rate will increase the average extent of disequilibrium if real disturbances associated with changes in the equilibrium value of the real exchange rate are generally more important than internal monetary disturbances in affecting the equilibrium value of the domestic price level and if the intervention authorities do not have a reliable means for estimating changes in the equilibrium value of the real exchange rate.

This chapter concludes, in section 5, with a discussion of some of the limitations and important underlying assumptions of this analysis of the effects of official intervention policies.

2. Model of Exchange Rate and Price Level Dynamics

To provide the basis for the analysis of alternative policies of official intervention in the foreign exchange market, it is useful to consider a slightly modified version of Dornbusch's (1976) model of exchange rate dynamics. Suppose that the condition for money market equilibrium in a small, open economy is described by the requirement,

$$m = k + p - h \cdot i \tag{1}$$

where m is the logarithm of the domestic nominal money supply, k represents the exogenous factors affecting the logarithm of domestic money demand, p is the logarithm of the domestic price level, i is the domestic nominal interest rate, and $h > 0$ is the interest semielasticity of money demand. The balance sheet constraint of the banking system implies that

$$m = d + f \tag{2}$$

where d is the logarithm of the domestic credit assets of the banking system and f is the logarithm of one plus the ratio of foreign exchange reserves to domestic credit assets of the banking system. The domestic nominal interest rate is linked to the world nominal interest rate, i^*, through the interest parity condition,

$$i = i^* + D^e(e) \tag{3}$$

where $D^e(e(t)) = E[(e(t + 1) - e(t)); t]$ is the expected rate of change of the exchange rate conditional on currently available information, with e defined as the logarithm of the price of a unit of world money in terms of domestic money. The world nominal interest rate is equal to the exogenously determined world real interest rate, r^*, plus the expected rate of change of the exogenously determined world price level;

$$i^* = r^* + D^e(p^*) \tag{4}$$

where p^* denotes the logarithm of the world price level in terms of world money. Substituting equations (2), (3), and (4) into (1) and solving for $D^e(e)$, it follows that the expected rate of change of the exchange rate must be consistent with the condition

$$D^e(e) = (1/h) \cdot [p - f - z] - D^e(p^*) \tag{5}$$

where

$$z = d - k + h \cdot r^*. \tag{6}$$

Since the exchange rate is a freely adjusting variable at each moment of time, the actual rate of change of the exchange rate, $D(e(t)) = e(t + 1) - e(t)$, may or may not equal its expected rate of change, $D^e(e)$. In contrast, the price level is assumed to be a slowly adjusting variable whose rate of change between t and $t + 1$ is predetermined in period t in accord with the rule

$$D(p) = b \cdot (e + p^* - p) + D^e(e + p^*), \, 0 < b < 1. \tag{7}$$

In this price adjustment rule, $e + p^*$ measures the equilibrium value of p, as determined by purchasing power parity, and b is the speed of adjustment of the price level in response to deviations from purchasing power parity. The additional term in the price adjustment rule, $D^e(e + p^*)$, allows the price level to adjust in anticipation of expected changes in its equilibrium value and thereby ensures that disequilibrium, as measured by the deviation from purchasing power parity, is not expected to grow over time. The actual extent of disequilibrium will grow between t and $t + 1$ only if the unexpected change in $e + p^*$, denoted by $D^u(e(t) + p^*(t))$ $= (e(t + 1) + p^*(t + 1)) - E[(e(t + 1) + p^*(t + 1)); t]$, outweighs the effect of the adjustment term, $b \cdot (e(t) + p^*(t) - p(t))$, in reducing the already existing disequilibrium at time t.[3]

Under the assumption of rational expectations, the expected time paths of p and e, conditional on information available at a given date, must be consistent with the difference equations (5) and (7), with the expected paths of z, f, and p^* treated as exogenous. Ignoring for notational simplicity the distinction between actual and expected values of variables, the dynamic system implied by these difference equations may be written as

$$\begin{bmatrix} -b - D & b + D \\ 1/h & -D \end{bmatrix} \cdot \begin{bmatrix} p \\ e \end{bmatrix} = \begin{bmatrix} -b \cdot p^* - D(p^*) \\ (1/h) \cdot (z + f) + D(p^*) \end{bmatrix} \tag{8}$$

where D is the forward difference operator. The characteristic roots of this dynamic system are

$$\lambda_1 = 1/h \quad \text{and} \quad \lambda_2 = -b. \tag{9}$$

Since this dynamic system has one forward-looking and one backward-looking dynamic process, this pattern of characteristic roots, one positive and one negative, guarantees that the system has a unique nonexplosive solution for the expected values of the price level and the exchange rate at any date $s \geq t$, conditional on information available at time t specifically,

$$p(s) = F(s) + [p(t) - F(t)] \cdot (1 - b)^{s-t} \tag{10}$$

$$e(s) = F(s) - p^*(s) - (1/hb) \cdot [p(t) - F(t)] \cdot (1 - b)^{s-t} \tag{11}$$

where

$$F(s) = (1 - \theta) \cdot \sum_{j=0}^{\infty} \theta^j \cdot [z(s+j) + f(s+j)] \tag{12}$$

with $\theta = h/(1 + h)$. It is understood that all of these results apply to conditional expectations based on information available at time t (the conditional expectation operator, $E(\ ; t)$, has been everywhere suppressed as a matter of t notational convenience).

In these results, $E(F(s); t)$ represents the expected value of the equilibrium price level at time s, based on information at time t. $F(s)$ itself is the discounted sum of current and future values of $z + f = d - k + h \cdot r^* + f$, which measure differences between the logarithm of the nominal money supply, $m = d + f$, and the exogenous components of the logarithm of money demand, $k - h \cdot r^*$. The discount factor can be expressed in the form

$$\theta = 1/[1 + (1/h)], \tag{13}$$

which makes it apparent that the characteristic root $\lambda_1 = 1/h$ plays a role in determining the expected equilibrium price level that is analogous to the role of the interest rate in the usual formula for discounted present value. It is noteworthy that the expression for the equilibrium price level that is defined by $F(s)$ is essentially the same as the expression for the equilibrium price level derived in Cagan's model of inflationary dynamics under the assumption of rational expectations.[4]

The expected equilibrium exchange rate in (11) is represented by

$F(s) - p^*(s)$. This is consistent with the idea embodied in the specification of the price adjustment rule that purchasing power parity defines the equilibrium relationship of the domestic price level, the exchange rate, and the world price level. The expected path of the divergence from purchasing power parity is given by

$$e(s) + p^*(s) - p(s) = -(1 + (1/hb)) \cdot [p(t) - F(t)] \cdot (1 - b)^{s-t}. \tag{14}$$

From this result it is apparent that the characteristic root $\lambda_2 = -b$ determines the rate at which the divergence from purchasing power parity is expected to decay with the passage of time.

The initial divergence from purchasing power parity at time t depends on the divergence between the actual price level, $p(t)$, which is predetermined by past events, and the equilibrium price level, $E(F(t);t)$, which reflects a discounted sum of current and expected future differences between the nominal money supply and the exogenous factors affecting money demand. The difference between $p(t)$ and $F(t)$ is reflected one for one in the initial deviation of the actual price level from its own equilibrium value and is reflected with a factor $-1/hb$ in the initial deviation of the exchange rate from its equilibrium value. Since the initial exchange rate at time t is a freely adjustable variable, the initial deviation of the exchange rate from its equilibrium value is not predetermined by past events. Rather, the deviation of $e(t)$ from its equilibrium value of $E(F(t);t) - p^*(t)$ is determined by the requirement for nonexplosive paths for the expected price level and the expected exchange rate subsequent to time t. Specifically, if the initial exchange rate were set at any value other than

$$e(t) = E(F(t);t) - p^*(t) - (1/hb) \cdot [p(t) - E(F(t);t)] \tag{15}$$

then the solutions for the expected paths of the price level and the exchange rate would necessarily include an explosive term of the form $A \cdot (1/\theta)^{s-t}$ where

$$A = e(t) - [E(F(t);t) - p^*(t) - (1/hb) \cdot [p(t) - E(F(t);t)]]. \tag{16}$$

Choice of the initial exchange rate to exclude this explosive term is justified by the argument that the equilibrium values of p and e should not be expected to exhibit exponentially explosive behavior independent of the expected behavior of the exogenous forcing variables that ought to influence the evolution of the equilibrium price level and exchange rate.[5]

The nature of the requirement that determines the initial exchange rate

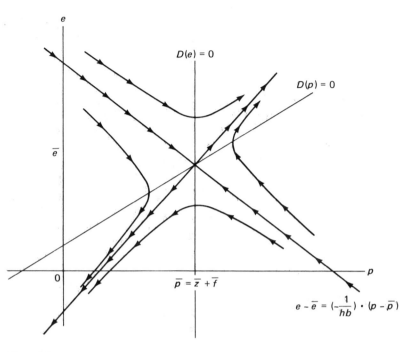

Figure 1.1
Adjustment path of price level and exchange rate

is illustrated in figure 1.1 for the case in which the exogenous forcing variables, $z, f,$ and p^*, are expected to remain constant at the values $\bar{z}, \bar{f},$ and $\bar{p}^*$. The vertical line along which $p = \bar{z} + \bar{f}$ shows the combinations of p and e for which the expected rate of change of the exchange rate, $D^e(e) = (1/h) \cdot (p - f - z) - D^e(p^*)$, is equal to zero. To the right of this line $D^e(e)$ is >0, and to the left of this line $D^e(e)$ is <0. The line along which $e = [1 - (1/hb)] \cdot p - \bar{p}^* + (1/hb) \cdot (\bar{z} + \bar{f})$ shows the combinations of p and e for which the rate of change of the price level, $D(p) = b \cdot (e + p^* - p) + D^e(e + p^*)$, is equal to zero.[6] Above this line $D(p)$ is >0, and below this line $D(p)$ is <0. The intersection of these two lines occurs at the long-run equilibrium point where $p = \bar{p} = \bar{z} + \bar{f}$ and $e = \bar{e} = \bar{p} - \bar{p}^*$. Consistent with the fact that the dynamic system determining the expected evolution of p and e has one stable and one unstable characteristic root, there is a unique stable branch in figure 1.1 that corresponds to the line along which $e - \bar{e} = (-1/hb) \cdot (p - \bar{p})$. For a given initial price level $p(t)$, if the initial exchange rate is chosen so that $e(t) = \bar{e} - (1/hb) \cdot (p(t) - \bar{p})$,

then the economy starts out at a point on this stable branch, and subsequently the point corresponding to $(p(s), e(s))$ moves along this stable
branch toward the long-run equilibrium point $(\bar{p}, \bar{e})$ at a rate equal to
the speed of adjustment of the price level in response to deviations from
purchasing power parity. For any other choice of the initial exchange
rate, the subsequent path of $(p(s), e(s))$ would not converge to the long-run
equilibrium point $(\bar{p}, \bar{e})$. The deviation from purchasing power parity
would still be eliminated at a rate equal to the speed of response of the
price level to deviations from purchasing power parity, as indicated by
the convergence the path of $(p(s), e(s))$ toward the line along which
$e = p - \bar{p}^*$. However, a common factor $A \cdot (1/\theta)^{s-t}$ in the solutions for
both $p(s)$ and $e(s)$ would drive the point $(p(s), e(s))$ further and further
away from the long-run equilibrium point. Choice of $e(t)$ so as to place
the initial point $(p(t), e(t))$ on the stable branch eliminates this explosive
bubble from the solution paths for $p(s)$ and $e(s)$.

If there were no alterations in expectations concerning the behavior of
the exogenous forcing variables z, f, and p^* due to new information
received with the passage of time, then the actual paths of p and e would
follow the expected paths described by (10) and (11). More generally,
however, alterations of expectations due to new information will induce
divergences between the actual behavior of p and e and the behavior that
was expected on the basis of previously available information. The relationship between the actual and expected behavior of p and e and the
role of new information in inducing divergences between the actual and
expected behavior of these variables is conveniently analyzed by decom-
posing the actual change in each of these variables between t and $t + 1$
into its expected and unexpected components.

The relevant expressions for the expected component of the changes in
the price level and the exchange rate are obtained immediately from the
results that describe the expected paths of p and e; specifically,

$$D^e(p(t)) = D^e(F(t)) - b \cdot [p(t) - E(F(t); t)] \tag{17}$$

$$D^e(e(t)) = D^e(F(t)) - D^e(p^*(t)) + (b/hb) \cdot [p(t) - E(F(t); t)] \tag{18}$$

where $D^e(F(t)) = E[(F(t + 1) - F(t)); t]$ is the expected change in the
common element in the equilibrium price level and the equilibrium exchange rate, as given by

$$D^e(F(t)) = (1 - \theta) \cdot \sum_{j=0}^{\infty} \theta^j \cdot E[D(z(t + j) + f(t + j)); t]$$

$$= (1 - \theta) \cdot [E(F(t + 1); t) - E(z(t) + f(t); t)] \qquad (19)$$

$$= [(1 - \theta)/\theta] \cdot [E(F(t); t) - E(z(t) + f(t); t)].$$

In addition to $D^e(F(t))$, the expected change in p is affected by the expected convergence of the price level toward its equilibrium value, as represented in the term $-b \cdot [p(t) - E(F(t); t)]$. The analogous term in the expression for the expected change in the exchange rate, $(b/hb) \cdot [p(t) - E(F(t); t)]$, represents the expected convergence of e toward its equilibrium value. The expected change in the equilibrium value of e includes the term $-D^e(p^*(t))$, as well as the term $D^e(F(t))$, because the exchange rate is expected to adjust in order to absorb changes in the world price level.

Since the price level is assumed to be a slowly adjusting variable whose rate of change between t and $t + 1$ is predetermined at time t, unexpected events occurring between t and $t + 1$ have no effect on the price level in $t + 1$. In other words the actual change in the price level, $D(p(t)) = p(t + 1) - p(t)$, is equal to the expected change in the price level, $D^e(p(t))$, as determined by (17). Unexpected events occurring between t and $t + 1$, however, do affect the equilibrium price level at $t + 1$, as indicated by the expression for the unexpected change in the equilibrium price level,

$$D^u(F(t)) = E(F(t + 1); t + 1) - E(F(t + 1); t)$$

$$\qquad\qquad\qquad\qquad (20)$$

$$= (1 - \theta) \cdot \sum_{j=0}^{\infty} \theta^j \cdot D^u(z(t + j) + f(t + j))$$

where $D^u(z(t + j) + f(t + j)) = E[(z(t + j + 1) + f(t + j + 1)); t + 1] - E[(z(t + j + 1) + f(t + j + 1); t]$. It is apparent that the source of the unexpected change in the equilibrium price level is new information received between t and $t + 1$ that alters expectations concerning the future behavior of the exogenous forcing variables, z and f, that are relevant for determining the equilibrium price level.

While new information that induces unexpected changes in the equilibrium price level has no immediate effect on the actual price level, it does have an immediate effect on the exchange rate, as indicated by the expression for the unexpected change in the exchange rate,

$$D^u(e(t)) = [1 + (1/hb)] \cdot D^u(F(t)) - D^u(p^*(t)). \qquad (21)$$

An unexpected change in $F(t)$ has more than a one-for-one effect on the exchange rate because $D^u(F(t))$ not only affects the equilibrium exchange rate on a one-for-one basis, it also affects the divergence between the equilibrium price level and the actual price level, and part of this effect spills over onto the exchange rate. This spillover effect is essentially Dornbusch's overshooting effect. As Dornbusch (1976) explains, when the equilibrium price level rises due to a permanent, unexpected increase in the money supply, the exchange rate initially rises more than proportionately in response to the increase in the money supply. This is because with the actual price level temporarily fixed, the increase in the money supply forces a reduction in the domestic nominal interest rate to maintain money market equilibrium. Maintenance of money market equilibrium with a lower domestic interest rate requires the expectation of a negative rate of change of e relative to what was expected before the money supply increase. For this expectation to be rational, it is necessary that the actual exchange rate rise by more than the equilibrium exchange rate in response to the money supply increase in order to allow for a subsequent decline of the exchange rate toward its new equilibrium value.

Finally, it is important to note the role of unexpected changes in the equilibrium price level in determining the extent of disequilibrium, as measured by the deviation from purchasing power parity,

$$v(t) = e(t) + p^*(t) - p(t) = [1 + (1/hb)] \cdot [E(F(t);t) - p(t)]. \tag{22}$$

The evolution of $v(t)$ is determined by the difference equation

$$D(v(t)) = -b \cdot v(t) + [1 + (1/hb)] \cdot D^u(F(t)). \tag{23}$$

The term $-b \cdot v(t)$ in this equation reflects the elimination of existing disequilibrium through the expected convergence of p and e toward their respective equilibrium values. The term $[1 + (1/hb)] \cdot D^u(F(t))$ is the innovation to disequilibrium resulting from unexpected change in the common element in the equilibrium price level and exchange rate. The solution of (23), given by

$$v(t) = \sum_{j=0}^{\infty} (1 - b)^j \cdot [1 + (1/hb)] \cdot D^u(F(t - j - 1)), \tag{24}$$

indicates that $v(t)$ depends on a discounted sum of past disturbances resulting from unexpected changes in the equilibrium price level.

3. Effects of Leaning against the Wind

An important objective of official intervention in the foreign exchange market is to moderate movements of the exchange rate and especially to limit movements of the exchange rate away from its economically appropriate value as indicated, for example, by purchasing power parity. A widely employed intervention policy for moderating exchange rate movements is a policy of leaning against the wind under which the authorities intervene in the foreign exchange market to oppose changes in the exchange rate, especially changes that they view as economically inappropriate. In general such a policy might be carried out by means of sterilized intervention, which has no effect on the domestic money supply. However, since the model of price and exchange rate dynamics described in section 2 embodies no mechanism through which sterilized intervention can affect the exchange rate of any other economic variable, the present analysis will focus on a policy of leaning against the wind implemented through nonsterilized intervention.[7] Specifically we will consider the effects of an intervention rule under which the foreign exchange reserve component of the money supply is changed in accord with the rule

$$f(t) = f(t-1) - \alpha \cdot (e(t) - e(t-1)). \tag{25}$$

In this rule, $\alpha > 0$ measures the strength of the intervention policy; the greater is α, the greater is the resistance offered by the authorities against movements in the exchange rate.

If the intervention policy (25) is expected to remain in force from period t onward, then the expected value of $f(s)$ for any $s \geq t$, based on information available at time t, must satisfy

$$E(f(s); t) = -\alpha \cdot E(e(s); t) + \alpha \cdot e(t-1) + f(t-1). \tag{26}$$

Taking this into account in the dynamic equations (5) and (7), it follows that the dynamic system that governs the evolution of the expected values of $p(s)$ and $e(s)$, conditional on information available at time t, can be written as

$$\begin{bmatrix} -b-D & b+D \\ 1/h & (\alpha/h)-D \end{bmatrix} \cdot \begin{bmatrix} p \\ e \end{bmatrix} = \begin{bmatrix} -b \cdot p^* - D(p^*) \\ (1/h) \cdot (z+u) + D(p^*) \end{bmatrix} \tag{27}$$

where $u = \alpha \cdot e(t-1) + f(t-1)$, which is predetermined at time t. The characteristic roots of this dynamic system are

$$\lambda_1 = (1 + \alpha)/h \qquad \text{and} \qquad \lambda_2 = -b. \tag{28}$$

Since this dynamic system, like the dynamic system (8), has one forward-looking and one backward-looking dynamic process, this pattern of characteristic roots, one positive and one negative, guarantees that the system has a unique nonexplosive solution for the expected values of $p(s)$ and $e(s)$ at any date $s \geq t$, conditional on the information available at time t. Suppressing the conditional expectations operator, $E(\ ; t)$, this solution is given by

$$p(s) = G(s) + [p(t) - G(t)] \cdot (1 - b)^{s-t} \tag{29}$$

$$e(s) = G(s) - p^*(s) - (1/(hb + \alpha)) \cdot [p(t) - G(t)] \cdot (1 - b)^{s-t} \tag{30}$$

where

$$G(s) = (1 - \mu) \cdot \sum_{j=0}^{\infty} \mu^j \cdot (1/(1 + \alpha)) \cdot [z(s + j) + u + \alpha \cdot p^*(s + j)] \tag{31}$$

with $\mu = h/(1 + h + \alpha)$.

In these results, $E(G(s); t)$ plays the same role as $E(F(s); t)$ in the earlier results (10) and (11) for the case of no official intervention; that is, $E(G(s); t)$ represents the expected value of the equilibrium price level at time s, based on information available at time t. Moreover the general form of $G(s)$ is the same as the general form of $F(s)$; both are discounted sums of the current and future values of the exogenous forcing variables that are relevant for determining the expected equilibrium price level. There are, however, three important differences between $G(s)$ and $F(s)$.

First, the discount factor μ in $G(s)$ is smaller than the discount factor θ in $F(s)$. This is so because the discount rate that is inversely related to the discount factor in both cases is equal to the positive characteristic root of the relevant dynamic system. In the absence of official intervention, this positive characteristic root is $1/h$, and, correspondingly, the discount factor θ, as given by (13), is equal to $1/[1 + (1/h)]$. With the intervention rule (25), the positive characteristic root becomes $(1 + \alpha)/h$, and the discount factor is given by

$$\mu = 1/[1 + ((1 + \alpha)/h)] < \theta. \tag{32}$$

Clearly the stronger is the intervention policy (the greater is α), the smaller will be the discount factor μ, and hence the smaller will be the weight assigned to future forcing variables, relative to current forcing variables, in determining the expected equilibrium price level (and exchange rate).

Second, in $G(s)$ the exogenous forcing variable $z(s + j)$, which measures the logarithmic difference between the domestic credit component of the money supply, $d(s + j)$, and the exogenous component of money demand, $k(s + j) - h \cdot r^*(s + j)$, is multiplied by a factor $1/(1 + \alpha)$, whereas in $F(s)$ this exogenous forcing variable is multiplied by a factor of unity. It follows that changes in the average expected level of z have a smaller effect on the expected equilibrium price level (and exchange rate) under the intervention policy (25) than they have in the absence of official intervention, with this effect becoming smaller and smaller as the intervention policy becomes stronger and stronger. The reason is that under the intervention policy (25), the effect on the equilibrium price level and exchange rate of changes in z is partially offset by changes in f (which imply offsetting changes in m), with this offset becoming greater the greater is α.

Third, the expected path of the world price level p^* has an effect on the expected equilibrium domestic price level under the intervention policy (25) but has no such effect in the absence of official intervention. The reason is that under the intervention policy (25), the foreign exchange reserve component of the domestic money supply is altered in response to all variations in the exchange rate, including variations needed to absorb changes in the world price level. Since changes in the world price level affect the domestic money supply through this policy of nonsterilized intervention, the expected path of the world price level affects the expected equilibrium path of the domestic price level.

The requirement of purchasing power parity as a condition for long-run equilibrium is reflected in the fact that the expected path of the equilibrium exchange rate is determined by $G(s) - p^*(s)$. The expected deviation of the exchange rate from this expected equilibrium value, $-(1/(hb + \alpha)) \cdot [p(t) - G(t)] \cdot (1 - b)^{s-t}$, is proportional to the expected deviation of the price level from its equilibrium value, $[p(t) - G(t)] \cdot (1 - b)^{s-t}$, with a factor of proportionality $-(1/(hb + \alpha))$ that is determined by the requirement for a nonexplosive solution for the expected paths of the price level and the exchange rate. The extent of these expected deviations from equilibrium depends on the initial deviation of $p(t)$ from its equilibrium value $E(G(t); t)$. With the passage of time these deviations from equilibrium are expected to decay with the factor $(1 - b)^{s-t}$ due to the adjustment of the price level in response to deviations from purchasing power parity. The expected speed of convergence of the price level and the exchange rate toward their respective equilibrium paths is not affected by the intervention rule (25) because this rule does not affect the negative characteristic root of the dynamic system that governs the expected paths of p and e.

Adoption of the intervention policy (25) could either increase or reduce the volatility of the domestic price level, depending on the nature and magnitude of variations in the exogenous variables z and p^*. If the world price level p^* is highly volatile or if movements in p^* are strongly positively correlated with movements in z, then the intervention policy (25) is likely to increase the volatility of the domestic price level because it makes the equilibrium domestic price level sensitive to variations in the world price level. This is the converse of the standard proposition that a flexible exchange rate helps to insulate an economy from disturbances originating in the rest of the world. If the world price level is quite stable, sensitivity of the equilibrium domestic price level to expected and actual variations in p^* will not be an important drawback of the intervention rule (25), and this rule will have the benefit of reducing the sensivity of the equilibrium domestic price level to variations in the average level of z by inducing offsetting changes in f. This reflects the standard argument that a fixed exchange rate is useful in stabilizing the domestic price level in the face of disturbances to the demand for domestic money or to the domestic credit component of the money supply. Moreover, since the intervention rule (25) makes the discount factor μ smaller than the discount factor θ, it makes the domestic price level less sensitive to expectations concerning future values of z, though it does so at the expense of making the price level relatively more sensitive to expectations concerning the current level of z.

Since the intervention rule (25) gears changes in f so as to offset changes in e, this rule should normally reduce the volatility of the exchange rate. The reason for this may be seen from the expressions for the expected and unexpected components of the change in the exchange rate:

$$D^e(e(t)) = D^e(G(t)) - D^e(p^*(t)) + [b/(hb + \alpha)] \cdot [p(t) - E(G(t); t)] \quad (33)$$

$$D^u(e(t)) = [1 + (1/(hb + \alpha))] \cdot D^u(G(t)) - D^u(p^*(t)) \quad (34)$$

where

$$D^e(G(t)) = (1 - \mu) \cdot \sum_{j=0}^{\infty} \mu^j \cdot (1/(1 + \alpha)) \cdot E[D(z(s + j) + \alpha \cdot p^*(s + j)); t]$$

$$(35)$$

$$D^u(G(t)) = (1 - \mu) \cdot \sum_{j=0}^{\infty} \mu^j \cdot (1/(1 + \alpha)) \cdot D^u(z(s + j) + \alpha \cdot p^*(s + j)) \qquad (36)$$

with $D^u(z(s + j) + \alpha \cdot p^*(s + j)) = E[z(s + j + 1) + \alpha \cdot p^*(s + j + 1);$
$t + 1] - E[z(s + j + 1) + \alpha \cdot p^*(s + j + 1); t]$.

Looking first at the terms $D^e(G(t)) - D^e(p^*(t))$, which determine the expected rate of change of the equilibrium value of the exchange rate, it is easily shown that for a constant expected rate of change of z, say $E[D(z(s + j)); t] = \zeta(t)$, and a constant expected rate of change of p^*, say $E[D(p^*(s + j)); t] = \pi^*(t)$, these terms reduce to $(1/(1 + \alpha)) \cdot [\zeta(t) - \pi^*(t)]$. Thus the stronger is the intervention policy, the smaller is the effect of any constant expected rate of change of z or p^* on the expected rate of change of the equilibrium value of the exchange rate. Further the factor $[b/(hb + \alpha)]$ that multiplies $[p(t) - E(G(t); t)]$ in the expression for $D^e(e(t))$ is clearly smaller the stronger is the intervention policy; and as indicated by the discussion of the volatility of the price level, $[p(t) - E(G(t); t)]$ is likely to be smaller with a stronger intervention policy provided that the world price level is not too volatile. Thus a stronger intervention policy has the potential for reducing the absolute size of all of the factors that influence the expected rate of change of the exchange rate.

With respect to the unexpected component of the change in the exchange rate, it is clear that a stronger intervention policy reduces the factor $[1 + (1/(hb + \alpha))]$ that multiplies $D^u(G(t))$. New information that alters by an amount Δz the expected level of z in all future periods affects $D^u(G(t))$ to the extent of $(1/(1 + \alpha)) \cdot \Delta z$, an effect that is clearly smaller the stronger is the intervention policy. Similarly a constant change Δp^* in the expected world price level affects the exchange rate to the extent of $[1 + (1/(hb + \alpha))] \cdot (\alpha/(1 + \alpha)) \cdot \Delta p^* - \Delta p^* = [-hb/(hb + \alpha)] \cdot \Delta p^*$, an effect that is smaller in absolute value the stronger is the intervention policy. Further since the factor multiplying $D^u(z(t + j))$ in (34) can be written in the form

$$(1 - \mu) \cdot \mu^j(1/(1 + \alpha)) = (1/(1 + h + \alpha)) \cdot (h/(1 + h + \alpha))^j, \qquad (37)$$

it follows that a stronger intervention policy reduces the effect on $D^u(e(t))$ of a change in expectation about any specific future $z(t + j + 1)$, with this reduction becoming greater the greater is j. This implies that new information that alters expectations concerning all future z's in the same direction will have a smaller effect on the exchange rate the stronger is the intervention policy. The only circumstance in which a stronger intervention policy is likely to increase the magnitude of unexpected changes in the exchange rate is if changes in expectations about the world price level are sufficiently greater in magnitude than changes in expectations concerning the z's so as to overwhelm all of the other effects of an increase in α that tend to reduce the magnitude of $D^u(e(t))$.

Finally we come to the effect of the intervention policy on the extent of disequilibrium, as measured by the deviation from purchasing power parity, $v(t) = e(t) + p^*(t) - p(t)$. Taking the difference between (30) and (29), it follows that

$$v(t) = [1 + (1/(hb + \alpha))] \cdot [E(G(t);t) - p(t)]. \tag{38}$$

Using the fact that the actual and expected change in the domestic price level is given by

$$D(p(t)) = b \cdot v(t) + D^e(e(t)) + D^e(p^*(t))$$
$$= b \cdot v(t) + D^e(G(t)) + [b/(hb + \alpha)] \cdot [p(t) - E(G(t);t)], \tag{39}$$

it is easily established that the rule governing the evolution of the deviation from purchasing power parity is

$$D(v(t)) = -b \cdot v(t) + [1 + (1/(hb + \alpha))] \cdot D^u(G(t)). \tag{40}$$

The solution of this difference equation,

$$v(t) = \sum_{j=0}^{\infty} (1 - b)^j \cdot [1 + (1/(hb + \alpha))] \cdot D^u(G(t - j - 1)), \tag{41}$$

indicates that the existing state of disequilibrium, as measured by $v(t)$, depends on a weighted sum of past disturbances resulting from unexpected changes in the equilibrium value of the domestic price level. Since the intervention rule does not affect the rate, $-b \cdot v(t)$, at which existing disequilibrium is eliminated, it is apparent that the effect of the intervention policy on the extent of disequilibrium depends on its effect on the magnitude of innovations to disequilibrium, as measured by $[1 + (1/(hb + \alpha))] \cdot D^u(G(t - j - 1))$. Clearly a stronger intervention policy reduces the average extent of disequilibrium by reducing the factor $[1 + (1/(hb + \alpha))]$ that multiplies $D^u(G(t - j - 1))$. Moreover an increase in α reduces the response of $D^u(G(t - j - 1))$ to a change in expectations about the average level of z or to any change in the same direction of expectations concerning all future z's. Also a stronger intervention policy reduces the response of $D''(G(t - j - 1))$ to uniform changes in the expected level of the world price level. Hence the only circumstance in which a stronger intervention policy is likely to increase the average extent of disequilibrium is if changes in expectations about the world price level are sufficiently large that their effect in increasing the magnitude of the disturbances $D''(G(t - j - 1))$ outweighs all of the other effects of an increase in α in reducing the average extent of disequilibrium.

4. Intervention to Stabilize the Real Exchange Rate

If the objective of intervention policy is to reduce the average extent of disequilibrium, as measured by divergences from purchasing power parity, then a policy that resists movements of the real exchange rate would seem to offer better prospects for success than the policy (25) that resists movements of the nominal exchange rate. For this purpose the *real exchange rate* is defined as the ratio of the domestic money price of world goods to the domestic money price of domestic goods. In terms of logarithms the level of the real exchange rate corresponds to the deviation from purchasing power parity, $v = e + p^* - p$. An intervention rule that resists movements of v is given by

$$f(t) = f(t - 1) - \beta \cdot (v(t) - v(t - 1)), \tag{42}$$

where $\beta > 0$ measures the strength of the intervention policy.

If this intervention policy is put into effect at time $t = 1$, it is easily established that the level of $f(t)$ at any time $t \geq 1$ is given by

$$f(t) = -\beta \cdot v(t) + \bar{f} \tag{43}$$

where $\bar{f} = \beta \cdot v(0) + f(0)$ is a constant. Using this fact, together with the basic dynamic equations (5) and (7), it follows that the dynamic system determining the evolution of the expected domestic price level and the expected exchange rate, conditional on information available at time t, can be written as

$$\begin{bmatrix} -b - D & b + D \\ (1 - \beta)/h & (\beta/h) - D \end{bmatrix} \cdot \begin{bmatrix} p \\ e \end{bmatrix} = \begin{bmatrix} -b \cdot p^* - D(p^*) \\ (1/h) \cdot (z + \bar{f}) + D(p^*) \end{bmatrix}. \tag{44}$$

The characteristic roots of this dynamic system,

$$\lambda_1 = 1/h \quad \text{and} \quad \lambda_2 = -b, \tag{45}$$

are the same as the characteristic roots of the original dynamic system (8). The solution for the expected path of the domestic price level given by (10) and all of the results concerning the expected and actual behavior of the domestic price level that were obtained in section 2 remain intact, indicating that the intervention rule (42) has no effect on the behavior of the domestic price level.

This interventional rule does, however, affect the behavior of the exchange rate. Specifically the solution for the expected path of the exchange rate is no longer given by (11) but rather by

$$e(s) = F(s) - p^*(s) - [(1 - \beta)/(hb + \beta)] \cdot [p(t) - F(t)] \cdot (1 - b)^{s-t}. \quad (46)$$

It is still the case, as in (11), that $F(s) - p^*(s)$ describes the expected equilibrium value of the exchange rate. The difference between (46) and (11) is in the coefficient that multiplies $[p(t) - F(t)] \cdot (1 - b)^{s-t}$ in the disequilibrium component of the expected exchange rate—that is, in the difference between the coefficient $-[(1 - \beta)/(hb + \beta)]$ and the coefficient $-(1/hb)$. It is clear that for any given deviation of $p(t)$ from its equilibrium value of $F(t)$, the expected deviation of the exchange rate from its expected equilibrium value becomes smaller as β is increased, up to the point where $\beta = 1$. When $\beta = 1$, the actual exchange rate $e(t) = E(F(t); t) + E(p^*(t); t) - 0 \cdot [p(t) - E(F(t); t]$ does not diverge from its equilibrium value at time t and is not expected to diverge from its equilibrium value at any future date. A value of $\beta > 1$ reverses the sign of the divergence of the exchange rate from its equilibrium value and makes the sign of this divergence the same as the sign of the divergence of $p(t)$ from its equilibrium value $E(F(t); t)$. In Dornbusch's terminology, $\beta > 1$ implies undershooting of the exchange rate rather than overshooting of the exchange rate in response to unexpected changes in the equilibrium domestic price level.

The intervention rule (42) also affects the behavior of real exchange rate or, equivalently, the behavior of the deviation from purchasing power parity. Specifically evaluating (46) and (10) at $s = t$ and introducing the suppressed operator $E(\ ; t)$ where appropriate, it follows that

$$v(t) = [(1 + hb)/(hb + \beta)] \cdot [E(F(t); t) - p(t)]. \quad (47)$$

Since the intervention policy (42) does not affect the behavior of either the equilibrium value of the domestic price level, $E(F(t); t)$, or the actual value of the domestic price level, $p(t)$, the only effect of this policy on $v(t)$ is through its effect on the factor $[(1 + hb)/(hb + \beta)]$. It is clear that the stronger the intervention policy, the smaller the deviation from purchasing power parity and, correspondingly, the smaller the variation in the real exchange rate. Indeed if the objective of the policy is to reduce the magnitude of disequilibrium as measured by deviations from purchasing power parity, it pays to adopt a rule that is stronger than the rule (with $\beta = 1$) that would eliminate deviations of the nominal exchange rate from its equilibrium value. With $\beta > 1$, deviations of the exchange rate from its equilibrium value are of the same sign as deviations between $p(t)$ and $E(F(t); t)$ and hence reduce the effect of deviations between $p(t)$ and $E(F(t); t)$ on the real exchange rate.

From this analysis it appears that the intervention policy (42) that resists movements in the real exchange rate can always be used to reduce deviations of the nominal exchange rate from its equilibrium value and that an even more aggressive policy of this type can reduce further the extent of disequilibrium as measured by the deviation from purchasing power parity. These very favorable conclusions about the effects of such an intervention policy, however, depend on an implicit assumption that there are no variations in the equilibrium value of the real exchange rate and hence that purchasing power parity always describes the equilibrium relationship of the nominal exchange rate, the world price level, and the domestic price level.

To analyze the implications of variations in the equilibrium value of the real exchange rate for the effects of intervention policy, it is necessary to modify slightly the specification of the basic dynamic system determining the evolution of the domestic price level and the nominal exchange rate. For this purpose $q(s)$ is defined as the logarithm of the exogenously determined equilibrium value of the real exchange rate at time s, while $v(s) = e(s) + p^*(s) - p(s)$ continues to represent the logarithm of the actual value of the real exchange rate at time s. At any moment of time t, economic agents have expectations concerning the present and future levels of $q(s)$, and these expectations are subject to change with the passage of time as new information is obtained about the underlying real economic conditions that influence the equilibrium value of the real exchange rate.[8]

With the possibility of a nonzero and varying value of q, it is no longer appropriate to think of the objective of the price adjustment process as achieving and maintaining purchasing power parity. Rather the object of the agents involved in the price-setting process would be to establish and maintain the appropriate equilibrium value of the domestic price level in relation to the domestic price of goods from the rest of the world. This is represented by replacing the price adjustment rule (7) with the rule

$$D(p) = b \cdot (e + p^* - q - p) + D^e(e + p^* - q). \tag{48}$$

The first term in this rule adjusts the domestic price level toward its equilibrium value, $e + p^* - q$, and the second term keeps the domestic price level on its expected equilibrium path once equilibrium is achieved.

In addition to modifying the price adjustment rule, it might be appropriate to allow for the possibility that variations in the equilibrium real exchange rate affect the demand for domestic money or are related to variations in risk premiums that affect the relationship between the domestic interest rate and the world interest rate. However, since these complicating factors do not contribute anything important to the present discussion of the effects of intervention policies, they will be ignored, and it will be assumed that equations (1) through (4) remain valid in the presence of a varying equilibrium real exchange rate.

With these assumptions it follows that the dynamic system controlling the evolution of the expected values of the domestic price level and the nominal exchange rate can be written as

$$\begin{bmatrix} -b - D & b + D \\ 1/h & -D \end{bmatrix} \cdot \begin{bmatrix} p \\ e \end{bmatrix} = \begin{bmatrix} b \cdot (q - p^*) + D(q - p^*) \\ (1/h) \cdot (z + f) + D^e(p^*) \end{bmatrix}. \tag{49}$$

It is noteworthy that this system is identical to the system (8) except for the presence of additional forcing variables q and $D(q)$ on the right-hand side of (49). The characteristic roots of this system, $\lambda_1 = 1/h$ and $\lambda_2 = -b$, are the same as the characteristic roots of the system (8). The unique nonexplosive solution of the system (49), however, is somewhat different from the corresponding solution of the system (8) because of the difference in the forcing variables. Specifically suppressing the operator $E(\; ; t)$, the solutions for the expected paths of p and e conditional on information available at time t are given by

$$p(s) = F(s) + H(s) - q(s) + [p(t) - F(t) - H(t) + q(t)] \cdot (1 - b)^{s-t} \tag{50}$$

$$e(s) = F(s) - p^*(s) + H(s)$$
$$- (1/hb) \cdot [p(t) - F(t) - H(t) + q(t)] \cdot (1 + b)^{s-t} \tag{51}$$

where $F(s)$ is still defined by (12) and where

$$H(s) = (1 - \theta) \cdot \sum_{j=0}^{\infty} \theta^j \cdot q(s + j) \tag{52}$$

with $\theta = h/(1 + h)$.

In these results the expected equilibrium value of the domestic price level is described by $F(s) + H(s) - q(s)$ rather than simply by $F(s)$ as was the case when q was implicitly assumed to be equal to zero always. The additional factor $H(s) - q(s)$ in the solution for $p(s)$ represents the influence of the current and expected future behavior of the equilibrium value of the real exchange rate on the equilibrium value of the domestic price level. It is interesting to note that if q is expected to remain constant, $H(s) = q(s)$ and the expected equilibrium price level given simply by $F(s)$. Thus it is only the deviation of the current expected level of q from the weighted average of expected current and future levels of q represented by $H(s)$ that has any influence on the expected equilibrium value of the domestic price level. In contrast the expected equilibrium value of the nominal exchange rate, $F(s) + H(s) - p^*(s)$, depends on the weighted average of expected current and future levels of q represented by $H(s)$ and not on the difference between $H(s)$ and $q(s)$. The significance of this result is apparent from the implied solution for the expected path of the real exchange rate, $v(s) = e(s) + p^*(s) - p(s)$:

$$v(s) = q(s) + [1 + (1/hb)] \cdot [F(t) + H(t) - q(t) - p(t)] \cdot (1 - b)^{s-t}. \quad (53)$$

Here we see that the expected value of the real exchange rate is influenced by the expected equilibrium value of the real exchange rate, as well as by the expected value of the disequilibrium divergence of the real exchange rate from its equilibrium value.

If the extent of disequilibrium is measured by the divergence of the real exchange rate from its equilibrium value, $x(t) = E[(v(t) - q(t)); t]$, then the dynamic process governing the evolution of disequilibrium is described by the difference equation

$$D(x(t)) = -b \cdot x(t) + [1 + (1/hb)] \cdot D^u[F(t) + H(t) - q(t)]. \quad (54)$$

This result is similar to the result (23), which is relevant when $q = 0$, in that the rate at which existing disequilibrium is eliminated is still equal to the speed of adjustment, b, of the domestic price level in response to disequilibrium and in that the factor $[1 + (1/hb)]$ that multiplies the unexpected change in the equilibrium value of the domestic price level is the same as it was in (23). The difference between (54) and (23) is that the unexpected change in the equilibrium value of the domestic price level (which determines the innovation to disequilibrium) now reflects not only $D^u[F(t)]$ but also $D^u[H(t) - q(t)]$; that is, the innovation to disequilibrium is now affected by changes in expectations about the behavior of the equilibrium value of the real exchange rate.

Two likely properties of the components of the disturbance term $D^u[F(t) + H(t) - q(t)]$ are relevant in establishing the probable result that an increase in the volatility of expectations concerning the equilibrium real exchange rate is likely to increase the average magnitude of disequilibrium. First, there is no strong reason to suppose that disturbances resulting from changes in expectations about the real economic conditions that influence the equilibrium real exchange rate (which are reflected in $D^u[H(t) - q(t)]$) and disturbances resulting from changes in expectations about money supply and money demand behavior (which are reflected in $D^u[F(t)]$) will result in strong negative correlation between $D^u[H(t) - q(t)]$ and $D^u[F(t)]$. This means that the real and monetary components of the disturbance term $D^u[F(t) + H(t) - q(t)]$ should not usually be assumed to offset each other; rather each component should be expected to contribute its own, largely independent part to the total disturbance. Second, although it is possible that $D^u[H(t) - q(t)]$ generally would be close to zero because $D^u[H(t)]$ is almost always exactly offset by $D^u[q(t)]$, this is not likely; it is more likely that the magnitude of $D^u[q(t)]$ will be larger than the magnitude of $D^u[H(t)]$. The circumstance in which $D^u[H(t)]$ would always be exactly offset by $D^u[q(t)]$ is if q were thought to follow a random walk and hence the change in expectations was always the same amount for each future q. However, since q refers to the equilibrium relative price of world goods in terms of domestic goods, it is not attractive to assume that q follows a random walk, with the implication that it moves outside any finite bound with probability one over a sufficiently long-time horizon. A more attractive assumption is that long-run movements in q occur only within reasonably modest finite bounds and that such long-run movements are generally smaller than and in the same direction as short-run movements in q. Under this assumption since $H(t)$ is a weighted average of expected current and future levels of q, $D^u[H(t)]$ should generally be of the same sign but of smaller magnitude than $D^u[q(t)]$. This conclusion will be assumed to be correct in subsequent discussion.

Allowance for the possibility of a nonzero and varying level of the equilibrium real exchange rate does not alter in a fundamental way the conclusions of section 3 concerning the effects of the intervention policy (25) that resists movements of the nominal exchange rate. The dynamic system (27) is modified by replacing the vector of forcing variables that appears on the right-hand side of (27) with the vector of forcing variables that appears on the right-hand side of (49). The unique nonexplosive solution for the expected paths of the domestic price level and the nominal exchange rate is given by

$$p(s) = G(s) + J(s) - q(s) + [p(t) - G(t) - J(t) + q(t)] \cdot (1 - b)^{s-t} \quad (55)$$

$$e(s) = G(s) + J(s) - p^*(s)$$
$$- [1/(hb + \alpha)] \cdot [p(t) - G(t) - J(t) + q(t)] \cdot (1 - b)^{s-t} \quad (56)$$

where $G(s)$ is defined by (31) and where

$$J(s) = (1 - \mu) \cdot \sum_{j=0}^{\infty} \mu^j \cdot (1/(1 + \alpha)) \cdot q(s + j) \quad (57)$$

with $\mu = h/(1 + h + \alpha)$.

Without going into the details of the analysis presented in section 3, it may be stated on the basis of these results that the main conclusions of that analysis remain valid provided that references to p^* are replaced with references to $p^* - q$. A stronger intervention policy (a higher α) reduces the sensitivity of the domestic price level to variations in z but increases its sensitivity to variations in $p^* - q$. A stronger intervention policy is likely to reduce the sensitivity of the nominal exchange rate to all types of disturbances. A stronger intervention policy is likely to reduce the average extent of disequilibrium, as measured by $x(t) = v(t) - q(t)$, provided that the increased sensitivity of the equilibrium price level to unexpected changes in $p^* - q$ is more than offset by the other effects of an increase in α that tend to reduce the magnitude of innovations to disequilibrium.

More important modifications are required for the analysis of the intervention rule (42) that resists movements of the real exchange rate. Formally the dynamic system that governs the expected evolution of the domestic price level and the exchange rate needs to be modified from the system (44) by altering the specification of the forcing variables to allow for nonzero and varying values of the equilibrium real exchange rate:

$$\begin{bmatrix} -b - D & b + D \\ (1 - \beta)/h & (\beta/h) - D \end{bmatrix} \cdot \begin{bmatrix} p \\ e \end{bmatrix} = \begin{bmatrix} b \cdot (q - p^*) + D(q - p^*) \\ (1/h) \cdot (z + \bar{f} - \beta \cdot p^*) + D(p^*) \end{bmatrix}. \quad (58)$$

The characteristic roots of this system are still $\lambda_1 = 1/h$ and $\lambda_2 = -b$. The unique nonexplosive solutions for the expected paths of the domestic price level and the exchange rate are given by

$$p(s) = F(s) + (1 - \beta) \cdot H(s) - q(s)$$
$$+ [p(t) - F(t) - (1 - \beta) \cdot H(t) + q(t)] \cdot (1 - b)^{s-t} \tag{59}$$

$$e(s) = F(s) + (1 - \beta) \cdot H(s) - p^*(s) + [(1 - \beta)/(hb + \beta)]$$
$$\cdot [p(t) - F(t) - (1 - \beta) \cdot H(t) + q(t)] \cdot (1 - b)^{s-t} \tag{60}$$

where $F(s)$ is defined by (12) and $H(s)$ is defined by (52), with $\theta = h/(1 + h)$.

The noteworthy feature of these results, in comparison with the results when $q = 0$, is that the expected path of the domestic price level is no longer independent of the strength of the intervention policy, as measured by β. When account is taken of a nonzero and varying equilibrium value of q, the value of β affects the path of $p(s)$ by affecting the term $(1 - \beta) \cdot H(s)$ in (59). This effect of an increase in β is likely to mean an increase in the sensitivity of unexpected changes in the domestic price level to changes in expectations about real economic conditions that influence the equilibrium real exchange rate. Formally the unexpected change in the equilibrium value of p is given by

$$D^u[p(t)] = D^u[F(t)] + D^u[(1 - \beta) \cdot H(t) - q(t)]. \tag{61}$$

If, as is reasonable to assume, $D^u[H(t)]$ is generally of the same sign but of smaller magnitude than $D^u[q(t)]$, then an increase in β will increase the magnitude of the disturbance term $D^u[(1 - \beta) \cdot H(t) - q(t)]$, which is associated with changes in expectation about real economic conditions that influence the equilibrium real exchange rate. If, as also seems reasonable, the monetary disturbance $D^u[F(t)]$ is not strongly negatively correlated with the real disturbance $D^u[(1 - \beta) \cdot H(t) - q(t)]$, then an increase in the magnitude of this real disturbance will increase the magnitude of unexpected changes in the equilibrium value of the domestic price level.

This effect of an increase in β is important in assessing the effect of the intervention rule (42) on the extent of disequilibrium, as measured by $x(t) = E[(v(t) - q(t)); t]$. The rule governing the evolution of $x(t)$ is

$$D(x(t)) = -b \cdot x(t) + [1 + ((1 - \beta)/(hb + \beta)] \cdot D^u[p(t)]. \tag{62}$$

The solution of this difference equation reveals that

$$x(t) = \sum_{j=0}^{\infty} (1 - b)^j \cdot [1 + ((1 - \beta)/(hb + \beta))] \cdot D^u[p(t - j - 1)]. \tag{63}$$

It is clear that a stronger intervention policy reduces the average expected size of $x(t)$ by reducing the common factor $[1 + ((1 - \beta)/(hb + \beta))]$ that multiplies each of the disturbances $D^u[p(t - j - 1)]$. If $q(s)$ were always zero, as assumed at the beginning of this section, this would be the only channel through which an increase in β affects the average level of $x(t)$, leading to the conclusion that a stronger intervention policy will reduce the average extent of disequilibrium. However, when we take account of the probable effect of an increase in β in increasing the magnitude of the disturbances $D^u[p(t - j - 1)]$, it no longer follows that a stronger intervention policy will necessarily reduce the average extent of disequilibrium. Indeed if real disturbances associated with unexpected changes in $H(s) - q(s)$ are sufficiently important relative to monetary disturbances associated with unexpected changes in $F(s)$ in generating unexpected changes in the equilibrium value of the domestic price level, a stronger intervention policy will increase the average extent of disequilibrium.

The property that a stronger intervention policy reduces the average extent of disequilibrium can be restored if the intervention policy is altered so as to resist movements in v relative to q rather than simply to resist all movements in v. Specifically it may be shown that an intervention rule of the form

$$f(t) = f(t - 1) - \gamma \cdot [x(t) - x(t - 1)], \quad \gamma > 0, \tag{64}$$

will have no effect on the expected or actual path of the domestic price level and will result in a state of disequilibrium determined by

$$x(t) = \sum_{j=0}^{\infty} (1 - b)^j \cdot [1 + ((1 - \gamma)/(hb + \gamma))] \cdot D^u[p(t - j - 1)] \tag{65}$$

where $D^u[p(s)] = D^u[F(s) + H(s) - q(s)]$ does not depend on γ. Since the only effect of an increase in γ is to reduce the common factor $[1 + ((1 - \gamma)/(hb + \gamma))]$ that multiples all of the disturbances $D^u[p(t - j - 1)]$, it is apparent that a stronger intervention policy of the form (64) will necessarily reduce the average extent of disequilibrium.

The difficulty with implementing such a policy is that the authorities may not have a very reliable measure of the equilibrium exchange rate. This is essentially the problem with the intervention policy (42) for which it is implicitly assumed that q remains close to zero. If this assumption is not too bad, then the intervention policy (42) will probably succeed in reducing the average extent of disequilibrium. Similarly if the authorities know that there are significant variations in the equilibrium value of the real exchange rate and have a reasonably accurate method for estimating q, then the intervention policy (64), using the authorities' estimates of q, should probably succeed in reducing the average extent of disequilibrium. But if the authorities are not very good at estimating the equilibrium real exchange rate, then the intervention policy (64) may add to the average extent of disequilibrium because the authorities fail to respond to actual changes in q that they do not perceive or respond to perceived changes in q that do not correspond to actual changes in the equilibrium real exchange rate.

5. Concluding Remarks

Since the main points of this chapter were summarized in the introduction, little purpose is served by reviewing these points here. Rather it is more useful to discuss some of the important limitations and underlying assumptions of the analysis.

First, the specific results for the effects of intervention policies that have been derived clearly depend on the specific formal representation of these policies and on the special properties of the model of price and exchange rate dynamics that has been used to analyze the effects of these policies. In principle a policy of leaning against the wind need not consist of a simple proportional response of the foreign exchange reserve component of the money supply to changes in the nominal or real exchange rate. Alternative specifications of this general type of intervention policy would lead to somewhat different results than those described here. Similarly alternative specification of the requirements for goods and asset market equilibrium and of the mechanism of price adjustment would lead to somewhat different formal results for the effects of particular intervention policies. The general conclusions of the analysis, however, should be reasonably robust to these alterations. A policy of resisting movements of the nominal exchange rate by offsetting changes in the money supply is likely to contribute to stability and reduce disequilibrium if exchange movements reflect primarily an excess response to internal disturbances rather than an equilibrium response to external disturbances. Similarly a policy that resists movements of the real exchange rate is likely to contribute to stability provided that movements of the real exchange rate are primarily a disequilibrium phenomenon rather than an equilibrium response to changing real economic conditions requiring adjustments of the relative price of world goods in terms of domestic goods.

Second, this chapter has been concerned exclusively with policies of nonsterilized intervention—that is, with official intervention that affects the domestic money supply by affecting the foreign exchange component of the money supply. Indeed, for the model considered, it would make no difference if the intervention policy were carried out by varying the domestic credit component of the money supply rather than the foreign exchange reserve component. In this model what matters is the size of the money supply, not its composition. For this reason there is no mechanism in the present model through which sterilized intervention, which affects only the composition of the money supply, can have any effect. This does not imply that there is no sensible model in which sterilized intervention can have meaningful effects, only that these effects cannot be analyzed in the model used in this chapter.

Third, it has been implicitly assumed that the intervention authorities always have reserves that are adequate to carry out their intervention policies. Since in the model used here variations in domestic credit are a perfect substitute for variations in foreign exchange reserves as the instrument for official intervention, this implicit assumption amounts to the requirement that domestic credit policy be consistent with maintaining an adequate level of reserves, given the intervention policy adopted by the authorities. For an intervention policy that is directed at influencing the nominal exchange rate, control of both the domestic credit and foreign exchange reserve components of the money supply ought to be sufficient to enforce the policy since the nominal exchange rate is a nominal price and monetary policy ought to be able to control one nominal price. There might not be, however, any monetary policy that would sustain an intervention policy directed at influencing the real exchange rate. This is not likely to be a problem with the policy (25) that resists changes in the real exchange rate, but it probably would be a problem for a policy that attempted to peg a value for the real exchange rate that differed permanently from its equilibrium value. In principle monetary policy cannot be relied on to fix permanently the values of relative commodity prices.

Fourth, the analysis has been concerned with intervention policies, as distinct from intervention action. This distinction is important because at any given date economic agents are responding not only to the actions that the policy authorities are taking on that date but also to expectations concerning the actions that the authorities will take in the future. Formally the analysis of the effects of an intervention policy, as opposed to a policy action, is captured by the assumption of rational expectations under which the entire expected future path of the authorities' actions, as determined by their intervention policy, affects the behavior of the price level and the exchange rate. In this formal framework we assess the effects of stronger or weaker policy rules, as represented by larger or smaller values of α and β, not the effects of particular policy actions.

Finally, this analysis ignores some important game theoretic issues that arise in connection with official intervention policies. In this chapter it has been assumed that the government's intervention policy is known by private economic agents who have complete confidence that the government will actually follow its announced policy. This ignores the possibility that governments may sometimes find it in their interest to depart from their previously announced policies and that private agents take some account of this possibility in forming their expectations about the government's future behavior.

Notes

1. The nature and source of disequilibrium in this analysis differ in some important respects from the nature and source of disequilibrium in a number of recent analyses of optimal official intervention and related policies; see in particular Flood (1979) and Eaton and Turnovsky (1983). In these analyses disequilibrium is explicitly measured as deviations of output from its normal level and such deviations are assumed to depend on deviations of the current price level from last period's expectation of the current price level. It follows that in these analyses, in contrast to the present analysis, disequilibrium cannot persist for even one period in the absence of unexpected disturbances. Obviously some of the specific conclusions of the present analysis would be modified if this alternative approach to specifying the nature and source of disequilibrium were adopted.

2. Official intervention policies of this type are examined in Branson (1977), Dornbusch (1980), and Quirk (1977).

3. It is shown in Mussa (1981) that for a price adjustment rule to have sensible properties in a rational expectations model of the general type under consideration, it should have both a forward-looking component that links the change in the price level to expected changes in its equilibrium value and a backward-looking component that adjusts the price level in response to existing disequilibrium.

4. For an analysis of various issues arising in the context of the rational expectations version of Cagan's (1956) model of the dynamics of inflation, see Sargent and Wallace (1973a) and Mussa (1975, 1978).

5. There is considerable controversy over the justification for excluding the explosive bubble term from the solution of rational expectations models like the present one; see Black (1974), Brock (1975), Sargent and Wallace (1973b), Flood and Garber (1980), McCallum (1983), Mussa (1976), and Obstfeld and Rogoff (1983). In the present discussion, it will be assumed that there are adequate grounds for excluding these terms whenever they appear.

6. Figure 1.1 illustrates the case where hb is > 1 and the $D(p) = 0$ locus is positively sloped. When hb is < 1, the $D(p)$ locus is negatively sloped. The stable branch of the dynamic system is negatively sloped in both of these cases, and its slope is always smaller, algebraically, than the slope of the $D(p) = 0$ locus.

7. In the present model there is no avenue through which sterilized intervention can have any effect on the exchange rate or the domestic price level since such intervention would affect only the composition of the central bank's assets, not the size of the domestic money supply. In a more elaborate model where private investors have distinct portfolio demands for domestic and foreign securities, sterilized intervention, which affects the supplies of these securities available to private investors, can affect the exchange rate and domestic price level. For a presentation and discussion of such models, see, for example, Branson, Haltunen, and Mason (1977) and Eaton and Turnovsky (1983). For a summary of empirical evidence on the capacity of sterilized intervention to affect exchange rates, see Obstfeld (1982).

8. A more complete model that allows for endogenous determination of the equilibrium path of the real exchange rate is presented in Mussa (1982).

References

Black, F., 1974, "Uniqueness of the Price Level in Monetary Growth Models with Rational Expectations," *Journal of Economic Theory* 7, no. 1 (January), 53–65.

Branson, W. H., 1976, "Leaning against the Wind as Exchange Rate Policy," paper presented at the Geneva Conference on Exchange Market Uncertainty, November.

Branson, W. H., Haltunen, H. and Mason, P., 1977, "Exchange Rates in the Short Run: The Dollar-Deutschemark Rate," *European Economic Review* 10, no. 4 (December), 303–324.

Brock, W. H., 1975, "A Simple Perfect Foresight Model of Money," *Journal of Monetary Economics* 1, no. 1 (January), 133–150.

Cagan, P., 1956, "The Monetary Dynamics of Hyperinflation," in M. Friedman (ed.), *Studies in the Quantity Theory of Money*. Chicago: University of Chicago Press.

Dornbusch, R., 1980, "Exchange Rate Economics: Where Do We Stand?" *Brookings Papers on Economic Activity* 1, 143–185.

Dornbusch, R., 1976, "Expectations and Exchange Rate Dynamics," *Journal of Political Economy* 84, no. 6 (December), 893–915.

Eaton, J., and Turnovsky, S. J., 1983, "The Forward Exchange Market, Speculation and Exchange Market Intervention," *NBER Working Paper* 1138, June.

Flood, R. P., 1979, "Capital Mobility and the Choice of Exchange Rate System," *International Economic Review* 20, no. 2 (June), 405–416.

Flood, R. P., and Garber, P., 1980, "Market Fundamentals versus Price Level Bubbles: The First Tests," *Journal of Political Economy* 88, no. 4 (August), 745–770.

MaCallum, B. T., 1983, "On Non-Uniqueness in Rational Expectations Models: An Attempt at Perspective," *Journal of Monetary Economics* 11, no. 2 (March), 139–168.

Mussa, M. L., 1982, "A Model of Exchange Rate Dynamics," *Journal of Political Economy* 90, no. 1 (February), 74–104.

Mussa, M. L., 1981, "Sticky Prices and Disequilibrium Adjustment in a Rational Model of the Inflationary Process," *American Economic Review* 71, no. 6 (December), 1020–1027.

Mussa, M. L., 1978, "On the Inherent Stability of Rationally Adaptive Expectations," *Journal of Monetary Economics* 4, no. 3 (July), 307–313.

Mussa, M. L., 1975, "Adaptive and Regressive Expectations in a Rational Model of the Inflationary Process," *Journal of Monetary Economics* 1, no. 4 (October), 423–442.

Mussa, M. L., 1976, *A Study in Macroeconomics*. Amsterdam: North Holland. Obstfeld, M., 1982, "Can We Sterilize? Theory and Evidence," *American Economic Review Papers and Proceedings* 72, no. 2 (May), 45–50.

Obstfeld, M., and Rogoff, K., 1983, "Speculative Hyperinflations in Maximizing Models: Can We Rule Them Out?" *Journal of Political Economy* 91, no. 4 (August), 675–687.

Quirk, P. J., 1977, "Exchange Rate Policy in Japan: Leaning against the Wind," *IMF Staff Papers* 24, no. 3 (November).

Sargent, T. J., and Wallace, N. J., 1973a, "Rational Expectations and the Dynamics of Hyperinflation," *International Economic Review* 14, no. 2 (June), 328–350.

Sargent, T. J., and Wallace, N. J., 1973b, "The Stability of Money and Growth with Perfect Foresight," *Econometrica*, 1043–1048.

2 Policy Decentralization and Exchange Rate Management in Interdependent Economies

Willem H. Buiter and Jonathan Eaton

1. Introduction

The demise of Bretton Woods and of the short-lived Smithsonian agreement has raised questions about exchange rate management by monetary authorities acting in isolation from one another. For instance, will individual monetary authorities have an incentive to stabilize the exchange rate? To what extent will monetary actions abroad disrupt domestic monetary policy? What are the gains from coordinating monetary policy?

The problems that arise when different agents pursue independent policies in interdependent economies have been explored by a number of authors. Aoki (1976), Cooper (1969), Hamada (1976), Allen and Kenen (1980), McFadden (1969), Patrick (1973), Kydland (1976), and Pindyck (1976), among others, have written on this issue. Different authors have focused on different aspects of decentralized policy formation. Three distinct types of decentralization and coordination can, in principle, be distinguished.

1. *Target* decentralization occurs when the two authorities have different objectives. Full coordination of targets requires that the authorities adopt a common objective. This does not necessarily imply that authorities then act on the basis of the same information. Furthermore even though authorities have a common set of objectives, they need not play a cooperative game in the formal sense; no binding preplay agreements on the choice of policy responses may have been established.

2. Decentralization of *nonstrategic information* occurs when authorities have access to different information concerning the state of the economy. Full coordination of such information requires that the authorities share this information. Each authority will then form expectations and policy in period t on the basis of the pooled information. This type of coordination need not imply that authorities adopt common objectives or that they formulate policy responses cooperatively.

3. Decentralization of *strategic information* arises whenever policy responses are chosen independently. This type of decentralization could arise even in situations in which authorities shared objectives and informa-

tion about the state of the economy but the optimal cooperative strategy is nonunique. It is analogous to the decentralization problem faced by an American football team that has snapped the ball without having called a play in the huddle. Coordination of strategic information means that authorities make binding, preplay agreements on their choice of policy responses, which they may do even though their targets and information about the state of the economy may differ. The Mundell (1962) assignment problem arises because of decentralization of this form.

The purpose of this chapter is to analyze the optimal design of monetary policy in interdependent economies when both targets and strategic information are decentralized. Previous analytic discussion of policy decentralization has been based on deterministic models. Furthermore, with the exception of Hamada (1976), who considers the problem in a classical, full-employment context, these models incorporate the traditional neo-Keynesian assumption of fixed prices. Studies incorporating stochastic elements have also used a neo-Keynesian framework and rely solely on simulation analysis (Pindyck 1976; Kydland 1976). None of the studies incorporates recent contributions to the theory of aggregate supply and expectations formation associated with the Lucas (1972) supply function.

We consider two monetary authorities pursuing domestic targets in two economies connected by trade both in real goods and in national monies. The model is presented in section 2. Each economy is characterized by a supply function of the Lucas type in which deviations of output from its natural level occur only because of deviations of the domestic price level from the value anticipated in the previous period. The natural level itself is stochastic. Agents in each economy hold domestic money for transactions purposes but may speculate on exchange rate movements by holding domestic or foreign money. We assume that money demands are also stochastic. The two economies are linked by a stochastic purchasing power parity relationship between the two price levels and the exchange rate.

Throughout we assume that the only contemporaneous variable observed by the two monetary authorities and the private sectors is the exchange rate. Incomes and price levels are observed only with a one-period lag. Each monetary authority's problem, then, is to infer from the observed current exchange rate the type of shocks affecting the economy and to set the current money supply to offset these shocks, taking into account the response of the foreign monetary authority to its actions.

In section 3 we assume that each country's monetary authority pursues the objective of stabilizing output around the average, or ex ante, natural level of output. In section 4 we modify the objective to one of stabilizing income around the actual but unobserved natural rate. This second objective is equivalent to minimizing price forecast errors and is more likely to lead to a policy of exchange rate stabilization. In section 5 we introduce exchange rate stabilization as an additional, independent goal.

Throughout we derive the policy rules that obtain if the monetary authorities pursue distinct targets independently. In sections 3 and 4 the optimal policy rules are not affected if authorities instead pursue a common objective cooperatively. This result does not extend to more general models such as the one considered in section 5.

A main purpose of the model is to provide insight into the design of optimal policies for managed floating. Models in which current policy can respond only to past information must implicitly assume that either the exchange rate or the money supply is fixed within the period: exchange rates are either fixed or the float is clean within the period (see Buiter 1979). Our model, however, allows for a contemporaneous money supply response to the current exchange rate.[1] Setting the money supply to fix the exchange rate and ignoring the exchange rate in setting the money supply constitute special cases of our model. Indeed we find that optimal monetary policy can involve exacerbating exchange rate movements.[2]

2. Two-Country Model of Monetary Policy and Exchange Rate Determination

We consider a model in which there are two countries, each with a monetary authority that manipulates the national money supply with the objective of stabilizing income in that country. Although the authorities pursue different objectives with different instruments, they share common information about the state of the world. Each authority establishes its money supply in response to this information, taking the other authority's response function as given.

The deviation of actual output from its long-run normal level in each country is proportional to the percentage deviation of the actual price level in that country from the price level anticipated in the previous period. In the home country we have

$$y_t = \Phi(p_t - p_{t|t-1}) + u_t^y \quad \Phi \geq 0 \tag{1}$$

while abroad

$$y_t^* = \Phi^*(p_t^* - p_{t|t-1}^*) + u_t^{*y} \quad \Phi^* \geq 0. \tag{2}$$

Here y_t denotes the logarithm of home country output and p_t the logarithm of the home country price level; $p_{t|t-1}$ denotes the expectation of p_t based on information available in period $t - 1$, and u_t^y denotes a Gaussian white noise disturbance term with variance $\sigma_{u^y}^2$. Equivalent magnitudes in the foreign country are denoted with an asterisk. In equations (1) and (2) we have normalized the expected logarithms of full employment income to equal zero. The actual or ex post natural levels of outputs, u_t^y and u_t^{*y} obtain when $p_t = p_{t|t-1}$ and $p_t^* = p_{t|t-1}^*$, respectively.

Justification for output supply equations of the form (1) and (2) is provided by Lucas (1972) and Sargent and Wallace (1975). Output equations of the form (1) and (2) would arise also if wage contracts are formed one period in advance. Wages in period t, it is assumed, cannot be modified by information that is not available before period t.[3] Other motivations of (1) and (2) involve imperfect observation of the contemporaneous aggregate price level.

We assume that citizens in each country must hold domestic money for transactions purposes but may speculate by holding foreign money. Overall money demand is thus given by a set of currency substitution money demand functions:

$$m_t - p_t = \alpha y_t - \beta(e_{t+1|t} - e_t) + u_t^m \quad \alpha, \beta \geq 0. \tag{3}$$

$$m_t^* - p_t^* = \alpha^* y_t^* + \beta^*(e_{t+1|t} - e_t) + u_t^{*m} \quad \alpha^*, \beta^* \geq 0. \tag{4}$$

Here m_t denotes the logarithm of nominal home country money balances in period t, e_t the logarithm of the spot price of foreign currency, and $e_{t+1|t}$ the value of e_{t+1} expected to occur in period t. The terms u_t^m and u_t^{*m} represent Gaussian white noise disturbances with variances $\sigma_{u^m}^2$ and $\sigma_{u^{*m}}^2$ respectively. The parameter α denotes the income elasticity of demand for real money balances and β the expected exchange rate appreciation elasticity. When $e_{t+1|t}$ is high relative to e_t, foreign money balances are more attractive.[4]

Finally we assume that the domestic and foreign price levels are connected by a stochastic purchasing power parity (PPP) relationship:[5]

$$p_t = e_t + p_t^* + u_t^e \tag{5}$$

where u_t^e represents a Gaussian white noise distribance with variance $\sigma_{u^e}^2$. Also, for simplicity, contemporaneous values of u_t^y, u_t^{*y}, u_t^m, u_t^{*m}, and u_t^e are assumed to be uncorrelated.

We assume that e_t is the only endogenous or exogenous variable observed contemporaneously. All past endogenous and exogenous variables are also part of the common private and public information set. The information set at time t when m_t is chosen, denoted by Ω_t, is therefore given by:[6]

$$\Omega_t = [e_\tau, p_{\tau-1}, p_{\tau-1}^*, y_{\tau-1}, y_{\tau-1}^*] \quad \tau \le t. \tag{6}$$

or equivalently by

$$\Omega_t = [e_\tau, y_{\tau-1}^y, u_{\tau-1}^{*y}, u_{\tau-1}^m, u_{\tau-1}^*, u_{\tau-1}^e] \quad \tau \le t. \tag{6'}$$

In addition both the authorities and the private sector know the true structure of the model, including the first and second moments of the distributions of the random disturbances. Expectations of p_t formed in period $t - 1$ are conditional on Ω_{t-1}, and expectations of e_{t+1} formed in period t are conditional on Ω_t. The foreign country has the same information set as the home country.

In period t the monetary authority in the home country chooses m_t to minimize

$$E(V_t|\Omega_t) = \sum_{\tau=t}^{\infty} \delta^{\tau-t} E[(y_\tau - \bar{y}_\tau)^2|\Omega_t] \quad 0 < \delta < 1. \tag{7}$$

The foreign monetary authority chooses m_t^* to minimize

$$E(V_t^*|\Omega_t) = \sum_{\tau=t}^{\infty} \delta^{*\tau-t} E[(y_\tau^* - \bar{y}_\tau^*)^2|\Omega_t] \quad 0 < \delta^* < 1. \tag{8}$$

$\bar{y}_\tau$ and $\bar{y}_\tau^*$ are target real output, at home and abroad, to be specified more precisely below. δ and δ^* are discount factors. Both m_t and m_t^* are chosen under the assumption that m_τ and m_τ^* minimize, respectively, $E(V_\tau|\Omega_\tau)$ and $E(V_\tau^*|\Omega_\tau)$ for all $\tau > t$.

By permitting money supplies to respond to the contemporaneous exchange rate out precluding the possibility of exchange rate contingent money wage contracts, known monetary rules will affect real output. In this model policymakers set money supplies by transfers and taxes. Direct exchange market intervention provides another mode that is consistent with our specification if the other country sterilizes the effect of exchange market intervention on its own money supply by transfers and taxes.

Equations (1) through (5) can be solved by substituting (1), (2), and (5) into (3) and (4) to obtain:

$$\begin{bmatrix} p_t \\ p_t^* \end{bmatrix} = B \begin{bmatrix} m_t + \alpha\phi p_{t|t-1} + \beta e_{t+1|t} + v_t + \beta u_t^e \\ m_t^* + \alpha^*\phi^* p_{t|t-1}^* - \beta^* e_{t+1|t} + v_t^* - \beta^* u_t^e \end{bmatrix} \Delta^{-1} \tag{9}$$

where

$$B \equiv \begin{bmatrix} \pi^* + \beta^* & \beta \\ \beta^* & \pi + \beta \end{bmatrix}$$

$$\pi \equiv 1 + \alpha\phi$$

$$\pi^* \equiv 1 + \alpha^*\phi^*$$

$$v_t \equiv -(\alpha u_t^y + u_t^m)$$

$$v_t^* \equiv -(\alpha^* u_t^{*y} + u_t^{*m})$$

$$\Delta \equiv \pi\pi^* + \beta\pi^* + \beta^*\pi.$$

Therefore, from the PPP relationship,

$$e_t = [\pi^*(m_t + \alpha\phi p_{t|t-1} + \beta e_{t+1|t} + v_t) - \pi(m_t^* + \alpha^*\phi^* p_{t|t-1}^*$$
$$- \beta^* e_{t+1|t} + v_t^*) - \pi\pi^* u_t^e]\Delta^{-1}. \tag{10}$$

Equations (9) and (10) represent reduced form expressions for the price levels and the exchange rate given past expectations of the current price levels and current expectations of the future exchange rate. We now turn to the design of monetary policy.

3. Optimal Monetary Policy: The Nash Solution

We first consider optimal monetary policy when each monetary authority follows a memoryless Nash strategy; that is, each monetary authority sets its money supply as a function only of the contemporaneous values of the state variàbles, taking as given the other monetary authority's money supply rule.

In this section, target output is the ex ante natural level of output.[7] We thus set $\bar{y}_\tau = \bar{y}_\tau^* = 0$ for all τ. Given the supply functions, equations (1) and (2), and the objective functions, equations (7) and (8), the authorities minimize

$$\sum_{\tau=t}^{\infty} \delta^{\tau-t} E[[\phi(p_\tau - p_{\tau|\tau-1}) + u_\tau^y]^2 |\Omega_t] \tag{11}$$

and

$$\sum_{\tau=t}^{\infty} \beta^{*\tau-t} E[[\phi^*(p_\tau^* - p_{\tau|\tau-1}^*) + u_\tau^{*y}]^2 |\Omega_t], \tag{12}$$

respectively.

We assume that each monetary authority sets its money supply as a linear, nonstochastic function of the information set. It is tedious but straightforward to show that the optimal money supply response is in fact of this form. In the appendix we show that the only element of the information set relevant for stabilization is the exchange rate. The monetary authority can achieve the same impact, however, by responding to any combination of current and lagged values of the exchange rate in appropriate proportion. For concreteness we consider only policies involving a response to the current exchange rate.[8] We thus consider policies of the form

$$m_t = ae_t, \tag{13}$$

$$m_t^* = a^* e_t. \tag{14}$$

Policy rules of this form are examples of contemporaneous or instantaneous feedback rules: policy variables respond to current observations of current endogenous variables. This formulation has been applied to stabilization policy by, for example, Poole (1970), Boyer (1978), McCallum and Whitaker (1979), Turnovsky (1982, 1983), Marston (1980), Frenkel and Aizenman (1982), and Canzoneri (1982). This specification is useful here because it allows an analysis of exchange rate management policies other than pure floating and fixed rates.

Since m_t and m_t^* respond only to e_t, all endogenous variables in our model depend, given expectations, only on current disturbances. Taylor (1977) has shown that models such as ours, which incorporate current or past expectations of future endogenous variables, have an infinite number of solutions in which current endogenous variables depend on the entire past history of exogenous variables. There is only one solution in which current variables depend on only a finite number of lagged variables, however. We restrict our analysis to this so-called minimal state solution in which no lagged variables appear. Thus e_t, y_t, y_t^*, p_t, and p_t^* depend linearly only on u_t so that

$$p_{t|t-1} = p_{t|t-1}^* = e_{t+1|t} = 0. \tag{15}$$

Since y_t and y_t^* do not depend on m_τ and m_τ^* for $t \neq \tau$, the authorities' problem reduces to one of choosing a to minimize $E(y_t^2|e_t)$ for the home country and a^* to minimize $E(y_t^{*2}|e_t)$ for the foreign country in each period t.

Each country will optimally choose its monetary policy rule, taking as given the rule of the other country. Considering the home country first, minimization of $E(y_t^2|e_t)$ is equivalent to choosing a money supply rule such that $E(y_t|e_t) = 0$,[9] given the rule followed by the foreign authority: a is chosen to satisfy:

$$E(y_t|e_t) = \Delta^{-1}\Phi[(\pi^* + \beta^*)ae_t + \beta a^* e_t + (\pi^* + \beta^*)E(v_t|e_t)$$
$$+ \beta E(v_t^*|e_t) + \pi^*\beta E(u_t^e|e_t)] + E(u_t^y|e_t) = 0. \tag{16}$$

The foreign country chooses its money supply rule (a^*) such that $E(y_t^*|e_t) = 0$ given the rule followed by the domestic authority (a):

$$E(y_t^*|e_t) = \Delta^{-1}\Phi^*[\beta^* ae_t + (\pi + \beta)a^* e_t + \beta^* E(v_t|e_t)$$
$$+ (\pi + \beta)E(v_t^*|e_t) - \pi\beta^* E(u_t^e|e_t)] + E(u_t^{*y}|e_t) = 0. \tag{17}$$

Equations (16) and (17) can be rewritten as reaction functions as in (18) and (19):

$$ae_t = -\left[\frac{\beta}{\pi^* + \beta^*}a^* e_t + E(v_t|e_t) + \frac{\beta}{\pi^* + \beta^*}E(v_t^*|e_t)\right.$$
$$\left. + \frac{\pi^*\beta}{\pi^* + \beta^*}E(u_t^e|e_t) + \frac{\Delta\Phi^{-1}}{\pi^* + \beta^*}E(u_t^y|e_t)\right] \tag{18}$$

$$a^* e_t = -\left[\frac{\beta^*}{\pi + \beta}ae_t + \frac{\beta^*}{\pi + \beta}E(v_t|e_t) + E(v_t^*|e_t) - \frac{\pi\beta^*}{\pi + \beta}E(u_t^e|e_t)\right.$$
$$\left. + \frac{\Delta\Phi^{*-1}}{\pi + \beta}E(u_t^{*y}|e_t)\right]. \tag{19}$$

Note from (18) and (19) that the domestic money supply responds negatively to the money supply abroad. An increase in the foreign money supply causes an appreciation of the exchange rate, creating expectations of depreciation, which reduce the demand for domestic currency. As all disturbances are independently, identically distributed, and there are no other sources of inertia in the model (specifically $m_{t|t-1} = 0$), rational expectations are regressive. To prevent the reduction in demand for domestic currency from raising the domestic price level, an accommodating reduction in domestic money supply must occur. Note also that given the money supply in the foreign country (m_t^*), the optimal domestic money supply in general responds to expectations of all types of shocks, both domestic and foreign and both monetary and real.

Noting that the optimal (least squares) predictor of some variable z_t given e_t is given by

$$E(z_t|e_t) = E(e_t)^{2-1} E(z_t e_t) \cdot e_t \tag{20}$$

we obtain

$$E(v_t|e_t) = \Delta \Lambda \pi^* \sigma_v^2 \sum{}^{-1} e_t, \tag{21a}$$

$$E(v_t^*|e_t) = -\Delta \Lambda \pi \sigma_{v*}^2 \sum{}^{-1} e_t, \tag{21b}$$

$$E(u_t^e|e_t) = -\Delta \Lambda \pi \pi^* \sigma_{u^e}^2 \sum{}^{-1} e_t, \tag{21c}$$

$$E(u_t^y|e_t) = -\Delta \Lambda \alpha \pi^* \sigma_{u^y}^2 \sum{}^{-1} e_t, \tag{21d}$$

$$E(u_t^{*y}|e_t) = \Delta \Lambda \alpha^* \pi \sigma_{u^*y}^2 \sum{}^{-1} e_t, \tag{21e}$$

$$\sum \equiv \pi^{*2}\sigma_v^2 + \pi^2\sigma_{v*}^2 + (\pi\pi^*)^2\sigma_{u^e}^2,$$

$$\Lambda \equiv 1 - \Delta^{-1}(\pi^*a - \pi a^*),$$

$$\sigma_v^2 \equiv E(v_t^2); \ \sigma_{v*}^2 \equiv E(v_t^{*2}); \ \sigma_{u^e}^2 \equiv E(u_t^{e2}); \ \sigma_{u^y}^2 \equiv E(u_t^{y2}); \ \sigma_{u^*y}^2 \equiv E(u_t^{*y2}).$$

Assuming the system given by (18) and (19) to be of full rank, the Nash equilibrium solution for a and a^* is given by:

$$a = \beta + \frac{\Phi^{-1}\alpha\pi\pi^*\sigma_{u^y}^2 - \pi^*\sigma_v^2}{\pi\pi^*\sigma_{u^e}^2 + \Phi^{-1}\alpha\pi^*\sigma_{u^y}^2 + \Phi^{*-1}\alpha^*\pi\sigma_{u^*y}^2}, \tag{22}$$

$$a^* = -\beta^* + \frac{-\Phi^{*-1}\alpha^*\pi\pi^*\sigma_{u^*y}^2 + \pi\sigma_{v*}^2}{\pi\pi^*\sigma_{u^e}^2 + \Phi^{-1}\alpha\pi^*\sigma_{u^y}^2 + \Phi^{*-1}\alpha^*\pi\sigma_{u^*y}^2}, \tag{23}$$

or, noting that $\sigma_v^2 = \alpha^2 \sigma_{uy}^2 + \sigma_{um}^2$ and $\sigma_{v*}^2 = \alpha*^2 \sigma_{u*y}^2 + \sigma_{u*m}^2$,

$$a = \beta + \frac{\Phi^{-1} \alpha \pi* \sigma_{uy}^2 - \pi* \sigma_{um}^2}{\pi \pi* \sigma_{ue}^2 + \Phi^{-1} \alpha \pi* \sigma_{uy}^2 + \Phi*^{-1} \alpha* \pi \sigma_{u*y}^2}, \tag{22'}$$

$$a* = -\beta* + \frac{-\Phi*^{-1} \alpha* \pi \sigma_{u*y}^2 + \pi \sigma_{u*m}^2}{\pi \pi* \sigma_{ue}^2 + \Phi^{-1} \alpha \pi* \sigma_{uy}^2 + \Phi*^{-1} \alpha* \pi \sigma_{u*y}^2}. \tag{23'}$$

β is the absolute value of the elasticity of demand for domestic money with respect to the expected proportional rate of depreciation of the domestic currency and $-\beta*$ the corresponding elasticity for the foreign currency. In a currency substitution framework they can be viewed as the exchange rate speculation elasticities of home and foreign currency, respectively. The first terms of (22) or (22') and (23) or (23') therefore suggest that monetary policy accommodates changes in the demand for money due to unanticipated changes in the exchange rate, thereby neutralizing the effect of unanticipated exchange rate changes on the price level. This policy helps to insulate the economy from real effects of unanticipated exchange rate changes. Remember that since $e_{t|t-1} = 0$, a monetary rule contingent on e_t is a monetary rule contingent on the deviation of the actual exchange rate in period t from the exchange rate for period t anticipated in period $t - 1$.

To the extent that monetary policy does accommodate swings in speculative demand, monetary authorities lean with the wind in the foreign exchange market; they expand the money supply when the price of domestic currency is lower than had been expected, and conversely (that is, $a > 0$ and $a* < 0$).[10] Such a policy will exacerbate movements in the exchange rate, as can be seen from equation (24), the reduced form expression for the exchange rate:

$$e_t = (\pi* v_t - \pi v_t* - \pi \pi* u_t^e)(\Delta - \pi* a + \pi a*)^{-1}. \tag{24}$$

The denominator of the second term on the right-hand side of (22') and (23') is positive. Thus an increase in the variability of the demand for domestic money (σ_{um}^2) will reduce the degree to which the authorities lean with the wind and may even reverse this policy. An unexpected increase in the demand for domestic money will be associated with an unanticipated appreciation of the home currency. Rather than contracting the money supply as would be optimal if the main sources of uncertainty were foreign, optimal monetary policy will at least in part accommodate the unexpected increase in the demand for money by expanding the money supply.

The variability of foreign money demand has no effect on optimal domestic monetary policy, however. This result may seem surprising since, from (16) and (17), foreign monetary shocks do affect domestic income and, from (18) and (19), domestic monetary policy, given foreign monetary policy, does respond to perceived shocks in the demand for foreign money. If foreign monetary authorities pursue an optimal monetary policy, however, they minimize the effect of their own monetary disturbances. Domestic monetary policy can then ignore such disturbances.

An increase in the variance of domestic output shocks raises the optimal degree to which monetary authorities should lean with the wind. A positive output shock raises the demand for money and appreciates the exchange rate. To offset the effect of a positive income shock, authorities should contract the money supply. Hence when exchange rate variation is caused in large part by instability in the supply of domestic output, monetary authorities should act to augment exchange rate changes.

The variability of foreign output shocks, unlike the variability of foreign monetary shocks, does affect the optimal intervention policy. A positive foreign output shock will tend to depreciate the exchange rate and engender a foreign monetary action that further depreciates the exchange rate. (In contrast a foreign monetary disturbance engenders an offsetting foreign monetary action.) Foreign output shocks thus create exchange rate variability that is unrelated to domestic disturbances. Any response designed to offset the effects of domestic shocks, as perceived through exchange rate variation, on domestic targets will be diminished because the foreign disturbances make the exchange rate a noisier indicator of those domestic disturbances. Thus as $\sigma_{y^*}^2$ rises, optimal domestic policy is aimed increasingly at accommodating speculative behavior.

For the same reason increased variability in shocks to the purchasing power parity relationship also reduces the extent to which monetary policy can offset the effects of domestic shocks on income. As $\sigma_{u^e}^2$ rises, policy increasingly should isolate the domestic price level from the effects of exchange rate speculation.

It is illuminating to consider monetary policy in four special cases of the model.

1. No domestic shocks. When $\sigma_{uy}^2 = \sigma_{um}^2 = 0$, there are no domestic

sources of disturbances in the home country. The only shocks it faces are exchange rate disturbances resulting either from the stochastic nature of the purchasing power parity relationship ($\sigma_{ue}^2 > 0$) or from uncertainty in the rest of the world ($\sigma_{u*m}^2, \sigma_{u*y}^2 > 0$). In this case (22′) reduces to $a = \beta$. (Similarly if there are no sources of disturbances internal to the foreign country, $\sigma_{u*y}^2 = \sigma_{u*m}^2 = 0$ and (23′) reduces to $a* = -\beta*$). The money supply rule is entirely accommodating. When the exchange rate depreciates unexpectedly, the money supply expands. In the absence of changes in the money supply, a depreciation of the exchange rate creates expectations of appreciation (since $e_{t+1|t} = 0$). These expectations increase the speculative demand for home country money, which lowers the home country price level and therefore income. To offset this, the monetary authority acts to accommodate exactly the higher money demand with a higher supply. Therefore a country facing temporary shocks largely from abroad through the exchange rate will adopt a monetary rule that exacerbates the exchange rate changes in order to stabilize real income.

2. No domestic shocks and no currency substitution. If there are no domestic shocks and if the demand for domestic currency is inelastic with respect to exchange rate changes (if $\sigma_{uy}^2 = \sigma_{um}^2 = \beta = 0$) then the optimal money supply is independent of the exchange rate ($a = 0$). Thus, except in the improbable event that the various components of (22′) cancel exactly, a policy of free floating is optimal if and only if the demand for money is inelastic and there are no domestic disturbances. Even if the demand for money does not depend on the expected change of the exchange rate (if $\beta = 0$) exchange rate changes signal in part domestic shocks to which the money supply should respond. This result is analogous to Poole's (1970) finding that in the closed economy IS-LM model, the optimal money supply is invariant to the interest rate if and only if the demand for money is interest inelastic and the economy is not subject to a variable demand for money.

3. No real or purchasing power parity shocks. When the only source of uncertainty is in the demand for either currency (when $\sigma_{uy}^2 = \alpha_{u*y}^2 = \sigma_{ue}^2 = 0$), then policy makes the supply of money perfectly elastic. The exchange rate is pegged. Turnovsky (1983) also obtains this result for a single small, open economy. This result is analogous to Poole's finding that for a closed economy, a policy of fixing the interest rate is optimal when the only source of disturbances is in the demand for money. Note that if pegging the exchange rate is the optimal policy for one country, it is so for both.

Unless the two countries peg at the same level, however, the model becomes inconsistent.

4. Infinitely elastic currency substitution. If individuals view domestic and foreign currency as perfect substitutes, then $\beta = \beta^* = \infty$, and a policy of pegging minimizes income variability even if the economy is subject to real disturbances. Otherwise the exchange rate becomes indeterminant. This can be seen from equation (10). Setting $\beta = \beta^* = \infty$, this expression reduces to $e_t = e_{t+1|t}$. Any exchange rate that remains constant over time is compatible with equilibrium (see Kareken and Wallace 1981). Again consistency requires that monetary authorities peg to the same exchange rate.

4. Optimal Exchange Rate Management When Minimizing the Price Forecast Error Is the Objective

So far we have assumed that the policy makers' objectives are to minimize output variation around the ex ante expected natural rates ($\bar{y}_t = \bar{y}_t^* = 0$). One might assume instead that policymakers are concerned with the deviation of income around the ex post actual natural rates ($\bar{y}_t = u_t^y$, $\bar{y}_t^* = u_t^{*y}$), which are unobserved contemporaneously. Such an objective is equivalent to minimizing price forecast errors since

$$y_t - u_t^y = \Phi(p_t - p_{t|t-1}) \tag{25}$$

and

$$y_t^* - u_t^{*y} = \Phi^*(p_t^* - p_{t|t-1}^*). \tag{26}$$

The alternative specification of objective functions as

$$\sum_{\tau=t}^{\infty} \delta^{\tau-t} E[(y_\tau - u_\tau)^2 | \Omega_t] \quad 0 < \delta < 1 \tag{27}$$

and

$$\sum_{\tau=t}^{\infty} \delta^{*\tau-t} E[(y_\tau^* - u_\tau^*)^2 | \Omega_t] \quad 0 < \delta^* < 1 \tag{28}$$

is plausible if one believes that price forecast errors themselves, rather than output fluctuations, are a primary source of inefficiency. If such a specification is adopted, optimal policy rules are derived for the home country by choosing a such that $E(y_t - u_t | \Omega_t) = 0$, given a^*, and for the foreign country by choosing a^* such that $E(y_t^* - u_t^*|\Omega_t) = 0$, given a. This yields

$$a = \beta - (\sigma_{u^m}^2 + \alpha^2 \sigma_{u^y}^2)/[(1 + \alpha\Phi)\sigma_{u^e}^2], \tag{29}$$

$$a^* = -\beta^* + (\sigma_{u^*m}^2 + \alpha^{*2}\sigma_{u^*y}^2)/[(1 + \alpha^*\Omega^*)\sigma_{u^e}^2]. \tag{30}$$

Three basic differences from our previous analysis emerge.

First, supply uncertainty now contributes toward the optimality of a policy of exchange rate stabilization (leaning against the wind in the exchange market) rather than the opposite. The reason is that an unanticipated increase in output will increase money demand, lower the price level, and cause the currency to appreciate. To eliminate the unanticipated price decline, money expansion is now appropriate, dampening the exchange rate change.

Second, the variability of foreign shocks, regardless of whether they are monetary or real in origin, has no effect on optimal domestic monetary policy. The domestic effects of foreign shocks of either type are minimized by optimal foreign monetary policy. In other words each monetary authority acts to offset the effects of local shocks on both itself and the other country.

Third, regardless of the variability of money demand or output supply in either economy, if the purchasing power relationship is nonstochastic, a policy of pegging the exchange rate is optimal.

5. Cooperative Pareto-Optimal Solution

So far we have assumed that each monetary authority acts independently to attain a domestic policy objective, taking the monetary policy of the other country as given. In this section we compare such policies with those that would arise if the two monetary authorities were to cooperate in setting monetary policy to attain a mutual objective. To derive the set of Pareto-optimal policies, we assume that policymakers jointly set monetary policy in period t to minimize an objective of the form

$$w \sum_{\tau=t}^{\infty} \delta^{\tau-t} E[(y_\tau^2|\Omega_\tau)|\Omega_t] + w^* \sum_{\tau=t}^{\infty} \delta^{*\tau-t} E[(y_\tau^{*2}|\Omega_\tau)|\Omega_t]$$

$$w, w^* > 0, 0 < \delta < 1 \tag{31}$$

in period t.

As section 4 demonstrated, however, current values of m_t and m_t^* do not affect values of y_τ and y_τ^* for $\tau > t$. Choosing m_t^* to minimize (31) is equivalent to choosing m_t and m_t^* to minimize

$$wE(y_t^2|\Omega_t) + w^*E(y_t^{*2}|\Omega_t)$$
$$= wE[(y_t - E(y_t|\Omega_t))^2|\Omega_t] + w^*E[(y_t^* - E(y_t^*|\Omega_t))^2|\Omega_t] \qquad (32)$$
$$+ w[E(y_t|\Omega_t)]^2 + w^*[E(y_t^*|\Omega_t)]^2.$$

From note 9 it follows that the first two terms of the right-hand side of expression (32) are independent of m_t and m_t^*. Minimizing (32) with respect to m_t and m_t^*, then, is equivalent to minimizing

$$wE[(y_t|\Omega_t)]^2 + w^*E[(y_t^*|\Omega_t)]^2. \qquad (33)$$

First-order conditions for a minimum are

$$wE\left(y_t\frac{dy_t}{dm_t}|\Omega_t\right) + w^*E\left(y_t^*\frac{dy_t^*}{dm_t}|\Omega_t\right) = 0, \qquad (34)$$

$$wE\left(y_t\frac{dy_t}{dm_t^*}|\Omega_t\right) + w^*E\left(y_t^*\frac{dy_t^*}{dm_t^*}|\Omega_t\right) = 0. \qquad (35)$$

From equation (A8) in the appendix and since all forward expectations are zero, dy_t/dm_t, dy_t^*/dm_t, dy_t/dm_t^*, and dy_t^*/dm_t^* are nonstochastic. These first-order conditions therefore obtain when m_t and m_t^* satisfy

$$E(y_t|\Omega_t) = E(y_t^*|\Omega_t) = 0. \qquad (36)$$

Since (34) and (35) are linear functions of m_t and m_t^*, the values of m_t and m_t^* that satisfy (36) constitute a unique solution. These are exactly the same values of m_t and m_t^* that satisfy the Nash equilibrium. In our model, then, the Nash solution is also the unique Pareto-optimal solution. This result is not surprising since, in our model, each country has one independent instrument, its money supply, and one independent target, the level of its income. In such a context there are no gains from policy coordination.

To show that the equivalence of the Nash and Pareto-optimal solutions does not generalize to systems in which there are more targets than instruments, consider a system in which one or both countries also have exchange rate stabilization as another goal; that is, in period t the home country seeks to minimize

$$E \sum_{\tau=t}^{\infty} \delta^{\tau-t} [E(y_\tau^2 + \omega e_\tau^2 | \Omega_\tau) | \Omega_t] \qquad \omega > 0, \quad 0 < \delta < 1 \tag{37}$$

while the foreign country minimizes

$$E \sum_{\tau=t}^{\infty} \delta^{*\tau-t} [E(y_\tau^{*2} + \omega^* e_\tau^2 | \Omega_\tau) | \Omega_t] \qquad \omega^* > 0, \quad 0 < \delta^* < 1. \tag{38}$$

First-order conditions for Nash equilibrium values of m_t and m_t^* are given by

$$E(y_t | \Omega_t) \frac{dy_t}{dm_t} + \omega e_t \frac{de_t}{dm_t} = 0, \tag{39}$$

and

$$E(y_t^* | \Omega_t) \frac{dy_t^*}{dm_t^*} + \omega^* e_t \frac{de_t}{dm_t^*} = 0. \tag{40}$$

With weights of w and w^* placed on the home and foreign countries' objective functions, however, first-order conditions for Pareto-optimal values of m_t and m_t^* are

$$wE(y_t | \Omega_t) \frac{dy_t}{dm_t} + w^* E(y_t^* | \Omega_t) \frac{dy_t^*}{dm_t} + (w\omega + w^*\omega^*) \frac{de_t}{dm_t} = 0, \tag{41}$$

$$wE(y_t | \Omega_t) \frac{dy_t}{dm_t^*} + w^* E(y_t^* | \Omega_t) \frac{dy_t^*}{dm_t^*} + (w\omega + w^*\omega^*) \frac{de_t}{dm_t^*} = 0. \tag{42}$$

These are not equivalent to (39) and (40) except when $\omega = \omega^* = 0$. In general, the Nash solution is not Pareto optimal.

If each authority's number of targets does not exceed the number of linearly independent instruments available to that authority, each target responds to each instrument, targets are not inconsistent, and the authorities' instruments are linearly independent of each other, then in a linear world each authority can use its own instruments to obtain an outcome independent of the other authority's rule. One authority could do no better in attaining its own targets if it had access to the other's instruments. When the number of targets that one authority pursues exceeds the number of instruments available to it, it could achieve its targets more precisely if it had access to the other authority's instruments as well.[11] The Pareto-optimal policy rules will depend in this case on the weights assigned to each authority's objective function in calculating global welfare.

In the above example, exchange rate stabilization constitutes a public good that is likely to be pursued inadequately under a decentralized solution. Comparing equation (39) to equation (41) and (40) to (42), note that the weight on the exchange rate effect relative to the home income effect in the first-order conditions for optimality rises from ω to $\omega + (w^*/w)\omega^*$ and from ω^* to $\omega^* + (w/w^*)\omega$ in moving from the decentralized Nash solution to the centralized Pareto-optimal solution.

6. Conclusion

This study of optimal monetary policy or exchange rate management in interdependent economies has abstracted from many real world complications in order to obtain a transparent structure. Nevertheless, a number of results are likely to be robust under further generalizations of the model.

1. Neither a fixed nor a freely floating exchange rate is likely to be optimal. Optimal monetary policy in general requires a finite response of the money supply to the exchange rate.

2. Output stabilizing monetary policy may well require leaning with the wind in the foreign exchange markets, expanding the money supply when the home currency depreciates, thus increasing the volatility of the exchange rate.

3. Depending on the nature of the objective function pursued abroad, optimal foreign monetary policy may allow the domestic monetary authority to establish an optimal intervention rule independent of the variance of some or all foreign disturbances.

4. There are likely to be gains from policy coordination when the number of targets exceeds the number of instruments.

Appendix 2A

Note that for any variable q one has $q_{t|t-i} \equiv E(q_t|\Omega_{t-i})$ and that $E[E(q_t|\Omega_{t-i})|\Omega_{t-i-j}] = E(q_t|\Omega_{t-i-j})$, $i, j \geq 0$. We thus obtain, from (9),

$$\begin{bmatrix} p_{t|t-i} \\ p^*_{t|t-i} \end{bmatrix} = B \begin{bmatrix} m_{t|t-i} + \alpha\Phi p_{t|t-i} + \beta e_{t+1|t-i} \\ m^*_{t|t-i} + \alpha^*\Phi^* p^*_{t|t-i} - \beta^* e_{t+1|t-i} \end{bmatrix} \Delta^{-1}. \tag{A1}$$

Subtracting (A1) for $i = 1$ from (9) yields:

$$\begin{bmatrix} p_t \\ p_t^* \end{bmatrix} - \begin{bmatrix} p_{t|t-1} \\ p_{t|t-1}^* \end{bmatrix}$$

$$= B \begin{bmatrix} m_t - m_{t|t-1} + \beta(e_{t+1|t} - e_{t+1|t-1}) + v_t + \beta u_t^e \\ m_t^* - m_{t|t-1}^* - \beta^*(e_{t+1|t} - e_{t+1|t-1}) + v_t^* - \beta^* u_t^e \end{bmatrix} \Delta^{-1}. \tag{A2}$$

Using

$$e_t = p_t - p_t^* - u_t^e \tag{A3}$$

which, since $u_{t+1|t}^e = u_{t+1|t-1}^e = 0$, implies, for $i > 0$,

$$e_{t+i|t} - e_{t+i|t-1} = p_{t+i|t} - p_{t+i|t-1} - (p_{t+i|t}^* - p_{t+i|t-1}^*) \tag{A4}$$

we may write (A2) as

$$\begin{bmatrix} p_t - p_{t|t-1} \\ p_t^* - p_{t|t-1}^* \end{bmatrix} = BD \begin{bmatrix} p_{t+1|t} - p_{t+1|t-1} \\ p_{t+1|t}^* - p_{t+1|t-1}^* \end{bmatrix} \Delta^{-1}$$

$$+ B \begin{bmatrix} m_t - m_{t|t-1} \\ m_t^* - m_{t|t-1}^* \end{bmatrix} \Delta^{-1} + B \begin{bmatrix} v_t + \beta u_t^e \\ v_t^* - \beta^* u_t^e \end{bmatrix} \Delta^{-1} \tag{A5}$$

where

$$D = \begin{bmatrix} \beta & -\beta \\ -\beta^* & \beta^* \end{bmatrix}.$$

From (A1) and (A4), however, note that

$$\begin{bmatrix} p_{t+i|t} - p_{t+i|t-1} \\ p_{t+i|t}^* - p_{t+i|t-1}^* \end{bmatrix} = ABD \begin{bmatrix} p_{t+i+1|t} - p_{t+i+1|t-1} \\ p_{t+i+1|t}^* - p_{t+i+1|t-1}^* \end{bmatrix} \Delta^{-1}$$

$$+ AB \begin{bmatrix} m_{t+i|t} - m_{t+i|t-1} \\ m_{t+i|t}^* - m_{t+i|t-1}^* \end{bmatrix} \Delta^{-1} \tag{A6}$$

where

$$A \equiv \left\{ I - B \begin{bmatrix} \alpha\Phi & 0 \\ 0 & \alpha^*\Phi^* \end{bmatrix} \Delta^{-1} \right\}^{-1}.$$

By repeated forward substitution and assuming stability, we may write (A6) as

$$\begin{bmatrix} p_{t+i|t} - p_{t+i|t-1} \\ p_{t+i|t}^* - p_{t+i|t-1}^* \end{bmatrix} = \sum_{j=i}^{\infty} C^{j-i} AB \begin{bmatrix} m_{t+j|t} - m_{t+j|t-1} \\ m_{t+j|t}^* - m_{t+j|t-1}^* \end{bmatrix} \tag{A7}$$

where $C \equiv ABD$.

Substituting (A7) into (A5) implies that

$$
\begin{bmatrix} p_t - p_{t|t-1} \\ p_t^* - p_{t|t-1}^* \end{bmatrix} = BD \sum_{j=1}^{\infty} C^j AB \begin{bmatrix} m_{t+j|t} - m_{t+j|t-1} \\ m_{t+j|t}^* - m_{t+j|t-1}^* \end{bmatrix} \Delta^{-1}
$$

$$
+ B \begin{bmatrix} m_t - m_{t|t-1} \\ m_t^* - m_{t|t-1}^* \end{bmatrix} \Delta^{-1} + B \begin{bmatrix} v_t + \beta u_t^e \\ v_t^* - \beta^* u_t^e \end{bmatrix} \Delta^{-1}.
$$

(A8)

We define the following: $u_t \equiv (u_t^y, u_t^{*y}, u_t^m, u_t^{*m}, u_t^e)$, $\tilde{u}_t \equiv u_t - E(u_t|\Omega_t)$, and $\tilde{e}_t \equiv e_t - E(e_t|\Omega_{t-1})$. We may thus define $\tilde{\Omega}_t \equiv (\tilde{e}_t, \tilde{u}_{t-1})$ as the new information available in period t. Since u_{t-i}, $i \geq 2$ is known at period $t-1$, $\tilde{e}_t$ and thus $\tilde{\Omega}_t$ can depend only on $\tilde{u}_{t-1}$ and u_t unless monetary policy is itself random. Revisions of expectations in period t about monetary policy can depend only on information newly available in period t: $\tilde{\Omega}_t$. Restricting ourselves to linear time-invariant nonstochastic policies, we may write

$$
m_{t+j|t} - m_{t+j|t-1} = \gamma_t \tilde{e}_t + \gamma' \tilde{u}_{t-1} \qquad j \geq 0 \tag{A9}
$$

and

$$
m_{t+j|t}^* - m_{t+j|t-1}^* = \gamma_j^* \tilde{e}_t + \gamma_j^{*'} \tilde{u}_{t-1} \qquad j \geq 0. \tag{A10}
$$

Substituting (A9) and (A10) into (A8) we obtain

$$
\begin{bmatrix} p_t - p_{t|t-1} \\ p_t^* - p_{t|t-1}^* \end{bmatrix} = BD \sum_{j=1}^{\infty} C^j AB \begin{bmatrix} \gamma_j \tilde{e}_t + \gamma_j' \tilde{u}_{t-1} \\ \gamma_j^* \tilde{e}_t + \gamma_j^{*'} \tilde{u}_{t-1} \end{bmatrix} \Delta^{-1}
$$

$$
+ B \begin{bmatrix} \gamma_0 \tilde{e}_t + \gamma_0' \tilde{u}_{t-1} \\ \gamma_0^* \tilde{e}_t + \gamma_0^{*'} \tilde{u}_{t-1} \end{bmatrix} \Delta^{-1} + B \begin{bmatrix} v_t + \beta u_t^e \\ v_t^* + \beta^* u_t^e \end{bmatrix} \Delta^{-1}.
$$

(A11)

Substituting (A11) into (11) and (12) it is clear that since u_t and u_{t-1}, and therefore $\tilde{e}_t$ and $\tilde{u}_{t-1}$, are orthogonal, policies for which γ_j' and $\gamma_j^{*'}$ are nonzero increase the minimum expected loss. Such policies introduce additional randomness in the form of the unobserved (as of last period) component of last period's disturbance into the current period price forecast error. We thus restrict ourselves to monetary policies that do not respond to $\tilde{u}_{t-1}$.

If, in fact, $\gamma_j' = \gamma_j^{*'} = 0$, then policy responds only to currently observed components of the current disturbances. Since these can be observed only by e_t, policy can respond only to e_t. We thus restrict ourselves to policies of the form

$$m_t = \sum_{\tau = -\infty}^{t} a_{t-\tau} e_\tau, \tag{A12}$$

$$m_t^* = \sum_{\tau = -\infty}^{t} a_{t-\tau}^* e_\tau. \tag{A13}$$

Substituting (A12) and (A13) into (A8) we obtain

$$\begin{bmatrix} p_t - p_{t|t-1} \\ p_t^* - p_{t|t-1}^* \end{bmatrix} = \Psi \Delta^{-1} e_t + B \begin{bmatrix} v_t + \beta u_t^e \\ v_t^* - \beta^* u_t^e \end{bmatrix} \Delta^{-1} \tag{A14}$$

where

$$\Psi \equiv BD \sum_{j=1}^{\infty} C^j A B \hat{a}_j + B \hat{a}_0,$$

$$\hat{a}_j \equiv \begin{bmatrix} a_j \\ a_j^* \end{bmatrix}; \quad \hat{a}_0 \equiv \begin{bmatrix} a_0 \\ a_0^* \end{bmatrix}.$$

Observe that any given values of Ψ and Ψ^* can be achieved by linear combinations of an infinite number of variations of the underlying policy parameters a_j and a_j^*. For example, a policy rule that sets $\hat{a}_j = 0, j \neq 0$, $\hat{a}_0 = \bar{a}_0$ will have the same effect on the objective functional as one that sets $\hat{a}_j = 0, j \neq 1$, and $\hat{a}_1 = (BDCAB)^{-1} B \bar{a}_0$. In general the government can achieve the same objective by responding only currently to current information (e_t) that it can achieve by responding to this information later. It is interesting to note that even if the governments were to have inferior information to the private sector in the sense that they learn e_t at a later date, they can achieve their objectives equally well. Turnovsky (1980) and Weiss (1982) provide other examples of this phenomenon. (See also Buiter 1980). For convenience we restrict curselves to current response only. We thus assume $a_j = a_j^* = 0, j \neq 0$.

Notes

Buiter would like to acknowledge financial support from the National Science Foundation. Much of Eaton's work on this chapter was done while he was visiting the Graduate Institute of International Studies, Geneva. Earlier versions were presented at the Ninety-second Annual Meeting of the American Economic Association, Atlanta, Georgia, December 1979, at the First Annual Conference of the Society for Economic Dynamics and Control in Cambridge, England, June 1979, and at the University of Warwick Summer Workshop in July 1980. Stanley Black, Marcus Miller, and Douglas Purvis made useful comments.

1. In this respect our model resembles that of Boyer (1978) and Roper and Turnovsky (1980); however, they consider a single open economy characterized by Keynesian unemployment. In a closed economy setting the current response issue has been studied by Woglom (1979) and McCallum and Whitaker (1979). In a recent paper Turnovsky (1983) derives optimal exchange market intervention rules for a small open economy characterized by a Lucas supply function. See also Frenkel and Aizenman (1982).

2. Turnovsky (1982, 1983) also finds a leaning with the wind policy to be optimal in some situations.

3. Contracts that do not allow wages to respond to contemporaneous data might arise because such data are not available symmetrically to workers and employers, leading to problems of moral hazard.

In fact the coefficients ϕ and ϕ^* may depend on the variance of the price level and hence on policy rules themselves. An increase in price level stability may lead to a greater use of long-term contracts embodying fixed nominal wages and prices—for example, raising ϕ and ϕ^*. We do not pursue this line of thought here but assume a short-run supply response independent of policy rules. This assumption is appropriate if, for example, the nature of long-term contracts and their significance in the economy are not affected by price variability over the range of variation relevant to our analysis. Flood and Marion (1982) discuss the implications of allowing output supply elasticities to depend on the variance of the price level. They consider only regimes of fixed and pure floating exchange rates, however. Their analysis, unlike ours, assumes that the aggregate price level is part of current information or that partial or complete wage indexation is feasible.

4. Barro (1978) also assumes that the demand for money responds to expected exchange rate changes in his model of monetary policy in a small open economy.

5. There are a number of reasons why the purchasing power parity relationship may be stochastic without creating possibilities for profitable commodity arbitrage. To illustrate one explanation, consider the standard two-country, two-commodity, two-factor Heckscher-Ohlin-Samuelson trade model appended to include a nontraded good produced in each country. With incomplete specialization and in the absence of transport costs, trade will cause exact purchasing power to hold with respect to traded goods alone and will also result in factor price equalization. The price of nontraded goods will be determined by competition in the nontraded goods sector. Random variation in relative productivities in the two sectors, if not perfectly correlated between the two countries, will cause the relative price of nontraded goods to vary independently in the two countries. The purchasing power parity relationship as applied to all goods, both traded and nontraded, therefore will be subject to random variation. Following this interpretation then, a positive value of u_t^e would imply that productivity in the nontraded goods sector at home is relatively lower, compared to that abroad, than is normally the case. The domestic price level is consequently higher.

6. We assume away all problems of nonuniqueness through extraneous information. The information sets of all agents therefore are limited to variables that appear in the structural model, given expectations—that is, to market fundamentals in the sense of Flood and Garber (1980). See also Taylor (1977).

7. Flood and Marion (1982) show that minimizing the deadweight loss due to wage contracts leads to an objective function somewhere between minimizing variability around the ex ante and ex post natural rates.

8. This case uniquely has the virtue of yielding time-consistent policies. A monetary policy that responds in period t to e_τ, $\tau < t$, does not affect y_t by this response but only y_τ. Since y_τ in period t is a bygone, time-consistent monetary authorities have no reason to stabilize output by expectations of future policy. At time t they may want the private sector to believe that they will respond in some particular way at some future period, but when that period comes they have no incentive to do so. Hence the private sector has no reason to believe them.

9. First note that

$$E(y_t^2|e_t) = E((y_t - E(y_t|e_t))^2|e_t) + [E(y_t|e_t)]^2.$$

In our model y_t and e_t are jointly normally distributed. Therefore, conditional on e_t, y_t is normally distributed with mean given by expression (16) and variance

$$E\{[y_t - E(y_t|e_t)]^2|e_t\} = E(y_t^2) - [E(y_t \cdot e_t)]^2/E(e_t)^2$$

(see Hogg and Craig 1978), pp. 63–65). Since this expression t contains only the unconditional variances and covariance of e_t and y_t, it is independent of the e_t actually observed.

10. See Harris and Purvis (1981) and Eaton and Turnovsky (1982) for a single economy model of exchange rate determination including permanent as well as transitory disturbances. Introducing permanent disturbances is likely to reduce the extent to which a policy of leaning with the wind is optimal since rational expectations consequently are less likely to be regressive. See also Eaton (1982) and Turnovsky (1982) for a discussion of this point.

11. This is also likely to be the case even if the number of targets does not exceed the number of instruments when the coefficients of the system are stochastic. See Brainard (1967).

References

Allen, Polly R., and Peter B. Kenen. 1980. *Asset Markets, Exchange Rates and Economic Integration: A Synthesis.* Cambridge: Cambridge University Press.

Aoki, Masanao. 1976. "On Decentralized Stabilization Policies and Dynamic Assignments Problem". *Journal of International Economics* 6 (May): 143–171.

Barro, Robert J. 1978. "A Stochastic Equilibrium Model of an Open Economy under Flexible Exchange Rates." *Quarterly Journal of Economics* 92 (February): 149–164.

Boyer, Russell S. 1978. "Optimal Foreign Exchange Market Intervention." *Journal of Political Economy* 86 (December): 1045–1055.

Brainard, William C. 1967. "Uncertainty and the Effectiveness of Policy." *America Economic Review Proceedings* 57 (May): 411–425.

Buiter, Willem H. 1979. "Optimal Foreign Exchange Market Intervention with Rational Expectations." In J. Martin and A. Smith, eds., *Trade and Payments Adjustment under Flexible Exchange Rates.* London: Macmillan.

Buiter, Willem H. 1980. "Monetary, Financial and Fiscal Policy under Rational Expectations." *IMF Staff Papers* 27 (December): 785–813.

Canzoneri, Matthew B. 1982. "Exchange Intervention in a Multiple Country World." *Journal of International Economics* 13 (November): 267–290.

Cooper, Richard N. 1969. "Macroeconomic Policy Adjustment in Interdependent Economies." *Quarterly Journal of Economics* 83 (February): 1–24.

Eaton, Jonathan. 1982. "Optimal and Time Consistent Exchange Rate Management in an Overlapping Generations Economy." *Economic Growth Center Discussion Paper* 413. Yale University (July).

Eaton, Jonathan, and Stephen J. Turnovsky. 1982. "Effects of a Monetary Disturbance on Exchange Rates with Risk Averse Speculation." *Journal of International Money and Finance* 1 (April): 21–37.

Flood, Robert P., and Peter M. Garber. 1980. "Market Fundamentals vs. Price Level Bubbles: The First Tests." *Journal of Political Economy* 88 (August): 745–770.

Flood, Robert P., and Nancy Peregrim Marion. 1982. "The Transmission of Disturbances under Alternative Exchange Rate Regimes with Optimal Indexing." *Quarterly Journal of Economics* 96 (February): 43–66.

Frenkel, Jacob A., and Joshua Aizenman. 1982. "Aspects of the Optimal Management of Exchange Rates." *Journal of International Economics* 13 (November): 231–256.

Hamada, Koichi. 1976. "A Strategic Analysis of Monetary Interdependence." *Journal of Political Economy* 84 (August): 677–700.

Harris, Richard G., and Douglas D. Purvis. 1981. "Diverse Information and Market Efficiency in a Monetary Model of the Exchange Rate." *Economic Journal* 91 (December): 829–847.

Hogg, Robert V., and Allan T. Craig. 1978. *Introduction to Mathematical Statistics*. 4th ed. New York: Macmillan.

Kareken, John H., and Neil Wallace. 1981. "Samuelson's Consumption Loan Model with Country Specific Fiat Money." *Quarterly Journal of Economics* 95 (May): 207–222.

Kydland, Fynn. 1976. "Decentralization Stabilization Policies: Optimization and the Assignment Problem." *Annals of Economic and Social Measurement* 5 (Spring): 249–261.

Lucas, Robert E., Jr. 1972. "Expectations and the Neutrality of Money." *Journal of Economic Theory* 4 (April): 103–124.

McCallum, Bennett, and John K. Whitaker. 1979. "The Effectiveness of Fiscal Feedback Rules and Automatic Stabilizers under Rational Expectations." *Journal of Monetary Economics* 5 (April): 171–186.

McFadden, Daniel. 1969. "On the Controllability of Decentralized Macroeconomic Systems: The Assignment Problem." In H. W. Kuhn and G. P. Szego, eds., *Mathematical Systems Theory and Economics I*. New York: Springer-Verlag.

Marston, Richard C. 1980. "Cross Country Effects of Sterilization, Reserve Currencies, and Foreign Exchange Intervention." *Journal of International Economics* 10 (February): 63–78.

Mundell, Robert A. 1962. "The Appropriate Use of Monetary and Fiscal Policy for Internal and External Balance." *IMF Staff Papers* 1 (March): 70–79.

Patrick, John D. 1973. "Establishing Convergent Decentralized Policy Assignments." *Journal of International Economics* 3 (February): 37–52.

Pindyck, Robert S. 1976. "The Cost of Conflicting Objectives in Policy Formulation." *Annals of Economic and Social Measurement* 5 (Spring): 239–248.

Poole, William. 1970. "Optimal Choice of Monetary Policy Instruments in a Simple Stochastic Macro Model." *Quarterly Journal of Economics* 84 (May): 197–216.

Roper, Don E., and Stephen J. Turnovsky. 1980. "Optimal Exchange Market Intervention in a Simple Stochastic Macro Model." *Canadian Journal of Economics* 13 (May): 296–309.

Sargent, Thomas J., and Neil Wallace. 1975. "Rational Expectations, the Optimal Monetary Instrument and the Optimal Money Supply Rule." *Journal of Political Economy* 83 (April): 241–254.

Taylor, John B. 1977. "Conditions for Unique Solutions in Stochastic Macroeconomic Models with Rational Expectations." *Econometrica* 35 (September): 1377–1385.

Turnovsky, Stephen J. 1980. "The Choice of Monetary Instruments under Alternative Forms of Price Expectations." *Manchester School* (March): 39–62.

Turnovsky, Stephen J. 1982. "Exchange Market Intervention under Alternative forms of Exogenous Disturbances." Mimeographed. University of Illinois (December).

Turnovsky, Stephen J. 1983. "Exchange Market Intervention Policies in a Small Open Economy." In J. Bhandari and B. H. Putnam, eds., *The International Transmission of Economic Disturbances*. Cambridge: MIT Press.

Weiss, Lawrence. 1982. "Information, Aggregation and Policy." *Review of Economic Studies* 49 (January): 31–42.

Woglom, Geoffrey R. H. 1979. "Rational Expectations and Monetary Policy in a Simple Macroeconomic Model." *Quarterly Journal of Economics* 93 (February): 91–106.

3 Optimal Exchange Market Intervention: Two Alternative Classes of Rules

Stephen J. Turnovsky

1. Introduction

The recent literature on exchange rate management posits rules describing how the domestic monetary authorities intervene in the foreign exchange market. The rules usually considered are of a very particular form. Typically they relate the level of change of foreign reserve holdings (or the domestic money supply) to contemporaneous movements in the exchange rate. The response of the monetary quantity to the exchange rate describes the nature of the intervention, and the question of the optimal intervention is then derived in the form of the optimal response coefficient. (See, among others, Boyer 1978; Cox 1980; Roper and Turnovsky 1980; Frenkel and Aizenman 1982; Turnovsky 1983; Black 1985; Driskill and McCafferty 1985.)

The argument frequently adopted in justifying intervention rules of this type is that the exchange rate is observable virtually instantaneously, thereby providing some information on the nature of the stochastic disturbances, which may be exploited in the determination of optimal policy. Although this is undoubtedly true, other financial variables, such as domestic and foreign interest rates, are also observable with similar frequency, and these contain additional pieces of information on the sources of the stochastic disturbances. Furthermore information on prices is also obtainable with much more frequency than, say, national income, which is usually considered to be the ultimate target variable the policy-makers wish to stabilize.

In this chapter we take up two related issues. First, we consider intervention rules in which the adjustment in the money supply depends on all of the observable monetary variables.[1] In our analysis these include the domestic and foreign interest rates, the domestic price level, and the exchange rate. The important point is that the assumed observability of each independent variable implies the observability of a different linear combination of the underlying stochastic disturbances influencing the economy, and this information should be taken into account in determining the intervention policy. An important feature of the analysis is that the incorporation of this additional information simplifies, rather than complicates, the determination of the optimal intervention decision. The reason is that the observability of certain stochastic variables means that their impact can in effect be neutralized directly, leaving the exchange rate free to accommodate to only a subset of the stochastic disturbances. In other words the optimal intervention problem, which can prove to be quite cumbersome even for the simplest stochastic model, can in fact be rendered quite manageable when the number of policy parameters is augmented.[2]

A second issue analyzed is the question of intervention by means of feedback rules, based on past information. The efficacy of such rules has been controversial in the rational expectations literature. Sargent and Wallace (1976) showed in their much celebrated article that under their assumptions, such feedback rules are ineffective. The robustness of this neutrality proposition has now been seriously questioned by a number of authors.[3] In particular Turnovsky (1980) has demonstrated that this proposition depends, among other things, on the dating of expectations in their definition of the expected rate of inflation. Specifically they define the expected rate of inflation over the period t to $t + 1$ to be conditioned on information available to time $t - 1$. If instead it is conditioned on information available at time t, at which time the actual price level is observed, then feedback rules based on past information are effective in stabilizing output; indeed by appropriate choice of policy, it is possible to stabilize output against all disturbances.

This latter informational assumption is appropriate for exchange rate models and in fact is assumed virtually uniformly throughout the rational expectations–exchange rate literature. Accordingly we shall show that the optimal feedback rule, based on past information, can outperform optimal rules based on current market information, at least insofar as stabilizing income is concerned.

2. Framework

We consider a small, open economy. The model is a simple but standard one, enabling us to focus on the main issues without undue complication. We assume that there is a single traded commodity, the price of which in terms of foreign currency is given. We also assume that the domestic bond is a perfect substitute for a traded world bond, on an uncovered basis. Thus purchasing power parity (PPP) and uncovered interest parity (UIP) are assumed to hold.

The model is summarized by the following set of equations, expressed in deviation form:

$$p_t = q_t + e_t, \tag{1a}$$

$$m_t - p_t = \alpha_1 y_t - \alpha_2 r_t + u_{1t} \quad \alpha_1 > 0, \alpha_2 > 0, \tag{1b}$$

$$r_t = \omega_t + (e^*_{t+1,t} - e_t), \tag{1c}$$

$$y_t = \gamma(p_t - p^*_{t,t-1}) + u_{2t} \quad \gamma > 0, \tag{1d}$$

$$m_t = \mu_1 e_t + \mu_2 e^*_{t+1,t} + \mu_3 \omega_t + \mu_4 q_t, \tag{1e}$$

$$m_t = \sum_{i=1}^{\infty} \phi_i z_{t-i}, \tag{1e$'$}$$

where

$p =$ domestic price level,
$q =$ foreign price level,
$e =$ exchange rate (measured in terms of units of domestic currency per unit of foreign currency),
$m =$ domestic nominal money supply,
$y =$ domestic real output,
$r =$ domestic nominal interest rate,
$q =$ foreign nominal interest rate,
$u_{1t} =$ stochastic disturbance in the demand for money,
$u_{2t} =$ stochastic disturbance in supply of domestic output,
$z_{t-i} =$ vector of exogenous or predetermined variables, yet to be specified,
$x^*_{t+s,t} =$ expectation of x_{t+s}, conditional on information available at time t, $x = p, e$.

All variables except r and q are expressed as logarithmic deviations from steady state levels; r and q are deviations in natural units; the subscript t refers to time.

The equations are straightforward. Equation (1a) is the purchasing power parity relationship, expressed in terms of logarithms; equation (1b) specifies the domestic money market equilibrium, with the demand for money depending positively on domestic income and negatively on the interest rate, together with the additive stochastic disturbance. Uncovered interest parity is described by (1c), while (1d) specifies the domestic supply of output to depend positively on the unanticipated component of the domestic price level, as well as on the additive disturbance u_{2t}.

The new features of the model are contained in the two alternative money supply rules, (1e) and (1e′). In either case we assume that the change in the money supply is brought about by the accumulation or decumulation of foreign reserves through intervention in the foreign exchange market, with the central bank's liabilities created against the purchase of domestic assets remaining fixed. The underlying notion behind (1e) is that the intervention depends on all of the financial variables assumed to be instantaneously observable: e_t, r_t, ω_t, and p_t. Thus we postulate $m_t = v_1 e_t + v_2 r_t + v_3 \omega_t + v_4 p_t$. Using the PPP condition (1a) and the UIP condition (1c), this equation is equivalent to the form (1e). The coefficients μ_i are the policy parameters, and their choice involves the stabilization decision. Note that the observability of e_t and p_t, together with PPP, implies the observability of the foreign price level q_t. The second rule (1e′), considered later in section 4, postulates the money supply to depend on past variables, which for the moment we simply summarize by z_{t-i}. In this case, the policy decisions involve the choice of the ϕ_i.

Finally, we have the stochastic specification. The two domestic stochastic disturbances u_{1t}, u_{2t} are assumed to have zero means and finite second moments and to be independently and identically distributed over time: $E(u_{it}) = 0$; $E(u_{it}^2) = \sigma_i^2$, $i = 1, 2$. The two foreign variables in the system ω_t, q_t are also assumed to be stochastic and to have similar properties: $E(\omega_t) = 0$; $E(\omega_t^2) = \sigma_\omega^2$ and $E(q_t) = 0$; $E(q_t^2) = \sigma_q^2$.

For simplicity we assume that all four stochastic disturbances are uncorrelated, although all of our results remain unchanged as long as only the two domestic variables are mutually uncorrelated. Moreover, even if these two variables are correlated, the results are affected in only fairly minor ways.

3. Optimal Contemporaneous Intervention Policy

In this section we derive the optimal intervention policy under the assumption that the monetary authorities operate in accordance with the rule (1e), which for obvious reasons we term a generalized contemporaneous intervention policy. We begin by solving the system (1a) through (1e) for given values of the intervention parameters, μ_i; we then determine the optimal values of these parameters.

Taking conditional expectations of the PPP condition (1a) and noting that q_t is identically and independently distributed, we have

$$p^*_{t,t-1} = e^*_{t,t-1}. \tag{2}$$

Next, substituting (2), (1a), (1c), (1d), and (1e) into (1b) leads to the following difference equation in e_t,

$$[1 + \alpha_2 + \alpha_1\gamma - \mu_1]e_t = (\alpha_2 + \mu_2)e^*_{t+1,t} + \alpha_1\gamma e^*_{t,t-1} + \varepsilon_t \tag{3}$$

where $\varepsilon_t \equiv -u_{1t} - \alpha_1 u_{2t} + (\alpha_2 + \mu_3)\omega_t - (1 + \alpha_1\gamma - \mu_4)q_t$. Using the method of undetermined coefficients yields the solution for e_t,

$$e_t = \left[\frac{(\alpha_2 + \mu_2)\delta + 1}{1 + \alpha_2 + \alpha_1\gamma - \mu_1}\right]\varepsilon_t + \delta[\varepsilon_{t-1} + \theta\varepsilon_{t-2} + \theta^2\varepsilon_{t-3} + \ldots] \tag{4}$$

where $\theta \equiv (1 + \alpha_2 - \mu_1)/(\alpha_2 + \mu_2)$ and δ is an arbitrary constant. The indeterminacy that characterizes all rational expectations models is embodied in the arbitrariness of this constant. If $|\theta| > 1$, then the only solution for e_t having a finite asymptotic variance, σ_e^2, is $\delta = 0$. Thus imposing the condition that σ_e^2 be finite uniquely determines the solution for e_t. This solution applies, for example, in the absence of any intervention ($\mu_1 = \mu_2 = 0$), when $\theta = (1 + \alpha_2)/\alpha_2 > 1$. On the other hand, since θ is a function of the policy parameters μ_1, μ_2 it is possible for these parameters to be chosen in such a way that $|\theta| < 1$. In this case σ_e^2 will be finite for all arbitrary values of δ, and the solution for e_t remains indeterminate under the finite variance criterion. Taylor (1977) has proposed a minimum variance criterion for determining in this case, but this is somewhat arbitrary since there is no obvious market mechanism to ensure that the variance is minimized in this way.[4] Another arbitrary, but more appealing, criterion is the minimal solution representation criterion, suggested recently by McCallum (1983). This is the notion that e_t is generated by the simplest stochastic process consistent with rational expectations. In this case this implies $\delta = 0$, irrespective of the magnitude of θ. Thus adopting this criterion, we find the solution for e_t simplifies to

$$e_t = \frac{\varepsilon_t}{1 + \alpha_2 + \alpha_1\gamma - \mu_1}. \tag{4'}$$

Taking conditional expectations of (4′) at time $t - 1$, we find $e^*_{t,t-1} = 0$. Using (1a) and (2) and substituting into the output supply function (1d), the solution for domestic output is given by the expression

$$y_t = \frac{1}{D}\{-\gamma u_{1t} + (1 + \alpha_2 - \mu_1)u_{2t} + \gamma(\alpha_2 + \mu_3)\omega_t + \gamma(\alpha_2 - \mu_1 + \mu_4)q_t\}$$

(5)

where $D \equiv 1 + \alpha_2 + \alpha_1\gamma + \mu_1$.

It is evident from (5) that the exchange market intervention parameters, μ_1, μ_3, μ_4, all influence how the stochastic disturbances impinge on the level of activity in the domestic economy. However, since the minimal solution we have chosen implies $e^*_{t+1,t} = 0$, the level of activity is independent of the remaining intervention parameter μ_2.

To determine the optimal intervention parameters it is necessary to introduce some criterion. Throughout we take the objective to be the minimization of σ_y^2, the variance of output. Although this criterion is a standard one, much of the recent rational expectations literature adopts an alternative of minimizing the variance of output about the level of output in a full information, frictionless economy. This latter criterion seems appropriate where one views the objective as being to undo the effects of rigidities such as wage contracts embodied in the supply function. But since the focus here is on actual fluctuations in output, we prefer to adopt the minimum variance criterion.[5]

It is evident from the solution for y_t given in (5) that the optimal values of the policy parameters, $\hat{\mu}_i$, can be attained recursively. First, given $\hat{\mu}_1$, the optimal values for $\hat{\mu}_3$ and $\hat{\mu}_4$ are simply obtained by setting the coefficients of ω_t and q_t in (5) to zero:

$$\hat{\mu}_3 = -\alpha_2,$$ (6a)

$$\hat{\mu}_4 = \hat{\mu}_1 - \alpha_2.$$ (6b)

It therefore follows immediately that by appropriate intervention in response to ω_t and q_t, it is possible to stabilize domestic output perfectly against all foreign disturbances. Substituting (6a) and (6b) into (5) and taking expectations, the variance of output, σ_y^2, given the choice of $\hat{\mu}_3$ and the conditionally optimal choice of $\hat{\mu}_4$, is

$$\sigma_y^2 = \frac{\gamma^2\sigma_1^2 + (1 + \alpha_2 - \mu_1)^2\sigma_2^2}{(1 + \alpha_2 + \alpha_1\gamma - \mu_1)^2}.$$ (7)

With σ_y^2 being independent of the intervention parameter μ_2, the remaining problem is to choose μ_1 to minimize (7). Carrying out the differentiation leads to the optimality condition

$$\hat{\mu}_1 = 1 + \alpha_2 - \frac{\gamma\sigma_1^2}{\alpha_1\sigma_2^2} \tag{8}$$

and combining (6b) and (8) we find

$$\hat{\mu}_4 = 1 - \frac{\gamma\sigma_1^2}{\alpha_1\sigma_2^2}. \tag{9}$$

Thus with $e_{t+1,t}^* = 0$, the optimal intervention rule can be expressed as

$$m_t = \left[1 + \alpha_2 - \frac{\gamma\sigma_1^2}{\alpha_1\sigma_2^2}\right]e_t - \alpha_2\omega_t + \left[1 - \frac{\gamma\sigma_1^2}{\alpha_1\sigma_2^2}\right]q_t. \tag{10}$$

Moreover substituting the optimal $\hat{\mu}_1$ into (7), it is seen that the corresponding minimized variance of output is

$$\hat{\sigma}_y^2 = \frac{\sigma_1^2\sigma_2^2}{\sigma_1^2 + \alpha_1^2\sigma_2^2}. \tag{11}$$

Several points about the solution merit comment. First, the optimality conditions (6a) and (6b), which eliminate the impact of the foreign disturbances ω_t and q_t, are obtained irrespective of whether these two disturbances are correlated. Moreover, having eliminated ω_t and q_t, their possible correlation with the domestic shocks becomes irrelevant. The only correlation that remains is that between u_{1t} and u_{2t}, and this affects the choice μ_1 in a simple manner. Second, by eliminating the foreign disturbances, the minimized variance of output reflects the variances of only the domestic stochastic disturbances.[6] Third, with $e_{t+1,t}^* = 0$, the interest rate parity condition (1c) reduces to

$$r_t = \omega_t - e_t. \tag{1c$'$}$$

In this case the domestic interest rate r_t contains no independent information over and above that contained in ω_t and e_t, this is the reason for the irrelevance of the intervention parameter μ_2.[7] Invoking (1c$'$) and the PPP condition (1a), the optimal intervention rule simplifies to

$$m_t = \left[1 - \frac{\gamma\sigma_1^2}{\alpha_1\sigma_2^2}\right]p_t - \alpha_2 r_t. \tag{12}$$

Thus the optimal intervention policy can be conveniently expressed in terms of responses in the domestic money supply to movements in the domestic nominal interest rate and the domestic price level. A 1 percentage point rise in the former should be met by a α_2 percentage reduction in the money supply, where, it will be recalled, α_2 is the semi-elasticity of the domestic demand for money with respect to the domestic interest rate. A 1 percent rise in the domestic price level should be ac-commodated by a less than 1 percent rise in the nominal money supply. The adjustment depends positively on the variance of the domestic real disturbance and inversely on the variance of the domestic monetary disturbance.

If one does not invoke the minimal information criterion but requires instead only that σ_e^2 be finite, the optimal intervention the can be charac-terized as follows:

$$m_t = \hat{\mu}_1 e_t + \hat{\mu}_2 e_{t+1,t}^* - \alpha_2 \omega_t + \left[1 - \frac{\gamma \sigma_1^2}{\alpha_1 \sigma_2^2}\right] q_t \tag{13}$$

where $\hat{\mu}_1$ and $\hat{\mu}_2$ satisfy

$$\frac{1 + \alpha_2 + \alpha_1 \gamma - \hat{\mu}_1}{(\alpha_2 + \hat{\mu}_2)\delta + 1} = \frac{\gamma[\sigma_1^2 + \alpha_1^2 \sigma_2^2]}{\alpha_1 \sigma_2^2} \tag{14a}$$

and if

$$\left|\frac{1 + \alpha_2 - \hat{\mu}_1}{\alpha_2 + \hat{\mu}_2}\right| < 1 \quad \text{then } \delta \text{ is arbitrary,} \tag{14b}$$

$$\left|\frac{1 + \alpha_2 - \hat{\mu}_1}{\alpha_2 + \hat{\mu}_2}\right| > 1 \quad \text{then } \delta = 0. \tag{14c}$$

In this case the intervention with respect to e_t and $e_{t+1,t}^*$ is indeterminate, although substituting (13) and (14), into the corresponding solution for y_t (not given), one can show that the minimized variance of output is again given by (11). Furthermore setting $\mu_2 = -\alpha_2$, (14c) implies $\delta = 0$, and hence (13) reduces to the solution obtained under the minimal condition—(12).

To see how output is determined, substitute the optimal rule (12) into the money market equilibrium condition (1b), which reduces to

$$\alpha_1 y_t + \frac{\gamma}{\alpha_1} \frac{\sigma_1^2}{\sigma_2^2} p_t = u_{1t}. \tag{15a}$$

This condition, together with the supply function (1d), which with $p^*_{t,t-1} = 0$ is

$$y_t - \gamma p_t = u_{2t} \tag{15b}$$

jointly determine domestic output y_t and the domestic price level p_t. In effect the appropriate choice of the interest rate coefficient $\hat{\mu}_3$ and the foreign price coefficient $\hat{\mu}_4$ in the intervention rule means that random fluctuations in these foreign variables are fully absorbed by the domestic money supply, thereby fully insulating the rest of the domestic economy from them. This leaves the intervention with respect to the exchange rate, say $(\hat{\mu}_1)$, as the remaining independent policy decision, which in effect is assigned to stabilize for the domestic disturbances.

In the absence of domestic monetary disturbances $(u_{1t} = 0, \sigma_1^2 = 0)$ and the money market equilibrium condition implies $y_t = $ for all t. Output is stabilized perfectly, with all the fluctuations in supply, u_{2t}, being borne by the price. In the absence of domestic supply disturbances $(u_{2t} = 0, \sigma_2^2 = 0)$, $y_t = p_t = 0$, for all t; that is, both output and price are perfectly stabilized. The fact that in either limiting case optimal intervention implies $\sigma_y^2 = 0$ can also be seen from (11) directly. It follows from the fact that with only one domestic disturbance, the observability of the exchange rate, together with the price level, implies the observability of this disturbance, and hence it can be stabilized exactly.

Finally, it is of interest of see the implications of the optimal intervention rule (12) for the exchange rate. This can be most easily obtained by solving (15a) and (15b) for p_t and invoking PPP. The result is

$$e_t = \frac{\alpha_1 \sigma_2^2 [u_{1t} - \alpha_1 u_{2t}]}{\gamma [\sigma_1^2 + \alpha_1^2 \sigma_2^2]} - q_t. \tag{16}$$

If the domestic monetary authorities intervene optimally, the exchange rate is independent of foreign interest rate fluctuations (which are absorbed in the domestic money supply) while it fully offsets fluctuations in the foreign price level. As long as the variance of supply disturbances is not zero, positive supply shocks lead to an appreciation of the exchange rate, while positive monetary disturbances will cause the exchange rate to depreciate.

4. Optimal Intervention Using Past Information

We now determine the optimal intervention policy on the assumption that the domestic monetary authorities intervene in accordance with a rule such as (1e′), which is based on only past information. For the moment we need not specify precisely the elements of the vector z_{t-i}. To solve the system, we begin as before by substituting (2), (1a), (1c), and (1d) into (1b). This yields the difference equation in e_t

$$(1 + \alpha_2 + \alpha_1 \gamma)e_t = \alpha_2 e^*_{t+1,t} + \alpha_1 \gamma e^*_{t,t-1} + \eta_t + m_t \tag{17}$$

where $\eta_t \equiv -u_{1t} - \alpha_1 u_{2t} + \alpha_2 \omega_t - (1 + \alpha_1 \gamma)q_t$ and is identically and independently distributed over time. By contrast since m_t is by assumption dependent on past information, it is not independently distributed over time. Applying the method of undetermined coefficients, the solution to (17) is

$$e_t = \frac{\eta_t + \sum\limits_{k=0}^{\infty} (m^*_{t+k,t} - m^*_{t+k,t-1})\lambda^k}{1 + \alpha_2 + \alpha_1 \gamma} + \frac{\sum\limits_{k=0}^{\infty} m^*_{t+k,t-1}\lambda^k}{1 + \alpha_2} \tag{18}$$

where $\lambda \equiv \alpha_2/(1 + \alpha_2)$ and $m^*_{t+k,t}$ is the prediction of the money supply for time $t + k$, formed at time t. We assume that $m^*_{t,t} = m_t$; that is, the prediction for the current money supply equals the actual money supply or, in other words, the current money supply is observable. It is important to note that with m_t based on only past information (not a function of e_t), (18) is the only stable solution to (17). Thus imposing the terminal condition that the asymptotic variance σ_e^2 be finite, the indeterminacies encountered in the previous policy do not arise. The solution for the current exchange rate consists of three components: the impact of the current stochastic disturbances through their effect on the composite disturbance η_t; the term involving the discounted sum of the $(m^*_{t+k,t} - m^*_{t+k,t-1})$, which measure the update to the forecast for the money supply for time $t + k$ on the basis of new information acquired at time t; and the discounted sum of the expected future money supplies.

As before, taking conditional expectations of (18) at time $t - 1$, using (1a) and (2) and substituting the relevant expressions into the output supply function implies the following solution for domestic output

$$y_t = \frac{\gamma \sum_{k=0}^{\infty} (m^*_{t+k,t} - m^*_{t+k,t-1})\lambda^k + u^y_t}{1 + \alpha_2 + \alpha_1 \gamma} \tag{19}$$

where $u^y_t = -\gamma u_{1t} + (1 + \alpha_2)u_{2t} + \gamma\alpha_2(\omega_t + q_t)$. Thus the solution for domestic output at time t depends on the composite output disturbance u^y_t and the discounted sum of the updates of the forecasts of the future money supplies.

Suppose now that the domestic monetary authorities' intervention rule is of the very simple feedback form,

$$m_t = \phi_1 u^y_{t-1}. \tag{20}$$

We assume that all stochastic disturbances impinging on the economy at time $t - 1$, say, are observed by the next period t. Thus the composite disturbance in domestic output, u^y_{t-1}, which incorporates all the underlying random disturbances occurring at time $t - 1$, is known at time t. Thus (20) is a simple rule whereby the authorities' decision is determined by the previous period's movements in the target variable, output.

Since u^y_t is identically and independently distributed over time, taking conditional expectations of (20) yields the following:

$$m^*_{t,t-1} = \phi_1 u^y_{t-1} = m_t, \tag{21a}$$

$$m^*_{t+k,t-1} = 0 \quad k = 1, 2, \ldots, \tag{21b}$$

$$m^*_{t+1,t} = \phi_1 u^y_t, \tag{22a}$$

$$m^*_{t+k,t} = 0 \quad k = 2, 3, \ldots. \tag{22b}$$

Now substitute (21) and (22) into the solution (20), and we find that the solution for current output reduces to

$$y_t = \frac{[\gamma\phi_1\lambda + 1]u^y_t}{1 + \alpha_2 + \alpha_1\gamma}. \tag{23}$$

The variance of income is minimized and indeed eliminated entirely by simply letting

$$\phi_1 = -\frac{1}{\gamma\lambda} = -\frac{(1 + \alpha_2)}{\gamma\alpha_2}; \tag{24}$$

that is, by following the money supply rule,

$$m_t = -\frac{(1 + \alpha_2)}{\gamma \alpha_2} u_{t-1}^y.$$ (25)

Thus the optimal money supply rule based on past information is to contract the money supply in response to positive disturbance in previous output and to expand it if output was low. The critical parameters determining the optimal response are the semielasticity of the demand for money with respect to the interest rate and price elasticity of output.

To see how the money supply rule (25) is able to eliminate all the fluctuations in domestic output, we embed the rule, together with its effects on expectations, into the complete system (19). To do this we first use (18) to calculate the conditional expectation $e_{t+1,t}^*$. In general, this is

$$e_{t+1,t}^* = \frac{1}{1 + \alpha_2} \sum_{k=0}^{\infty} m_{t+k+1,t}^* \lambda^k$$ (26)

and given the rule (25), this reduces to

$$e_{t+1,t}^* = -\frac{u_t^y}{\gamma \alpha_2} = \frac{m_{t+1,t}^*}{1 + \alpha_2} = \frac{m_{t+1}}{1 + \alpha_2}$$ (27a)

and, for prices, to

$$p_{t,t-1}^* = -\frac{u_{t-1}^y}{\gamma \alpha_2} = \frac{m_{t,t-1}^*}{1 + \alpha_2} = \frac{m_t}{1 + \alpha_2}.$$ (27b)

Thus the knowledge that the monetary authorities will contract the money supply in response to a positive disturbance in the previous period's output causes domestic agents to expect a positive disturbance in the previous period's output to lead to an appreciation of the exchange rate, which, given PPP, translates directly to corresponding expected price movements. These expectational effects are less than proportional to the anticipated (and actual) change in the money supply.

Substituting (27a) and (27b) into the basic model (1), this can be reduced to three equations:

$$p_t = q_t + e_t,$$ (28a)

$$(1 + \alpha_2)p_{t,t-1}^* - p_t = \alpha_1 y_t + \frac{u_t^y}{\gamma} + \alpha_2 e_t + u_{1t} - \alpha_2 \omega_t,$$ (28b)

$$y_t = \gamma[p_t - p_{t,t-1}^*] + u_{2t}.$$ (28c)

Consider now the money market equilibrium relationship (28b). In particular observe that the effect of the expected exchange rate on the demand for money (which operates by UIP) is given by the expression $u_t^y/\gamma = -u_{1t} + (1 + \alpha_2)u_{2t}/\gamma + \alpha_2(\omega_t + q_t)$. Note that it incorporates the fluctuations in the demand for money u_{1t} and in the foreign interest rate ω_t and precisely neutralizes the independent additive effects these two variables have on domestic money demand. Moreover, using PPP, (27a) and (27b) can be combined to yield

$$(1 + \alpha_2)\left[p_t - p_{t,t-1}^* + \frac{u_{2t}}{\gamma} \right] + \alpha_1 y_t = 0. \tag{28b'}$$

It is clear that equations (28b') and (28c) describe two equations in output y_t and the unanticipated component of the price level, $p_t - p_{t,t-1}^*$, and it is evident that the only solution to this pair of equations is

$$y_t = 0. \tag{29a}$$

$$p_t = p_{t,t-1}^* - \frac{u_{2t}}{\gamma} = -\frac{u_{t-1}^y}{\gamma\alpha_2} - \frac{u_{2t}}{\gamma}. \tag{29b}$$

The corresponding solution for the exchange rate is obtained by invoking PPP and is

$$e_t = e_{t,t-1}^* - \frac{u_{2t}}{\gamma} - q_t = -\frac{u_{t-1}^y}{\gamma\alpha_2} - \frac{u_{2t}}{\gamma} - q_t. \tag{29c}$$

In particular the exchange rate exactly offsets the stochastic fluctuations in the foreign price level. We find that the stochastic fluctuations in the money demand and foreign interest rate are fully absorbed by the expected exchange rate; domestic price disturbances are fully absorbed by the domestic price level; foreign price disturbances are fully absorbed by the exchange rate. These facts permit output to be stabilized perfectly during each period.

Note also that equations (27b), (29b), and (27a), (29c) may be combined to yield

$$m_t = (1 + \alpha_2)p_t + \frac{(1 + \alpha_2)}{\gamma}u_{2t}, \tag{30a}$$

$$m_t = (1 + \alpha_2)e_t + (1 + \alpha_2)\left[q_t + \frac{u_{2t}}{\gamma} \right]. \tag{30b}$$

Although the monetary authorities choose m_t on the basis of past information, the contemporaneous response in the price level and exchange rate makes the policy equivalent to one in which the money supply is adjusted to the current price level (or exchange rate), together with current output supply shocks. In particular (30b) can be viewed as being equivalent to a stochastic leaning with the wind policy, in which the money supply is increased by $(1 + \alpha_2)$ percent for every 1 percent depreciation of the exchange rate.

We have demonstrated that the optimal money supply rule (25) is capable of eliminating all of the variance in y_t, thereby stabilizing it perfectly. We now show that this rule is just one of an infinite number of policies capable of achieving this. Any rule of the form

$$m_t = \phi_i u_{t-1}^y \quad i = 1, 2, \ldots \tag{31}$$

so that the monetary authorities respond to disturbances in output i periods in the past will do equally well. For this rule, the conditional expectations of (31) imply the following relationships

$$m_{t+k,t-1}^* = \phi_i u_{t+k-i}^y \quad k = 1, \ldots, i-1, \tag{32a}$$

$$m_{t+k,t-1}^* = 0 \quad k = i, \ldots, \tag{32b}$$

$$m_{t+k,t}^* = \phi_i u_{t+k-i}^y \quad k = 1, \ldots, i, \tag{33a}$$

$$m_{t+k,t}^* = 0 \quad k = i+1, \ldots. \tag{33b}$$

The solution for output is therefore

$$y_t = \frac{[\gamma\phi_i\lambda^i + 1]u_{t-i}^y}{1 + \alpha_2 + \alpha_1\gamma} \tag{34}$$

and the variance of output is reduced to zero by setting

$$\phi_i = -\frac{1}{\gamma\lambda^i} = -\frac{1}{\gamma}\left[\frac{1 + \alpha_2}{\alpha_2}\right]^i. \tag{35}$$

In other words output can be stabilized fully if the monetary authorities follow a rule relating the money supply to disturbances in output pertaining to an arbitrary number of periods in the past, namely:

$$m_t = -\frac{1}{\gamma}\left[\frac{1 + \alpha_2}{\alpha_2}\right]^i u_{t-i}^y. \tag{36}$$

All that is now required is that the response to a disturbance of a given magnitude must now be intensified by a factor λ^i for each period in the past.

The explanation for this result is basically the same as for the one-period lag already discussed. To see this, we first substitute the expressions for the expectations of the future money supplies into (26):

$$e_{t+1,t}^* = -\frac{1}{\gamma\alpha_2}\left[u_t^y + \left[\frac{1+\alpha_2}{\alpha_2}\right]u_{t-1}^y + \ldots + \left[\frac{1+\alpha_2}{\alpha_2}\right]^{i-1} u_{t-i+1}^y\right]. \tag{37}$$

It is seen that with the monetary rule based on shocks occurring with an i period lag, the expectations of the exchange rate become a function of these shocks distributed over the previous i periods. Considering (37) at the previous time $t-1$ and noting (36), we can easily show

$$e_{t+1,t}^* = -\frac{u_t^y}{\gamma\alpha_2} + \left[\frac{1+\alpha_2}{\alpha_2}\right]e_{t,t-1}^* - \frac{m_t}{\alpha_2}. \tag{38}$$

Now substituting (38) into the money market equilibrium condition, recalling the definition of u_t^y, and invoking PPP and (2), this reduces to equation (28b'). Thus as before (28b'), together with the supply function (28c), determine the solutions for $y_t = 0$ and $p_t = p_{t,t-1}^* - u_{2t}/\gamma$ together with $e_t = e_{t,t-1}^* - u_{2t}/\gamma - q_t$. The only difference is that the expectations for $p_{t,t-1}^*$, $e_{t,t-1}^*$ are now functions of past disturbances u_{t-k}^y extending over i periods:

$$e_{t,t-1}^* = p_{t,t-1}^* = -\frac{1}{\gamma\alpha_2}\sum_{k=0}^{i-1}\left[\frac{1+\alpha_2}{\alpha_2}\right]^k u_{t-k}^y.$$

One final point worth noting is that although all such rules we have been considering do equally well in terms of stabilizing output, that is not so with respect to price stability. It is clear that the longer the lag embodied in the policy rule, the more past disturbances get built into price expectations and the larger the variance of the price level. Thus the policy rule, which uses information with only a one-period lag, is optimal from the viewpoint of maximizing price stability among those policies that treat the elimination of fluctuations in income as the primary objective.

5. Conclusions

This chapter has dealt with two aspects of exchange market intervention pertaining to the appropriate utilization of available information. First, the existing literature restricts itself to rules in which the intervention is based on the current (and perhaps past) behavior of the exchange rate. It seems reasonable to argue that in designing their intervention policies, the monetary authorities will also take account of information on other financial variables and prices available with virtually the same frequency as the exchange rate and which provide further independent information on the sources of the stochastic disturbances impinging on the economy. When one takes this additional information into account, the determination of the optimal intervention rule becomes much simpler than has been previously argued. Basically this is because the information contained in these variables can be exploited, leaving the exchange rate free to accommodate to only a subset of them. In the particular model we have considered, we have shown that the optimal intervention can stabilize domestic output perfectly against foreign disturbances, leaving it to fluctuate in response to only domestic disturbances. The optimal income-stabilizing intervention policy contains an element of nonuniqueness, reflecting the indeterminacy of the underlying rational expectations solution. If one resolves this indeterminacy by invoking the minimal information solution strategy, the optimal rule is of a very simple and convenient form. Specifically the monetary authorities are required to respond appropriately to only the domestic interest rate and to the domestic price level.

The second issue considered is intervention using feedback rules based on only past information. Here we have demonstrated that perfect stabilization of output can be achieved for all disturbances simultaneously, if the monetary authorities intervene appropriately in response to past stochastic movements in the target variable, income. This rule is not unique, and the appropriate adjustment to any past stochastic fluctuation in output will be equally effective in stabilizing domestic output. In all cases the rule is very simple, with the intervention parameter involving just the semielasticity of the demand for money with respect to the interest rate and the elasticity of supply with respect to an unanticipated price change. Price fluctuations, on the other hand, are exacerbated by longer delays in the policy rule, in which case if price stability is also a consideration, the optimal rule should be based on the most recently available information.

The fact that a feedback rule based on past information on the target variable, output, can outperform a rule based on contemporaneous information on the financial and price variables is of some interest. It suggests that greater stability in real activity may be achieved by ensuring that reliable information is obtained on the past real fluctuations of the economy rather than trying to use contemporaneous financial data to filter information on the current stochastic disturbances.

Notes

1. Note that Eaton and Turnovsky (1984) introduce intervention rules based on both the forward and spot exchange rates.

2. See, for example, Turnovsky (1983).

3. A review of this literature is contained in MaCallum (1980).

4. In Turnovsky (1983) we chose to determine δ so as to minimize the one-period variance of the exchange rate. For reasons discussed in Turnovsky, this leads to complications in the determination of the optimal policy.

5. This criterion was first proposed by Gray (1976) and has been used by a number of authors in the wage indexation literature; see, for example, Marston (1984) and Flood and Marion (1982).

6. Notice also that the minimized variance of output, $\hat{\sigma}_y^2$, is independent of γ, the slope of the supply curve. Thus given the optimal intervention scheme, any wage indexation scheme, which from the wage indexation literature has been shown to operate by changing γ, is thereby rendered redundant.

7. Note that for a solution in which $\delta \neq 0$, the policy parameter μ_2 will affect the stability of output.

References

Black, S. W. 1985. "The Effect of Alternative Intervention Policies on the Variability of Exchange Rates." In J. S. Bhandari (ed.), *Exchange Rate Management under Uncertainty*. Cambridge, Mass.: MIT Press.

Boyer, R. 1978. "Optimal Foreign Exchange Market Intervention." *Journal of Political Economy* 86:1045–1056.

Cox, W. M. 1980. "Unanticipated Money, Output, and Prices in the Small Economy." *Journal of Monetary Economics* 6:359–384.

Driskill, R., and S. McCafferty. 1985. "Exchange Market Intervention under Rational Expectations with Imperfect Capital Substitutability." In J. S. Bhandari (ed.), *Exchange Rate Management under Uncertainty*. Cambridge, Mass.: MIT Press.

Eaton, J., and S. J. Turnovsky. 1984. "The Forward Exchange Market, Speculation and Exchange Market Intervention." *Quarterly Journal of Economics* 99:45–69.

Flood, R. P., and N. P. Marion. 1982. "The Transmission of Disturbances under Alternative Exchange Rate Regimes with Optimal Indexing." *Quarterly Journal of Economics* 97:43–66.

Frenkel, J., and J. Aizenman. 1982. "Aspects of the Optimal Management of Exchange Rates." *Journal of International Economics* 13:231–256.

Gray, J. A. 1976. "Wage Indexation: A Macroeconomic Approach." *Journal of Monetary Economics* 2:221–235.

Marston, R. C. 1984. "Real Wages and the Terms of Trade: Alternative Wage Indexation Rules for an Open Economy." *Journal of Money, Credit, and Banking* 16: 285–301.

McCallum, B. T. 1980. "Rational Expectations and Macroeconomic Stabilization Policy: An Overview." *Journal of Money, Credit, and Banking* 12:716–746.

McCallum, B. T. 1983. "On Non-uniqueness in Rational Expectations Models: An Attempt at Perspective." *Journal of Monetary Economics* 11:139–168.

Roper, D. E., and S. J. Turnovsky. 1980. "Optimal Exchange Market in a Simple Stochastic Macro Model." *Canadian Journal of Economics* 13:296–309.

Sargent, T. J., and N. Wallace. 1976. "Rational Expectations and the Theory of Economic Policy." *Journal of Monetary Economics* 2:169–183.

Taylor, J. 1977. "Conditions for Unique Solutions in Stochastic Macroeconomic Models with Rational Expectations." *Econometrica* 45:1377–1385.

Turnovsky, S. J. 1980. "Choice of Monetary Instrument under Alternative Forms of Price Expectations." *Manchester School* 48:39–62.

Turnovsky, S. J. 1983. "Exchange Market Intervention Policies in a Small Open Economy." In J. S. Bhandari and B. Putnam (eds.), *Economic Interdependence and Flexible Exchange Rates*. Cambridge, Mass.: MIT Press.

4 The Effect of Alternative Intervention Policies on the Variability of Exchange Rates: The Harrod Effect

Stanley W. Black

1. Introduction

According to Lucas (1976), changes in governmental policy can be expected to lead to changes in private behavior because private agents optimize their actions subject to a different set of environmental conditions. Harrod (1965) hypothesized that adoption of a floating exchange rate regime would deter speculators from taking foreign currency positions because of increased uncertainty about the future value of the exchange rate. Although Harrod's argument was developed for the purpose of comparing pegged with floating exchange rates, the general point needs to be taken into account in evaluating the effects of alternative government intervention policies within a regime of floating exchange rates. For example, McKinnon (1979, chap. 7) has argued that the supply of stabilizing speculation has been inadequate during the period of floating exchange rates since 1973. This chapter analyzes the Harrod effect within a stochastic exchange rate model whose focus is deliberately limited in order to allow the problem to be tractable.

The model used to determine the exchange rate is based on the balance of payments, what may be called the "good old theory," modified as in Black (1973) to take account of imperfect substitutability of assets denominated in different currencies and rational expectations under imperfect information.[1] The basic rationale for using this theory is that empirical evidence appears to support its underlying assumptions, in contrast to monetary models based on assumptions of short-run purchasing power parity and/or perfect substitutability of assets denominated in different currencies.

The data from the 1970 as marshaled by Frenkel (1981) do not support the purchasing power parity hypothesis because of sticky domestic prices and/or changes in real factors. If investors were risk neutral with respect to exchange risk or if they demanded a constant or predictable risk premium, then uncovered interest differentials between assets denominated in different currencies should equal the expected rate of change of the exchange rate plus the risk premium. But Hansen and Hodrick (1980) appear to find a variable risk premium rather than a stable and predictable one.

The model presented here attempts to capture these aspects of reality, albeit in a highly simplified framework. Prices (and output) are assumed to be exogenous to the model, while fluctuations in exchange rates are induced by random shocks in both real and financial sectors and changes in monetary policy. These factors cause fluctuations in both competitiveness, affecting the current account, and in expected returns, affecting the capital account. Changes in the willingness of speculators to assume risk and therefore changes in the risk premium depend on changes in the perceived amount of short-term risk in the model, which depends on both government policies and the variability of shocks to the system. A major question of interest is under what conditions government intervention in the exchange market, whether sterilized or unsterilized, will induce private speculators to assume larger or smaller positions in foreign currency, under rational expectations.

2. Behavior of Speculators

In this model the representative private speculator is assumed to be a domestic resident who holds foreign assets or incurs foreign liabilities in the amount f_t at the end of period t, where f_t is denominated in units of foreign currency. If e_t is the logarithm of the price in period t of foreign currency in units of domestic currency, r_t is the interest rate on domestic assets held or liabilities owed at the end of period t, and r_t^* is the interest rate on foreign assets held or liabilities owed at the end of period t, then the rate of return to the domestic investor net of opportunity cost per unit of f_t is given by[2]

$$r_t^* + e_{t+1} - e_t - r_t. \tag{1}$$

The profit in domestic currency of holding f_t is then

$$\Pi_{t+1} = f_t(e_{t+1} - e_t + r_t^* - r_t). \tag{2}$$

The representative speculator is assumed to choose f_t to maximize an expected utility function, which is characterized by a constant absolute risk aversion factor ϕ:

$$U = E_t\Pi_{t+1} - \frac{\phi}{2} V_t\Pi_{t+1}, \tag{3}$$

where $E_t\Pi_{t+1}$ and $V_t\Pi_{t+1}$ are the conditional expected profit and its variance, given information available at time t. Therefore we have

$$E_t\Pi_{t+1} = f_t(E_t e_{t+1} - e_t + r_t^* - r_t), \tag{4}$$

$$V_t\Pi_{t+1} = E_t[f_t(e_{t+1} - E_t e_{t+1})]^2 = f_t^2 \sigma_{e,1}^2, \tag{5}$$

where $\sigma_{e,1}^2$ is the conditional variance of the next-period exchange rate. Given the quadratic form of (5), the second-order condition for a maximum is satisfied, and the solution for the speculator's optimum foreign asset holding is

$$f_t = \frac{1}{\phi\sigma_{e,1}^2}[E_t e_{t+1} - e_t + r_t^* - r_t] = \beta[E_t e_{t+1} - e_t + r_t^* - r_t]. \tag{6}$$

Equation (6) makes clear the dependence of the representative speculator's risk-bearing behavioral parameter β on his degree of risk-aversion ϕ and on the one-period variability of the exchange rate $\sigma_{e,1}^2$, as

$$\beta = \frac{1}{\phi\sigma_{e,1}^2}. \tag{7}$$

3. Interest Rate Determination

The foreign interest r^* is assumed to be exogenous, but domestic interest rates can be affected by changes in domestic monetary policy or by changes in foreign reserves arising from nonsterilized intervention. For analytical convenience, the demand for money is taken to be of the form

$$\frac{M_t}{P_t Y_t} = k - \mu r_t \tag{8}$$

where M_t is the end of period stock of high-powered money, P_t is the (exogenous) price level in period t, and Y_t is the exogenous level of domestic output in period t. P and Y are assumed constant henceforth.

The supply of high-powered money is composed of domestic credit D_t and foreign reserves x_t valued at a constant exchange rate $\bar{H}$, as valuation effects are assumed to be fully absorbed by the central bank:

$$M_t = D_t + \bar{H}x_t. \tag{9}$$

Central bank intervention in the exchange market is assumed to take the form of changes in reserves Δx_t, which are sterilized according to a coefficient ρ. Thus the level of domestic credit is equal to an exogenous component D_o attributable to domestic policy targets less the sterilization effect,

$$D_t = D_o - \rho \bar{H} x_t. \tag{10}$$

Solving (3.1) through (3.3), we find the interest rate to be

$$r_t = \frac{1}{\mu}\left(k - \frac{D_o}{PY}\right) - \frac{(1-\rho)\bar{H}}{\mu PY} x_t = \bar{r} - \frac{1-\rho}{\mu\varepsilon} x_t, \tag{11}$$

where $\varepsilon = PY/\bar{H}$. Thus nonsterilized intervention affects the interest rate.

4. Exchange Rate Determination

The exchange rate is assumed to be determined to equilibrate the demand and supply for foreign exchange, as expressed in the balance of payments. The current account, measured in terms of foreign currency, is assumed for simplicity to depend on the current ratio of foreign to domestic prices and a random disturbance term,

$$c_t = \alpha(e_t + p_t^* - p_t) + u_t, \tag{12}$$

where p_t and p_t^* are the logarithms of the exogenous prices of foreign and domestic goods, respectively. The random disturbance term u_t is assumed to have mean zero, constant variance σ_u^2, and zero autocorrelation. Other forms of current account, including dependence on the expected future exchange rate and lagged terms giving rise to a J-curve, could be allowed for at the cost of some clarity in the results.

The demand to hold foreign assets is aggregated from (6) together with a disturbance term

$$f_t = \beta(r_t^* - r_t + E_t e_{t+1} - e_t) + v_t, \tag{13}$$

where the financial disturbance term v_t is assumed to follow a random walk whose increments Δv_t have mean zero, constant variance σ_v^2, zero autocorrelation, and are uncorrelated with u_t.[3] Equation (13) represents a short-run stock equilibrium condition, in which asset holders are willing to hold the stocks of foreign assets they actually have. Its first difference represents the outflow of private capital.

Central bank purchases of foreign exchange are assumed to respond partly according to a leaning against the wind rule and partly to deviations from a target exchange rate $\tilde{e}$, according to

$$\Delta x_t = -\gamma(e_t - e_{t-1}) - \delta(e_t - \tilde{e}).$$ (14)

The balance of payments equation is

$$c_t = \Delta f_t + \Delta x_t,$$ (15)

which is converted into an equilibrium condition by substituting into it (12) through (14).

5. Solution of the Model

The model is solved under the assumptions that p, p^*, r^*, and $\bar{r}$ are exogenous. From (11) $\Delta r_t = -(1 - \rho)\Delta x_t/\mu\varepsilon$, to allow for the effects of nonsterilized intervention. The first difference of (13) is, then,

$$\Delta f_t = \beta(E_t e_{t+1} - e_t - E_{t-1} e_t + e_{t-1}) + \frac{\beta(1 - \rho)}{\mu\varepsilon}\Delta x_t + \Delta v_t,$$

making it evident that nonsterilized intervention ($\rho < 1$) has an additional interest rate effect on capital flows, an effect that is absent when intervention is sterilized. Thus nonsterilized purchases of foreign currency increase the domestic monetary base and lower domestic interest rates, leading to additional private purchases of foreign currency, which are complementary to and strengthen the central bank's purchases in their effect on the balance of supply and demand. Having made this point, I will now assume complete sterilization ($\rho = 1$).

Substituting from (12) through (14) into (15), we obtain

$$\alpha(e_t + p^* - p) + u_t = \beta(E_t e_{t+1} - e_t - E_{t-1} e_t + e_{t-1})$$
$$- \gamma(e_t - e_{t-1}) - \delta(e_t - \tilde{e}) + \Delta v_t.$$ (16)

To solve this equation by the method of undetermined coefficients, we let

$$e_t = \bar{e} + \sum_{i=0}^{\infty} \Pi_i(u_{t-i} - \Delta v_{t-i}),$$ (17)

whence

$$E_{t-1}e_t = \bar{e} + \sum_{i=1}^{\infty} \Pi_i(u_{t-i} - \Delta v_{t-i}). \tag{18}$$

Substituting (17) and (18) into (16), we find from the constant terms that

$$\bar{e} = \frac{\delta}{\alpha + \delta}\tilde{e} + \frac{\alpha}{\alpha + \delta}(p - p^*) = \frac{\delta}{\alpha + \delta}\tilde{e} + \frac{\alpha}{\alpha + \delta}\bar{\bar{e}}, \tag{19}$$

where $\bar{\bar{e}} = p - p^*$ is the long-run purchasing power parity exchange rate. Of course, if the central bank chooses a target exchange rate $\tilde{e} \neq p - p^*$, it will observe a continuous gain or loss of reserves, abstracting from the random shocks.

Equating coefficients on $u_t - \Delta v_t$, we find

$$(\alpha + \gamma + \delta + \beta)\Pi_o + 1 - \beta\Pi_1 = 0. \tag{20}$$

Equating coefficients on $u_{t-1} - \Delta v_{t-1}, u_{t-2} - \Delta v_{t-2}$, and so on, we find the recursive relationships

$$(\alpha + \gamma + \delta + \beta)\Pi_1 - \beta(\Pi_2 - \Pi_1) - (\beta + \gamma)\Pi_0 = 0,$$
$$(\alpha + \gamma + \delta + \beta)\Pi_2 - \beta(\Pi_3 - \Pi_2) - (\beta + \gamma)\Pi_1 = 0 \dots . \tag{21}$$

The second-order difference equation in (21) is assumed to have a solution of the form $\Pi_i = \Pi_o\lambda^i$. From (20) this yields

$$\Pi_0 = \frac{-1}{\alpha + \gamma + \delta + \beta(1 - \lambda)}. \tag{22}$$

The difference equations (21) take the form

$$\lambda^2 - \left(2 + \frac{\alpha + \gamma + \delta}{\beta}\right)\lambda + \left(1 + \frac{\gamma}{\beta}\right) = 0, \tag{23}$$

a well-known equation with two positive real roots whose product is $1 + \gamma/\beta$. The boundary condition $\lim_{i\to\infty} \Pi_i < \infty$ will be adopted to rule out speculative bubbles, by assumption. This implies discarding the root of (23) that exceeds unity and using instead

$$\lambda = 1 + \frac{\alpha + \gamma + \delta}{2\beta} - \frac{\alpha + \gamma + \delta}{2\beta}\sqrt{1 + \frac{4\beta(\alpha + \delta)}{(\alpha + \gamma + \delta)^2}}, \tag{24}$$

which is less than unity. The general solution of (16) is, then,

$$e_t = \frac{\alpha}{\alpha + \delta}(p - p^*) + \frac{\delta}{\alpha + \delta}\tilde{e} + \Pi_o\sum_{i=0}^{\infty} \lambda^i(u_{t-i} - \Delta v_{t-i}). \tag{25}$$

From (25) we can calculate the unconditional variance of the exchange rate about its long-run equilibrium value $\bar{\bar{e}} = p - p^*$ as

$$\sigma_e^2 = \frac{\delta^2}{(\alpha + \delta)^2}(\tilde{e} - \bar{\bar{e}})^2 + \frac{(\sigma_u^2 + \sigma_v^2)/(1 - \lambda^2)}{[\alpha + \gamma + \delta + \beta(1 - \lambda)]^2}. \tag{26}$$

This will depend on intervention policy both directly through γ and δ and indirectly through variations in the dynamics as expressed in λ and through variations in private risk bearing as expressed in β. To these issues we turn in the next section.

In order to examine variations in risk bearing, we must find the one-period variance of the exchange rate. Subtracting (18) from (17), we have $e_t - E_{t-1}e_t = \Pi_o(u_t - \Delta v_t)$, so that the conditional variance based on information available to speculators at time $t - 1$ is simply

$$\sigma_{e,1}^2 = \frac{\sigma_u^2 + \sigma_v^2}{[\alpha + \gamma + \delta + \beta(1 - \lambda)]^2}. \tag{27}$$

6. Intervention Policies and the Harrod Effect

The Harrod effect refers to the response of speculators' willingness to bear risk to changes in the variability of exchange rates. From (7) and (27) we have

$$\frac{\sigma_u^2 + \sigma_v^2}{[\alpha + \gamma + \delta + \beta(1 - \lambda)]^2} = \frac{1}{\beta\phi}. \tag{28}$$

This relationship will enable us to determine how β changes with changes in γ and δ. However, it is also necessary to take account of changes in λ, according to (24). Thus we must solve (24) and (28) jointly for β and λ. To begin (28) can be transformed by taking the square root of both sides into

$$\frac{\alpha + \gamma + \delta}{\sqrt{\beta}} + \sqrt{\beta}(1 - \lambda) = \sqrt{\phi(\sigma_u^2 + \sigma_v^2)}, \tag{29}$$

or

$$\lambda = 1 + \frac{\alpha + \gamma + \delta}{\beta} - \frac{\sqrt{\phi(\sigma_u^2 + \sigma_v^2)}}{\sqrt{\beta}}. \tag{30}$$

We can now eliminate λ by equating (30) to (24) and after some simplification obtain

$$[\phi(\sigma_u^2 + \sigma_v^2) - (\alpha + \delta)]\beta = [(\alpha + \gamma + \delta)\sqrt{\phi(\sigma_u^2 + \sigma_v^2)}]\sqrt{\beta}. \tag{31}$$

If we assume that $\phi(\sigma_u^2 + \sigma_v^2) > \alpha + \delta$, then the quadratic equation in $\sqrt{\beta}$ has two roots, $\sqrt{\beta} = 0$ and the positive root[4]

$$\sqrt{\beta} = \frac{(\alpha + \gamma + \delta)\sqrt{\phi(\sigma_u^2 + \sigma_v^2)}}{\phi(\sigma_u^2 + \sigma_v^2) - (\alpha + \delta)}, \tag{32}$$

which yields

$$\beta = \frac{(\alpha + \gamma + \delta)^2 \phi(\sigma_u^2 + \sigma_v^2)}{[\phi(\sigma_u^2 + \sigma_v^2) - (\alpha + \delta)]^2}. \tag{33}$$

Substitution back into (30) yields

$$\lambda = 1 - \frac{\alpha + \delta}{2}\left(\frac{\phi(\sigma_u^2 + \sigma_v^2) - (\alpha + \delta)}{\alpha + \gamma + \delta}\right) < 1. \tag{34}$$

These values of β and λ account fully for the effects of changes in intervention policy on the dynamics of the model and the behavior of speculators.

The following comparative static results are easy to derive from (33):

$$\frac{\partial \beta}{\partial[\phi(\sigma_u^2 + \sigma_v^2)]} < 0, \quad \frac{\partial \beta}{\partial \gamma} > 0, \quad \frac{\partial \beta}{\partial \delta} > 0.$$

Thus increased intrinsic variability of disturbances or increased risk aversion will decrease the willingness of speculators to bear risk, as is only to be expected. The Harrod effect is directly obtained for both leaning against the wind and target intervention, as risk bearing increases with intervention. It can also be seen that $\partial \lambda/\partial \gamma > 0$, but it turns out that $\partial \lambda/\partial \delta$ is indeterminate in sign.

We can also examine the effect of intervention on the level of uncertainty, as measured by the one-period conditional variance of the exchange rate, $\sigma_{e,1}^2$. From (33) and (34), we find that

$$\beta(1 - \lambda) = \frac{(\alpha + \delta)(\alpha + \gamma + \delta)}{\phi(\sigma_u^2 + \sigma_v^2) - (\alpha + \delta)}, \tag{35}$$

so that $\partial \beta(1 - \lambda)/\partial \gamma > 0$ and $\partial \beta(1 - \lambda)/\partial \delta > 0$. It is then evident from (27) that in the case at hand, intervention clearly reduces the level of uncertainty about the exchange rate. The overall variability of the exchange rate about its equilibrium level $\bar{e}$ is, however, given by (26). Target intervention (δ) will have an ambiguous effect on σ_e^2 unless the target $\tilde{e}$ is equal to $\bar{\bar{e}}$, and in fact choice of a mistaken target can increase the variance substantially, especially if it is pursued with considerable effort (high δ). In this case it remains true that risk taking by private speculators increases with δ, but now the speculators are betting against the central bank. Leaning against the wind, by contrast, unambiguously reduces the overall variability of the exchange rate since it raises $\beta(1 - \lambda)$ and reduces λ.

Harrod also expressed the view that abandonment of pegged exchange rates might paradoxically increase the use of reserves as stabilizing private speculators withdraw from the market. This conclusion is much harder to verify. From (14) the expectation of Δx_t is $(\alpha\delta/\alpha + \delta)(\tilde{e} - \bar{\bar{e}})$. Through tedious calculations, its variance may be shown to be

$$
\sigma_{\Delta x}^2 = \delta^2 \left[\frac{\alpha^2}{(\alpha + \delta)^2}(\tilde{e} - \bar{\bar{e}})^2 + \frac{(\sigma_u^2 + \sigma_v^2)/(1 - \lambda^2)}{[\alpha + \gamma + \delta + \beta(1 - \lambda)]^2} \right]
$$
$$
+ 2\gamma(\gamma + \delta) \left[\frac{(1 - \lambda - \lambda^2)(\sigma_u^2 + \sigma_v^2)/(1 - \lambda^2)}{[\alpha + \gamma + \delta + \beta(1 - \lambda)]^2} \right].
$$

(36)

Evidently there are two forces at work in opposite directions here: the direct effect of increased intervention, from the coefficients outside the brackets, and the indirect effects of increased private risk bearing in reducing the variance of the exchange rate, inside the brackets. The possibility of a Harrod paradox appears to exist.

7. Conclusion

This chapter has demonstrated the theoretical existence of the Harrod effect within a simple framework that reflects at least some of the relevant empirical features of exchange markets. The model is too limited in scope to address the larger question of the desirability of intervention in exchange markets, for it leaves variables such as output and prices as exogenous. Nevertheless I would argue on the basis of these results that it is no longer possible to consider testing an exchange rate theory with constant coefficients over periods that include significant changes in intervention policy, even if the theory assumes that such policies have no effects, for there is an alternative hypothesis under which such policies do have effects.

Notes

This paper arose out of work begun at the 1981 Warwick Summer Workshop. Discussions with Stephen Turnovsky, Marcus Miller, Richard Marston, Jacques Melitz, and Art Benavie were helpful, but the usual disclaimer applies.

1. Other recent users of this model include Driskill and McCafferty (1980a, 1980b).

2. This may be derived by taking the logarithm of $H_{t+1}(1 + r_t^*)/H_t(1 + r_t)$, where H_t is the price of foreign currency in units of domestic currency, using the approximation $\log(1 + r) \cong r$ and the definition $e_t = \log H_t$.

3. Under these conditions the variance of v, and hence f, becomes unbounded over time.

4. It is interesting to observe that the problem of nonuniqueness noted by Driskell and McCafferty (1980a) does not arise in this model, presumably because of the absence of the J-curve.

References

Black, Stanley W. 1973. *International Money Markets and Flexible Exchange Rates*. Studies in International Finance 32. Princeton: International Finance Section, Princeton University.

Driskill, Robert, and McCafferty, Stephen. 1980a. "Speculation, Rational Expectations, and Stability of the Foreign Exchange Market." *Journal of International Economics* 10:91–102.

Driskill, Robert, and McCafferty, Stephen. 1980b. "Exchange-Rate Variability, Real and Monetary Shocks, and the Degree of Capital Mobility under Rational Expectations." *Quarterly Journal of Economics* 95:577–586.

Frenkel, Jacob A. 1981. "The Collapse of Purchasing Power Parities during the 1970's." *European Economic Review* 16:145–165.

Hansen, Lars Peter, and Hodrick, Robert J. 1980. "Forward Exchange Rates as Optimal Predictors of Future Spot Rates: An Econometric Analysis." *Journal of Political Economy* 88:829–853.

Harrod, Roy F. 1965. *Reforming the World's Money*. London: Macmillan.

Lucas, Robert E., Jr. 1976. "Econometric Policy Evaluation: A Critique." In Karl Brunner and Allan Meltzer (eds.), *The Phillips Curve and Labor Markets*. Amsterdam: North Holland.

McKinnon, Ronald I. 1979. *Money in International Exchange*. New York, Oxford University Press.

5 Exchange Market Intervention under Rational Expectations with Imperfect Capital Substitutability

Robert Driskill and Stephen A. McCafferty

1. Introduction

Recently some notable economists have argued that high international capital substitutability and mobility has exacerbated the transmission of international disturbances even with flexible exchange rates, causing excessive relative price variability (see Tobin 1978). Recent work substantiates these claims when the disturbances are monetary in nature (see Driskill and McCafferty 1980; Eaton and Turnovsky 1982; and Turnovsky and Bhandari 1982). This same work, however, also shows that relative price variability is reduced by high capital substitutability and mobility when the fundamental disturbances are real. The result that high capital substitutability has differential effects on relative-price variability depending on where the underlying shocks originate has important implications for recent policy prescriptions. In particular Tobin (1978) has argued for a tax on international exchange transactions, presumably believing such a tax would limit capital flows. (Recent work by Rennhack 1982 suggests, though, that such a tax will have ambiguous effects on capital flows.) Even if a tax were successful, though, it would be counterproductive if shocks were predominantly real.

In this chapter we argue that appropriate exchange market intervention policies can succeed in reducing relative-price variability, regardless of the source of the underlying shocks to the system. That such policies succeed results from the intervention authorities not behaving as profit-maximizing speculators but rather from their leaning against the wind and using a feedback rule on past stocks.

2. The Model: Overview

Our strategy is first to develop the model without intervention—that is, to develop a pure floating rate model. We use this model to illustrate the the asymmetric effects of capital substitutability, depending on whether the fundamental shocks to the system are real or monetary. We then amend the model by incorporating an intervention rule and show how such an intervention rule reduces relative-price variability.

The basic model is one of partial equilibrium, focusing on the foreign exchange market and abstracting from the simultaneous determination of the exchange rate and other macroeconomic variables. Specifically we take price levels, real outputs, and interest rates as exogenous and, for price levels and outputs, fixed and suppressed. Interest rates, though, are assumed stochastic. The three building blocks of the model without exchange market intervention are a net foreign asset demand specification, a trade balance specification, and the market-clearing condition. The net demand for foreign assets, B, is assumed proportional to the expected relative rate of return between domestic and foreign bonds:

$$B_t = \eta[E_t e_{t+1} - e_t - r_t] \quad \eta > 0 \tag{1}$$

where e is the (log) exchange rate, r is the exogenous interest differential, and $E_t(\cdot)$ is the conditional expectations operator. The trade balance surplus, T_t, is assumed an increasing function of the exchange rate:

$$T_t = \alpha e_t + u_t \quad \alpha > 0 \tag{2}$$

where u_t is a white noise random variable without official intervention, the market-clearing condition is simply:

$$\Delta B_t = T_t. \tag{3}$$

Once the stochastic processes governing the behavior of the exogenous variables are specified, the model can be solved for the stochastic process governing the behavior of the exchange rate. For our purposes the simple assumption that the exogenous interest differential vibrates randomly about its mean suffices. More complicated mean-regression stochastic specifications leave our qualitative results unchanged. With this assumption, straightforward application of the method of undetermined coefficients gives us:

$$e_t = \pi_0 e_{t-1} - \pi_0 r_t + \pi_0 r_{t-1} - \frac{(1 - \pi_0)}{\alpha} u_t \tag{4}$$

where

$$\pi_0 = 1 + \tfrac{1}{2}\frac{\alpha}{\eta} - \tfrac{1}{2}\frac{\alpha}{\eta}\sqrt{1 + \frac{4\eta}{\alpha}}. \tag{5}$$

Analysis of the model shows that when the underlying shocks are trade-balance shocks, increases in η, the measure of asset substitutability, reduce exchange rate variance. On the other hand when the shocks are monetary, increases in η increase exchange rate variance. Consequently policies that affect the degree of capital substitutability may have undesirable consequences for exchange rate variability.

3. Exchange Market Intervention: Existence of a Solution

We append to the basic model an exchange market intervention function. Of course, a wide variety of intervention rules conceivably could be relevant, but we focus on a linear rule that reflects concern for both exchange rate variance and reserve stock variance. Specifically we assume that the change in the stock of foreign assets held by the central bank, ΔG_t, is negatively related to the current exchange rate and to their foreign asset holdings last period, G_{t-1}:

$$\Delta G_t = -\gamma e_t - (1 - \delta)G_{t-1}; \quad \gamma > 0, 0 \leq \delta \leq 1. \tag{6}$$

The first part of the rule reflects leaning against the wind behavior by the central bank; the second part can be interpreted as reflecting concern about the level of reserve stocks. When $\delta = 1$ and intervention policy is independent of the level of reserves, it turns out that G has unbounded variance. Thus a condition for finite variance for reserve stocks is that $\delta < 1$.

Our intervention rule (6) embodies as special cases a pure float or a fixed exchange rate. A pure float is obtained when $\gamma = 0$ and $\delta = 1$; a fixed exchange rate is maintained with $\gamma = \infty$ and $\delta = 1$. Some empirical evidence on the use of such a rule by the Belgo-Luxemburg Economic Union is presented by Adam (1982).

Under intervention rule (6), the market clearing equation becomes:

$$T_t = \Delta B_t + \Delta G_t. \tag{7}$$

Using (1), (2), and (6), this condition yields the following exchange rate equation:

$$e_t(\eta + \alpha + \gamma) = \eta E_t e_{t+1} - \eta E_{t-1} e_t + \eta e_{t-1} - \eta r_t$$
$$+ \eta r_{t-1} + (\delta - 1)G_{t-1} - u_t. \tag{8}$$

Given that u_t and r_t are white noise random variables, the solution to (8) will have the form:

$$e_t = \pi_0 e_{t-1} + \pi_1 G_{t-1} + \pi_2 r_t + \pi_3 r_{t-1} + \pi_4 u_t \tag{9}$$

where the π_i are as yet undetermined coefficients. Using (9) to get expressions for $E_t e_{t+1}$ and $E_{t-1} e_t$ and substituting these expressions into (8), we have:

$$e_t[\eta(1 - \pi_0 + \gamma\pi_1) + \alpha + \gamma] = e_{t-1}[\eta(1 - \pi_0)]$$
$$+ G_{t-1}[-\eta\pi_1(1 - \delta) + \delta] \tag{10}$$
$$+ r_t(\eta\pi_3 - \eta) + r_{t-1}(-\eta\pi_3 + \eta) - u_t.$$

For (9) and (10) to be consistent, we must have:

$$\pi_0 = \frac{\eta(1 - \pi_0)}{\eta(1 - \pi_0) + \eta\gamma\pi_1 + \alpha + \gamma}, \tag{11a}$$

$$\pi_1 = \frac{-\eta\pi_1(1 - \delta) + \delta - 1}{\eta(1 - \pi_0) + \eta\gamma\pi_1 + \alpha + \gamma}, \tag{11b}$$

$$\pi_2 = \frac{\eta(\pi_3 - 1)}{\eta(1 - \pi_0) + \eta\gamma\pi_1 + \alpha + \gamma}, \tag{11c}$$

$$\pi_3 = \frac{-\eta(\pi_3 - 1)}{\eta(1 - \pi_0) + \eta\gamma\pi_1 + \alpha + \gamma}. \tag{11d}$$

$$\pi_4 = \frac{-1}{\eta(1 - \pi_0) + \eta\gamma\pi_1 + \alpha + \delta}. \tag{11e}$$

(11a) and (11b) constitute a coupled, nonlinear system of equations in π_0 and π_1. Inspection of (11c, 11d, and 11e) shows that once π_0 and π_1 are solved as functions of the structural parameters η, α, γ, and δ, the other π_i follow directly. Hence we turn to solving (11a) and (11b).

First consider relation (11a). Let $X = (\eta\gamma\pi_1 + \alpha + \gamma)$, an increasing, positive function of π_1. Straightforward differentiation of (11a) shows that:

$$\frac{d\pi_0}{dX} = \frac{\pi_0}{-2\eta(1 - \pi_0) - X}. \tag{12}$$

Now, rearranging (11a), and using our substitution for X, we find that:

$$-\eta(1 - \pi_0) - X = \frac{\eta(1 - \pi_0)}{\pi_0}. \tag{13}$$

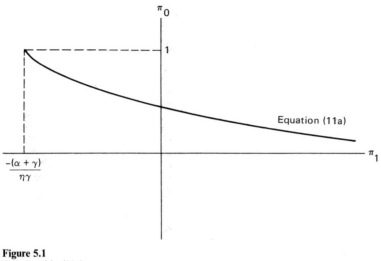

Figure 5.1
Relationship (11a)

Clearly for $0 < \pi_0 < 1$, $(-2\eta(1 - \pi_0) - X) < 0$, and so $d\pi_0/dX < 0$. Hence, for $0 < \pi_0 < 1$, $d\pi_0/d\pi_1 < 0$. Evaluating (11a) at $\pi_1 = -(\alpha + \gamma)/\eta\gamma$, we have $\pi_0 = 1$. As $\pi_1 \to \infty$, $\pi_0 \to 0$. Finally, at $\pi_1 = 0$, $\pi_0 = 1 + \frac{1}{2}\frac{(\alpha + \gamma)}{\eta} - \frac{1}{2}\frac{(\alpha + \gamma)}{\eta}\sqrt{1 + \frac{4\eta}{\alpha + \gamma}}$. Note that this value of π_0 differs from that applicable to the nonintervention model only by the addition of γ to every α term (see equation 5).

This information lets us graph relationship (11a) as in figure 5.1. π_0 is a decreasing, monotonic function of π_1, taking a maximum value of 1 at $\pi_1 = -(\alpha + \gamma)/\eta\gamma$. For values of $\pi_1 < -(\alpha + \gamma)/\eta\gamma$, π_0 is either imaginary or less than -1; these values of π_0, it turns out, are incompatable with stability of the dynamic system.

Now consider relationship (11b). This can be rewritten as the following relationship, with π_0 as an explicit function of π_1:

$$\pi_0 = 1 + \gamma\pi_1 + \frac{\alpha + \gamma}{\eta} + (1 - \delta) + \frac{(1 - \delta)}{\eta\pi_1}. \tag{14}$$

This function is graphed in figure 5.2. The important points to note are that when $\pi_1 = -(\alpha + \gamma)/\eta\gamma$, $\pi_0 = 1 + (1 - \delta)\alpha/\alpha + \gamma > 1$, and for $\pi_1 \geq 0$, $\pi_0 > 1$. Hence when we superimpose figure 5.2 on figure 5.1, we see that a unique intersection of (11a) and (11b) exists, with $0 < \pi_0 < 1$ and $\pi_1 < 0$. This is depicted in figure 5.3.

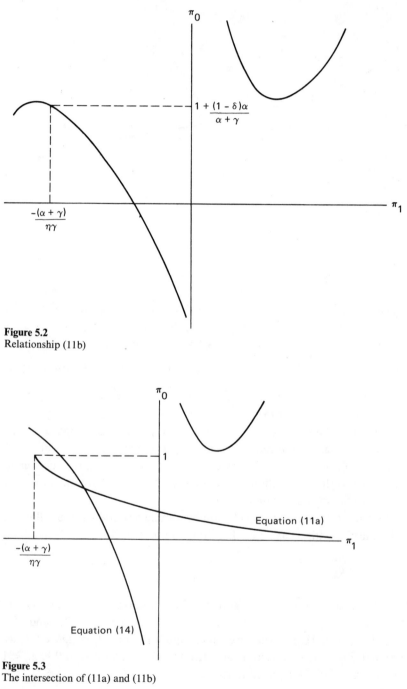

Figure 5.2
Relationship (11b)

Figure 5.3
The intersection of (11a) and (11b)

4. Dynamic Stability

From section 3, we know a unique pair (π_0, π_1) exists that satisfies the model. In this section we show that the model is dynamically stable; the deterministic part of the model converges to a steady state.

The deterministic part of model is given by:

$$e_t = \pi_0 e_{t-1} + \pi_1 G_{t-1}, \tag{15a}$$

$$G_t = -\gamma \pi_0 e_{t-1} + (-\gamma \pi_1 + \delta) G_{t-1}. \tag{15b}$$

The stability of system (15) is most readily demonstrated graphically. First consider the $\Delta G = 0$ line derived from (15b):

$$\bar{e} = \frac{1 - \delta + \gamma \pi_1}{-\gamma \pi_0} \bar{G}. \tag{16}$$

This line will be positively or negatively sloped depending on whether $(1 - \delta + \gamma \pi_1) > 0$, since $\pi_0 > 0$. If we evaluate equation (14) where $\pi_1 = -(1 - \delta)/\gamma$, we find:

$$\pi_0 = 1 + \frac{\alpha}{\eta} + 1 - \delta > 1. \tag{17}$$

This means that the intersection of (11a) and (11b) must be at some value of $\pi_1 > -(1 - \delta)/\gamma$ (see figure 5.4). Hence the $\Delta G = 0$ line is negatively sloped.

Now consider the $\Delta e = 0$ line derived from (15a):

$$\bar{e} = \frac{\pi_1}{1 - \pi_0} \bar{G}. \tag{18}$$

For $0 < \pi_0 < 1$, this line is negatively sloped. Straightforward calculations show also that:

$$\frac{\pi_1}{1 - \pi_0} > \frac{-\gamma \pi_1 + \delta - 1}{\gamma \pi_0}. \tag{19}$$

Hence, the $\Delta G = 0$ line is steeper than the $\Delta e = 0$ line.

Figure 5.5 presents the phase diagram depicting the $\Delta G = 0$ and $\Delta e = 0$ loci, along with the associated arrows of movement. Clearly the system is stable. Two other points warrant mentioning. First, if $\delta = 1$ and there is no feedback from previous reserve stocks to current intervention pur-

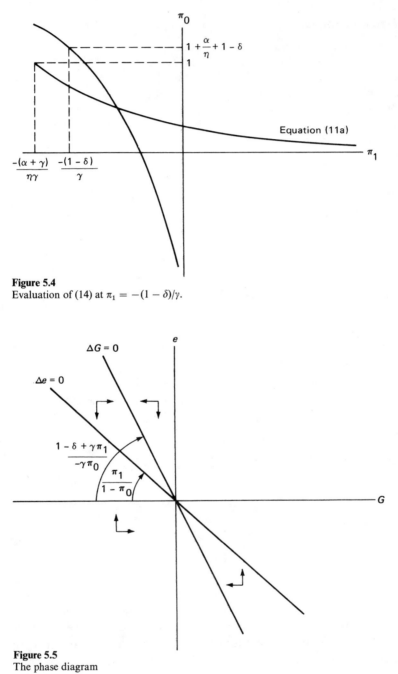

Figure 5.4
Evaluation of (14) at $\pi_1 = -(1 - \delta)/\gamma$.

Figure 5.5
The phase diagram

chases, the system is unstable in the sense that the stationary state level of G is undetermined. The stochastic analogue to this is that G follows a random walk and hence has unbounded variance. The exchange rate, though, will still be well behaved. Second, if both π_0 and π_1 are negative, the system will be unstable. This is the confirmation of our earlier comment concerning the existence and uniqueness of a stable pair (π_0, π_1).

5. Comparative Statics: Effects on π_0 of Changes in γ and δ

Our goal now is to investigate the effects of changes in the intervention parameters γ and δ on exchange rate and reserve stock variance. We first find the effects of these changes on π_0.

Consider first relationship (11a), whose graph appears in figure 5.1. Taking π_1 as parametrically given, we can differentiate with respect to π_0 and γ to find:

$$\frac{\partial \pi_0}{\partial \gamma} = \frac{\pi_0(1 + \eta\pi_1)}{-2\eta(1 - \pi_0) - \eta\gamma\pi_1 - \alpha - \gamma}. \tag{20}$$

The numerator of (20) is negative since $\{-\eta(1 - \pi_0) - \eta\gamma\pi_1 - \alpha - \delta\} = -\eta(1 - \pi_0)/\pi_0$. The denominator of (20) will be positive if $(1 + \eta\pi_1) > 0$. Now if $\pi_1 = -1/\eta$, π_1 lies to the right of $[-(\alpha + \gamma)/\eta\gamma]$, which marks the point at which $\pi_0 = 1$ in relationship (11a). Evaluating the value of π_0 associated with $\pi_1 = -1/\eta$ in relationship (11b), we find $\pi_1 = 1 + \alpha/\eta > 1$. Hence at $\pi_1 = -1/\eta$, line (11b) lies above (11a), and their intersection must occur at some $\pi_1 > -1/\eta$. This is illustrated in figure 5.6. Hence

$$\left(\frac{\partial \pi_0}{\partial \gamma}\right)$$

in equation (20) is negative; an increase in γ shifts down the line in figure 5.1 representing (11a).

Turning to relationship (11b), we find, taking π_1 as parametrically given, that:

$$\frac{\partial \pi_0}{\partial \gamma} = \pi_1 + \frac{1}{\eta} > 0. \tag{21}$$

Consequently increases in γ shift up the line in figure 5.1 representing (11b). The net result from shifts of both curves depicted in figure 5.6 is a decline in the equilibrium value of π_0.

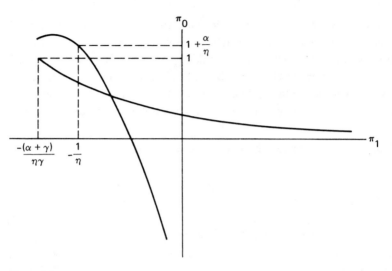

Figure 5.6
Evaluation of (14) at $\pi_1 = -1/\eta$

For changes in δ, the effect on π_0 is straightforward. Since δ does not appear in (11a), this curve does not shift at all. Differentiation of (11b), again taking π_1 as parametrically given, yields:

$$\frac{\partial \pi_0}{\partial \delta} = \frac{\eta\pi_1 + 1}{-\eta\pi_1} > 0 \qquad (22)$$

since $(\eta\pi_1 + 1) > 0$, as we showed earlier. This means a decrease in δ shifts down the (11b) curve in figure 5.1, leading to an equilibrium pair (π_0, π_1) at a larger π_0.

6. Comparative Statics: Effects on Variances

Knowing how change in γ and δ affects π_0, we are ready to investigate their effects on the one-period or forecast variances of the exchange rate and reserves. While we would like to obtain results on asymptotic variances, these are too complicated to solve at the moment.

First, note that by making use of (11a), we can write π_2, π_3, π_4 as the following explicit functions of π_0:

$$\pi_2 = -\pi_0, \qquad (23a)$$

$$\pi_3 = \pi_0, \tag{23b}$$

$$\pi_4 = \frac{-\pi_0}{\eta(1 - \pi_0)}. \tag{23c}$$

Now the forecast variance of the exchange rate, σ_e^2 is just:

$$\sigma_e^2 = \pi_0^2 \sigma_r^2 + \frac{\pi_0^2}{\eta^2(1 - \pi_0)^2} \sigma_u^2 \tag{24}$$

where σ_r^2 and σ_u^2 are the variances of r and u, respectively. Hence for given values of η and α, increases in π_0 increase exchange rate variance. Given our results from section 5, we can say that increases in γ decrease exchange rate variance, and decreases in δ increase exchange rate variance, regardless of where the shocks originate.

To investigate reserve variance, note that, from (6), we can write the reduced form for G_t as:

$$G_t = -\gamma \pi_0 e_{t-1} + (-\gamma \pi_1 + \delta) G_{t-1} + \gamma \pi_0 r_t - \gamma \pi_0 r_{t-1} + \frac{\gamma \pi_0}{\eta(1 - \pi_0)} u_t. \tag{25}$$

The forecast variance of reserves, σ_G^2, is then:

$$\sigma_G^2 = \gamma^2 \pi_0^2 \sigma_r^2 + \frac{\gamma^2 \pi_0^2}{\eta^2(1 - \pi_0)^2} \sigma_u^2. \tag{26}$$

The effects of decreases in δ on reserve variance are clear: decreases in δ increase π_0 and thus increase σ_G^2. What is interesting here is that decreases in δ presumably decrease asymptotic reserve variance, at least in the neighborhood of $\delta = 1$. It appears then that the potential exists for some tension between short-horizon and longer-horizon concerns about reserve variance, but without analytic results about longer-horizon variances, we are left with conjecture.

The result that increased feedback from past reserve stocks to current intervention increases both exchange rate and reserve stock variability is, on reflection, not so disconcerting. On average we would expect that when the exchange rate is above its longer-run value, reserve stocks are below; a shock that pushes e, say, above its long-run value calls forth a sale of reserve assets, pushing them below their long-run level. Given the rule (6), this means that a smaller δ (larger feedback) tends to reduce the volume of intervention purchases for a given value of the exchange rate. This in turn increases the one-period exchange rate variance, which calls forth an increased one-period reserve variance, as the authorities lean against the wind. Over the longer haul, though, some feedback is necessary to tie down the long-run level of reserves.

Finally, consider the effect on reserve variance of changes in γ. As already developed, increases in γ decrease the one-period exchange rate variance since it decreases the equilibrium value of π_0. This reduced exchange rate variance, though, is created by larger intervention, so we should expect reserve variance to increase. It turns out we are unable to support this conjecture analytically for arbitrary values of δ. For a small increase in γ from an initial position of $\gamma = 0$, though, we can indeed show this to be true; that is, at $\gamma = 0$,

$$\frac{\left[\dfrac{\gamma\pi_0}{d\eta(1-\pi_0)}\right]}{d\gamma} = \frac{\pi_0}{\eta(1-\pi_0)} > 0 \tag{27}$$

and

$$\frac{d(\gamma\pi_0)}{d\gamma} = \pi_0 > 0. \tag{28}$$

Thus for the measure of leaning against the wind, the intervention authorities do face a trade-off between exchange rate and reserve variability.

7. Conclusions

Policy-induced disruptions of the free flow of capital may have the undesirable effect of exacerbating exchange rate variability if the shocks are primarily real, as opposed to monetary, in origin. Leaning against the wind intervention policy can dampen exchange rate variability no matter where the shocks originate. Without a feedback rule on past reserve stocks, though, such an intervention rule is not viable in the long run since reserves will follow a random walk. With a feedback rule, reserves will have finite asymptotic variance, and the authorities can still reduce exchange rate variance.

References

Adam, Marie-Christine. 1982. "Asset Markets and Foreign Exchange Intervention: A Model of the Belgo-Luxemburg Economic Union." *Journal of Policy Modelling* 4(2):223–242.

Driskill, R., and S. McCafferty. 1980. "Exchange Rate Variability, Real and Monetary Shocks, and the Degree of Capital Mobility under Rational Expectations." *Quarterly Journal of Economics* (November): 577–586.

Eaton, J., and S. Turnovsky. 1982. "Effects of Monetary Disturbances on Exchange Rates with Risk Averse Speculation." *Journal of International Money and Finance* 1:21–37.

Rennhack, R. 1982. "Taxation of Capital Flows and Stabilization Policy." Mimeographed. Yale University.

Tobin, J. 1978. "A Proposal for International Monetary Reform." Cowles Foundation Discussion Paper 506 (October).

Turnovsky, S., and Bhandari, J. 1982. "The Degree of Capital Mobility and the Stability of an Open Economy under Rational Expectations." *Journal of Money, Credit, and Banking* 3 (August): 303–326.

6 Exchange Rate Management with Rational Expectations but Diverse Precisions

Jerome L. Stein

1. Introduction and Summary

Four major issues arise in discussion of exchange rate management. First, who is better able to locate the equilibrium price of foreign exchange: the government or the private sector? Does exchange rate management mean that the government attempts to defend a disequilibrium rate of exchange? Second, do the private agents exhibit unduly high degrees of risk aversion so that random variations in the balance of payments produce unduly large movements in the exchange rate? Third, are the anticipations of the private agents highly volatile so that they impart an undesirable degree of volatility to the current exchange rate? Fourth, does the free exchange market tend to produce variations in the exchange rate that reduce the variance of output resulting from variations in the exogenous variables (Stein 1963, 1979: 25–32)?

In this chapter I focus on the second and third points and consider a world where all agents including the government have Muth rational expectations such that the forecast errors have zero expectations and no structure. The variances of the forecast errors differ among the agents due to their heterogeneous information. Government exchange rate management does not attempt to defend a disequilibrium rate of exchange because on average each agent including the government has correct anticipations. The government acts like an optimizing speculator, but it selects the parameters of its utility function to achieve an optimal allocation of resources.

To summarize, when each agent acts optimally, a stock demand function is derived relating the current price of foreign exchange $p(t)$ to the stock $S(t)$ of net claims against foreigners. The rate of change of the stock is the balance of payments on current account. The sum of the past current accounts is the stock of net claims against foreigners. The price of foreign exchange adjusts very quickly to equate the stock demand to the stock in existence. Balance of payments surpluses or deficits produce changes in the stock of net claims and thereby in the price of foreign exchange.

The intercept of the stock demand function is the present value of a weighted average of the price of foreign exchange anticipated by the market to prevail during the subsequent period. Although the market forecast error is zero on average, there will be price fluctuations due to the variance of the market forecast error, which implies shifts of the stock demand function, as well as variations in the stock of net claims against foreigners, which are associated with movements along the stock demand function.

Assume that real output is given so that the fourth issue can be ignored. An optimal allocation of resources implies that the current price of foreign exchange equals the present value of the next period's price of foreign exchange less a risk premium. This means that an optimal allocation of resources implies a zero forecast error. Given the stock of net claims against foreigners, social loss is related to the variance of the market forecast error.

The average market forecast error ε_m is a weighted average of the error of the private sector ε_p and the error of the government ε_G. Variable g is the ratio of the government's holding of net claims against foreigners relative to the private sector's holdings. This is a control variable, which underlies the government's demand function: $\varepsilon_m = (\varepsilon_p + g\varepsilon_G)/(1 + g)$. The optimal degree of government intervention is the value of control variable g, which minimizes the variance of ε_m. When the errors of the government and private sector are independent, then the optimal value of g is g^*: $g^* = \text{var}\,\varepsilon_p/\text{var}\,\varepsilon_G$. The ratio of government to private holdings should equal the ratio of the variance of the forecast error of the private sector to that of the government.

Although these variances are unobservable, there is an algorithm for the government to find the optimum parameter g^* of its demand function. The expected profits of the government from its foreign exchange operations, net of a risk premium, denoted by $E\pi_1^G$, are: $E\pi_1^G = g\gamma\,\text{var}\,\varepsilon_G(g^* - g)/(1 + g)^2\,\text{var}\,p$, where γ is the sum of parameters of private demand functions. The government can locate the optimal value of its demand parameter g^* by raising (lowering) g if it is making profits (losses). When the expected profits net of a risk premium are zero, then government intervention is at its optimal value.

A glossary of symbols is found at the end of the chapter.

2. Stock Demand for Net Claims Against Foreigners

Basic Considerations

Consider two market baskets: domestic securities and foreign securities. The composition of each portfolio, which consists of assets of different degrees of risk, is ignored in the process of aggregation. The object is to determine the demand for the stock of net claims against foreigners: the stock of net assets less the stock of liabilities to foreigners.

The yield on the portfolio of domestic assets is r_H per unit of time. It can be either the interest rate on bonds plus the capital gain or the yield on equities. The comparable yield on foreign assets is denoted by r_F, when the returns are measured in foreign currency. These returns are received at time $t + 1$; hence $r_i(t + 1)$ is a stochastic variable. The yield on foreign assets, measured in domestic currency, depends on whether the assets are hedged in the forward market. Let $p(t)$ be the logarithm of the dollar price of foreign exchange and $q_{t+1}(t)$ the logarithm of the dollar price of forward foreign exchange that matures at time $t + 1$. With continuous compounding, the yield on a hedged foreign exchange asset (or cost of a hedged foreign exchange liability) is $q_{t+1}(t) - p(t) + r_F(t + 1)$. It is the sum of the forward premium $q_{t+1} - p(t) \gtreqless 0$ and the foreign yield $r_F(t + 1)$. The yield on an unhedged foreign asset (or cost of an unhedged foreign liability) is $p(t + 1) - p(t) + r_F(t + 1)$. The term $p(t + 1) - p(t)$ is the percentage change in the price of foreign exchange.

Let an economic unit with one dollar of wealth allocate it among domestic assets, unhedged foreign assets, and hedged foreign assets. Equation (1) describes the return where ξ_1 of wealth is invested in unhedged foreign assets, ξ_2 is invested in hedged foreign assets and $1 - \xi_1 - \xi_2$ in domestic assets. Fraction ξ_i is positive if it is an asset and negative if it is a liability

$$R = \xi_1[p(t + 1) - p(t) + r_F(t + 1)] + \xi_2[q_{t+1}(t) - p(t) + r_F(t + 1)] + (1 - \xi_1 - \xi_2)r_H(t + 1). \tag{1}$$

Alternatively the return can be written as equation (1a), where $r(t + 1)$ represents the domestic less foreign yields $r_H(t + 1) - r_F(t + 1)$. The return expected by the ith agent is described by equation (1b), where E is the expectations operator:

$$R = \xi_1[p(t + 1) - p(t) - r(t + 1)] + \xi_2[q_{t+1}(t) - p(t)$$
$$- r(t + 1)] + r_H(t + 1), \tag{1a}$$

$$ER = \xi_1[E_i p(t + 1; t) - p(t) - Er] + \xi_2[q_{t+1}(t) - p(t) - Er] + Er_H. \tag{1b}$$

At time t the stochastic variables are $p(t + 1)$ and $r_i(t + 1)$. The spot price $p(t)$ and forward price $q_{t+1}(t)$ are known.

The term in (1b) $E_i p(t + 1; t)$ is the expected price of foreign exchange at $t + 1$ when the expectation is taken by the ith agent at time t. The variance of the interest rate differential is denoted by $\operatorname{var} r$.

Assume that the yield differential $r \equiv r_H(t + 1) - r_F(t + 1)$ between domestic and foreign assets has a mean of Er and is independent of the domestic yield:

$$\operatorname{cov}(r_H - r_F, r_H) = 0. \tag{2a}$$

Moreover assume that the covariances between the price of foreign exchange $p(t + 1)$, the yield differential r, and the domestic yield are zero:

$$\operatorname{cov}(p(t + 1), r) = \operatorname{cov}(p(t + 1), r_H) = 0. \tag{2b}$$

The covariance between the price of foreign exchange and the yield differential is ambiguous; hence it is assumed to be zero (2b). There are two counterbalancing effects. (1) Let the yield differential r rise. If it were anticipated, there would be a capital inflow, which would lower the price of foreign exchange. Hence $\operatorname{cov}(p, r)$ tends to be negative. (2) A rise in the price of foreign exchange may induce a rise in the yield differential to offset the rise in the price. Hence $\operatorname{cov}(p, r)$ tends to be positive. Considering counterbalancing forces (1) and (2) together, the covariance between the price of foreign exchange and the yield differential is assumed to be zero:

Using (2a) and (2b), the variance of the return is equation (3):

$$\operatorname{Var} R = \xi_1^2 \operatorname{var} p + (\xi_1 + \xi_2)^2 \operatorname{var} r + \operatorname{var} r_H. \tag{3}$$

Assume that everyone has the same distribution function for the yield differential even though all assets are risky. The choice variables are ξ_1 and ξ_2 for foreign assets and hence $1 - \xi_1 - \xi_2$ for domestic assets.

Optimization and Market Clearing

Optimization   Assume that the ith agent selects fractions ξ_1 and ξ_2 to maximize expected utility function (4) of expected return ER (equation (1b)) and variance var R (equation (3)). The coefficient of absolute risk aversion is α_i.

$$E(U) = ER - (\alpha_i/2)\text{var}\, R. \tag{4}$$

The optimal fraction ξ_1^i of wealth held in unhedged foreign assets (denoted by subscript 1) is described by equation (5), and the optimal fraction ξ_2^i of wealth held in hedged foreign assets (denoted by subscript 2) is described by equation (6) when the yield differential is uncertain. When the yield differential is certain, var $r = 0$, then (6a) is obtained:

$$\xi_1^i = [E_i p(t+1;t) - q_{t+1}(t)]/\alpha_i \,\text{var}\, p, \tag{5}$$

$$\xi_2^i = [q_{t+1}(t) - p(t) - Er]/\alpha_i \,\text{var}\, r - [E_i p(t+1;t) - q_{t+1}(t)]/\alpha_i \,\text{var}\, p \tag{6}$$

$$\text{when var}\, r \neq 0,$$

$$q_{t+1}(t) - p(t) - r = 0, \qquad \text{when var}\, r = 0. \tag{6a}$$

Add (5) and (6) to derive the ith agent's demand for the total net claims against foreigners per dollar of wealth W_i, whether hedged or unhedged:

$$\xi_1^i + \xi_2^i = [q_{t+1}(t) - p(t) - Er]/\alpha_i \,\text{var}\, r; \qquad \text{when var}\, r \neq 0. \tag{7}$$

Market Clearing   To determine the market clearing spot price and forward price, two conditions must be satisfied. First, the total demand by all agents for the stock of net claims against foreigners must be equal to the stock in existence, denoted by $S(t)$. Equation (8) described this condition. To avoid revaluing the stock of net claims against foreigners when ever the price of foreign exchange varies, assume that foreigners do not invest in dollar assets. Residents of the United States either own foreign assets or owe foreign liabilities:

$$\sum_{i=1}^{G} (\xi_1 + \xi_2)^i W_i(t) = S(t). \tag{8}$$

The left-hand side is the sum of the demands for total net claims of the G agents, and the right-hand side is the stock $S(t) \gtreqless 0$ in existence.

Second, the total supply of forward contracts by all of the G agents must be zero. Quantity $\xi_2^i W_i(t)$ is the demand for hedged net claims against foreigners, which is the supply of forward contracts. Equation (9) describes the market clearing in the forward market:

$$\sum_{i=1}^{G} \xi_2^i W_i(t) = 0. \tag{9}$$

In this formulation no dichotomy is made between hedgers and speculators. The excess supply of forward foreign exchange by the ith agent is $\xi_2^i W^i(t)$. Agents will be on different sides of the market only insofar as their price anticipations $E_i p(t + 1; t)$ differ. In formulations where there is a dichotomy between hedgers and speculators (Stein et al. 1983), agents can be on opposite sides of the market although they have the same price anticipations.

Quantities ξ_1^i and ξ_2^i are described by optimization equations (5) and (6). Solve the two market clearing equations (8) and (9) for the spot price $p(t)$ and the forward price $q_{t+1}(t)$. Equation (8) implies equation (10), and equations (8) and (9) imply equation (11):

$$q_{t+1}(t) - p(t) - Er = \left[\operatorname{var} r \middle/ \sum_{i=1}^{n} (w_i/\alpha_i) \right] [S(t)/W(t)], \tag{10}$$

$$S(t)/W(t) = \sum_{i=1}^{G} [E_i p(t + 1; t) - q_{t+1}(t)](w_i/\alpha_i)/\operatorname{var} p, \tag{11}$$

where $w_i \equiv w_i/W$ is the relative wealth of the ith agent.

Equation (10) states that the differential between the forward premium $q_{t+1}(t) - p(t)$ and the expected yield differential Er is equal to a risk premium. If the yield differential were known with certainty, then the risk premium would be zero, and the interest rate parity condition would hold. In the case considered here the assets are market baskets of securities with different maturities and risks of default. Moreover the foreign government may impose exchange restrictions. Hence, $\operatorname{var} r$ is strictly positive.

It has been shown that the interest rate parity theory holds in the special case where the yield differential between a domestic and a foreign asset is known with certainty, in the Eurocurrency market. Otherwise the deviation from interest rate parity is described by equation (10). To simplify the equations, it is often convenient (but not necessary) to consider the special case where $\operatorname{var} r = 0$.

Equation (11) is the market clearing equation that determines the forward price.

Solve equation (11) for the forward price and derive equation (12). It is a weighted average of the anticipated prices less a positive or negative risk premium, which is a function of the stock of the net claims against foreigners $S(t)$, the price variance $\sigma^2 \equiv \mathrm{var}\,p$, and risk aversion relative to wealth w_i/α_i:

$$q_{t+1}(t) = \left[\sum_{i=1}^{G} (w_i/\alpha_i) E_i p(t+1;t) - \sigma^2 S(t)/W(t) \right] \Big/ \sum_{i=1}^{G} (w_i/\alpha_i). \tag{12}$$

Equation (10), a general version of the interest rate parity theory, determines the differential between the forward price $q_{t+1}(t)$ and the current spot price $p(t)$. Equation (12) determines the level of the forward price in terms of a weighted average of anticipated prices and an endogenous risk premium, which depends on the stock of net claims against foreigners, risk, and risk aversion.

Combining (10) and (12), the spot price $p(t)$ is described by equation (13). If yield differential were known with certainty, then (13a) is derived.

$$p(t) = \left[\sum_{i=1}^{n} (w_i/\alpha_i) E_i p(t+1;t) - \sigma^2 S(t)/W(t) \right] \Big/ \sum_{i=1}^{n} (w_i/\alpha_i) - Er$$

$$- \left[\mathrm{var}\, rS(t)/W(t) \right] / \sum_{i=1}^{n} (w_i/\alpha_i), \tag{13}$$

$$p(t) = \left[\sum_{i=1}^{G} (w_i/\alpha_i) E_i p(t+1;t) / \sum_{i=1}^{n} (w_i/\alpha_i) - Er \right]$$

$$- \sigma^2 S(t)/W(t) \sum_{i=1}^{G} (w_i/\alpha_i). \tag{13a}$$

The spot price, which equates the demand for the stock of net claims against foreigners to the stock in existence, is equal to the present value of a weighted average of anticipated prices during the next period adjusted for the interest differential less a positive or negative risk premium.[1]

Figure 6.1 describes this equation, which is stock demand function $D_1 D_1'$. The vertical axis is the logarithm of the spot price, and the horizontal axis is the stock of net claims $S(t) \gtreqless 0$ against foreigners (per unit of wealth). The vertical intercept is the term in square brackets: the present value of a weighted average of the anticipated price. At any time the stock

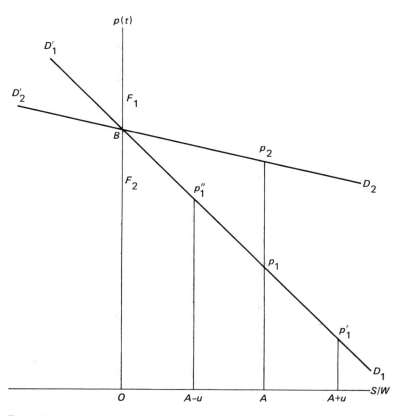

Figure 6.1
The stock demand function relates the price of foreign exchange $p(t)$ to the ratio of the
stock of net claims against foreigners per unit of wealth. The intercept is the present value
of the price of foreign exchange next period plus the average market forecast error.

of net claims is known. Then the market clearing spot price of foreign exchange is p_1.

Equation (13) or (13a) is the fundamental equation describing the stock equilibrium that prevails at all times.

Rational Expectations with Diverse Precisions

For people to be on opposite sides of the forward market in this model, price anticipations must differ. Otherwise the market would clear without any transactions.

It is assumed that the anticipated price $E_i p(t + 1; t)$ for each agent is a random variable distributed normally around the subsequently realized price $p(t + 1)$. There are $G - 1$ private agents, and the Gth agent is the government denoted by G. The forecast error $\varepsilon_i(t + 1)$ between the anticipated price and the subsequently realized price is normally distributed with a mean of zero (14b). If each agent made repeated forecasts of the subsequent period's price, then he would be correct on average. The variances of the forecast errors (var ε_i) are assumed to differ among agents. The second moment of the distribution of the random variable $E_i p(t + 1; t)$ around the common mean $p(t + 1)$ differs among the agents. Some have higher precisions (reciprocal of variance) than do others.

The rational expectations assumptions are described by (14b) and (14c). On average each agent's forecasts are correct and the forecast errors are not serially correlated. If the underlying structure that generates $p(t + 1)$ were stationary, then there should not be significant differences in the distribution of $E_i p(t + 1; t)$ among agents. The interesting situation concerns the case where the underlying distribution that generates $p(t + 1)$ has changed:

$$E_i p(t + 1; t) - p(t + 1) = \varepsilon_i(t + 1),$$

$$i = 1, 2, \ldots, G, \tag{14a}$$

$$\varepsilon_i(t + 1) \quad \text{is} \quad N(0, \text{var } \varepsilon_i), \tag{14b}$$

$$E\varepsilon_i(t)\varepsilon_i(t + 1) = 0. \tag{14c}$$

The variances of the distribution differ because people have differential information, resulting from different degrees of experience and involvement in the foreign exchange market. The theoretical rationale for the view that the variances of the forecast error of the agents differ is based on Bayesian inference.

Let there be a normally distributed population with an unknown mean M and a specified precision (the reciprocal of the variance) of $s = 1/\sigma^2$. At time $t - 1$ agents have prior estimates of this normal distribution. The mean of the normal prior distribution is $\mu(t - 1)$ and the precision of the prior distribution is $\tau(t - 1)$. At time $t - 1$ the agent takes a sample of size n from the population and obtains a mean of $\bar{x}(t - 1)$.

The question is, What is the variance of the mean of the prior distribution $\mu(t - 1)$ around the unknown population mean M? The following table indicates the relation of this problem of statistical inference to the problem at hand:

Distribution	Mean	Precision $\equiv$ 1/variance
population	$M \equiv p(t + 1)$	s
prior	$\mu(t - 1) \equiv E_i p(t + 1; t)$	$\tau(t - 1)$

The mean of the population M corresponds to the subsequently realized price $p(t + 1)$. The mean of the prior distribution $\mu(t - 1)$ corresponds to the expected price $E_i p(t + 1; t)$. The uncertainty is reflected in the two precisions. The subsequently realized price is distributed normally around mean $M \equiv p(t + 1)$ with a variance of $1/s$. The anticipated price is distributed around $\mu(t - 1) \equiv E_i p(t + 1; t)$ with a variance of $1/\tau(t - 1)$.

The sample size n that an agent draws has a mean of $\bar{x}(t - 1)$. This reflects the information that he obtains at time $t - 1$ about the population distribution. A large sample size indicates that the agent has more bits of information about the population. On the basis of the sample the agent revises his prior distribution of the population and obtains a posterior distribution of next period's price. Equations (15a) and (15b) describe the posterior mean and precision (DeGroot 1970: 167):

$$\mu(t) = [\tau(t - 1)/\tau(t - 1) + ns]\mu(t - 1) + [ns/\tau(t - 1) + ns]\bar{x}(t - 1),$$

(15a)

$$\tau(t) = \tau(t - 1) + ns.$$

(15b)

The new prior for the mean $\mu(t)$ is (15a), a weighted average of the preceding prior $\mu(t - 1)$ and the current sample mean $\bar{x}(t - 1)$. The new prior for the precision is the original prior plus ns.

Consider the variance of the prior estimate $\mu(t)$ of the unknown population mean: $E[\mu(t) - M]^2$. This is a way of determining how quickly the new prior $\mu(t)$ converges to the unknown population mean M. Theorem 1 is proved.

THEOREM 1.   *For very low initial precisions ($\tau(0)$ is small) $E[\mu(t) - M]^2 = (\sigma^2/n)/t$. The variance of the prior estimate of the mean around the population mean is positively related to the variance of sample means $\sigma^2/n \equiv 1/sn$ and negatively related to the number of samples (t).*

Proof Define a variable $y(t) \equiv \mu(t) - M$, the difference between the prior estimate of the population mean $\mu(t)$ and the unknown population mean M. Then (15a) can be written as:

$$y(t + 1) = [\tau(t)/\tau(t) + ns]y(t) + [ns/\tau(t) + ns][\bar{x}(t) - M]. \tag{16a}$$

By induction on t it can be proved that:

$$y(t) = [\tau(0)/\tau(t - 1) + ns]y(0) + [ns/\tau(t - 1) + ns]\sum_{h=0}^{t-1}[\bar{x}(h) - M]. \tag{16b}$$

The expectation of (16b) is the first term on the right-hand side. Therefore since the variance of the distribution of sample means is $\sigma^2/n = 1/ns$:

$$\text{var } y(t) = [ns/\tau(t - 1) + ns]^2 t/ns \tag{16c}$$
$$= nst/[\tau(t - 1) + ns]^2.$$

From (15b), the precision of the prior distribution is:

$$\tau(t - 1) = \tau(0) + ns(t - 1) \tag{16d}$$

Substitute (16d) into (16c) and derive:

$$\text{var } y(t) = nst/[\tau(0) + nst]^2. \tag{16e}$$

For small initial precision $\tau(0)$,

$$\text{var } y(t) \approx 1/nst = (\sigma^2/n)/t. \quad \text{Q.E.D.} \tag{16f}$$

The variance of the prior estimate of the mean $E_i p(t + 1; t)$ around the unknown population mean $p(t + 1)$ depends on two variables: the noisiness of the system as measured by $\sigma^2 = 1/s$, which is the variance of the subsequently realized price, and the amount of information nt. The latter is the product of the sample size n that was just taken and the number t of samples. As nt grows, the price estimate converges to the population mean. If the population distribution were stationary, the nt term grows over time and every agent's prior converges to the population mean. The problem arises when the population distribution has changed so that nt differs among agents, thereby producing a variance of priors around the new unknown mean.

Consider two agents who are in the foreign exchange market: Exxon and a medium-sized German bank. Neither knows the new equilibrium rate of exchange M. Exxon transacts foreign exchange in almost every location and in large volume. This is equivalent to drawing many samples (t), and each is of a large size (n). From theorem I the variance of Exxon's prior around the population mean M would be less than that of the medium-sized bank. This is the rationale behind the assumption that the error variances differ among agents when the population distribution has changed. The agents with more experience and larger volume have higher prior precisions than do novices or those with small volumes of transactions. The differences in the priors $E_i p(t + 1; t)$ generated in this fashion explain why some agents are short and others are long forward exchange.

Rational Expectations Stock Demand Function

Assume that the $(G - 1)$ private agents plus the government (denoted by G) have rational expectations as described by equations (14). Each of the G agents has expectations that are correct on average. Write equation (13a) using the rational expectations assumptions (14) and derive (17). The price variance $\operatorname{var} p$ is written as σ^2. In this case $Er = r$, since the yields are known:

$$p(t) = p(t + 1) + \frac{\sum\limits_{i=1}^{G} (w_i/\alpha_i)\varepsilon_i(t + 1)}{\sum\limits_{i=1}^{G} (w_i/\alpha_i)} - \frac{\sigma^2 S(t)/W(t)}{\sum\limits_{i=1}^{G} (w_i/\alpha_i)} - r. \tag{17}$$

It is convenient to simplify notation in (17). Let ε_p be a weighted average of the private forecast errors (18a), g be the weight of the government relative to that of the private sector (18b), and γ be the sum of the weights of the private sector (18c):

$$\varepsilon_p \equiv \sum\limits_{i=1}^{G-1} (w_i/\alpha_i)\varepsilon_i(t + 1) \bigg/ \sum\limits_{i=1}^{G-1} (w_i/\alpha_i), \tag{18a}$$

$$g \equiv (w_G/\alpha_G) \bigg/ \sum\limits_{i=1}^{G-1} (w_i/\alpha_i) \equiv (w_G/\alpha_G)/\gamma, \tag{18b}$$

$$\gamma \equiv \sum\limits_{i=1}^{G-1} (w_i/\alpha_i). \tag{18c}$$

Then equation (17) can be written as (19):

$$p(t) = p(t + 1) - r + (\varepsilon_p + g\varepsilon_G)/(1 + g) - \sigma^2 S(t)/W(t)\gamma(1 + g). \qquad (19)$$

The average market forecast error ε_m is:

$$\varepsilon_m = (\varepsilon_p + g\varepsilon_G)/(1 + g). \qquad (20)$$

Coefficient γ represents the magnitude of the private demand that depends on the private wealth per unit of risk aversion; g represents the magnitude of government operations relative to that of the private sector; and ε_m is the average market forecast error.

The weights (w_i/α_i) underlying the private error ε_p are given by the coefficients of risk aversion and the distribution of wealth of the private sector. Weight $g \equiv (w_G/\alpha_G)/\gamma$ is a control variable of the government, which determines its own risk aversion and scope of operations. The object of this chapter is to determine the optimal value of g or (w_G/α_G). Consequently for the private sector w_i/α_i is given by the utility function and wealth, whereas $w_G/\alpha_G \equiv g\gamma$ is a control variable for the government.

Figure 6.1 describes the stock demand function, equation (19), which determines the current spot price $p(t)$. The intercept is the present value of next period's price $p(t + 1) - r$ plus the average market error ε_m as defined by (20).

The value of g selected by the government affects both the intercept and the slope of stock demand function (19). The intercept is discussed below in detail. Figure 6.1 can serve to illustrate the importance of g in determining the slope.

If the stock of net claims against foreigners per unit of wealth is $0A$ and the present value of next period's price $p(t + 1) - r$ is $0B$, then on average the price $p(t) = p_1$ will be the market clearing spot price. At that price the demand for the stock of net claims is equal to the stock in existence. The spot price $p(t)$ differs from the present value of next period's price $p(t + 1) - r$ by risk premium $0B - Ap_1$.

A rise in the government demand parameter g lowers the risk premium, the difference between the present value of the expected price and the current price. Insofar as the government purchases net claims against foreigners, the position at risk of the private sector diminishes. Consequently a smaller risk premium per unit is demanded and the "backwardation" between the present value of the expected price and the current price declines. Graphically the expected stock demand function becomes flatter;

the spot price rises from p_1 to p_2 when the stock of net claims is $0A$ and the government increases its weight from g_1 to g_2.

3. Rate of Change of the Stock

The rate of change of the stock of net claims against foreigners is the current account of the balance of payments (ignoring unilateral transfers). The current account is the excess supply of traded goods $B(t)$, as described by equation (21). It depends on the ratio of the prices of traded goods in domestic currency to the price of nontraded goods and the excess demand for money. (See Connolly and Taylor 1982; Stein 1980, p. 571.) The greater the ratio of the price of traded goods in domestic currency $p + z_F - z_H$, the greater the excess supply of traded goods and hence the current account. Coefficient β_0 represents the strength of the substitution effect. The greater the excess demand for money $vz_H + (1 - v)(z_F + p) + l(\cdot) - m$, the greater the excess supply of all goods. Coefficient β_F represents the effect of a rise in the excess demand for money on the excess supply of traded goods.

$$B(t) = \beta_0[p(t) + z_F(t) - z_H(t)] + \beta_F[vz_H(t)$$
$$+ (1 - v)(z_F(t) + p(t)) + l(\cdot) - m(t)] + u \qquad (21)$$

where

z_H, z_F	logarithm of prices of traded (F), nontraded (H) goods,
m	logarithm of domestic money,
v	weight of nontraded goods in price index,
$l(\cdot)$	logarithm of demand for real balances,
u	disturbance or other factors, $Eu = 0$,
p	logarithm of price of foreign exchange, and
$vz_H + (1 - v)(z_F + p)$	weighted logarithm of price level.

The excess supply of nontraded goods $H(t)$ has a similar form but is constructed so that the excess supply of all goods $B(t) + H(t)$ is proportional to the excess demand for money:

$$H(t) = -\beta_0[p(t) + z_F(t) - z_H(t)] + \beta_H[vz_H(t) + (1 - v)z_F(t)$$
$$+ (1 - v)p(t) + l(\cdot) - m(t)] + u_H. \qquad (22)$$

Define the flow equilibrium price of foreign exchange P_e as the price of foreign exchange that prevails when the expected excess supplies of traded and nontraded goods are both zero:

$$EB(t) = EH(t) = 0. \tag{23}$$

It is apparent that the flow equilibrium price of foreign exchange $p(t) = P_e$ is the ratio of the price of nontraded to traded goods. In logarithms P_e satisfies

$$P_e(t) = z_H(t) - z_F(t). \tag{24}$$

It follows from (21)–(24) that the current account can be written as equation (25).

$$B(t) = [\beta_0 + \beta_F(1 - v)][p(t) - P_e] + u \equiv c[p(t) - P_e] + u. \tag{25}$$

The current account, which is the rate of change of the stock of net claims against foreigners, is a multiple $c \equiv \beta_0 + \beta_F(1 - v)$ of the difference between the current price of foreign exchange $p(t)$ and the flow equilibrium price P_e, plus a disturbance term. When the price of foreign exchange is equal to its flow equilibrium value, on average the balance on current account will be zero. This is equation (26) in discrete time:

$$S(t + 1) - S(t) = c[p(t) - P_e(t)] + u(t + 1). \tag{26}$$

Equations (26) and (27), which is (19) and definition (20), where wealth is normalized at unity, constitute the basic model that determines the spot price and the stock of net claims against foreigners:

$$p(t) = [p(t + 1) + \varepsilon_m(t + 1)] - r - \sigma^2 S(t)/\gamma(1 + g) \tag{27}$$

or

$$p(t) = E_m p(t + 1) - r - \sigma^2 S(t)/\gamma(1 + g), \tag{27a}$$

where $E_m p(t + 1) \equiv p(t + 1) + (\varepsilon_p + g\varepsilon_G)/(1 + g)$ is a weighted average of the prices anticipated by the market to prevail during the next period. It is the sum of the price that does prevail $p(t + 1)$ plus the weighted average market error ε_m, defined in (20). The intercept of stock demand function (27) is the present value of the anticipated market price $E_m p(t + 1) - r$, which is a stochastic variable.

Flow equilibrium price $P_e(t)$ is determined by macroeconomic equation

(24), and nominal interest rate differential r is predetermined. Once the spot price $p(t)$ and the stock of net claims against foreigners are determined, from (26) and (27), the forward price $q_{t+1}(t)$ is determined by equation (10). The model is now complete.

4. Solution of the Model

Steady-State Solution

The model—equations (26) and (27)—can be solved for the equilibrium values of the variables and their trajectories to the equilibrium. Define the equilibrium as a situation where, on average, the stock of net claims against foreigners (per unit of wealth) is constant:

$$E[S(t + 1) - S(t)] = 0. \tag{28}$$

Equations (26) and (27) imply that, in equilibrium, the price of foreign exchange p is equal to the flow equilibrium price P_e as described by (24). The price of foreign exchange at any time $p(t)$ produces stock equilibrium (equation (19) or (27)), and its steady-state value also produces flow equilibrium.

In the steady state there will be an equilibrium stock of net claims against foreigners denoted by S_e. This is obtained by solving (27) when the expected change in price and expected forecast errors are zero. The equilibrium stock satisfies (29):

$$[\sigma^2/\gamma(1 + g)]S_e = -r = r_F - r_H. \tag{29}$$

The equilibrium stock of net claims is such that the risk premium (left-hand side of (29)) is equal to the foreign less domestic interest rate (right-hand side of (29)). If nominal interest rates are equal, then the equilibrium stock of net claims is zero.

Dynamics of the Exchange Rate

Stock demand equation (19) or (27a) takes the intercept $E_m p(t + 1) \equiv p(t + 1) + \varepsilon_m$ as a parameter. The object of the rational expectations approach is to derive the value of the intercept of a stock demand function from the structure of the model. Then an explicit dynamical process is obtained.

The dynamics are most easily analyzed by measuring the stock $S(t)$ as a deviation from its equilibrium value S_e as defined in equation (30):

$$s(t) \equiv S(t) - S_e. \tag{30}$$

Equations (31) and (32) describe the dynamic process. The former is based on (27a) and (30) and the latter is based on (26) and (30):

$$p(t) = E_m p(t + 1) - \sigma^2 s(t)/\gamma(1 + g), \tag{31}$$

$$s(t + 1) - s(t) = c[p(t) - P_e(t)] + u(t + 1). \tag{32}$$

At time t the only information that agents have are the current stock $s(t)$, the flow equilibrium price $P_e(t)$, and the structure of the model: equations (31) and (32). They do not know $u(t + 1)$ but know that it has a zero mean. The rational expectations solution is as follows (Stein 1980: appendix B).

Postulate a relation between the current spot price $p(t)$ and the current stock $s(t)$, as described by (33). The object is to determine the parameters V_0 and V_1.

$$p(t) = V_0 + V_1 s(t). \tag{33}$$

Parameter V_0 will be the intercept of the stock demand function when expectations are endogenous, and V_1 is the corresponding slope.

Take the expectation of next period's price, from (33) and derive (34):

$$Ep(t + 1; t) = V_0 + V_1 Es(t + 1; t). \tag{34}$$

From (32) the expected stock is derived:

$$Es(t + 1; t) = s(t) + c[p(t) - P_e(t)]. \tag{35}$$

Substitute (33) into (35) to derive:

$$Es(t + 1; t) = s(t) + c[V_0 + V_1 s(t) - P_e(t)]. \tag{36}$$

The expected price $Ep(t + 1; t)$ is obtained by substituting (36) into (34) to obtain (37):

$$Ep(t + 1; t) = V_0 + V_1 \{s(t) + c[V_0 + V_1 s(t) - P_e(t)]\}. \tag{37}$$

The crucial assumption for a rational expectations analysis is (38); the average market anticipated price $E_m p(t + 1; t) \equiv p(t + 1) + (\varepsilon_p + g\varepsilon_G)/(1 + g)$ in (31) is equal to the expected price from the model $Ep(t + 1; t)$ in (34):

$$E_m p(t + 1; t) \equiv p(t) + (\varepsilon_p + g\varepsilon_G)/(1 + g) = Ep(t + 1; t). \tag{38}$$

In that case substitute (33) and (37) into (31) to obtain (39):

$$cV_1[V_0 + V_1 s(t) - P_e(t)] \equiv \sigma^2 s(t)/\gamma(1 + g). \tag{39}$$

This is an identity in $s(t)$, so coefficients V_0 and V_1 are to be chosen so that (39) is always true. These coefficients must satisfy (40a) and (40b):

$$V_1^2 \equiv \sigma^2/c\gamma(1 + g), \tag{40a}$$

$$V_0 \equiv P_e(t). \tag{40b}$$

There are two solutions for the slope V_1 of stock demand function (33): one is positive and the other negative. If the stock demand function is negatively sloped or if the dynamical system is stable, then the stock demand function (33) is described by (41):

$$p(t) = P_e(t) - \sigma s(t)/\sqrt{c\gamma(1 + g)}.. \tag{41}$$

The vertical intercept is the flow equilibrium price $P_e(t)$, and the slope is a function of risk, risk aversion, the speed of response of the current account to the exchange rate, and the magnitude of government operations.

The dynamics can be seen graphically (Stein 1980: figures 1–3). A description is as follows. Given the flow equilibrium price P_e and the current stock $s(t)$, the stock demand function (equation (41)) determines the spot price $p(t)$. At that price the expected percentage change in price is equal to the opportunity cost (r) plus a risk premium $\sigma^2 s(t)/\gamma(1 + g)$, as described by (27a).

Given the price of foreign exchange determined by the stock demand function (41), the current account of the balance of payments is determined by (26). This is the change in the stock.

As long as $p(t)$ exceeds flow equilibrium price P_e, the stock rises on average as a result of current account surpluses. The stock demand function is negatively sloped. Consequently the spot price must decline to induce the public to hold the larger stock. In this manner the spot price converges in a statistical sense to the flow equilibrium price.

There are two problems with the rational expectations solution to this dynamic system. First, the derivation of the rational expectations stock demand function (41) assumes that on average the agents know the flow equilibrium price (as well as weights γ and g). Assume that P_e is given over an interval. As a result there will be no variance to the stock demand function (41). Given the stock $s(t)$, there is no variance to the spot price. The only reason why the price foreign exchange varies is that the stock changes and the price varies along the given stock demand function. This is an implausible description of the foreign exchange market.

It was argued above that when the mean (M) of the population changes, the variance of the prior estimate of the mean $\mu(t)$ of an agent depends on the variance of the population and the total number (nt) of items sampled from the population. Population mean M corresponds here to P_e, and agents have different values of nt. When P_e has changed, the agents will have different prior estimates of the new P_e. The priors of the agents will change over time and will differ among agents as described by $E(\mu(t) - M)^2$ in equation (16f). If the new $P_e \equiv M$ remains constant then, as nt rises, all the priors converge to the true value of P_e.

At any time after the value of P_e has changed, when nt is not large, agents will have different prior estimates of P_e. Consequently agents will have different solutions for the stock demand equation (41) based on their different prior estimates of P_e.

The second problem is that the system has been analyzed on the assumption that the negative root V_1 (in (39)) has been selected, and the economy is always on the negatively sloped stock demand function. Mathematically the stock demand function (41) is the stable eigenvector of dynamical system (31)–(32). There is to my knowledge, however, no logically satisfactory way to ensure that in the presence of stochastic disturbances ($\varepsilon_p, \varepsilon_G, u$) the economy is always on the stable eigenvector. It may start off on the stable eigenvector, but forecast errors and the exogenous disturbances will produce deviations from the stable eigenvector. What economic mechanism, in a world of uncertainty, will put the economy back on it?[2]

In view of the serious instability problem of a rational expectations model, an alternative approach is taken to analyze the effects of government demand management.

Variance of Foreign Exchange Rate

In equation (41) the prior estimate of the flow equilibrium price is $P_e(t)$. On the basis of the previous analysis, the difference between the prior estimate and the true value of the flow equilibrium price P_e is a weighted average of the market forecast errors ε_m:

$$P_e(t) - P_e = \varepsilon_m = (\varepsilon_p + g\varepsilon_G)/(1 + g). \tag{42}$$

Each agent in the system obtains a stock demand function based on his prior estimate of the flow equilibrium price. Aggregating the functions, the market stock demand function is obtained.[3] Its intercept is a weighted average of the agents' priors. Assumption (42) states that the intercept $P_e(t)$ differs from the true unknown flow equilibrium price P_e by a weighted average of forecast errors ε_m, which has a zero mean.

Consequently the stock demand function that determines the spot price is (43):

$$p(t) = [P_e + (\varepsilon_p + g\varepsilon_G)/(1 + g)] - \sigma s(t)/\sqrt{c\gamma}(1 + g). \tag{43}$$

We are working with a stable dynamical system: (32), (43).

Consider the variance of $p(t)$. Given the stock $s(t)$ at time t, the variance of the price $\operatorname{var} p(t) = \sigma^2$ is equation (44):

$$\sigma^2 = [\operatorname{var} \varepsilon_p + g^2 \operatorname{var} \varepsilon_G + 2gE\varepsilon_p\varepsilon_G]/(1 + g)^2 = \operatorname{var} \varepsilon_m. \tag{44}$$

The underlying sources of disturbance in the short-run model are the stochastic term u in the balance of payments equation (26) and the flow equilibrium price $P_e(t)$. Forecast errors will be made because $u(t)$ and P_e are not known. For expositional simplicity, it is convenient to assume that the variance of the forecast error of each agent $\operatorname{var} \varepsilon_i$ is a multiple k_i of the underlying variance $\operatorname{var} P_e$ and that[4] $\operatorname{var} u = \operatorname{var} P_e$:

$$\operatorname{var} \varepsilon_i = k_i \operatorname{var} u = k_i \operatorname{var} P_e, \quad i = p, G. \tag{45}$$

Let b represent the slope of a regression of the government forecast error ε_G on the private forecast error ε_p:

$$\varepsilon_G = b\varepsilon_p + \eta; \quad E\eta = 0, \tag{46a}$$

$$b = E\varepsilon_p\varepsilon_G/\operatorname{var} \varepsilon_p. \tag{46b}$$

Using (46) in (44), the conditional price variance σ^2 can be expressed as (47):

$$\sigma^2 = [k_p(1 + 2bg) + g^2 k_G] \operatorname{var} u/(1 + g)^2. \tag{47}$$

When the errors of the agents are independent $b = 0$, equation (47a) is obtained:

$$\sigma^2 = [k_p + g^2 k_G] \operatorname{var} u/(1 + g)^2. \tag{47a}$$

Equation (47) or (47a) describes the conditional price variance as defined by (44). (See Figlewski 1982 for an analysis a similar problem.)

If the expectations are taken before the stock $s(t)$ is known, then there are two sources of disturbances: the average market forecast error ε_m and the disturbance u to the current account. Assume that $E(\varepsilon_m, u) = 0$, these disturbances are independent.

The variance of the price $p(t)$ in (43) would then be equation (48), when ε_m and u are independent:

$$\sigma^2 = \operatorname{var} p(t) = \operatorname{var} \varepsilon_m + [\sigma^2/c\gamma(1 + g)]\operatorname{var} u. \tag{48}$$

Using the definition of ε_m and (45),

$$\sigma^2 = (k_p + g^2 k_G)\operatorname{var} P_e/(1 + g)^2 + \sigma^2 \operatorname{var} u/c\gamma(1 + g). \tag{49}$$

Equation (48) indicates that there are two sources of price variance. The first term $\operatorname{var} \varepsilon_m(t + 1)$ concerns the price forecast errors of the agents. The second term reflects the fluctuations in the stock of net claims against foreigners. A graphic interpretation of these two sources of price variance is given in figure 6.1, based on equation (19) or the closed form solution (43).

Given the intercept, which is an anticipated price, the price of foreign exchange adjusts to equate the stock of net claims demanded to the stock in existence. Variations in the stock $S(t)$ produce movements along the stock demand curve DD' (19) or (43). If the stock fluctuates between $A - u$ and $A + u$ as a result of the current account of the balance of payments, then the price of foreign exchange will fluctuate between p_1'' and p_1' on stock demand curve $D_1 D_1'$. This is the source of variation $[\sigma^2/c\gamma(1 + g)]\operatorname{var} u$ in (49) where the term in brackets is the absolute value of the slope of the stock demand function.

The price variance σ^2 appears on both sides of (49) for the following reason. A high price variance raises the risk premium and thereby increases the steepness of the stock demand function. A large expected return is required to induce agents to maintain a given position. Variations in the stock ($\operatorname{var} u$) along a given stock demand function produce a price variance directly related to the steepness of the stock demand function, which in turn depends on the price variance. For this reason the resulting price variance (left-hand side of (49)) is affected by the steepness of the curve, which is a function of the price variance (the second term on the right-hand side of (49)).

Given the stock of net claims, the price of foreign exchange is affected by the market's anticipated price of foreign exchange. Variations in the forecast error $\varepsilon_m(t + 1)$ are reflected by vertical shifts of the stock demand function say between F_1 and F_2. The variance of the market error is described by the first term on the right-hand side of equation (48).

For the reasons discussed, if the flow equilibrium price P_e remains constant, then the priors of the agents will converge to the true population mean. Consequently the variance of ε_m in the rational expectations stock demand equation (43) will decline steadily (see (16f)).

5. Optimum Degree of Government Intervention

Conditional Variance Is the Expected Social Loss

When resources are allocated optimally, the current price of foreign exchange $p(t)$ should equal the present value of its price during the subsequent period. Insofar as there is a socially optimal risk premium, for example, as described in (27) $[\sigma^2/\gamma(1 + g)]S(t) \gtreqless 0$, the optimal allocation of resources requires that the current price equal the present value of the price next period adjusted for a socially optimal risk premium.

The optimum price $p^*(t)$, conditional on the price $p(t + 1)$, is:

$$p^*(t) = p(t + 1) - r - [\sigma^2/\gamma(1 + g)]S(t) \tag{50}$$

assuming that the last term is a socially optimal risk premium. The actual price $p(t)$ is given by (27), repeated here:

$$p(t) = p(t + 1) + \varepsilon_m(t + 1) - r - [\sigma^2/\gamma(1 + g)]S(t). \tag{27}$$

Ex post, the misallocation of resources is directly related to:

$$p(t) - p^*(t) = \varepsilon_m. \tag{51}$$

Alternatively the optimum price $p^*(t)$ is given by rational expectations stock demand function (41) when people know the true flow equilibrium price P_e. At any time, however, the market price $p(t)$ is given by stock demand equation (43) when the weighted average of the agents' priors is $P_e(t) = P_e + \varepsilon_m$. Hence the misallocation of resources is directly related to $p(t) - p^*(t) = \varepsilon_m$, the average market forecast error.

There is reason to consider a multiple K of the mean square forecast error as a measure of the misallocation or social loss.[5] Multiple K is related to the elasticities of appropriate demand and supply curves.

The expected social loss is proportional to the variance of the forecast error:

$$E(L) = K \text{var } \varepsilon_m. \tag{52}$$

The optimal allocation of resources is associated with a minimum variance of the market forecast error. In the problem considered in this chapter, the control variable is g the ratio of the government position to that of the private sector. The control variable $g \equiv (w_G/\alpha_G)/\sum_{i=1}^{G-1}(w_i/\alpha_i)$ is equivalent to the choice of utility function and wealth constraint of the government. Whereas the risk aversion α_i and wealth w_i of the private sector are basic parameters, the government selects its w_G/α_G to achieve a social optimum. The problem of exchange rate management is taken to be the choice of g, which minimizes social loss $E(L)$. Let g^* represent the magnitude of g that minimizes var ε_m, the variance of the market forecast error. A minimum of var ε_m, as described by (20) and (46), occurs when g is g^*:

$$g^* = (1-b)k_p/(k_G - bk_p) \gtreqless 0. \tag{53}$$

If the errors of the private and government sectors are independent ($b = 0$), then g^* is:

$$g^* = k_p/k_G > 0. \tag{54}$$

Theorem 2 describes this situation.

THEOREM 2. *If the forecast errors of the government and private sector are independent, then the degree of government intervention that minimizes the conditional price variance, or expected social loss, is equal to the ratio of the error variance of the private sector to that of the government sector.*

Figure 6.2 graphs var ε_m equation (47a) in the case where var $P_e(t)$ in (43) is equal to var u and the private sector on average has a lower error variance than the government. It can just as easily serve to describe the opposite case, by interchanging k_p and k_G. Equation (47a) is a rational function of g, which achieves a minimum below the variance of either group alone. The error variance is minimized when the ratio of the government position to the private position is equal to the ratio of variance of the private error to that of the government error.

When var ε_m/var u is minimal at $g = g^*$, then the minimal value of the error variance var ε^* is:

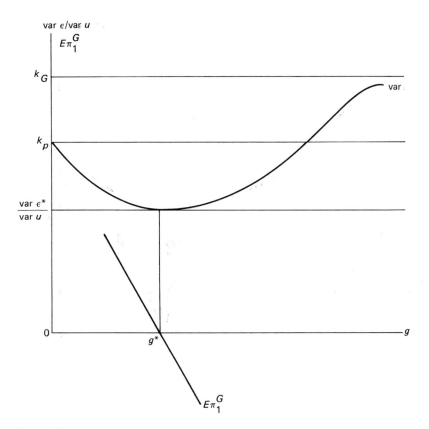

Figure 6.2
The variance of the market error var ε_m/var u and the expected profits of the government $E\pi_1^G$ are plotted against the ratio of the government's to the private positions. At $g = g^*$, the variance of the market error is minimal, and expected profits (net of risk premium) are zero.

$$\text{var } \varepsilon_m^* / \text{var } u = (k_G/k_p + k_G)k_p < k_p, \tag{55}$$

which is less than k_p.

The interesting conclusion is that there exists an optimum degree of participation of the government in the exchange market to minimize the error variance. The latter has been identified as a social loss. As long as regression coefficient b in (46a) is less than unity, the optimum degree of government intervention g^* is strictly positive. If $b = 1$, such that the error of the government is equal to the error of the private sector plus a pure noise term, then the optimal degree of government intervention is zero.

We may state a corollary to theorem II.

COROLLARY. *If the difference between the government and the private forecast error is noise, with a zero expectation, then the optimal value of g is zero. The government should not intervene in the foreign exchange market.*

Profits from Government Intervention

The optimum fraction of the stock of net claims against foreigners to be held by the government (equation (53) or (54)) depends on unobservable quantities k_p and k_G (var ε_p and var ε_G). It is now proved that the profits from government intervention are directly related to $(g^* - g)$, the difference between the unobserved optimal quantity g^* and the actual quantity g. To find the optimal degree of government intervention, the value of $g = (w_G/\alpha_G)/\gamma$ should be raised (lowered) according to whether the government is making profits (losses) on its operations. When expected profits in excess of a risk premium are zero, then $g = g^*$. The proof is as follows.

Total profits from the government purchases and sales of claims against foreigners $\pi_1^G(t)$ is the product of profit per unit $p(t + 1) - p(t) - r$ and the government's position $\xi_1^G(t)W^G(t)$. When the government optimizes, its position is described by (5). Using the rational expectations hypothesis (14), the government profit is (56):

$$\pi_1^G(t) = [p(t + 1) - p(t) - r][p(t + 1) + \varepsilon_G$$
$$\qquad - q_{t+1}(t)]W^G(t)/\alpha_G \text{ var } p. \tag{56}$$

When the yields on domestic and foreign assets are relatively certain, the interest rate parity condition holds:

$$q_{t+1}(t) - p(t) = r = r_H - r_F.$$ (6a)

Substitute (6a) and the definition $g\gamma \equiv w^G/\alpha_G$ into (56) to derive:

$$\pi_1^G(t) = [p(t+1) - p(t) - r][p(t+1) - p(t) - r + \varepsilon_G]g\gamma/\text{var}\, p.$$ (57)

Market equilibrium condition (19) states:

$$p(t+1) - p(t) - r = [\sigma^2/\gamma(1+g)]S(t)/W(t) - (\varepsilon_p + g\varepsilon_G)/(1+g).$$ (19)

The present value of the actual percentage change in price $p(t+1) - p(t) - r$ is the sum of a risk premium and the market forecast error. When $S(t) = 0$, the profits are equation (58):

$$\pi_1^G(t) = \frac{g\gamma}{\text{var}\, p}\left[\frac{(\varepsilon_p + g\varepsilon_G)^2}{(1+g)^2} - \frac{(\varepsilon_G\varepsilon_p + g\varepsilon_G^2)}{(1+g)}\right],$$ (58)

when $S(t) = 0$.

Expected profits when $b = E\varepsilon_p\varepsilon_G = 0$ (to make it comparable with (54)) are:

$$E\pi_1^G(t) = [g\gamma\,\text{var}\,\varepsilon_G/(1+g)^2\,\text{var}\,p](g^* - g).$$ (59)

We have proved theorem 3.

THEOREM 3. *Expected profits from government operations in foreign exchange are positively related to $(g^* - g)$.*

In the neighborhood of $g = g^*$ and $S(t) = 0$, the expected profit is described by curve $E\pi_1^G$ in figure 6.2. To achieve the optimal degree of government intervention, the government should expand (contract) its w_G/α_G if it is making profits (losses). When its expected profits (in excess of the risk premium) are zero, then g is at its optimum value g^*. The government can determine the optimal values of the parameters in its demand function.

There are several noteworthy aspects to theorems 1 and 2. First, when the expectations of each agent including the government are rational and forecast errors are independent, then the optimal degree of government intervention in the foreign exchange market is strictly positive. The ratio of government w_G/α_G to private sector $\sum_{i=1}^{G-1}(w_i/\alpha_i)$ is equal to the ratio of the variance of the error of the private sector to that of the government sector. Second, the optimal w_G/α_G degree of government intervention is zero if the government's forecast error ε_G is equal to the private market's forecast error ε_p plus a noise term. Third, the profits from the government operations in excess of a risk premium are positively related to $(g^* - g)$, the difference between the optimal and current level of intervention. Figure 6.2 describes these conclusions.

Qualifications

The analysis of the optimal degree of government exchange rate management presented in this chapter is amenable to three qualifications.

First, the magnitude of governmental operations affects the two components of the variance in equation (49). A rise in the magnitude of government intervention $g = (w_G/\alpha_G)/\sum_{i=1}^{G-1}(w_i/\alpha_i)$ reduces the absolute value of the slope $\sigma^2/\gamma(1 + g)$ of the stock demand function because it shares risks with the private sector. This is the second term in equation (49). Since the risk premium of the private agents is a function of the magnitude of the position at risk, the risk premium declines as the government shares in the risk. This risk sharing, which rotates the stock demand function in figure 6.1 from $D_1 D_1'$ to $D_2 D_2'$, reduces the variations in the price resulting from fluctuations in the stock.

A trade-off exists between the first and second term of variance in (49). If the government expands its involvement by increasing g above g^*, it reduces the risk premium and the variance due to fluctuations in the stock (the second term in equation (49)); however, it raises the error variance (first term). In the analysis the misallocation of resources was measured by the error variance var ε_m, and the magnitude of the risk premium was ignored. A question for further research is, What is a socially optimal risk premium?

Second, the value of the flow equilibrium price of foreign exchange P_e was assumed to be independent of the magnitude of the government intervention in the foreign exchange market. Price P_e was shown to be equal to the purchasing power parity. It was implicitly assumed that g does not affected relative price levels. Such an assumption may be valid only under restrictive assumptions.

Third, the rational expectations hypothesis that underlines this analysis assumes that both the government and the private sector have forecast errors with zero means. The usual saddle point instability problem implied by rational expectations is unresolved. Alternative approaches using asymptotically rational expectations (Stein 1982: 87–92) are not amenable to these instability problems. Moreover the history of currency devaluations questions the assumption that the government has rational expectations. It is not apparent that the government has less information and is less rational than the private sector. Therefore the Muth expectations hypothesis is a debatable assumption.

The rectification of these qualifications may provide an agenda for further research in the subject of exchange rate management under uncertainty.

Notes

I am deeply indebted to my colleagues George Borts and Harl Ryder and Yukio Takahashi of Tohoku University, Japan, for criticisms of an earlier draft.

1. The receipts are $\sum_{i=1}^{G} (w_i/\alpha_i) E_i p(t+1; t)/\sum_{i=1}^{G} (w_i/\alpha_i) + r_{F'}$, a weighted average of the anticipated price of foreign exchange plus the foreign yield. Discount it by the domestic yield r_H. Hence the present value of a weighted sum of the anticipated prices inclusive of foreign interest is the term in square brackets.

2. A logically satisfactory solution may involve the use of suboptimal feedback control as developed by Infante and Stein (1973). This problem is currently being studied.

3. The summation is vertical, along the price axis. Thus at the market price, some agents have speculative long positions and others short positions.

4. The assumption var $P_e(t) = $ var u permits me to use figure 6.1 to describe either stock demand equation (27a) or rational expectations stock demand equation (43).

5. There is a deeper reason for considering the variance of the forecasting error a measure of social loss. In a forward pricing model, it was proved (Stein 1981) that expected social loss $E(L)$, measured as the sum of producer and consumer surplus, is a multiple K of the square of the forecast error between the subsequently realized price $p(t+1)$ and the forward price $q_{t+1}(t)$:

$$E(L) = KE[p(t+1) - q_{t+1}(t)]^2. \tag{a}$$

When the interest rate differential is known with certainty, the forward rate is:

$$q_{t+1} = p(t) + r. \tag{b}$$

Substitute (b) into (a) to obtain a measure of social loss (c).

$$E(L) = K[p(t+1) - r - p(t)]^2. \tag{c}$$

Glossary

$p(t)$	logarithm of the dollar price of foreign exchange
$q_{t+1}(t)$	logarithm of the dollar price of forward foreign exchange that matures at time $t+1$

$S(t)$	stock of net claims against foreigners; the sum of the balance of payments on current account
$r_F(t)$, $r_H(t)$	yield on a foreign (F) or domestic (H) asset
$r(t) \equiv r_H(t) - r_F(t)$	yield differential between domestic and foreign assets
E	expectations operator
α_i	coefficient of absolute risk aversion
W_i	wealth of ith agent; W total wealth
$w_i \equiv W_i/W$	relative wealth of ith agent
$\varepsilon_i(t+1)$	deviation between $E_i p(t+1;t)$ and $p(t)$
$E_i p(t+1;t)$	price anticipated at time t by the ith agent to prevail at $t+1$
$\gamma_i \equiv (w_i/\alpha_i)/\sum_{i=1}^{G-1}(w_i/\alpha_i)$	relative holdings of the ith agent
$\gamma = \sum_{i=1}^{G-1}(w_i/\alpha_i)$	the summation is over the $G-1$ private agents
$g = (w_G/\alpha_G)/\gamma$	ratio of government to private holdings of net claims
$\varepsilon_m = (\varepsilon_p + g\varepsilon_G)/(1+g)$	average market error, a weighted average of private error ε_p and government error ε_G
$\sigma^2 = \operatorname{var} p$	price variance
z_i	logarithm of the price of traded goods (F) or nontraded goods (H)
P_e	true flow equilibrium price of foreign exchange
$P_e(t)$	weighted average anticipated flow equilibrium price $P_e + \varepsilon_m$
$s(t) = S(t) - S_e$	deviation of stock of net claims from its equilibrium value
$k_i = \operatorname{var} \varepsilon_i/\operatorname{var} u \quad i = p, G.$	It is assumed in the figures that $\operatorname{var} P_e = \operatorname{var} u$
u	stochastic term in the current account balance

References

Connolly, Michael, and Dean Taylor. 1982. "Crawling Pegs and Exchange Rate Crises." Working paper.

DeGroot, Morris. 1970. *Optimal Statistical Decisions.* New York: McGraw-Hill.

Figlewski, Stephen. 1982. "Information Diversity and Market Behavior." *Journal of Finance* 37:87–102.

Infante, Ettore F., and Jerome L. Stein. 1973. "Optimal Growth with Robust Feedback Control." *Review of Economic Studies* 40:47–60.

Stein, Jerome L. 1963. "The Optimum Foreign Exchange Market." *American Economic Review* 53:384–402.

Stein, Jerome L. 1979. "Assessing the Efficiency of Free Foreign Exchange Markets." In *International Finance and Trade I,* edited by Marshall Sarnat and Giorgio P. Szego. Cambridge, Mass.: Ballinger.

Stein, Jerome L. 1980. "The Dynamics of Spot and Forward Prices in an Efficient Foreign Exchange Market with Rational Expectations." *American Economic Review* 70:565–583.

Stein, Jerome L. 1981. "Speculative Price: Economic Welfare and the Idiot of Chance." *Review of Economics and Statistics* 63:223–232.

Stein, Jerome L. 1982. *Monetarist, Keynesian and New Classical Economics.* Oxford: Basil Blackwell.

Stein, Jerome L., et al. 1983. "A Theoretical Explanation of the Empirical Studies of Futures Markets in Foreign Exchange and Financial Instruments: A Review Article." *Financial Review* 18:1–32.

7 Informational Regimes, Economic Disturbances, and Exchange Rate Management

Jagdeep S. Bhandari

1. Introduction

This chapter is concerned with the role of the availability of macro-economic information in determining the impact of various structural disturbances in an open economy. Another issue of interest concerns the selection of an optimal exchange rate intervention stance under alternative informational regimes. The framework of analysis is a two-country currency-substitution rational expectations model.

The debate over the choice of the optimal exchange rate policy in a stochastic context, although relatively new, has already attracted a great number of contributions. A general conclusion that emerges from this literature is that floating (fixed) exchange rates are usually preferable from the point of view of externally (domestically) occurring disturbances, although a more precise statement is contingent on the exact source (whether nominal or real) as well as the relative magnitudes of the underlying disturbances. Some papers that reach these conclusions are Boyer (1978), Roper and Turnovsky (1980), Turnovsky (1983), Frenkel and Aizenman (1982), Bhandari and Driskill (1981), and Weber (1981).[1] Other lines of inquiry in the context of exchange rate management have included investigation of the effects of intervention on persistence and stability of the economy (as in Mussa 1985; Bhandari 1982a; Bhandari and Driskill 1983) and the implications of assorted issues such as wage-price stickiness or wage indexation for the choice between fixed and floating rates (see, for example, Marston 1982; Bhandari 1982b).[2]

The informational assumptions made in these papers (which are a critical ingredient of such models) usually involve full contemporaneous information (as in Turnovsky 1983; Weber 1981; Marston 1982), or, if information gaps are introduced, then these are such that either agents cannot distinguish between permanent and transitory innovations in exogenously generated variables or, if several innovations occur simultaneously, the current period realizations of these disturbances are not contemporaneously observable (see, for example, Barro 1978; Bhandari 1981; Saidi 1980; Frenkel and Aizenman 1982). Prevailing economic reality, however, suggests that this may be too harsh an interpretation of the incompleteness of current information and that contemporaneous information on at least some macrovariables is in fact currently available. For example, observations on asset market variables such as interest rates and exchange rates are available on a daily basis in the financial page of any major newspaper. A slightly longer lag applies to money supply data, currently reported in the United States with an eight-day lag. These preliminary estimates are then revised, over a period of several weeks or even months. On the other hand, data on contract market variables such as prices or GNP are available quarterly at best and are subject to revision over a much longer period of time. These facts suggest that the information set of individuals contains differentiated current information rather than either full or no current information, as has been commonly assumed. The current observations of asset market variables permit rational agents to infer the values of certain (combination) random variables and thus allows for greater forecasting efficiency. The information-aggregator role of observations of an economy-wide interest rate or of a preliminary estimate of the aggregate money supply in the context of a closed economy has been previously considered by Barro (1980) and Boschen and Grossman (1980), respectively. These ideas were extended to the case of an open economy in Bhandari (1982a). An important aspect of the extension of these ideas to an open economy is the new information provided by observations of the exchange rate and the foreign interest rate, in addition to the domestic interest rate. In the present currency substitution framework, however, no interest-bearing stores of value exist so that the exchange rate is the sole global information-aggregator variable. In one part of the paper, though, I allow national aggregate price levels to play the role of locally observed variables in the sense that agents in each country observe their own national price levels in addition to the globally observed exchange rate.

What impact do alternative informational regimes have on the transmission properties of various structural disturbances and on the selection of an optimal exchange rate policy? These are the issues addressed in this chapter. In order to investigate these questions, I construct and analyze a two-country, discrete-time rational expectations model. The framework is related to that developed earlier in Bhandari (1982a), but this chapter goes much further in investigating the implications of four alternative informational regimes. In addition, this chapter avoids the informational asymmetries between the two countries present in the earlier effort by applying alternative information assumptions symmetrically across countries, where relevant. The richer detail of the present model, however, does result in computational complexities in that closed-form solutions generally are not available. Despite this, certain qualitative properties of interest do emerge.

The alternative informational regimes considered in this chapter are: (1) the case of full current information in both economies (designed to serve as a benchmark case); (2) a case of incomplete but symmetrical information in which agents in both countries observe the current exchange rate but no other current variables; (3) a situation of differentiated asymmetrical information wherein, in addition to the exchange rate, agents observe the national price level in their own country[3] (Their information set does not contain current observations on the price level prevailing in the other country; (hence information on price levels is only asymmetrically available); and (4) a scenario that allows for a divergence between the information sets of the intervention authorities and of private agents. Specifically it is assumed in this fourth case that the authorities possess superior information with respect to the realizations of various random disturbances, as compared with private agents. In each of the previous three cases (1 through 3) the authorities share the same information set as private agents.

Several new results emerge from this investigation.

1. Under full information, it is relatively straightforward to obtain closed-form solutions. In principle exchange rate policies that are procyclical or countercyclical are both feasible. However, the successful pursuit of a procyclical policy may be circumscribed by problems of potential instability in the money supply process. Ironically procyclical policies are stable only if they are sufficiently activist in nature. Countercyclical policies are always stable. These conclusions thus validate the results reached by Turnovsky (1983) in the context of a small economy model. Under a regime of freely floating exchange rates, a domestic monetary expansion may not lead to domestic nominal depreciation. However, a sufficient condition to ensure this normal response is that the ratio of domestically held domestic money to total domestic money supply be greater than a certain critical magnitude. If parameter values across the two countries are identical, then this critical magnitude is one-half. In the normal case the domestic price level increases while

that in the foreign country decreases; negative transmission can be said to have occurred. Portfolio shifts in favor of domestic currency (on the part of either domestic or foreign residents) lead to effects qualitatively similar to a contraction of domestic money supply. A domestic expenditure expansion implies real and nominal exchange appreciation in the normal case. Depending on the magnitude of the elasticity of substitution between the two currencies, as well as on the degree of financial openness, it is possible for this disturbance to lead to stronger inflation effects in the foreign (passive) economy as compared with the home economy. Analogous results obtain for a foreign expenditure expansion. Finally, it is possible to compute analytical expressions for the optimal degree of exchange rate intervention in the case of full information. Illustrative numerical calculations (for the case of real disturbances) show that the optimal degree of intervention is extremely sensitive to the financial parameters of the model, such as the degree of financial openness, substitutability between the two currencies, and so forth. It is much less sensitive to the underlying structural variances of the model. If the underlying disturbances in the economy are monetary (portfolio) in origin, then the optimal intervention stance dictates a regime of pegged exchange rates.

2. If the current information set of agents worldwide is limited to observations of the exchange rate (i.e., regime (b) is considered), the exchange rate and price effects resulting from an aggregate monetary expansion (in the absence of exchange market intervention) are muted but not qualitatively reversed. By contrast portfolio shifts now result in sharper nominal exchange rate and price movements. Real disturbances, on the other hand, imply a trade-off between the magnitudes of exchange rate and price adjustments. Thus the appreciation resulting from a domestic real disturbance is sharper than that in the full information case; the domestic price effect is of a smaller magnitude. Because of the nonlinearities involved, it is not possible now to obtain closed-form solutions for the optimal degree of intervention. Such a statement is also valid for the other incomplete informational regimes considered in this chapter.

3. The regime of asymmetrical incomplete information is considerably more complex to analyze than any of the others. In part this is due to the problems of nonlinearities encountered in this case. These problems notwithstanding, certain results of interest do emerge. For example, it

can be shown that the asymmetrical information effect of an aggregate monetary expansion is bounded only between the full information and limited (symmetrical) information effects, if the underlying monetary variance is sufficiently small. For large values of the latter, it is possible for the asymmetric information effect to exceed the full information impact. These results have the following implication: as information sets are smoothly expanded to include additional information, economic variables may display discontinuous behavior in the sense that limited information sets may replicate the implications of full information sets less closely than information sets incorporating even more limited information.

4. The final regime analyzed is one in which the authorities possess superior information with respect to the current realization of random disturbances, while private agents are limited to a global observation of the exchange rate. It can be shown that intervention poses problems of nonuniqueness in this case. Although a closed-form solution for the optimal degree of intervention is available, it is seen to involve a highly nonlinear equation.

There are other results of interest and these are discussed in the text.

2. Analytical Framework

The hypothetical world of this model consists of two roughly equal-sized economies, referred to as the domestic and foreign economies. In order to avoid the complexities associated with incorporating interest-bearing assets, the present framework is of the currency-substitution variety. There are additional simplifications, introduced as the model is presented.

Since both economies are assumed to hold each other's currencies (in addition to their own currencies), it is necessary to specify portfolio equilibrium relationships. By definition the total domestic portfolio (L) is comprised of domestically held domestic money (M_d) and domestically held foreign currency (M_d^*). Thus,

$$L = M_d + E M_d^* \tag{1}$$

where E is the exchange rate (number of units of domestic currency per unit foreign currency). Since the model is most conveniently specified in logarithmic form, it is necessary to log linearize (1). A first-order logarithmic Taylor approximation to (1) is given by

$$l = \beta m_d + (1 - \beta)(e + m_d^*) \qquad (2)$$

where lower-case letters denote logarithmic values, while $\beta \equiv (M^d/L)^o$ is the initial ratio of domestic currency in the total domestic portfolio. Clearly β can be identified as (the inverse of) the degree of financial openness. Similarly the foreign portfolio is described by

$$L^* = M_f^* + \frac{M_f}{E} \qquad (3)$$

where M_f^* and M_f denote the quantities of foreign and domestic currencies, respectively, that are held in foreign portfolios. Equation (3) may be log linearized as

$$l^* = \beta^* m_f^* + (1 - \beta^*)(m_f - e) \qquad (4)$$

where $\beta^* = (M_f^*/L^*)^o$ is the analogous initial value. If the domestic economy is the United States, then $(1 - \beta^*)$ can be regarded as the dollarization ratio (see Ortiz 1983).

Next consider the derivation of asset demand functions. Following Canto and Miles (1983) it is assumed that agents in each country attempt to maximize the extent of money services derived from a given portfolio. For domestic agents, the maximization problem may be stated as max $S = [\alpha M_d^{-\rho} + (1 - \alpha)(EM_d^*)^{-\rho}]^{-1/\rho}$ subject to $M^o = M_d(1 + i_d) + EM_d^*(1 + i_f)$ where i_d and i_f are the implicit rates of return on domestic and foreign currency, respectively, and ρ is related to the elasticity of substitution between currencies (from the view point of domestic agents) by $\sigma = 1/(1 + \rho)$. The analogous problem for foreign portfolio owners is max $S^* = [\alpha^* M_f^{*-\rho^*} + (1 - \alpha^*)(M_f/E)^{-\rho^*}]^{-1/\rho^*}$ subject to $M^{o*} = [M_f^*(1 + i_f) + M_f/E(1 + i_d)]$. Since money pays no explicit interest, the relevant implicit adjacent rate of return is defined by

$$i_d = i_f + (\bar{E}_t, e_{t+1} - e_t) \qquad (5)$$

from the point of view of domestic agents and

$$i_d = i_f + (\bar{E}_t^*, e_{t+1} - e_t) \qquad (6)$$

from the viewpoint of foreign investors. The symbols $\bar{E}_t$ and $\bar{E}_t^*$ denote domestic and foreign expectational operators respectively. In general,

$\bar{E}_t \neq \bar{E}_t^*$, except for the case of worldwide full information, in which case these expectations coincide.

It can be shown that the maximization problems stated above imply the following asset demand functions for domestic currency,

$$m_d = l - (1 - \beta)\sigma(\bar{E}_t, e_{t+1} - e_t) + (1 - \beta)z_t \tag{7}$$

$$(m_f - e) = l^* - \beta^*\sigma^*(\bar{E}_t^*, e_{t+1} - e_t) + \beta^*z_t^* \tag{8}$$

where z_t and z_t^* are log additive stochastic shift terms that capture increases in relative demands for domestic currency on the part of domestic and foreign agents, respectively.[4] It is not necessary for the analysis that follows to report demand functions for foreign currency. Thus equilibrium in the world market for domestic currency necessarily ensures equilibrium in the market for foreign currency, and I focus only on the former.

Equilibrium in the world market for domestic currency is described by

$$M_d + M_f = M \tag{9}$$

where M denotes the supply of domestic currency. Equation (9) may be log linearized as

$$\gamma m_d + (1 - \gamma)m_f = m \tag{10}$$

where $\gamma \equiv (M_d/M)^o$, denotes the initial ratio of domestically held domestic currency to total domestic money supply. It is possible to relate γ to β; this relation is

$$\frac{\gamma}{\beta} = \left(\frac{L}{M}\right)^o. \tag{11}$$

It is necessary now to specify the functional forms for domestic and foreign portfolios l and l^*. For simplicity I assume that total real portfolios are log linearly proportional to real incomes. Under the assumption that the elasticity of real portfolio demand with respect to real income is unity, the expressions for l and l^* may be written simply as

$$l = p + y \tag{12}$$

$$l^* = p^* + y^* \tag{13}$$

where y and y^* denote real incomes in the two countries. Substituting (7), (8), (12), and (13) into (10) now yields the desired form for the world equilibrium condition for domestic currency:

$$m_t = \gamma[p_t + y_t - (1 - \beta)\sigma(\bar{E}_t, e_{t+1} - e_t) + (1 - \beta)z_t]$$
$$+ (1 - \gamma)[e_t + p_t^* + y_t^* - \beta^*\sigma^*(\bar{E}_t^*, e_{t+1} - e_t) + \beta^*z_t^*]. \tag{14}$$

It is clear from equation (14), as well as from (7) and (8), that expected depreciation of domestic currency by either domestic or foreign agents reduces demand for domestic currency but at different rates, depending on whether domestic or foreign agents' expectations are considered. In an incomplete information setting, it is possible for domestic and foreign agents' expectations about the future course of exchange rates to deviate, even in qualitative terms (sign $(\bar{E}_t, e_{t+1} - e_t) \neq \text{sign}(\bar{E}_t^*, e_{t+1} - e_t)$, is possible).

In order to complete the description of the asset sector of the model, it is necessary to specify the stochastic process governing aggregate domestic money supply. For most of this chapter I assume that money supply follows the following stochastic feedback control rule,

$$m_t = m_{t-1} + v_t - \mu(e_t - e^o) \tag{15}$$

where the term $-\mu(e_t - e^o)$ prescribes a systematic countercyclical response to the state of the current exchange rate in relation to its target value e^o, while v_t may be interpreted as an aggregate monetary disturbance (by contrast, z_t is a relative shift) attributable, perhaps, to policy error. Thus, $\mu \to o$ corresponds to freely flexible exchange rates, while $\mu \to \pm\infty$ implies a regime of pegged exchange rates. The dynamic implications of an alternative intervention rule based on rates of change are also briefly considered for the full information regime. This alternative rule is specified by

$$m_t = m_{t-1} + v_t - \mu(e_t - e_{t-1}). \tag{16}$$

The next step in the formulation of the model is the specification of the real sector in each economy. I assume that the use of the Lucas supply function is no longer contentious; that is, aggregate supply in each country is described by

$$y_t = \bar{y} + s(p_t - \bar{E}_{t-1}, p_t) \tag{17}$$

$$y_t^* = \bar{y}^* + s^*(p_t^* - \bar{E}_{t-1}, p_t^*) \tag{18}$$

where $\bar{y}$ and $\bar{y}^*$ are trend levels of output, which will be subsequently suppressed. Aggregate demand in each country is given definitionally by the level of consumption plus the net trade surplus (ignoring the investment and government components of aggregate expenditure in the interest of simplicity). Assuming that consumption depends only on income, while imports are determined by the relevant real exchange rate and aggregate consumption, it can be shown that the relevant logarithmic reduced forms of the aggregate demand functions are given by

$$y_t = u + \delta(e_t + p_t^* - p_t) + \alpha y_t^* + \xi_t \tag{19}$$

$$y_t^* = u^* - \delta^*(e_t + p_t^* - p_t) + \alpha^* y_t + \xi_t^* \tag{20}$$

where the u's subsume constant terms, while ξ_t and ξ_t^* denote log additive stochastic disturbance terms. The parameters δ, δ^*, α, and α^* are related to other structural parameters of the model by

$$\delta \equiv \frac{e_x(x_1 + m_2 - 1)}{1 - \hat{c}_1(1 - \hat{m}_1)}; \; \delta^* \equiv \frac{e_x^*(x_1 + m_2 - 1)}{1 - \hat{c}_1^*(1 - \hat{m}_1^*)}$$

$$\alpha \equiv \frac{e_x x_2 c_1^*}{1 - \hat{c}_1(1 - \hat{m}_1)}; \; \alpha^* \equiv \frac{e_x^* m_1 c_1}{1 - \hat{c}_1^*(1 - \hat{m}_1^*)}$$

where $(x_1 + m_2 - 1)$ is the Marshall-Lerner expression, e_x and e_x^* are the (initial) ratios of exports to income in each country, x_2 the elasticity of domestic exports with respect to foreign consumption (recall that domestic exports are foreign imports, which are related to foreign consumption), m_1 the elasticity of domestic imports with respect to domestic consumption, $\hat{c}_1$ and $\hat{c}_1^*$ the marginal propensities to consume, and $\hat{m}_1$ and $\hat{m}_1^*$ the marginal propensities to import.[5]

Equations (17) through (20) along with (14) and (15) comprise six relations in y, y^*, p, p^*, e, and m. The description of the model is completed by specifying domestic and foreign information sets.

Various alternative informational regimes are considered in the next section.

3. Full Information Case

The first informational regime considered involves full contemporaneous information on all current variables on the part of both domestic and foreign agents. Given the linear structure of the model, it is clear that the ultimate solutions to the state vector $[e_t p_t p_t^*]$ will be linear in the vector of predetermined exogenous variables: $[m_{t-1} e^o v_t \xi_t \xi_t^* z_t z_t^*]$. Thus, the conjectured solutions to the state vector are

$$e_t = \pi_1 m_{t-1} + \pi_2 e^o + \pi_3 v_t + \pi_4 \xi_t + \pi_5 \xi_t^* + \pi_6 \xi_t + \pi_7 z_t^* \qquad (21)$$

$$p_t = U_1 m_{t-1} + U_2 e^o + U_3 v_t + U_4 \xi_t + U_5 \xi_t^* + U_6 z_t + U_7 z_t^* \qquad (22)$$

$$p_t^* = W_1 m_{t-1} + W_2 e^o + W_3 v_t + W_4 \xi_t + W_5 \xi_t^* + W_6 z_t + W_7 z_t^* \qquad (23)$$

where $\{\pi_i, U_i, W_i\}$, $i = 1, 2, \ldots, 6$ are undetermined reduced-form coefficients. The solutions to these coefficients are obtained by reducing the structural model to three relations involving each of the three state variables and then equating net coefficients identically to zero. These three relations involve the domestic and foreign commodity market clearing conditions along with the domestic currency market equilibrium relation. Since the procedure for deriving these solutions is well known by now, it suffices to report these solutions and to discuss their properties.

The stability of the economy—in particular the stability of the money supply process—is governed by the coefficients $\{\pi_1, U_1, W_1\}$. These solutions can be shown to be given by

$$W_1 = 0, \pi_1 = U_1 = \frac{-(1 + \mu) \pm [(1 + \mu)^2 + 4du]^{1/2}}{2d\mu} \qquad (24)$$

where $d \equiv [\gamma(1 - \beta)\sigma + (1 - \gamma)\beta^* \sigma^*]$. It is seen, using (15), that the domestic money supply process can be expressed as

$$m_t = (1 - \mu\pi_1)m_{t-1} + (1 - \mu\pi_3)v_t + \ldots \qquad (25)$$

Since (25) is a first-order difference equation, stability requires that

$$(1 - \mu\pi_1) < 1 \text{ and } (1 - \mu\pi_1) > -1. \qquad (26)$$

In order to make progress in analyzing the condition stated in (26), it is convenient first to classify various configurations of π_1 and μ according to the following three cases:

1. If $\mu > 0$, then $\pi_1^+ > 0$ and $\pi_1^- < 0$ (where π_1^+ is the root selected by the $(+)$ sign in (24) and π_1 the root corresponding to the $(-)$ sign).
2. If $\mu < 0$ and if $(1 + \mu) < 0$, then $\pi_1^+ < 0$ and $\pi_1^- < 0$.
3. If $\mu < 0$ and if $(1 + \mu) > 0$, then $\pi_1^+ > 0$ and $\pi_1^- > 0$.

Now consider the stability criterion (26). In case 1, it is clear that the negative root π_1^- violates the first part of the stability criterion and consequently must be rejected. The positive root π_1^+ trivially satisfies $(1 - \mu\pi_1) < 1$ and can also be shown (by contradiction) to fulfill $(1 - \mu\pi_1) > -1$. It is clear that given a countercyclical policy stance ($\mu > 0$), stability requires that the unique positive root π_1^+ be selected. Further, since π_1^+ is always real, dynamic adjustment is of the monotonic variety in this case.

By contrast a procyclical intervention policy ($\mu < 0$) may be associated with complex roots and consequently oscillatory adjustment. For expository purposes, however, assume that both roots are real so that $[(1 + \mu)^2 + 4d\mu] > 0$. Now the first part of the stability criterion requires that $\mu\pi_1 > 0$. With $\mu < 0$, it is necessary that $\pi_1 < 0$, which in turn requires that $(1 + \mu) < 0$. This implies that case 3 is incompatible with stability. We are left therefore with case 2 in which $(1 + \mu) < 0$ and both roots π_1^+ and π_1^- are negative. Using the second part of the stability criterion now ($\mu\pi_1 < 2$), it is readily demonstrated that $\mu\pi_1^+ < 2$ is never fulfilled, given real roots, while $u\pi_1^- < 2$ requires that

$$\mu < -(2 + 4d). \tag{27}$$

Thus a procyclical policy implies that the unique root π_1^- be chosen and that the degree of intervention be sufficiently activist in nature, as prescribed by (27).[6]

In conclusion stable values of u are everywhere except in the closed interval $[0, -(2 + 4d)]$. The effect of variations in various structural parameters on the stability of the economy is also apparent. Specifically larger values of d (due to larger values of the elasticity of substitution σ or σ^* or to lower values of β, for example) imply that the range of values for which procyclical policies are unstable is extended. In this sense a higher degree of substitutability between currencies (from the viewpoint of either domestic or foreign agents) is clearly destabilizing.

An increase in the target exchange rate e^o leads to price and exchange rate effects as summarized by the coefficients $\{\pi_2, U_2, W_2\}$. These are

$$W_2 = 0; \pi_2 = U_2 = \frac{\mu(1 + d\pi_1)}{1 + \mu(1 + d\pi_1)}. \tag{28}$$

Under a countercyclical exchange rate policy, a devaluation of the exchange rate target leads to a less than proportionate depreciation of the actual current exchange rate, with the remainder of the effect occurring in the next period. With a procyclical policy, on the other hand, the current exchange effect may be larger than the initial devaluation.

Consider next the implications of a current, unexpected expansion in domestic money supply as represented by a positive value of the aggregate disturbance term v_t. It is convenient at this stage (and for what follows) to impose identity of commodity market parameters between the two countries: $s = s^*$, $\delta = \delta^*$, and $\alpha = \alpha^*$. The exchange rate and price effects of this aggregate monetary disturbance are now given by

$$\pi_3 = \frac{1 + d\pi_1}{[\mu + 1 - \gamma + (1 + s)F_3(1 - 2\gamma) + d(1 + \pi_1\mu)]};$$ (29)

$$\pi_3|_{\mu=0} = \frac{1 + d}{[1 - \gamma + (1 + s)F_3(1 - 2\gamma) + d]}$$

$$W_3 = F_3\pi_3 \,;\, u_3 = -F_3\pi_3$$

where

$$F_3 \equiv -\frac{\delta}{s(1 + \alpha) + 2\delta} < 0.$$

It is immediately clear from inspection of the expression for $\pi_{3|\mu=0}$ that owing to the sign ambiguity in the denominator of the latter, it is possible for the exchange rate to depreciate or to appreciate following an aggregate monetary expansion. The reason for this ambiguity lies in the fact that domestic monetary expansion leads to increased domestic currency holdings in both countries, and depending on portfolio preferences, as summarized by γ and d, it is possible for the seemingly perverse effect of appreciation to occur. A sufficient condition to rule out this outcome, however, is that $\gamma \geq \frac{1}{2}$. Thus if domestic residents hold half or more of total domestically issued currency, then an aggregate monetary expansion produces the normal effect of exchange depreciation. It should be emphasized, however, that this is not a necessary condition, and such an effect may also occur for $\gamma < \frac{1}{2}$ as long as d is sufficiently large. In the normal case exchange depreciation increases domestic aggregate demand while reducing foreign aggregate demand; see (19) and (20). The restoration of commodity equilibrium consequently requires price inflation in the domestic economy and price deflation in the foreign economy. Finally, the effect of the aggregate monetary disturbance on the real exchange rate is given by

$$(\pi_3 + W_3 - U_3) = \frac{s(1 + \alpha)\pi_3}{s(1 + \alpha) + 2d}.$$

It is possible, of course, to examine the sensitivity of these various impact effects with respect to various structural parameters, but this is left to the interested reader.

The impact effects of a transitory, unexpected increase in domestic aggregate demand (as represented by $\xi_t > 0$) are given by

$$\pi_4 = \frac{-(1 + s)[\gamma k_4 + (1 - \gamma)h_4]}{[\mu + 1 - \gamma + (1 + s)F_3(1 - 2\gamma) + d(1 + \pi_1\mu)]}; \qquad (30)$$

$$\pi_4|_{\mu=0} = \frac{-(1 + s)[\gamma k_4 + (1 - \gamma)h_4]}{[1 - \gamma + (1 + s)F_3(1 - 2\gamma) + d]}$$

where $k_4 \equiv (\delta + s)/s(1 - \alpha)$ $[s(1 + \alpha) + 2\delta]$; $h_4 \equiv (\delta + \alpha s)/s(1 - \alpha)$ $[s(1 + \alpha) + 2\delta]$ and $W_4 = F_3\pi_4 + h_4$; $U_4 = -F_3\pi_4 + k_4$.

It is apparent from the above expression for $\pi_4|_{\mu=0}$ that the conventionally expected effect of spot appreciation (with $\mu = 0$) following domestic expenditure expansion is not necessarily guaranteed. Two conditions are now sufficient in order to ensure this outcome. First, the denominator of $\pi_4|_{\mu=0}$ must be positive, and this requires $\gamma \geq \frac{1}{2}$ and/or a large value of d. In addition both k_4 and h_4 must be positive, for which it is necessary that $\alpha < 1$. As is clear from the definition of the latter, there is no necessary presumption for this to be so. Two other points about the expressions reported in (30) deserve comment. First, each of the effects is decreasing in d, second, it is quite possible for magnified transmission to occur, in the sense that $W_4 > U_4$ may occur. Such an outcome cannot be ruled out, especially if d is low, so that $|\pi_4|$ is large. Finally, if nominal appreciation occurs, then there is also real appreciation, since

$$(\pi_4 + W_4 - U_4) = \frac{s(1 + \alpha)\pi_4}{s(1 + \alpha) + 2\delta} + (h_4 - k_4)$$

where

$$(h_4 - k_4) = -\frac{1}{s(1 + \alpha) + 2\delta} < 0.$$

The effects of an unanticipated expenditure in the foreign country ($\xi_t^* > 0$) are similar, but not identical, to those of domestic expenditure expansion. Specifically,

$$\pi_5 = \frac{-(1 + s)[\gamma h_4 + (1 - \gamma)k_4]}{[\mu + 1 - \gamma + (1 + s)F_3(1 - 2\gamma) + d(1 + \pi_1\mu)]} \tag{31}$$

$$\pi_5|_{\mu=0} = \frac{-(1 + s)[\gamma h_4 + (1 - \gamma)k_4]}{[1 - \gamma + (1 + s)F_3(1 - 2\gamma) + d]}$$

$$W_5 = F_3\pi_5 + k_4; \ U_5 = -F_3\pi_5 + h_4.$$

A comparison of (30) and (31) indicates that the same types of considerations are involved in determining the qualitative impacts in both cases. The reason why real disturbances originating in either country may lead to exchange appreciation is that both disturbances lead to an increase in the demand for domestic currency (by an increase in domestic nominal income in the $\xi_t > 0$ case and through increased foreign nominal income in the $\xi_t^* > 0$ case). In either case continued equilibrium in the market for domestic currency requires appreciation (and expected depreciation) to reduce total demand to the fixed level of supply under floating rates; see equation (14). The qualitative effects are different, though, since nominal appreciation directly reduces foreign demand for domestic currency (see (8)), but this direct effect does not operate on domestic demand for domestic currency (see (7)). It can be shown, however, that if $\gamma > \frac{1}{2}$, then $|\pi_4| > |\pi_5|$; that is, a domestic real disturbance leads to sharper nominal appreciation than an equivalent foreign real disturbance, if the majority of domestic currency is held in domestic portfolios.

Finally, consider the impacts of relative shifts in portfolio preferences as represented by the random terms $z_t > 0$ and $z_t^* > 0$. Both of these disturbances capture an increased relative demand for domestic currency (on the part of domestic and foreign residents, respectively). It is to be expected, therefore, that in either case domestic currency must appreciate against foreign currency. The relevant effects are given by

$$\pi_6 = \frac{-\gamma(1 - \beta)}{[\mu + 1 - \gamma + (1 + s)F_3(1 - 2\gamma) + d(1 + \pi_1\mu)]}; \tag{32}$$

$$\pi_6|_{\mu=0} = \frac{-\gamma(1 - \beta)}{[1 - \gamma + (1 + s)F_3(1 - 2\gamma) + d]}$$

$$W_6 = F_3\pi_6; \ U_6 = -F_3\pi_6,$$

$$\pi_7 = \frac{-(1-\gamma)\beta^*}{[\mu+1-\gamma+(1+s)F_3(1-2\gamma)+d(1+\pi_1\mu)]}; \qquad (33)$$

$$\pi_7\big|_{\mu=0} = \frac{-(1-\gamma)\beta^*}{[1-\gamma+(1+s)F_3(1-2\gamma)+d]}$$

$$W_7 = F_3\pi_7; \; U_7 = -F_3\pi_7.$$

In either case, the foreign price level increases (since F_3 is negative), while domestic prices fall. Finally, it can be shown that $\gamma > \frac{1}{2}$ is again a sufficient condition to ensure that $|\pi_6| > |\pi_7|$.

I now briefly consider the nature of the optimal intervention stance. In order to proceed, it is necessary to define an appropriate loss function. Since there is no separate role for foreign monetary policy in this model (owing to its currency-substitution nature), it seems reasonable to interpret domestic monetary policy as a world monetary instrument. Accordingly a reasonable loss function might be one that minimizes the variance of world output:

min var(ω_t) where

$$\omega_t = hy_t + (1-h)(y_t^* + e_t + p_t^* - p_t); \; 0 \le h \le 1$$

where h is the weight attached by the policymaker to domestic output.

Consider first the case in which the principal random disturbances are portfolio shocks—z_t and z_t^*. In this case it can be shown that the variance of world output is var(ω_t) $= (\pi_6^2 x^2 \sigma_z^2 + \pi_7^2 x^2 \sigma_{z*}^2)$ where $x \equiv [(1-h)sF_3 - hsF_3 + (1-h)(1+2F_3)]$. Since $\mu \to \pm\infty$ ensures that $\pi_6 \to 0$ and $\pi_7 \to 0$, it is clear that irrespective of the weight h, the optimum policy is one of pegged exchange rates. Such a policy completely eliminates the variance in domestic and foreign output that is attributable to portfolio disturbances. The optimality of pegged exchange rates, given predominantly monetary disturbances, has also been noted by other authors (see Turnovsky 1983, for example).

Matters are somewhat more complex when the principal disturbances in the world economy are real in origin (ξ_t and ξ_t^*). A corner solution is no longer optimal in this case, and in general, the optimal degree of intervention depends on relative structural variances, as well as on structural parameters, including the policy-determined weight h. I limit my discussion here to examining a few sample cases. For expository purposes it is useful to specialize the analysis further at this point by assuming that $h = 1$ and that $\gamma = \frac{1}{2}$. The latter assumption ensures that $\pi_4 = \pi_5$ (see (30) and (31)). The optimality condition can be shown to reduce to

$$\frac{k_4 - f_3 \pi_4}{h_4 - f_3 \pi_4} = -\frac{\sigma_{\xi*}^2}{\sigma_\xi^2} \equiv -n$$

which, on substituting for π_4, leads to

$$2\mu^* + 2\pi_1 \mu^* d = -\frac{(1 + s)(k_4 + h_4)(1 + n)F_3}{(k_4 + h_4 n)} - (1 + 2d) \tag{34}$$

where n is the ratio of structural variances as defined. Because of the square root form of π_1, it is necessary to assign numerical magnitudes to various parameters in order to assess the implications of (34). For the numerical examples that follow, it is assumed that the real parameters of the model are given by $s = 3$, $\alpha = 0.50$, $\delta = 0.30$. Equation (34) now yields the following values for the optimal degree of intervention:

1. $d = 2$, $\sigma_{\xi*}^2/\sigma_\xi^2 = 0.10$; $\mu^* = -4.6208$ (unstable).
2. $d = 2$, $\sigma_{\xi*}^2/\sigma_\xi^2 = 1$; $\mu^* = 3.8963$ (stable).
3. $d = 2$, $\sigma_{\xi*}^2/\sigma_\xi^2 = 10$; $\mu^* = 3.2194$ (stable).
4. $d = 20$, $\sigma_{\xi*}^2/\sigma_\xi^2 = 1$; $\mu^* = 531.0081$ (stable).
5. $d = 0.20$, $\sigma_{\xi*}^2/\sigma_\xi^2 = 1$; $\mu^* = -0.3383$ (unstable).

These examples illustrate several facts. First, the optimality criterion may dictate either a countercyclical or a procyclical policy stance. For the numbers chosen for these examples, the optimal procyclical policy is always unstable; it fails to satisfy (27). The practical implications of this are clear; in examples 1 and 5 the policymaker must be satisfied with only partial attainment of the objective if stability is to be preserved. Second, in general, the optimal intervention stance is much more sensitive to the financial parameters of the model (as captured by d) than to underlying structural variances. Third, higher values of d result in an increasingly activist policy stance, while a larger foreign real variance (relative to domestic real variance) reduces the optimal value of μ^*.

It is useful to consider briefly the implications of the alternative intervention rule (based on rates of growth) stated in equation (16). It is not difficult to see that the use of the latter implies that the exchange rate solution must now be of the form $e_t = \pi_1 m_{t-1} + \pi_2 e_{t-1} + \ldots$. This equation, along with the money supply adjustment equation, $m_t = (1 - \mu\pi_1)m_{t-1} + \mu(1 - \pi_2)e_{t-1} + \ldots$, implies that dynamic adjustment is now guided by a second-order difference equation system rather than a first-order system as discussed previously. The principal consequence of utilizing such a rule therefore is that the dynamics of the model are more complex, with resulting complications for the stability condition.

4. Limited (Symmetrical) Information Case

In this section I consider the implications of limiting the current information set of both domestic and foreign agents to an observation of the current exchange rate. Neither prices nor the aggregate money supply level are currently observable by either agent. Because domestic and foreign agents share the same current information set, it is clear that $\bar{E}_t, e_{t+1} = \bar{E}_t^*, e_{t+1}$; that is, both agents' expectations of the future exchange rate are identical. The essential difference between this regime and the full information case involves the conditional expectation of the global monetary disturbance v_t. While in the full information case, $\bar{E}_t$, $v_t = \bar{E}_t^*$, $v_t = v_t$, in the present case

$$\bar{E}_t, v_t = \bar{E}_t^*, v_t = \frac{\theta_v}{\pi_3} \left[\pi_3 v_t + \pi_4 \xi_t + \pi_5 \xi_t^* + \pi_6 z_t + \pi_7 z_t^* \right] \tag{35}$$

where

$$\theta_v \equiv \frac{\pi_3^2 \sigma_v^2}{\pi_3^2 \sigma_v^2 + \pi_4^2 \sigma_\xi^2 + \pi_5^2 \sigma_{\xi^*}^2 + \pi_6^2 \sigma_z^2 + \pi_7^2 \sigma_{z^*}^2} \geq 0 \text{ but } \leq 1;$$

that is, θ_v is the fraction of total variance attributable to global monetary variance.

The change in the current information set does not alter the solutions to $\{\pi_i, U_i, W_i\}$, $i = 1, 2$. Thus there is no change in the stability propositions discussed earlier. The coefficients corresponding to the comparative static properties of the model are altered, however, and the new coefficients are given by

$$\pi_3' = \frac{1 + d\pi_1 \theta_v}{[\mu + 1 - \gamma + (1 + s)F_3(1 - 2\gamma) + d(1 + \pi_1\mu)]}; \tag{36}$$

$$\pi_3'|_{\mu=0} = \frac{1 + d\theta_v}{[1 - \gamma + (1 + s)F_3(1 - 2\gamma) + d]},$$

$$W_3' = F_3\pi_3'; \quad U_3' = -F_3\pi_3',$$

$$\pi'_4 = \frac{-(1+s)\left[\gamma k_4 + (1-\gamma)h_4\right]}{\left[\mu + 1 - \gamma + (1+s)F_3(1-2\gamma) + d(1+\pi_1\mu) - \dfrac{d\pi_1\theta_v}{\pi_3}\right]}; \tag{37}$$

$$\pi'_4\big|_{\mu=0} = \frac{-(1+s)\left[\gamma k_4 + (1-\gamma)h_4\right]}{\left[1 - \gamma + (1+s)F_3(1-2\gamma) + d - \dfrac{d\theta_v}{\pi_3}\right]}$$

$$W'_4 = F_3\pi'_4 + h_4; \; u'_3 = -F_3\pi'_4 + k_4,$$

$$\pi'_5 = \frac{-(1+s)\left[\gamma h_4 + (1-\gamma)k_4\right]}{\left[\mu + 1 - \gamma + (1+s)F_3(1-2\gamma) + d(1+\pi_1\mu) - \dfrac{d\pi_1\theta_v}{\pi_3}\right]}; \tag{38}$$

$$\pi'_5\big|_{\mu=0} = \frac{-(1+s)\left[\gamma h_4 + (1-\gamma)k_4\right]}{\left[1 - \gamma + (1+s)F_3(1-2\gamma) + d - \dfrac{d\theta_v}{\pi_3}\right]}$$

$$W'_5 = F_3\pi'_5 + k_4; \; U'_5 = -F_3\pi'_5 + h_4,$$

$$\pi'_6 = \frac{-\gamma(1-\beta)}{\left[\mu + 1 - \gamma + (1+s)F_3(1-2\gamma) + d(1+\pi_1\mu) - \dfrac{d\pi_1\theta_v}{\pi_3}\right]}; \tag{39}$$

$$\pi'_6\big|_{\mu=0} = \frac{-\gamma(1-\beta)}{\left[1 - \gamma + (1+s)F_3(1-2\gamma) + d - \dfrac{d\theta_v}{\pi_3}\right]}$$

$$W'_6 = F_3\pi'_6; \; U'_6 = -F_3\pi'_6,$$

$$\pi'_7 = \frac{-(1-\gamma)\beta^*}{\left[\mu + 1 - \gamma + (1+s)F_3(1-2\gamma) + d(1+\pi_1\mu) - \dfrac{d\pi_1\theta_v}{\pi_3}\right]}; \tag{40}$$

$$\pi'_7\big|_{\mu=0} = \frac{-(1-\gamma)\beta^*}{\left[1 - \gamma + (1+s)F_3(1-2\gamma) + d - \dfrac{d\theta_v}{\pi_3}\right]}$$

$$W'_7 = F_3\pi'_7; \; U'_7 = -F_3\pi'_7.$$

Consider first the impact of an aggregate monetary expansion on the exchange rate under flexible exchange rates. A comparison of the coefficients π_3 (relevant to the full information case) and π'_3 reveals that $\pi'_3 < \pi_3$, since $\theta_v < 1$. Thus the extent of exchange depreciation resulting from a domestic moentary expansion is reduced by comparison with the full information case. As a result the magnitudes of both domestic and foreign price effects are also reduced. Such an outcome is not difficult to understand. Because the monetary disturbance is not currently observable, agents, both domestic and foreign, attribute part of the current change to other real and portfolio disturbances, all of which would have led to spot appreciation if currently perceived. Not surprisingly the magnitude of the current depreciation is muted. Finally, as θ_v increases, agents increasingly identify the current shock with a monetary disturbance, enhancing the resulting exchange depreciation.

By contrast a domestic expenditure expansion now leads to sharper spot appreciation than in the full information case: $|\pi_4'| > |\pi_4|$.[7] As a result the foreign price inflationary effect (W_4') is enhanced, and the extent of domestic inflation (U_4') is reduced. An identical statement is also true of foreign expenditure innovations: $|\pi_5'| > |\pi_5|$. Finally, comparing π_6' and π_7' with their full information counterparts, it is clear that the lack of full information also enhances the extent of spot appreciation attendant on portfolio disturbances (of either domestic or foreign origin). Since the price level effects are directly proportional to the exchange rate movement in this case, it follows that sharper domestic deflation and foreign inflation effects result. The effect of underlying structural variances on these impact multipliers conforms with intuition. For example, as the domestic real variance σ_ξ^2 increases, it can be shown that the term (θ_v/π_3) declines, implying a reduced extent of spot appreciation following either type of portfolio disturbance. Finally it can be demonstrated that each of the impact effects is decreasing in the parameter d, as in the full information case.

I now briefly consider the rule of exchange market intervention in the limited information setup. For the case of portfolio shocks, a regime of pegged exchange rates is again optimal in the sense that $u \rightarrow \pm\infty$ ensures that π_6', $\pi_7' \rightarrow 0$.[8] With real shocks alone, it is no longer possible to obtain closed-form solutions for the optimal value of μ, even numerically. Assume for simplicity that $\gamma = \frac{1}{2}$, so that $\pi_4' = \pi_5'$ as previously. The optimality condition then reduces to $(U_4'/U_5') = -(\sigma_{\xi*}^2/\sigma_\xi^2)$. After a substantial amount of manipulation, this condition can be reduced to

$$\mu^* = \frac{(A + B)(A + B + 2)}{4(1 + d) + 2(A + B)} \tag{41}$$

where

$$A \equiv \frac{(1 + s)(k_4 + h_4)(1 + n)F_3}{(k_4 + h_4 n)} - (1 + 2d); \, n \equiv (\sigma^2_{\xi*}/\sigma^2_{\xi}),$$

$$B \equiv \frac{2d\theta_v\pi_1(\mu + 1 - \gamma + d + d\pi_1\mu)}{1 + d\pi_1\theta_v}.$$

Since π_1 is itself a quadratic function of μ, equation (41) is highly nonlinear in μ and no unique solution for μ^* can be found.[9] Thus one of the implications of limited information appears to be the fact that the authorities' task of intervening in a rational manner is greatly complicated. These nonuniqueness problems also exist even when the authorities possess superior information than do private agents regarding the realizations of current randon disturbances.

5. Asymmetrical Information Regime

The next informational regime analyzed involves more current information than in the previous section. Specifically I assume now that agents in each country are able to observe their own national price level and aggregate money supply level but not the price and money supply levels in the other country. In addition every agent observes the current exchange rate. In a sense, therefore, I have now included observations of the local price level (appropriately interpreted) in current information sets. The inclusion of domestic money supply observations in domestic but not foreign current information sets can easily be justified on the basis of prevailing economic reality. Weekly movements in the U.S. money supply are reported in U.S. financial media with virtually no mention of, say, German money supply movements. It is important to realize at this stage, however, that the currency-substitution nature of the present model imposes a type of asymmetry on the model in the sense that foreign money supply is not relevant to the analysis. In this sense it is possible to interpret domestic money supply as global money supply. By this interpretation domestic agents may be said to be better informed than foreign agents.[10] Thus the current information set of domestic agents is characterized by $I_t = \{m_t, p_t, e_t\}$ and that of foreign agents by $I_t^* = \{p_t^*, e_t\}$.

The essential implication of incorporating differential (asymmetric) information is that now $\bar{E}_t$, $e_{t+1} \neq \bar{E}_t^*$, e_{t+1}; that is, domestic and foreign expectations about the future exchange rate diverge in the present case (as opposed to the limited but symmetrical information case considered above). Owing to the fact that only the global monetary shock v_t is of a permanent nature, while each of ξ_t, ξ_t^*, z_t, and z_t^* are transitory, it is only the conditional expectations $\bar{E}_t(v_t)$ and $\bar{E}_t^*(v_t)$ that matter in the analysis.

It is clear at the outset that since domestic agents observe both m_t and e_t currently, the monetary innovation v_t is fully observable to the latter; $\bar{E}_t$, $v_t = v_t$ (see equation (15)). Domestic agents, however, cannot currently observe z_t, z_t, ξ_t, and ξ_t^* separately, but the conditional expectations of the latter do not matter for the analysis and will not be discussed here. Matters are somewhat more complicated for the formation of foreign agents' conditional expectation of the current monetary shock, $\bar{E}_t^*(v_t)$. To simplify matters further, I assume that there are no portfolio shocks z_t and z_t^*. In this absence, the foreign agents' information problem involves the inference of three expectations $(\bar{E}_t^*, v_t, \bar{E}_t^*, \xi \text{ and } \bar{E}_t^*, \xi^*)$ from two pieces of current information. One piece of current information is obtained by rearranging the money market equilibrium condition and is, in terms of reduced-form coefficients,

$$(k_o U_3 - 1)v_t + (k_o U_4)\xi_t + (k_o U_5)\xi_t^* \tag{42}$$

where $k_o \equiv \gamma(1 + s)$. The second piece of information involves the foreign commodity market clearing condition. When appropriately rearranged in reduced form, it can be shown that the combination term $(k_1 U_3)v_t + (k_1 U_4 + \alpha)\xi_t + (k_1 U_5 + 1)\xi_t^*$ where $k_1 \equiv \delta(1 - \alpha)$ is currently observed. These two pieces of information are now used to form conditional expectations by

$$\begin{bmatrix} \bar{E}_t^*(v_t) \\[6pt] \bar{E}_t^*(\xi_t) \\[6pt] \bar{E}_t^*(\xi_t^*) \end{bmatrix} = \begin{bmatrix} (k_o U_3 - 1)\sigma_v^2 & k_1 U_3 \sigma_v^2 \\[6pt] k_o U_4 \sigma_\xi^2 & (k_1 U_4 + \alpha)\sigma_\xi^2 \\[6pt] k_o U_5 \sigma_{\xi*}^2 & (k_1 U_5 + 1)\sigma_{\xi*}^2 \end{bmatrix} \begin{bmatrix} \dfrac{A11}{\Delta} & \dfrac{A12}{\Delta} \\[10pt] \dfrac{A21}{\Delta} & \dfrac{A22}{\Delta} \end{bmatrix}$$

$$\begin{bmatrix} (k_o U_3 - 1)v_t + k_o U_4 \xi_t + k_o U_5 \xi_t^* \\[18pt] (k_1 U_3)v_t + (k_1 U_4 + \alpha)\xi_t + (k_1 U_5 + 1)\xi_t^* \end{bmatrix} \tag{44}$$

where

$$\Delta \equiv \sigma_v^2 \sigma_\xi^2 [(k_1 U_3)(k_o U_4) - (k_1 U_4 + \alpha)(K_o U_3 - 1)]^2$$
$$+ \sigma_v^2 \sigma_{\xi*}^2 [(k_1 U_3)(k_o U_5) - (k_1 U_5 + 1)(k_o U_3 - 1)]^2$$
$$+ \sigma_\xi^2 \sigma_{\xi*}^2 [(k_1 U_4 + \alpha)(k_o U_5) - (k_1 U_5 + 1)(k_o U_4)]^2 > 0$$

and

$$A11 \equiv [(k_1 U_3)^2 \sigma_v^2 + (k_1 U_4 + \alpha)^2 \sigma_\xi^2 + (k_1 U_5 + 1)^2 \sigma_{\xi*}^2]$$

$$A12 \equiv -[(k_o U_3 - 1)k_1 U_3 \sigma_v^2 + (k_o U_4)(k_1 U_4 + \alpha)\sigma_\xi^2$$
$$+ (k_o U_5)(k_1 U_5 + 1)\sigma_{\xi*}^2]$$

$$A21 = A12$$

$$A22 = [(k_o U_3 - 1)^2 \sigma_v^2 + (k_o U_4)^2 \sigma_\xi^2 + (k_o U_5)^2 \sigma_{\xi*}^2].$$

Thus, the relevant conditional expectation $(\bar{E}_t^*(v_t))$ is

$$\bar{E}_t^*(v_t) = \sigma_v^2 C_1 [(k_o U_3 - 1)v_t + k_o U_4 \xi_t + k_o U_5 \xi_t^*]$$
$$+ \sigma_v^2 C_2 [k_1 U_3 v_t + (k_1 U_4 + \alpha)\xi_t + (k_1 U_5 + 1)\xi_t^*] \tag{45}$$

where

$$C_1 \equiv \left[(k_o U_3 - 1)\frac{A11}{\Delta} + k_1 U_3 \frac{A12}{\Delta} \right];$$

$$C_2 \equiv \left[(k_o U_3 - 1)\frac{A12}{\Delta} + k_1 U_3 \frac{A22}{\Delta} \right].$$

It is now possible to state the explicit solutions for $\{\pi_i, W_i, U_i\}$, $i = 3, 4, 5$ for the asymmetrical information case.[11]

$$\hat{\pi}_3 = \frac{1 + [\gamma(1 - \beta)\sigma - (1 - \gamma)\beta^*\sigma^*\sigma_v^2 C_1]\pi_1}{[\mu + 1 - \gamma + (1 + s)F_3(1 - 2\gamma) + d(1 + \pi_1 \mu) + (1 - \gamma)\beta^*\sigma^*\pi_1 \sigma_v^2(C_1 k_o + C_2 k_1)F_3]}$$

$$\hat{\pi}_3|_{\mu=0} = \frac{1 + [\gamma(1 - \beta)\sigma - (1 - \gamma)\beta^*\sigma^*\sigma_v^2 C_1]}{[1 - \gamma + (1 + s)F_3(1 - 2\gamma) + d + (1 - \gamma)\beta^*\sigma^*\sigma_v^2(C_1 k_o + C_2 k_1)F_3]} \tag{46}$$

$$\hat{W}_3 = F_3 \hat{\pi}_3; \ \hat{U}_3 = -F_3 \hat{\pi}_3,$$

$$\hat{\pi}_4 = \frac{-(1 + s)[\gamma k_4 + (1 - \gamma)h_4] + (1 - \gamma)\beta^*\sigma^*\pi_1 \sigma_v^2[(C_1 k_o + C_2 k_1)k_4 + C_2\alpha]}{[\mu + 1 - \gamma + (1 + s)F_3(1 - 2\gamma) + d(1 + \pi_1 \mu) + (1 - \gamma)\beta^*\sigma^*\pi_1 \sigma_v^2(C_1 k_o + C_2 k_1)F_3]}$$

$$\hat{\pi}_4|_{\mu=0} = \frac{-(1 + s)[\gamma k_4 + (1 - \gamma)h_4] + (1 - \gamma)\beta^*\sigma^*\sigma_v^2[(C_1 k_o + C_2 k_1)k_4 + C_2\alpha]}{[1 - \gamma + (1 + s)F_3(1 - 2\gamma) + d + (1 - \gamma)\beta^*\sigma^*\sigma_v^2(C_1 k_o + C_2 k_1)F_3]} \tag{47}$$

$$\hat{W}_4 = F_3 \hat{\pi}_4 + h_4; \ \hat{U}_4 = -F_3 \hat{\pi}_4 + k_4,$$

$$\hat{\pi}_5 = \frac{-(1+s)[\gamma h_4 + (1-\gamma)k_4] + (1-\gamma)\beta^*\sigma^*\pi_1\sigma_v^2[(C_1 k_o + C_2 k_1)h_4 + C_2]}{[\mu + 1 - \gamma + (1+s)F_3(1-2\gamma) + d(1+\pi_1\mu) + (1-\gamma)\beta^*\sigma^*\pi_1\sigma_v^2(C_1 k_o + C_2 k_1)F_3]}$$

$$\hat{\pi}_5|_{\mu=0} = \frac{-(1+s)[\gamma h_4 + (1-\gamma)k_4] + (1-\gamma)\beta^*\sigma^*\sigma_v^2[(C_1 k_o + C_2 k_1)h_4 + C_2]}{[1 - \gamma + (1+s)F_3(1-2\gamma) + d + (1-\gamma)\beta^*\sigma^*\sigma_v^2(C_1 k_o + C_2 k_1)F_3]} \tag{48}$$

$$\hat{W}_5 = F_5\hat{\pi}_5 + k_4; \quad \hat{U}_5 = -F_3\hat{\pi}_5 + h_4.$$

At the outset it may be noted that these solutions are not in closed form since each includes the terms C_1 and C_2. In turn the latter are functions of $\hat{\pi}_3$, $\hat{\pi}_4$, and $\hat{\pi}_5$ (via $\hat{U}_i$). Thus, (46) through (48) are of the form

$$\hat{\pi}_3 = a(\hat{\pi}_3, \hat{\pi}_4, \hat{\pi}_5),$$

$$\hat{\pi}_4 = b(\hat{\pi}_3, \hat{\pi}_4, \hat{\pi}_5),$$

$$\hat{\pi}_5 = c(\hat{\pi}_3, \hat{\pi}_4, \hat{\pi}_5);$$

that is, they form a simultaneous set of highly nonlinear equations in the relevant reduced-form coefficients. These complications notwithstanding, it is possible to note certain qualitative properties of interest. Consider first the case wherein aggregate monetary variance σ_v^2 is small compared to the underlying real variances. In this case π_3' and $\hat{\pi}_3$ reduce approximately to (under flexible exchange rates)[12]

$$\pi_3' \simeq \frac{1}{1 - \gamma + (1+s)F_3(1-2\gamma) + d}, \tag{36'}$$

$$\hat{\pi}_3 \simeq \frac{1 + \gamma(1-\beta)\sigma}{1 - \gamma + (1+s)F_3(1-2\gamma) + d}. \tag{46'}$$

Comparing these expressions with the full information coefficient stated in (29) and recalling the definition of d, it is clear that

$$\pi_3 > \hat{\pi}_3 > \pi_3'. \tag{49}$$

According to the relation stated in (49), the exchange rate impact of global monetary innovations increases monotonically as information sets are expanded to incorporate additional current information. This appealing property, however, is contingent on the monetary variance is being small. Examination of the expression for $\hat{\pi}_3$ reveals that if σ_v^2 is large enough, specifically $\sigma_v^2 > 1/|C_1|$, while $C_1 < 0$ and $(C_1 k_o + C_2 k_1) > 0$, then $\hat{\pi}_3 > \pi_3$ is certainly possible. Because of the complicated forms in which C_1 and C_2 appear, it is not straightforward to evaluate these conditions more precisely. However, the crucial implication that deserves note at this point is that except in special cases (for example, in which σ_v^2 is very small), it is possible for economic variables to display discontinuous behavior as information sets are smoothly expanded. Thus, an informational regime embodying very limited current information may replicate the behavior of a full information regime more closely than one that incorporates more complete (but not full) information.

Similar statements are true of the other coefficients $\hat{\pi}_4$ and $\hat{\pi}_5$, which correspond to the exchange rate impacts of real disturbances. In the case of domestic expenditure innovations, for example, a very low value of σ_v^2 results in an exchange rate impact approximately equal across all information regimes. With higher values of the global monetary variance, however, the asymmetric information regime may generate less (absolute) appreciation than the full information case, while the limited (symmetrical) information case results in sharper spot appreciation. Clearly further investigation of this phenomenon is required.

6. Superior Information

The final regime I consider involves superior information on the part of the policymaker. Here the authorities are presumed to be able to observe the relevant stochastic disturbances currently. Meanwhile the current information set of private agents worldwide is limited to observations of the exchange rate.

The essential operational implication of the authorities' possessing superior information is that the monetary feedback rule may now be conditioned directly on observations of the random disturbances Thus equation (15) is now modified to

$$m_t = m_{t-1} - \mu_1 \xi_t - \mu_2 \xi_t^* + v_t. \tag{50}$$

According to (50) aggregate money supply responds directly to the real disturbances ξ_t and ξ_t^* according to the feedback parameters μ_1 and μ_2, respectively. The global disturbance v_t is capable of at least two interpretations: either it may be regarded as the policy error associated with intervention, or it may be interpreted as the unsystematic component of monetary policy ($(m_{t-1} - \mu_1 \xi_t - \mu_2 \xi_t^*)$ being the systematic component).

Because of the form of the feedback rule (50), it is now necessary for private agents to compute conditional expectations of all relevant disturbances, based on an observation of e_t.

The coefficients corresponding to the comparative static properties of the model can now be shown to be given by

$$\pi_3^* = \frac{1 + d\theta_v}{\left[1 - \gamma + d + (1 + s)F_3(1 - 2\gamma) + d\left(\mu_1 \dfrac{\theta_\xi}{\pi_4} + \mu_2 \dfrac{\theta_{\xi*}}{\pi_5}\right)\right]} \tag{51}$$

$$W_3^* = F_3\pi_3^*; \quad U_3^* = -F_3\pi_3^*,$$

$$\pi_4^* = \frac{-[\mu_1(1 + d\theta_\xi) + \gamma(1 + s)k_4 + (1 - \gamma)(1 + s)h_4]}{\left[1 - \gamma + d + (1 + s)F_3(1 - 2\gamma) + d\left(\mu_2 \dfrac{\theta_\xi^*}{\pi_5} - \dfrac{\theta_v}{\pi_3}\right)\right]} \tag{52}$$

$$W_4^* = F_3\pi_4^* + h_4; \quad U_4^* = -F_3\pi_4^* + k_4,$$

$$\pi_5^* = \frac{-[\mu_2(1 + d\theta_\xi^*) + \gamma(1 + s)h_4 + (1 - \gamma)(1 + s)k_4]}{\left[1 - \gamma + d + (1 + s)F_3(1 - 2\gamma) + d\left(\mu_1 \dfrac{\theta_\xi}{\pi_4} + \mu_2 \dfrac{\theta_{\xi*}}{\pi_5}\right)\right]} \tag{53}$$

$$W_5^* = F_3\pi_4^* + k_4; \quad U_5^* = -F_3\pi_5^* + h_4.$$

where θ_v, θ_ξ, and $\theta_{\xi*}$ are the fractions of total variance attributable to various disturbances; that is,

$$\theta_v \equiv \frac{\pi_3^2\sigma_v^2}{\pi_3^2\sigma_v^2 + \pi_4^2\sigma_\xi^2 + \pi_5^2\sigma_{\xi*}^2};$$

$$\theta_\xi = \frac{\pi_4^2\sigma_\xi^2}{\pi_3^2\sigma_v^2 + \pi_4^2\sigma_\xi^2 + \pi_5^2\sigma_{\xi*}^2} \quad \text{and} \quad \theta_{\xi*} = (1 - \theta_v - \theta_\xi).$$

Examination of equations (51)–(53) reveals that the latter are not available in closed form. In order to provide an example of the type of nonuniqueness problems posed by such an informational regime, consider the case of real disturbances alone—$\theta_v = 0$. Given the parameter configuration $\gamma = \frac{1}{2}$, $d = 2$, $\theta_\xi = \theta_{\xi*} = \frac{1}{2}$ along with $\mu_2 = 0$, it can be shown that the optimality condition determining μ_1^* reduces to

$$\frac{[0.0588\pi_4^* + 0.4314][2.5\pi_4 + \mu_1]^3}{[0.5099\pi_4^* + 0.2353\mu_1][1.3334\mu_1]} = -\frac{\sigma_{\xi*}^2}{\sigma_\xi^2} \tag{54}$$

where $\pi_4^* = -[0.80\mu_1 + 0.5333]$.

Equation (54) is a quartic in μ_1, which may potentially yield four distinct values of μ_1^*. It would be fortuitous indeed if application of the stability criterion alone were to result in a single admissible value of the latter. In general it is clear that criteria other than the stability condition need to be invoked in order to discriminate between competing admissible values of the intervention parameter.

7. Conclusion

This chapter has focused on the implications of alternative information regimes in determining the impact of various structural disturbances, as well as in determining the optimal intervention stance in the context of a two-country currency-substitution framework. By and large the previous literature on exchange market intervention has employed full current information models. The results of this chapter (based on part analytical and part numerical methods) indicate that it is only in this case that unique solutions generally can be found for the optimal degree of intervention. In all other informational regimes (including regimes involving superior information on the part of the intervention authorities), either closed-form solutions do not exist at all or, alternatively, troublesome problems of nonuniqueness may occur. An important result that emerges from the comparison of various informational regimes is that the acquisition of progressively more complete current information by economic agents does not imply that the economy's behavior converges smoothly to that of the full information state. This does have a seemingly disturbing policy implication: the free provision of additional current information to private agents by the authorities is not necessarily the best strategy to adopt in eliminating the welfare loss due to incomplete information.

Notes

I am greatly indebted to Jacob Frenkel for pointing out a crucial error in a previous version of this chapter.

1. See also Flood and Marion (1982), Eaton and Turnovsky (1984), and Cox (1980).

2. See also Henderson (1982) who examines the role of exchange market intervention as part of a more general financial policy package. Several other references are cited in the latter and also in Branson and Henderson (1983).

3. Such a scenario can readily be justified on the basis of the fact that popular sources of financial information, such as newspapers and newscasts, invariably report movements in the domestic price level index, with almost no mention of foreign financial developments.

4. These equations—(7) and (8)—are derived by using the following money demand functions that emerge from the maximization problem

$$[m_d - (e + m_d^*)] = -\sigma(i_d - i_f) + z_t$$
$$[m_f^* - (m_f - e)] = \sigma^*(i_d - i_f) - z_t^*$$

along with (2) and (4). Notice that z_t captures an increase in the relative demand for domestic currency by domestic agents, while z_t^* measures a decrease in the foreign relative demand for foreign currency (and hence a switch in favor of domestic currency).

5. In terms of natural units, aggregate demand is given by $Y = C + X - R \cdot M$ where $R \equiv (EP^*/P)$, and $Y^* = C^* + M - \dfrac{X}{R}$ since $X^* = M$ and $R^*M^* \equiv (X/R)$. Equations (14) and (20) result from log linearizing these expresssions after substituting from the hypothesized functions $\ln C \equiv c_1 y$; $\ln C^* \equiv c_1^* y^*$; $\ln X \equiv x = x_1(e + p^* - p) + x_2 c^*$ and $\ln M \equiv m = m_1 c - m_2(e + p^* - p)$.

6. Note that (27) encompasses $\mu < -1$.

7. This is because of the additional negative term in the denominator of π_4'. I have not been able to rule out a sign reversal in the latter, owing to the additional term. The possibility of this perverse effect is not related to θ_v in an obvious manner since π_3' is itself a function of θ_v.

8. Since $\pi_3' \to 0$ as $u \to \pm\infty$, it is necessary to use L'Hôpital to demonstrate this statement.

9. If either $\theta_v \to 0$ or $d \to 0$, then π_6' and π_7' converge to their full information counterparts π_6 and π_7. In this case (41) reduces precisely to the full information solution (34) (when rearranged).

10. See also Stein (1985) and Flood and Hodrick (1985), both of whom incorporate differential information scenarios.

11. There is no change in the solutions for π_1 and π_2, which are as stated in the full information case.

12. Strictly speaking, π_3' and $\hat{\pi}_3$ are given by

$$\pi_3' = \frac{1 + \varepsilon \cdot d}{1 - \gamma + (1 + s)F_3(1 - 2\gamma) + d} \; ; \; \hat{\pi}_3 = \frac{1 + \gamma(1 - \beta)\sigma + (1 - \gamma)\beta^*\sigma^*C_1\varepsilon}{1 - \gamma + (1 + s)F_3(1 - 2\gamma) + d}$$

where ε is an arbitrarily small constant.

References

Barro, R. J. 1978. "A Stochastic Equilibrium Model of an Open Economy under Flexible Exchange Rates." *Quarterly Journal of Economics* 92:149–164.

Barro, R. J. 1980. "A Capital Market in an Equilibrium Business Cycle Model." *Econometrica* 48:1393–1417.

Bhandari, J. S. 1981. "A Stochastic Macroequilibrium Approach to a Floating Exchange Rate Economy with Interest-Bearing Assets." *Weltwirtschaftliches Archiv* 117:1–19.

Bhandari, J. S. 1982a. "Informational Efficiency and the Open Economy." *Journal of Money, Credit and Banking* 14:457–478.

Bhandari, J. S. 1982b. "Staggered Wage Setting and Exchange Rate Policy in an Economy with Capital Assets." *Journal of International Money and Finance* 1:275–1292.

Bhandari, J. S., and R. Driskill. 1981. "A Stochastic Equilibrium Model of the Open Economy Under Controlled Floating." Mimeographed. Carbondale, Ill.: Southern Illinois University.

Bhandari, J. S., and R. Driskill. 1983. "Some Problems Relating to the Existence of Equilibrium in an Economy with Exchange Rate Indexation." Mimeographed. New Haven: Yale University.

Boschen, J. F., and H. I. Grossman. 1980. "Monetary Information and Macroeconomic Fluctuations." National Bureau of Economic Research Working Paper 498.

Boyer, R. 1978. "Optimal Foreign Exchange Market Intervention." *Journal of Political Economy* 86:1045–1056.

Branson, W., and D. Henderson. 1983. "The Specification and Influence of Asset Markets." In *Handbook of International Economics*, P. Kenen and R. Jones, eds. Amsterdam: North Holland.

Canto, V., and M. Miles. 1983. "Exchange Rates in a Global Monetary Model with Currency Substitution and Rational Expectations." In *Economic Interdependence and Flexible Exchange Rates*, edited by J. S. Bhandari and B. H. Putnam. Cambridge: MIT Press.

Cox, W. M. 1980. "Unanticipated Money, Output and Prices in the Small Economy." *Journal of Monetary Economics* 6:359–1384.

Eaton, J., and S. J. Turnovsky. 1984. "The Forward Exchange Market, Speculation and Exchange Market Intervention." *Quarterly Journal of Economics*, 99, 45–69.

Flood, R., and N. Marion. 1982. "The Transmission of Disturbances under Alternative Exchange Rate Regimes with Optimal Indexing." *Quarterly Journal of Economics* 97:43–66.

Flood, R., and R. Hodrick. 1984. "Central Bank Intervention in a Rational Open Economy: A Model with Asymmetric Information." In *Exchange Rate Management under Uncertainty*, ed. J. S. Bhandari. Cambridge: MIT Press.

Frenkel, J. A., and J. Aizenman. 1982. "Aspects of the Optimal Management of Exchange Rates." *Journal of International Economics* 13:231–256.

Henderson, D. 1982. "Exchange Market Intervention Operations: Their Role in Financial Policy and Their Effects." Mimeographed. Washington, D.C.: Federal Reserve Board.

Marston, R. 1982. "Wages, Relative Prices and the Choice between Fixed and Flexible Exchange Rates." *Canadian Journal of Economics* 15:87–103.

Mussa, M. 1985. "Official Intervention and Exchange Rate Dynamics." In J. S. Bhandari, ed., *Exchange Rate Management under Uncertainty*. Cambridge: MIT Press.

Ortiz, G. 1983. "Currency Substitution in Mexico." *Journal of Money, Credit, and Banking* 15:174–185.

Roper, D. E., and S. J. Turnovsky. 1980. "Optimal Exchange Market Intervention in a Simple Stochastic Macro Model." *Canadian Journal of Economics* 13:296–309.

Saidi, N. 1980. "Fluctuating Exchange Rates and the International Transmission of Economic Disturbances." *Journal of Money, Credit and Banking* 12:575–591.

Stein, J. 1984. "Exchange Rate Management with Rational Expectations But Diverse Precisions." In J. S. Bhandari, ed., *Exchange Rate Management under Uncertainty*. Cambridge: MIT Press.

Turnovsky, S. J. 1983. "Exchange Market Intervention Policies in a Small Open Economy." In *Economic Interdependence and Flexible Exchange Rates*, edited by J. S. Bhandari and B. H. Putnam. Cambridge: MIT Press.

Weber, W. 1981. "Output Variability under Monetary Policy and Exchange Rate Rules." *Journal of Political Economy* 89:733–751.

8 Central Bank Intervention in a Rational Open Economy: A Model with Asymmetric Information

Robert P. Flood and Robert J. Hodrick

1. Introduction

The purpose of this chapter is to discuss central bank intervention and feedback monetary policy in a rational expectations model of an open economy. The development of the model parallels that in Flood and Hodrick (1983b) except that the information sets of economic agents are different. The information structure adopted here corresponds to the asymmetric information structure explored in Flood and Hodrick (1983a).

In our previous work (1983b) we constructed an open-economy model useful for interpreting observed fluctuations in output, inventories, prices, and exchange rates. The model was constructed to be consistent with the empirical regularities that characterize fluctuations in these magnitudes discovered in studies of business and inventory cycles and in studies of prices and exchange rates.[1]

In this chapter we adopt an asymmetric information structure and explore whether a relatively poorly informed monetary authority can design a set of incentives for the well-informed agents that induces these agents, through their market actions, to reveal information to the rest of the economy that is useful in stabilizing the real economy.

At the center of our model is the optimization problem of domestic firms facing uncertain demand. The representative firm must set its price at the beginning of the period without knowledge of actual demand that occurs during the period. Although firms have less than full information about the current state of the economy, they do observe market clearing prices in asset markets as well as prices being charged by other firms. Consequently firms use this information to make inferences about what demand will actually occur, and they set their prices to maximize the present value of profits.[2] Each period firms make two sequential decisions. First, they set their prices based on incomplete information. Second, after they have received orders for their products, they decide how much of the orders to meet out of current production and how much out of inventories.

Our investigation yields both positive and normative results. On the positive side we provide a new channel for the effects of monetary disturbances on the real economy, and our model matches the impact effects of the Dornbusch (1976) model, which is based on sticky nominal prices, but it provides alternative dynamics. Both the positive and the normative results are produced by a confusion by price setters concerning the true nature of disturbances impinging on asset markets, and the dynamics are due to optimal price and inventory management in the future. On the normative side we find that fixed exchange rates provide higher conditional output variance than do freely floating exchange rates. A free float, however, is not an optimal monetary policy since the monetary authority can manipulate the relatively well-informed agents into revealing stabilizing information.

Our analysis is presented in the next five sections. Section 2 develops our model, and section 3 presents the solution of the model. In section 4 we examine the model's dynamics, and in section 5 we examine the effects of changing the variances of our underlying disturbances. In section 6 we discuss exchange rate regime choice and monetary policy in the context of our model and contrast the model's results with some of our previous work. Section 6 is followed by some concluding remarks and our technical appendixes.

2. The Open Economy Macromodel

This section presents an open economy macroconomic model based in part on the decision problems of rational profit-maximizing firms. The development parallels that in Flood and Hodrick (1983b) except that the information sets of economic agents are different. The information structure corresponds to that in Flood and Hodrick (1983a). These informational assumptions are made explicit later in this section. In the first part of the section we develop quasi-reduced forms for the average relative price of the home good across firms, the aggregate output of the home good, and the aggregate inventory stock. These are quasi-reduced forms in the sense that they depend on firms' beliefs regarding the stochastic state of the economy. In the second part of the section we close the model with the discussion of equilibrium in asset markets and the demonstration of how firms gain information about their environment from the asset markets.

The economy is postulated to be a typical medium-sized open economy as in the discussions of Dornbusch (1976) and Mussa (1982). Output of the economy is distinct from the output of the rest of the world, but the bonds of the economy are postulated to be perfect substitutes for the assets in the rest of the world. In the model some irrevocable decisions are made sequentially within a period, and the firms' decisions are based on incomplete information. At the beginning of the period agents choose their asset portfolios for the period, and firms choose their prices for the period.[3] Later in the period actual demand is realized; firms must meet it at their posted prices either by sales out of stocks of inventories or by current production. Firms respond optimally given their information and the knowledge that end-of-period inventories will influence profitability in future periods.

Demand in the Goods Market

The J firms in the economy each face a demand curve of the form

$$D_t^j = (1/J)D_t - J\beta_4(R_t^j - \bar{R}_t) + e_t^j \qquad j = 1, \ldots, J \tag{1}$$

where D_t is economy-wide demand, $D_t = \sum_{j=1}^{J} D_t^j$, R_t^j is the relative price charged by firm j, and $\bar{R}_t$ is the average economy-wide relative price, $\bar{R}_t = (1/J)\sum_{j=1}^{J} R_t^j$.

The relative prices are the firms' domestic currency prices of their products divided by the price level, which is a function of the domestic currency prices of home and foreign goods. Economy-wide demand, D_t, is the sum of domestic demand, $\rho_0 - \rho_1\bar{R}_t + \rho_2 X_t$ and foreign demand, $\rho_0^* - \rho_1^*\bar{R}_t$, where ρ coefficients are positive parameters and X_t is the level of real expenditure by domestic residents. The disturbance term e_t^j is a stochastic shock to the demand function facing firm j. We assume that each firm knows its own relative demand shock, but we assume that the relative shocks have no influence in the aggregate—that is, $\sum_{j=1}^{J} e_t^j = 0$. Real expenditure is assumed to depend positively on real income, $\bar{R}_t Y_t$, with the specification given by the following linearization:

$$X_t = \kappa_1\bar{R}_t + \kappa_2 Y_t + u_t \qquad \kappa_1, \kappa_2 > 0 \tag{2}$$

where u_t is an aggregate expenditure disturbance assumed to be white noise.[4]

Firms' Pricing, Production, and Inventory Holding

Firm j faces the demand curves given by (1). If it charges the average economy-wide relative price, $R_t^j = \bar{R}_t$, then its demand is its share of aggregate demand, $(1/J)D_t$, plus its relative demand disturbance. If the firm charges a higher (lower) relative price than the average, its demand is reduced (increased) by the amount $J\beta_4(R_t^j - \bar{R}_t)$. The larger is $J\beta_4$, the greater is the firm's price sensitivity to deviations from the average relative price. In the limit ($J\beta_4 \to \infty$), each firm chooses to charge the average price.[5]

A firm produces output, Y_t^j, and holds inventories, N_t^j, such that

$$Y_t^j = D_t^j + N_t^j - N_{t-1}^j \tag{3}$$

describes the law of motion of end-of-period inventories. Firms face production costs that are an increasing convex function of the firm's output and an increasing function of aggregate output, $Y_t = \sum_{j=1}^{J} Y_t^j$, and that depend positively on a known aggregate stochastic shock, k_t.[6] The specific functional form for production costs is $(\gamma_0 + k_t)Y_t^j + \gamma_1 Y_t Y_t^j + (\gamma_2/2)(Y_t^j)^2$ with the γ parameters defined to be positive constants. Firms hold inventories to smooth the cost of production, but holding inventories is also costly. Inventory costs are incurred on beginning-of-period inventories and are assumed to depend positively on own inventories and positively on aggregate inventories, $N_t = \sum_{j=1}^{J} N_t^j$. The specific functional form for inventory costs is $\delta_1 N_{t-1} N_{t-1}^j + (\delta_2/2)(N_{t-1}^j)^2$, with the δ parameters defined to be positive constants.[7]

Our specific functional forms should be thought of as tractable approximations to more complex real behavior. Since the functions contain aggregate output and inventories, production costs increase for the typical firm when aggregate production rises, and inventory storage costs increase when economy-wide inventories rise. These properties reflect the presumed positive association of average real wages and aggregate output and the positive effect of aggregate inventories on storage space rents. Because we allow negative inventories, the term $\delta_1 N_{t-1} N_{t-1}^j$ could be negative if firm j has inventories that differ in sign from the aggregate. The importance of such terms is minimal when each firm does not deviate very much from the average.

The firms' first-stage contingency plans are found from the following maximization problems:

$$\max_{\{R_{t+i}^j, N_{t+i}^j\}} E_t^j \sum_{i=0}^{\infty} \{D_{t+i}^j R_{t+i}^j - (\gamma_0 + k_{t+i} + \gamma^1 Y_{t+i}) Y_{t+i}^j - (\gamma_2/2)(Y_{t+i}^j)^2$$

$$- \delta_1 N_{t+i-1} N_{t+i-1}^j - (\delta_2/2)(N_{t+i-1}^j)^2\} \sigma^i \quad j = 1, \ldots, J \tag{4}$$

which are subject to an inital stock of inventories for each firm and to the relationships (1) and (3). The discount rate σ is a constant between zero and unity.[8] The operator E_t^j denotes the mathematical expectation conditional on the information available to firm j at the beginning of the period. Each firm is assumed to know all economy-wide price information, the economy-wide cost shock, and its own relative demand shock.

In finding the firms' optimal solutions to (4), we postulate that each firm ignores its influence on economy-wide variables such as $\bar{R}_{t+i}$, N_{t+i}, and Y_{t+i}. Such a strategy is exactly profit maximizing only in the limit as $J \to \infty$, and there is nothing in the model that prevents such an interpretation.[9]

The problem stated in (4) implies a pair of linear Euler equations and a transversality condition for each of the J firms. These equations are recorded in appendix 8A and may be used to find the firm-specific decisions. Since our concern is with the aggregate economy, we record here only the aggregate Euler equations, which are obtained by summing the firm-specific Euler equations. The derivation in appendix 8A indicates that we can substitute the operator E_t^G, which is based on the common information set of all firms in the goods market to form the aggregate Euler equations, which are:

$$E_t^G\{D_{t+i} - J^2\beta_4\bar{R}_{t+i} + J^2\beta_4(\gamma_0 + k_{t+i} + \gamma_1 Y_{t+i})$$

$$+ \gamma_2 J\beta_4(D_{t+i} + N_{t+i} - N_{t+i-1})\} = 0, \tag{5a}$$

$$E_t^G\{-J(\gamma_0 + k_{t+i} + \gamma_1 Y_{t+i}) - \gamma_2(D_{t+i} + N_{t+i} - N_{t+i-1})$$

$$+ \sigma J(\gamma_0 + k_{t+i+1} + \gamma_1 Y_{t+i+1}) + \sigma\gamma_2(D_{t+i+1} + N_{t+i+1} - N_{t+i}) \tag{5b}$$

$$- \sigma(\delta_1 J N_{t+i} + \delta_2 N_{t+i})\} = 0.$$

Because prices are set based on beginning-of-period information, the planned value $E_t^G\bar{R}_t$ and actual $\bar{R}_t$ will coincide. Since firms can respond to unanticipated demand by altering their contingency plans, the planned value of end-of-period inventories, $E_t^G N_t$, will coincide with actual inventories only if there is no unanticipated demand. Since aggregate output

Table 8.1
Quasi-reduced form coefficients π_{ij}

	1. N_{t-1}	2. k_t	3. $E_t^G w_t$
R_t	$\pi_{R1} < 0$	$0 < \pi_{R2}$	$0 < \pi_{R3}$
$E_t^G N_t$	$0 < \pi_{N1} < 1$	$\pi_{N2} < 0$	$\pi_{N3} < 0$

is given by $Y_t = N_t - N_{t-1} + D_t$, the solutions for inventories and prices provide the solution for output.

Before presenting the quasi-reduced form solutions for output, it is convenient to reformulate the demand function to incorporate the dependence of demand on expenditure and real income. Substituting the law of motion for aggregate output and the expenditure function in (2) into D_t, we obtain

$$D_t = \beta_0 - \beta_1 \bar{R}_t + \beta_2 (N_t - N_{t-1}) + \beta_3 w_t \tag{6}$$

where $\beta_0 = (\rho_0 + \rho_0^*)/(1 - \kappa_2 \rho_2)$, $\beta_1 = (\rho_1 + \rho_1^* - \rho_2 \kappa_1)/(1 - \kappa_2 \rho_2)$, $\beta_2 = \kappa_2 \rho_2/(1 - \kappa_2 \rho_2)$, $\beta_3 = 1/(1 - \kappa_2 \rho_2)$, and $w_t \equiv \rho_2 u_t$. Since we assume that $\kappa_2 \rho_2 < 1$ and $(\rho_1 + \rho_1^* - \kappa_1 \rho_1) > 0$, all the β coefficients are positive. Substituting (6) into (5a) and (5b) and using the law of motion of aggregate inventories to eliminate Y_t allows us to solve for $\bar{R}_t$ and $E_t^G N_t$.

Since w_t and k_t are white noise disturbance terms, we conjecture solutions to the Euler equations of the form

$$\bar{R}_t = \pi_{R0} + \pi_{R1} N_{t-1} + \pi_{R2} k_t + \pi_{R3} E_t^G w_t \tag{7a}$$

and

$$E_t^G N_t = \pi_{N0} + \pi_{N1} N_{t-1} + \pi_{N2} k_t + \pi_{N3} E_t^G w_t. \tag{7b}$$

The values of the π coefficients of equations (7a) and (7b) are found by the method of undermined coefficients. These values are recorded in appendix 8B and their algebraic signs are given in table 8.1.

The signs of the π coefficients of equations (7a) and (7b) make good intuitive sense. When beginning-of-period aggregate retail inventories are high, firms set relative prices lower on average. Average relative prices are higher the higher are production costs, and firms increase relative prices on average in response to expected increases in aggregate demand. Since $0 < \pi_{N1} < 1$, expected aggregate inventories evolve according to a stable autoregression, and when production costs are high, firms expect to draw down inventories as they also expect to do when they anticipate an increase in demand.

After firms set prices, they are confronted with actual demand. We assume that firms may not alter their posted prices after they see demand. They may, however, alter their contingency plans for inventory accumulation.[10] The actual inventory decision for period t is found by returning to (4) and optimizing with respect to N_t^j taking R_t^j, $\bar{R}_t$, w_t, and N_{t-1}^j, as given and using the solutions for $E_t^G N_{t+i+1}$ and $E_t^G \bar{R}_{t+i+1}$ for all $i > 0$ found in (7a) and (7b).

The inventory decision is found from the Euler equation

$$E_t^{G'}\{Y_t - \sigma Y_{t+1} + [J/(J\gamma_1 + \gamma_2)]k_t + \sigma\mu N_t\} = 0 \tag{8}$$

where $E_t^{G'}$ is the expectation operator conditional on full information for period t and $\mu = (J\delta_1 + \delta_2)/(J\gamma_1 + \gamma_2)$.

Because actual inventories will differ from expected inventories only due to differences of w_t from $E_t^G w_t$, the solution for actual inventories can be written as

$$N_t = \pi_{N0} + \pi_{N1} N_{t-1} + \pi_{N2} k_t + \pi_{N3} E_t^G w_t + \pi_{N4}(w_t - E_t^G w_t). \tag{9}$$

Using (8) and (9) and the previous results we find $-1 < \pi_{N4} < \pi_{N3} < 0$. The value of π_{N4} is recorded in appendix 8B. Aggregate inventories respond more strongly to unexpected demand than to expected demand because firms respond to expected demand by changing their relative prices and their expected inventory response. When actual demand occurs, the firms must respond optimally given their set prices. The inability to raise relative prices in response to an unexpected shift in demand leads to larger responses of inventory and production that when firms can decrease demand by increasing prices.

Aggregate output is given by $Y_t = D_t + N_t - N_{t-1}$. Using our previous results we derive the quasi-reduced form

$$Y_t = \pi_{Y0} + \pi_{Y1} N_{t-1} + \pi_{Y2} k_t + \pi_{Y3} E_t^G w_t + \pi_{Y4}(w_t - E_t^G w_t). \tag{10}$$

The π_Y coefficients are presented in appendix 8B, and their algebraic signs are recorded in table 8.2. Both larger beginning-of-period inventories and higher production costs decrease aggregate output. An increase in $E_t^G w_t$ produces an increase in $\bar{R}_t$ and a higher quantity demanded along the shifted demand curve. Firms plan on meeting this partly out of inventories and partly out of current production. The fact that $\pi_{Y4} > \pi_{Y3}$ indicates

Table 8.2
Quasi-reduced form coefficients π_{Yj}

	1. N_{t-1}	2. k_t	3. $E_t^G w_t$	4. $(w_t - E_t^G w_t)$
Y_t	$\pi_{Y1} < 0$	$\pi_{Y2} < 0$	$0 < \pi_{Y3}$	$0 < \pi_{Y3} < \pi_{Y4}$

that the response of aggregate output to unexpected demand is stronger than to expected demand since expected demand is reflected in relative prices and unexpected demand is not.

This completes the development of the quasi-reduced forms of the goods market. The true reduced forms for relative prices, inventories, and output require elimination of the expectation $E_t^G w_t$. Agents determine this variable by using their knowledge of the entire economy, which includes the asset markets. We turn now to the development of the information structure and the asset markets.

Information Structure and the Asset Markets

The economy portrayed here is assumed to be small in the world capital market, where all securities are perfect substitutes, and small in the markets for foreign-produced goods. The country is assumed to be large in the markets for domestically produced goods and for domestic money. Thus the country takes foreign interest rates and the foreign prices of foreign-produced goods as exogenous.

Asset markets are assumed to be in equilibrium at the beginning of the period. The principal equations describing the asset markets are the following:

$$m_t - p_t = -\alpha_1 i_t + \alpha_2 \tilde{X}_t + z_t \qquad \alpha_1, \alpha_2 > 2, \tag{11a}$$

$$i_t = i_t^* + E_t^A s_{t+1} - s_t, \tag{11b}$$

$$p_t = \theta \bar{h}_t + (1 - \theta)(\bar{h}_t^* + s_t) \qquad 0 < \theta < 1, \tag{11c}$$

$$m_t = m_{t-1} + v_t. \tag{11d}$$

Equation (11a) is money market equilibrium. The logarithm of the supply of real money balances, $m_t - p_t$, equals the logarithm of the demand for real money balances, $-\alpha_1 i_t + \alpha_2 \tilde{X}_t + z_t$. In (11a) m_t is the logarithm of nominal transactions balances, p_t is the logarithm of the nominal price level defined in (11c), i_t is the nominal interest rate, $\tilde{X}_t$ is an expenditure scale variable defined below, and z_t is a white noise disturbance term to the demand for money. According to (11c) p_t is a weighted average of the logarithms of the average domestic currency price of domestic goods, $\bar{h}_t$, and the average domestic currency price of foreign goods, $\bar{h}_t^* + s_t$, where $\bar{h}_t^*$ is the logarithm of the average foreign currency price of foreign goods and s_t is the logarithm of the exchange rate quoted as the domestic currency price of a unit of foreign currency. Goods units are chosen such that the relative price of the home good, $\bar{R}_t$, is approximated as $\bar{R}_t = \bar{h}_t - \bar{p}_t + 1$. Equation (11d) indiçates that the supply of money is exogenous and follows a random walk with innovation v_t. We first solve the model with this assumed money supply process before turning in later sections to discussions of intervention and alternative exchange rate regimes. Equation (11b) is capital market equilibrium. The nominal interest rate obeys uncovered interest rate parity. The expected nominal return on domestic assets equals the expected nominal domestic currency return on foreign assets, which is the foreign interest rate, i_t^*, plus the expected rate of change in the exchange rate.[11] The information set in the conditional expectation operator E_t^A is defined precisely below.

The demand for money is specified in the spirit of the models of Clower (1967) and Lucas (1980), which require individuals to obtain cash in advance of purchasing goods during a period. We do not examine the microfoundations of money demand here but instead postulate that money demand is sensitive to the opportunity cost of holding money given by the nominal interest rate and that the scale variable in money demand is aggregate planned expenditures in the economy, $\tilde{X}_t$.

Planned real expenditure of an agent depends on his expected real income, which in turn depends on his information set. We assume that the n agents of the economy each observes a random disturbance, u_t^i, to his expenditure savings decision at the beginning of the period. This disturbance is composed of two uncorrelated white noise components, b_t^i and a_t^i, $u_t^i = b_t^i + a_t^i$. Further, we impose $\sum_{i=1}^{n} b_t^i = 0$. Thus, u_t^i contains an individual specific component, b_t^i, that contributes nothing to the aggregate expenditure disturbance, and it contains the individual's contribution to the aggregate disturbance, a_t^i, such that $\sum_{i=1}^{n} u_t^i = \sum_{i=1}^{n} a_t^i = u_t$. We also assume that the variance of b_t^i is sufficiently large compared to the variance of a_t^i that the agent can make no useful inference about the aggregate expenditure disturbance even though he observes his actual disturbance. Of course information sets also differ as to whether the agent works in the goods market, in which case he has the information set I_t^G, or the asset market, in which case he has the information set I_t^A. Consequently aggregate expected expenditure depends on the number of agents, n_a, that are asset market specialists.

Aggregate expected expenditure therefore is

$$\tilde{X}_t = \sum_{i=1}^{n} E_t^i X_t^i = \kappa_1 \bar{R}_t + \kappa_2 Y_t + \kappa_2 (n_a/n)(E_t^A Y_t - E_t^G Y_t) + \sum_{i=1}^{n} u_t^i. \qquad (12)$$

Asset market specialists know the actual aggregate disturbances; hence a useful quasi-reduced form for $\tilde{X}_t$ is

$$\tilde{X}_t = \pi_{X1} N_{t-1} + \pi_{X2} k_t + \pi_{X3} E_t^G w_t + \pi_{X4}(w_t - E_t^G w_t) + u_t \qquad (13)$$

where the π_{Xi} coefficients are recorded in appendix 8B and $\pi_{X1} < 0$, π_{X2} is ambiguous in sign, $0 < \pi_{X3}$, and $0 < \pi_{X4}$.

All agents in the model are assumed to have complete information about current prices in the economy, including the nominal prices of all firms and the market clearing nominal interest rate and exchange rate. All agents also know the actual values of all variables dated $t - 1$ and earlier. The only difference between the information sets I_t^A and I_t^G is with respect to knowledge of aggregate disturbance in period t. Asset market specialists are assumed to have complete knowledge of all aggregate period t disturbances, u_t, which is proportional to w_t, v_t, and z_t, while goods market specialists are assumed to have no additional aggregate information about the disturbances beyond what they can infer from observing prices, interest rates, and exchange rates. In summary $I_t^G = \{p_t, \bar{h}_t, i_t, s_t, i_t^*, \bar{h}_t^*, m_{t-1}, I_{t-1}^A\}$ and $I_t^A = \{u_t, v_t, z_t, I_t^G\}$.

Before turning to the formal solution of the model, it is useful to summarize informally the working of the model. At the beginning of each period nominal prices are set by firms simultaneously as the asset markets clear. Each firm chooses its relative price given the decisions of other firms. At this stage price-setting agents do not know the values of the aggregate disturbances u_t, v_t, and z_t. Some agents who specialize in the asset markets are assumed to know these disturbances, and their knowledge is reflected in the nominal interest rate and the exchange rate. Price setters know the structure of the economy and are able to infer a value of the demand disturbance from their observations; it is the inferred value of w_t, $E_t^G w_t$, that affects the pricing decision. After prices are set, the actual values of the demand disturbance and the other disturbances are revealed to agents. As actual demand is realized, the firm chooses an optimal value of production and inventory decumulation in order to meet the demand at its fixed price. The actual quantity demanded is determined in part by the prices that firms set under partial information.

3. Solution of the Model

In this section we provide the model's reduced form solutions for the level of output, inventories, the exchange rate, the average relative price of the domestic good, and the average nominal price of the domestic good. First we discuss the nature of the inference problem faced by firms and investigate the information that firms learn from the clearing of asset markets. Price setters will be able to extract two signals of the three underlying aggregate disturbances, and we assume that these inferences, $E_t^G u_t$, $E_t^G v_t$, and $E_t^G z_t$, are linear least-squares projections of the respective disturbances onto the information set I_t^G. Since firms are concerned only with determining an expected value of the expenditure disturbance u_t, which is proportional to the domestic demand disturbance, w_t, only the inference regarding w_t is presented.

Since w_t is a white noise disturbance, only the new information or innovation to the information set I_t^G is useful for predicting its value. The innovation to the information set arises because of the innovations in v_t, w_t, and z_t, and its source is the clearing of the domestic money market and the international capital market. Firms observe two distinct linear combinations of the three fundamental disturbances.

The first linear combination of the disturbances that is contained in I_t^G is found from the money market. Equilibrium in the money market can be written as

$$m_{t-1} + v_t - p_t = -\alpha_1 i_t + \alpha_2 [\pi_{X1} N_{t-1} + \pi_{X2} k_t + (\pi_{X3} - \pi_{X4}) E_t^G w_t] + \alpha_3 w_t + z_t \tag{14}$$

where $\alpha_3 \equiv [\alpha_2 \pi_{X4} + (\alpha_2/\rho_2)] > 0$. Since I_t^G contains m_{t-1}, p_t, i_t, and $\bar{R}_t$ as well as the parameters α_1, α_2, and α_3, and because I_t^G is used to form the prediction $E_t^G y_t$, I_t^G contains

$$g_{1t} = v_t - \alpha_3 w_t - z_t, \tag{15}$$

which is the incipient excess supply of money. Prices and interest rates adjust to clear the money market in response to the innovation g_{1t}.

The second linear combination of the fundamental disturbances that is contained in I_t^G is found from the equilibrium in the international capital market. Since the asset market is dominated by the well-informed asset market specialists, who set the forward rate equal to their expected future spot rate, agents in the goods market observe $E_t^A s_{t+1}$ directly. Given their knowledge of the economy, this observation provides price setters with an additional linear combination of the fundamental disturbances; but in order to determine the value of this variable, it is necessary to discuss the reduced form of the endogenous variables of the model.

Given the assumed time-series properties of the exogenous stochastic processes of the model and ignoring constant terms, reduced form equations have the form

$$Q_t = \lambda_{QN} N_{t-1} + \lambda_{Qk} k_t + \lambda_{Qm} m_{t-1} + \lambda_{Qv} v_t + \lambda_{Qw} w_t + \lambda_{Qz} z_t \tag{16}$$

for $Q_t = N_t, Y_t, \bar{R}_t, s_t,$ and $\bar{h}_t$. Consequently asset market participants know the value of N_t that will be determined at the end of the period, and they form the following prediction of the exchange rate in period $t + 1$:

$$E_t^A s_{t+1} = \lambda_{sN} N_t + \lambda_{sm}(m_{t-1} + v_t). \tag{17}$$

Since lagged money is in the information set and because the logarithm of the money supply follows a random walk, it will turn out that $\lambda_{sm} = 1$. From (9) it is clear that the new information in $E_t^A s_{t+1}$ is

$$g_{2t} = \lambda_{sN} \pi_{N4} w_t + v_t, \tag{18}$$

which is the linear combination of the fundamental innovations that price setters learn from observing the expected future spot rate of the asset market specialists.

The variables g_{1t} in (15) and g_{2t} in (18) contain the information about w_t that is available to price setters at the beginning of period t. Agents use these two variables to form a linear least-squares projection of w_t onto g_{1t} and g_{2t}:

$$E_t^G w_t = \phi_{w1} g_{1t} + \phi_{w2} g_{2t} \tag{19}$$

where $\phi_{w1} = -(\alpha_3 + \lambda_{sN} \pi_{N4})\sigma_v^2 \sigma_w^2/\Delta$, $\phi_{w2} = -\phi_{w1} + \lambda_{sN} \pi_{N4} \sigma_w^2 \sigma_z^2/\Delta$, and $\Delta = (\alpha_3 + \lambda_{sN} \pi_{N4})^2 \sigma_v^2 \sigma_w^2 + (\sigma_v^2 + \lambda_{sN}^2 \pi_{N4}^2 \sigma_w^2)\sigma_z^2$.

The full reduced form for the real sector of the model, $\bar{R}_t, N_t,$ and Y_t, can now be found by substituting (19) into (7a), (9), and (11). The solutions for $s_t, i_t,$ and $\bar{h}_t$ are found from the money market equilibrium, from capital market equilibrium, and from the definition of the relative price,

Table 8.3
λ_{ij} Reduced form coefficients

	N_{t-1}	k_t	m_{t-1}	v_t	w_t	z_t
N_t	$0 < \lambda_{NN} < 1$	$\lambda_{Nk} < 0$	$\lambda_{Nm} = 0$	$\lambda_{Nv} < 0$	$\lambda_{Nw} < 0$	?
Y_t	$\lambda_{YN} < 0$	$\lambda_{Yk} < 0$	$\lambda_{Ym} = 0$	$0 < \lambda_{Yv}$	$0 < \lambda_{Yw}$	?
$\bar{R}_t$	$\lambda_{RN} < 0$	$0 < \lambda_{Rk}$	$\lambda_{Rm} = 0$	$\lambda_{Rv} < 0$	$0 < \lambda_{Rw}$	?
s_t	$0 < \lambda_{sN}$	$\lambda_{sk} < 0$	$\lambda_{sm} = 1$	$0 < \lambda_{sv}$	$\lambda_{sw} < 0$	$\lambda_{sz} < 0$
$\bar{h}_t$	$\lambda_{hN} < 0$	$0 < \lambda_{hk}$	$\lambda_{hm} = 1$	$0 < \lambda_{hv}$	$\lambda_{hw} < 0$	$\lambda_{hz} < 0$

$\bar{R}_t = h_t - p_t + 1$. The signs of the reduced form λ coefficients are presented in table 8.3. The actual values of the reduced form coefficients are presented in appendix 8C. The dynamics of the model are described in the next section.

4. Dynamics of the Model

Because the money supply, money demand, and domestic demand disturbances are unobservable by firms, each of these shocks produces a response of the economy that deviates from the full information solution. A variable is said to overshoot (undershoot) when the absolute value of its immediate response to a disturbance is greater than the absolute value of the corresponding full information benchmark.

The reduced form coefficients in table 8.3 indicate that the beginning-of-inventory stock, N_{t-1}, the logarithm of the money supply from the previous period, m_{t-1}, and the stochastic disturbances k_t, v_t, w_t, and z_t are the state variables of the system.

Effects of m_{t-1}

We assume that actual money is known with a one-period lag. Therefore the lagged money stock does not influence the real sector of the economy, and since the logarithm of the money supply is assumed to follow a random walk, the exchange rate and the domestic price of the home good change equiproportionately to known changes in m_{t-1}. Consequently $\lambda_{Nm} = \lambda_{Ym} = \lambda_{Rm} = 0$, and $\lambda_{sm} = \lambda_{hm} = 1$.

Effects of N_{t-1}

The dynamic path of the economy is induced by innovations in the exogenous stochastic processes: the production cost disturbance, k_t, which is known to firms, and the money supply shock, v_t, the domestic demand disturbance, w_t, and the money demand disturbance, z_t, which are not known to firms at time t. These four disturbances shock the system away from its full information steady state. Any disturbance is propagated through time by the optimal responses of firms to changes in their inventory stocks. Since $0 < \lambda_{NN} < 1$, the aggregate inventory stock converges over time in a stable autoregression back to its steady-state value after an initial disturbance. When inventories are above (below) average, firms decrease (increase) their relative prices ($\lambda_{RN} < 0$) and decrease (increase) their production ($\lambda_{YN} < 0$) to deplete (replenish) inventories. The relative price change is accomplished partly by a decrease (increase) in the nominal price of the home good ($\lambda_{hN} < 0$) and partly by a depreciation (appreciation) of the currency ($0 < \lambda_{sN}$). These inventory dynamics accompany all transitions back to the steady state.

Effects of k_t

Consider now how the economy responds to an observed increase in the cost of production. Since this is a temporary disturbance, firms find it optimal to increase their relative prices ($0 < \lambda_{Rk}$), cut their production ($\lambda_{Yk} < 0$), and draw down their inventory stocks ($\lambda_{Nk} < 0$). The change in the relative price is produced by an increase in the nominal domestic price and an appreciation of the currency.[12] Since firms observe the cost disturbance, there is no deviation of the response of the economy from its full information equilibrium.

Effects of v_t

Now examine the response of the economy to a hypothetical increase in the money supply unobserved by firms assuming that $w_t = z_t = 0$. From (19), notice that $E_t^G(w_t) = (\phi_{w1} + \phi_{w2})v_t < 0$, indicating that agents misperceive the money supply increase as a reduction in real goods demand. This occurs because agents' observations on the changes in equilibrium asset prices are consistent with both an increase in the supply of money and a decrease in expenditure, which decreases the demand for money. Agents do perceive an increase in the money supply, as indicated by examining the linear least-squares projection of v_t onto the two sources of information, g_{1t} and g_{2t}:

$$E_t^G v_t = \phi_{v1} g_{1t} + \phi_{v2} g_{2t} \tag{20}$$

where $\phi_{v1} = \lambda_{sN}\pi_{N4}(\alpha_3 + \lambda_{sN}\pi_{N4})\sigma_v^2\sigma_w^2/\Delta$, $\phi_{v2} = [\alpha_3(\alpha_3 + \lambda_{sN}\pi_{N4})\sigma_v^2\sigma_w^2$ $+ \sigma_v^2\sigma_z^2]/\Delta$, and Δ is the same as that given after equation (19). When $v_t > 0$ and $w_t = z_t = 0$, agents perceive $E_t^G v_t = (\phi_{v1} + \phi_{v2})v_t$ and $0 < (\phi_{v1} + \phi_{v2}) < 1$. Therefore agents perceive an increase in the money supply, but they rationally attribute part of the changes in equilibrium asset prices, which reequilibrate the asset market after an increase in v_t, to a fall in expenditure.

Since firms expect a fall in demand, they lower their relative prices $\bar{R}_t(\lambda_{Rv} < 0)$. Firms are anticipating an increase in inventories and a reduction in output since they think the demand curve has shifted. When real demand is realized, it occurs along the unshifted demand curve since $w_t = 0$ in the hypothetical case under discussion. Because firms lowered their relative prices, demand is now unexpectedly high; firms meet this unforeseen increase in demand by an optimal combination of an increase in production ($\lambda_{Yv} > 0$) and a decrease in inventories ($\lambda_{Nv} < 0$).

The innovation in the money supply has effects on the exchange rate and the nominal domestic price that arise from several sources. First, the full information response of these variables to an increase in the money supply is an equiproportional increase given that the money supply follows a random walk. Second, with incomplete information, firms lower their relative prices by raising their nominal price less than the proportionate change in the exchange rate. The third effect arises because goods market agents expect a decrease in real income while asset market agents expect an increase in real output. This has an ambiguous effect on money demand. Finally the agents anticipate an increase in the relative price in the future, which will be accomplished partly by an appreciation of the currency. This expected appreciation positively affects money demand, reducing the magnitude of the other effects.

The total effect of an increase in v_t on the exchange rate is given by

$$\lambda_{sv} = 1 + \{[\lambda_{sN}\pi_{N4}\sigma_w^2\sigma_z^2/\Delta(1 + \alpha_1)][-(\theta/(1 - \theta))\pi_{R3}$$
$$- \alpha_2(\pi_{X3} - \pi_{X4}) + \alpha_1\lambda_{sN}(\pi_{N3} - \pi_{N4})]\}$$

(21)

which is written as the full information response plus a term reflecting the sum of effects arising under asymmetric information. In Dornbusch (1976) monetary shocks induce overshooting of the exchange rate because goods prices are predetermined and interest rates and exchange rates adjust to keep the money and capital markets in equilibrium. An increase in the money supply increases real balances, and the interest rate falls to clear the money market. This produces a depreciation of the currency that is greater than the proportionate increase in the money supply so that the currency can be expected to appreciate, thereby maintaining capital market equilibrium. Here there need not be overshooting. The relative price effect that arises under asymmetric information contributes toward overshooting, but the influences from money demand are either ambiguous or offsetting. Both the fall in the relative price and the potential decrease in money demand from an anticipated fall in real income by goods market agents serve to depreciate the currency. The anticipated increase in output by asset market agents, which increases their money demand, and the general expected increase in the relative price of the home good, which induces an expected appreciation of the currency, serve to offset the other effects. If these latter channels are sufficiently strong, the exchange rate need not overshoot in response to an innovation in the money supply. Overshooting is more likely the smaller is α_1, the semielasticity of the demand for money with respect to the interest rate.[13] Overshooting in the Dornbusch model is also larger the smaller is α_1.

The effect of v_t on the nominal domestic price is given by

$$\lambda_{hv} = 1 + \{[(\alpha_3 + \lambda_{sN}\pi_{N4})\sigma_w^2\sigma_z^2/\Delta(1 + \alpha_1)][((1 + \alpha_1 - \theta)/(1 - \theta))\pi_{R3}$$

$$- \alpha_2(\pi_{X3} - \pi_{X4}) + \alpha_1\lambda_{sN}(\pi_{N3} - \pi_{N4})]\} \tag{22}$$

which is also written as its full information response plus a term due to the influence of incomplete information. The same effects as were discussed for the exchange rate operate on the nominal domestic price, but here they contribute toward price undershooting. Both the relative price decrease and the expected correction of the relative price in the future cause the domestic price to increase by less than the percentage increase in v_t. The anticipated fall in real income for agents in the goods market works, though, to increase all nominal prices through its influence on money demand. The increase in output expected by asset market agents increases their demand for money, which contributes toward undershooting.

In the discussions that follow, we will assume that

$$[-(\theta/(1 - \theta))\pi_{R3} - \alpha_2(\pi_{X3} - \pi_{X4}) + \alpha_1\lambda_{sN}(\pi_{N3} - \pi_{N4})] < 0$$

and that

$$\{[(1 - \theta + \alpha_1)/(1 - \theta)]\pi_{R3} - \alpha_2(\pi_{X3} - \pi_{X4}) + \alpha_1\lambda_{sN}(\pi_{N3} - \pi_{N4})\} > 0.$$

With these signs, the exchange rate overshoots with respect to its full information response, and the nominal domestic price undershoots in response to an increase in the money supply.

Effects of w_t

Now consider the effects of a positive shock to real expenditure under the hypothetical situation in which $v_t = z_t = 0$. When a positive but unobservable real shock occurs, $w_t > E_t^G w_t > 0$, since $E_t^G w_t = (-\alpha_3 \phi_{w1} + \lambda_{sN} \pi_{N4} \phi_{w2}) w_t = \{[(\alpha_3 + \lambda_{sN} \pi_{N4})^2 \sigma_v^2 \sigma_w^2 + \lambda_{sN}^2 \pi_{N4}^2 \sigma_w^2 \sigma_z^2]/\Delta\} w_t$. Firms expect an increase in demand and raise their relative prices ($\lambda_{Rw} > 0$), but because $w_t > E_t^G w_t$, they are surprised by the magnitude of demand and increase output ($\lambda_{Yw} > 0$) and deplete inventories ($\lambda_{Nw} < 0$) by more than expected. The increase in real demand for goods arising from the expenditure disturbance is also misinterpreted as a decrease in the supply of money, $E_t^G v_t = (\lambda_{sN} \pi_{N4} \sigma_v^2 \sigma_z^2/\Delta) < 0$. Consequently when firms increase their relative prices, part of the increase in the nominal domestic price is offset by a reduction in all nominal prices due to the perceived decrease in the money supply. The appreciation of the currency that normally accompanies the increase in relative prices is also further exacerbated by the perceived decrease in v_t. The actual coefficients λ_{hw} and λ_{sw}, which give the responses of domestic prices and the exchange rate, are given in appendix 8C. As can be seen by examining these coefficients, the response of the exchange rate to a demand disturbance is smaller in absolute value than its full information counterpart. This is undershooting. This occurs even though the effect of misperceived money reinforces the decrease in the exchange rate due to the relative price effect because the actual demand disturbance is larger than perceived, making the actual change in the exchange rate less than its full information value.

When the direct effect of the relative price change would cause the nominal domestic price to increase, there is also price undershooting in response to a w_t disturbance. If agents knew the true disturbance, they would raise h_t by more because of a demand disturbance, and they would not lower it due to a perceived decrease in the money supply.

Effects of z_t

The effects of the disturbance to the demand for money are ambiguous in the model. Since z_t is transitory, it has no effect on the well-informed agents' expected future spot exchange rate. Participants in the goods market notice this lack of change, but they are confused as to whether a money demand disturbance has occurred or whether there have been offsetting money supply and expenditure disturbances, which could be either both positive or both negative. The goods market participants form $E_t^G z_t = [(\sigma_v^2 \sigma_z^2 + \lambda_{sN}^2 \pi_{sN}^2 \sigma_w^2 \sigma_z^2)/\Delta] z_t$, and $0 < |E_t^G z_t| < |z_t|$. Therefore a positive money demand disturbance is perceived partly as such by agents, but part of the incipient excess demand for money that was eliminated by the observed changes in prices, the interest rate, and the exchange rate is attributed by agents to movements in money and expenditure. Goods market participants form $E_t^G v_t = -\phi_{v1} z_t = [-\lambda_{sN} \pi_{N4}(\alpha_3 + \lambda_{sN} \pi_{N4})\sigma_v^2 \sigma_w^2/\Delta] z_t$ and $E_t^G w_t = -\phi_{w1} z_t = [(\alpha_3 + \lambda_{sN} \pi_{N4})\sigma_v^2 \sigma_w^2/\Delta] z_t$, which both depend on the magnitude of α_3 relative to the absolute value of $\lambda_{sN} \pi_{N4}$. In either case agents attribute part of the excess demand for money to $(E_t^G v_t - \alpha_3 E_t^G w_t) = -(\alpha_3 + \lambda_{sN} \pi_{N4})^2 \sigma_v^2 \sigma_w^2/\Delta < 0$, but when $\alpha_3 > |\lambda_{sN} \pi_{N4}|$, they think that the money supply and expenditure have risen, and when $|\lambda_{sN} \pi_{N4}| > \alpha_3$, they think that both have fallen. Assuming that the latter case characterizes the economy, agents would lower their relative prices in response to an unperceived disturbance to the demand for money. Firms would then be surprised by the magnitude of actual demand and would increase output and decrease their inventory stocks.

If agents had complete information, the exchange rate and all nominal domestic prices would fall by $[1/(1 + \alpha_1)]$ in response to the positive disturbance to the demand for money. When agents think that both the money supply and expenditure have fallen, however, there is exchange rate undershooting since

$$\lambda_{sz} = -[1/(1 + \alpha_1)]$$

$$+ \{[(\alpha_3 + \lambda_{sN} \pi_{N4})\sigma_v^2 \sigma_w^2/\Delta(1 + \alpha_1)][-((\theta/(1 - \theta))\pi_{R3} \quad (23)$$

$$- \alpha_2(\pi_{X3} - \pi_{X4}) + \alpha_1 \lambda_{sN}(\pi_{N3} - \pi_{N4})]\}$$

and domestic price overshooting since

$$\lambda_{hz} = -[1/(1 + \alpha_1)] - \{[(\alpha_3 + \lambda_{sN} \pi_{N4})]\sigma_v^2 \sigma_w^2/\Delta(1 + \alpha_1)] \cdot$$

$$[((1 + \alpha_1 - \theta)/(1 - \theta))\pi_{R3} - \alpha_2(\pi_{X3} - \pi_{X4}) + \alpha_1 \lambda_{sN}(\pi_{N3} - \pi_{N4})]\}.$$

$$(24)$$

This completes our discussion of the reduced form coefficients of the model. In the next section we discuss how these coefficients are affected by changes in the underlying variances of the fundamental stochastic processes.

5. Effects of Changing Variances

An interesting aspect of the described economy is that the reduced form coefficients of the innovations to the supply of money, real expenditure, and the demand for money are functions of the variances of these exogenous processes. Consequently overshooting or undershooting of the full information response changes with changes in the stochastic environment of the economy.

These changes occur because the goods market agents interpret the information in g_{1t} and g_{2t} in different ways depending on their stochastic environment. Instead of developing a full taxonomy of all possible effects, we make a few general observations and provide an example of the results by examining the effects on the coefficients of $\bar{R}_t$ and Y_t of a change in σ_v^2.

In general as the variance of a particular exogenous variable approaches zero, the effects of the other two disturbances approach their full information values. This is true because the uninformed agents continue to observe two separate pieces of information that they know are caused by only two shocks in the limit. Given the structure of the economy, they become fully informed. The behavior of the reduced form coefficients of the variable whose variance is going to zero, on the other hand, is quite different. As the variance becomes smaller, agents attribute less and less of any of their observations to that particular source. Hence the response of the economy moves away from its full information response. If there is overshooting (undershooting), it is exacerbated.

What matters for the signal extraction problems is the ratio of the variances. As the variance of a particular disturbance become larger, its importance as a source of variance in the two signals increases, and agents are able to obtain more precise information about that source of shocks to the economy while becoming less well informed about the other two disturbances. To see this clearly, we examine the effects of changing the variance of the money supply, σ_v^2, on the response of the relative price to the three disturbances.

When σ_v^2 increases, agents know that monetary shocks are a more important part of their stochastic environment. Consequently they are able to estimate v_t more precisely, and v_t has a reduced effect on $\bar{R}_t$, which is translated into a reduced real effect on Y_t and N_t. The increase in the variance of the supply of money makes it more difficult for agents to infer w_t and z_t, and consequently the effect of w_t on $\bar{R}_t$ is smaller and the effect of z_t on $\bar{R}_t$ is larger. Undershooting of $\bar{R}_t$ with respect to w_t and overshooting of $\bar{R}_t$ with respect to z_t are exacerbated.

An interesting aspect of this analysis is the effect of an increase in σ_v^2 on the overall volatility of real output. We define the volatility of a particular variable, x_t, to be the variance of its one-step-ahead prediction error. Letting $\bar{x}_t = E_{t-1}(x_t)$, the definition of volatility is

$$V_{t-1}(x_t) = E_{t-1}(x_t - \bar{x}_t)^2, \tag{25}$$

where the $t - 1$ information set contains all information dated $t - 1$ or earlier.

Under this definition the volatility of Y_t is

$$V_{t-1}(Y_t) = \lambda_{Yk}^2 \sigma_k^2 + \lambda_{Yv}^2 \sigma_v^2 + \lambda_{Yw}^2 \sigma_w^2 + \lambda_{Yz}^2 \sigma_z^2 \tag{26}$$

where the λ coefficients are given in appendix 8C. Using these coefficients one finds

$$V_{t-1}(Y_t) = \lambda_{Yk}^2 \sigma_k^2 + \pi_{Yw}^2 \sigma_w^2 + [(\pi_{Y4}^2 - \pi_{Y3}^2)\sigma_v^2 \sigma_w^2 \sigma_z^2/\Delta]. \tag{27}$$

The first two terms in (28) represent the volatility of real output under full information; the third term arises because firms have less than full information when they must set their prices. An increase in the variance of v_t, w_t, or z_t increases this third term, which indicates that the volatility of real output is larger the more volatile is any aspect of the economy. This result contrasts sharply with the Lucas (1972) framework and is a reflection of the sticky price nature of our model.

6. Exchange Rate Regime Choice and Monetary Policy

Our analysis so far has been based on a freely floating exchange rate with an exogenous supply of money. It is interesting to ask the extent to which monetary policy rules, including rules for fixing the exchange rate or simply intervening in the foreign exchange markets, influence the conditional variance of output. The conditional variance measure we use is

$$V(Y_t) = E(Y_t - E_t^G Y_t)^2. \tag{28}$$

Notice from (10) that $Y_t - E_t^G Y_t = \pi_{Y4}(w_t - E_t^G w_t)$. Consequently a policy designed to minimize (28) is equivalent to a policy designed to minimize

$$V(w_t) = E(w_t - E_t^G w_t)^2, \tag{28a}$$

since π_{Y4} is a structural parameter. Recall that agents in the goods market use the two signals g_{1t} and g_{2t} to form $E_t^G w_t$. Therefore the effect of a policy on (28a) depends on its influence on the information content of these signals.

As a benchmark consider the value of (28a) under freely floating exchange rates. Using (19) and the definitions of g_{1t} and g_{2t} gives

$$V(w_t)|_{\text{free float}} = (1 + \phi_{w1}\alpha_3 - \phi_{w2}\lambda_{sN}\pi_{N4})^2\sigma_w^2 + (\phi_{w1} + \phi_{w2})^2\sigma_v^2 + \phi_{w1}^2\sigma_z^2. \tag{29}$$

The important point to note about this expression is that it lies between 0 and σ_w^2. The expression is greater than zero since neither ϕ_{w1} nor ϕ_{w2} equals zero. The expression must be less than σ_w^2 for the same reason: ϕ_{w1} and ϕ_{w2} were calculated to minimize (28a), and choosing nonzero optimal values for these coefficients implies that g_{1t} and g_{2t} provide useful information about w_t. Hence the value of $V(w_t)$ in (29) must be less than σ_w^2, its value with $\phi_{w1} = \phi_{w2} = 0$.

Against this benchmark consider first the policy of fixing s_t at $\bar{s}$ indefinitely. Such a policy destroys all information signals reaching goods market participants. Recall that g_{1t} is the incipient excess supply in the money market. Under flexible exchange rates, interest rates, exchange rates, prices, and real income adjust to eliminate this incipient excess supply, and in the adjustment, information is passed to firms about the innovations in the economy. With a fixed exchange rate, the supply of money is demand determined, and the incipient excess supply of money is zero. The money supply innovation is the money demand innovation, making $g_{1t} = 0$ for all values of v_t, w_t, z_t. Further, g_{2t}, the information contained in $E_t^A s_{t+1}$, is also affected. Under permanently fixed exchange rates, $E_t^A s_{t+1} = \bar{s}$ for all values of v_t, w_t, and z_t.[14] Consequently, g_{2t} carries no information about w_t. Since neither information source provides news to the goods market agents, they will calculate $E_t^G w_t = 0$, and the conditional variance of w_t is

$$V(w_t)|_{\text{fixed}} = \sigma_w^2, \tag{30}$$

which must be larger than (29).

In order to peg the exchange rate, the monetary authority must buy and sell foreign exchange, and a distinction must be made among changes in the money supply that are due to domestic credit, foreign exchange intervention, and the money multiplier. Let the logarithm of the transactions balances of the economy be

$$m_t = mm_t + \omega b_t + (1 - \omega)d_t \tag{31}$$

where mm_t is the logarithm of the money multiplier, b_t is logarithm of the book value of international reserves, and d_t is the logarithm of domestic credit. Assume that $mm_t = mm_{t-1} + v_{1t}$ and that domestic credit follows the process $d_t = d_{t-1} + v_{2t}$ where v_{1t} and v_{2t} are white noise processes. Under a free float, $b_t = \bar{b}$ and $v_t = v_{1t} + (1 - \omega)v_{2t}$. Under fixed exchange rates, b_t is endogenous and moves to clear the money market. If the monetary authority announces its current foreign exchange intervention, firms in the goods market will know b_t when the money market clears. The announcement of intervention restores g_{1t} to its value under freely floating exchange rates since

$$\omega b_t = -mm_t - (1 - \omega)d_t - \alpha_1 i_t + \alpha_2 \tilde{X}_t + z_t \tag{32}$$

from which agents can infer $g_{1t} = v_t - \alpha_3 w_t - z_t$. However, since the exchange rate is assumed to be fixed forever at $\bar{s}$, $E_t^A s_{t+1} = \bar{s}$ for all values of the disturbances, and $E_t^A s_{t+1}$ still provides no additional information during a regime of permanently fixed exchange rates. Thus while fixing the exchange rate need not remove all information sources concerning w_t if intervention is announced, it does remove some information and will raise the values of (28a) compared to a free float.

A free float without monetary policy feedback is clearly better than a fixed rate, but is it the first-best policy? Our model is one with hierarchical information sets, and the work of Weiss (1980) in similar models alerts us to search for an optimal feedback policy. Let us assume that the monetary authority uses only information from the past but that it may use any past information. The problem facing the authority is to design a policy such that the well-informed agents, acting in their own interests, will reveal to the poorly informed agents a maximum of information concerning w_t.[15] For this problem it is sufficient for the authority to consider rules of the form

$$m_t = m_{t-1} + cv_{t-1} + v_t, \tag{33}$$

where c is to be determined to minimize (28a). Rules of this form will not influence g_{1t}, but such rules will yield

$$g_{2t} = \lambda_{sN}\pi_{N1}w_t + (1 + c)v_t. \tag{34}$$

By setting $c = -1$, the monetary authority makes $g_{2t} = \lambda_{SN}\pi_{N1}w_t$, which conveys full information concerning w_t to the goods market. Consequently (28a) becomes its minimum value, zero.

To understand the intuition behind the optimality of setting $c = -1$, remember that g_{2t} is extracted from $E_t^A s_{t+1}$. By setting $c = -1$, the monetary authority promises an exact offset of this period's monetary disturbance in the next period. Consequently the monetary disturbance, on its own, does not influence the well-informed agents' expectation of next period's exchange rate. When the goods market agents see $E_t^A s_{t+1}$, they know it contains no new information about the money supply shock. Its new information is due entirely to the real disturbance, w_t. Even though the monetary authority does not know the current disturbances, its policy creates an environment in which the well-informed agents reveal their information.

In summary we obtain the following results concerning foreign exchange market intervention and monetary policy:

1. A freely floating exchange rate always performs better than a fixed one because fixing the exchange rate destroys information in the money market. Releasing the extent of foreign exchange intervention restores the money market information but does not restore the forward market information.

2. A free float is not a first-best monetary policy. Even if the monetary authority does not have current information, it can condition policy on past data to induce the well-informed agents to reveal a maximum of information.

Flood and Hodrick (1983b) presented a model quite similar to the current one. The substantive difference between our previous work and the present chapter is that previously we did not postulate the existence of well-informed asset market participants. In Flood and Hodrick (1983b) all agents had identical information sets that corresponded essentially to the information set of the goods market agents in this chapter.

By comparing the policy implications of the two papers, we discover the importance of the well-informed agents in an economy's performance. In the previous paper we found that all foreign exchange market intervention or monetary feedback policies were equivalent to each other, and all such policies were superior to a fixed exchange rate regime unless the monetary authority announced its foreign exchange intervention. If such intervention were announced, then fixed rates became equivalent to all other monetary policies.

The central difference between the current chapter and the previous paper is the appearance here of the information signal g_{2t}, which is the information content of $E_t^A s_{t+1}$. In the previous paper all agents had identical information so $E_t^A s_{t+1} = E_t^G s_{t+1}$ and $g_{2t} = 0$ for all values of the disturbances and for all policies. Currently, though, $E_t^A s_{t+1}$ is an independent information source. Because fixed rates destroy this source, they are inferior to flexible rates even when intervention is announced. Further the information content of this information source can be manipulated by a monetary authority to reveal a maximum amount of information concerning specific variables important for stabilizing real output.

7. Concluding Remarks

We have presented an open economy model of the business cycle based on optimizing behavior of inventory-holding firms. Prices are sticky in our model in the sense that they do not respond fully to new disturbances because price-setting agents are not fully aware of the disturbances in the economy at the time prices are set. In our setup some agents, however, are fully aware of these disturbances, and therefore an interesting policy problem arises. How does a monetary authority design a monetary policy such that the well-informed agents, acting in their own self-interest, will reveal a maximum amount of information to the relatively poorly informed price setters? We find that a policy of fixed exchange rates is the worst possible policy for revealing information. Any floating exchange rate scheme will dominate fixed rates. A pure floating rate, however, is dominated by an optimal feedback policy where the monetary authority reacts to past money supply disturbances.

Appendix 8A The Representative Firm's Problem

This appendix provides the solutions to the representative firm's maximization problem given by (4) in the text, demonstrates that summing these solutions produces the aggregate Euler equations (5a, b), and explains the steps necessary to obtain the solutions in table 8.1.

The firm's problem is rewritten here as (A1):

$$\max_{\{R^j_{t+i}, N^j_{t+i}\}} E^j_t \sum_{i=0}^{\infty} \{D^j_{t+i}R^j_{t+i} - (\gamma_0 + k_{t+i} + \gamma_1 Y_{t+i}) Y^j_{t+i} - (\gamma_2/2)(Y^j_{t+i})^2$$

$$- \delta_1 N_{t+i-1} N^j_{t+i-1} - (\delta_2/2)(N^j_{t+i-1})^2 \} \sigma^i \qquad j = 1, 2, \ldots, J \tag{A1}$$

subject to

$$Y^j_t = D^j_t + N^j_t - N^j_{t-1}, \tag{A2}$$

$$D^j_t = (1/J)D_t - J\beta_4(R^j_t - \bar{R}_t) + e^j_t, \tag{A3}$$

and an initial level of inventories, N^j_{t-1}. The operator $E^j_t(\cdot)$ is the expectation operator conditional on information in the goods market of firm j, which is common across firms except that each firm knows its own relative demand shock e^j_t. In (A3), $D_t = \beta_0 - \beta_1 \bar{R}_t + \beta_2(N_t - N_{t-1}) + \beta_2 w_t$ is the quasi-reduced form for aggregate demand derived in (6). A solution to the problem is found by differentiating (A1) with respect to R^j_{t+1} and N^j_{t+i}, $i = 0, 1, 2, \ldots$, setting the derivative equal to zero and imposing the transversality condition. In the maximization it is assumed that each firm is small enough such that it takes as given the economy-wide average price, $\bar{R}_t \equiv \sum_{j=1}^{J} R^j_t/J$, the economy-wide output, $Y_t \equiv \sum_{j=1}^{J} Y^j_t$, and economy-wide level of inventories, $N_t \equiv \sum_{j=1}^{J} N^j_t$.

Differentiating with respect to R^j_{t+i} and N^j_{t+i} gives the following system of stochastic Euler equations:

$$E^j_t\{(1/J)D_{t+i} + e^j_{t+i} - 2J\beta_4 R^j_{t+i} + J\beta_4 \bar{R}_{t+i} + (\gamma_0 + k_{t+i} + \gamma_1 Y_{t+i})J\beta_4$$

$$+ J\beta_4\gamma_2[N^j_{t+i} - N^j_{t+i-1} + (1/J)D_{t+i} + e^j_{t+i} - J\beta_4(R^j_{t+i} - \bar{R}_{t+i})]\} = 0, \tag{A4a}$$

$$E^j_t\{-(\gamma_1 Y_{t+i} + k_{t+i} + \gamma_0) - \gamma_2[(1/J)D_{t+i} + e^j_{t+i} - J\beta_4(R^j_{t+i} - \bar{R}_{t+i})$$

$$+ N^j_{t+i} - N^j_{t+i-1}] + \sigma(\gamma_1 Y_{t+i+1} + k_{t+i+1} + \gamma_0) + \sigma\gamma_2[(1/J)D_{t+i+1}$$

$$+ e^j_{t+i+1} - J\beta_4(R^j_{t+i+1} - R_{t+i+1}) + N^j_{t+i+1} - N^j_{t+i}] - \sigma[\delta_1 N_{t+i}$$

$$+ \delta_2 N^j_{t+i}]\} = 0 \qquad i = 0, 1, 2, \ldots. \tag{A4b}$$

Following Sargent (1979), the appropriate transversality condition is found by examining the finite horizon problem, differentiating with respect to the final inventory stock, N_{t+T}^j, and taking the limit as T goes to infinity. The transversality condition is

$$\lim_{T\to\infty} \{E_t^j[-(\gamma_1 Y_{t+T} + k_{t+T} + \gamma_0) - \gamma_2(D_{t+T}^j + N_{t+T}^j - N_{t+T-1}^j)]\sigma^T\} = 0.$$
$$(A5)$$

In a finite horizon world, the firm would be tempted to meet its entire final period demand out of its negative inventory stock since it would accept payment today but never deliver the goods and never incur any inventory carrying cost. This tendency remains in the infinite horizon problem, but the transversality condition prevents inventories from growing faster than the rate $1/\sigma$.

The aggregate Euler equations in the text (5a, b), are found summing (A4a, b) across the J firm in the economy using the definitions of Y_t, N_t, $\bar{R}_t$, and the fact that $\sum_{j=1}^J e_t^j = 0$. Because the e_t^j sum to zero and are not useful for forecasting the future, the summation can be simplified by substituting the common information set I_t^G for the firm-specific set, which is I_t^G plus e_t^j.

A solution to the two Euler equations requires several steps. First, solve (5a) for $E_t^G \bar{R}_{t+i}$ and substitute this into (5b). The resulting equation is a second-order difference equation in $E_t^G N_{t+i}$. The solution to the equation is readily obtained by the method of undetermined coefficients. Conjecture that the solution will have the form of (7b). Substitute this into the equation to eliminate terms in $E_t^G N_t$ and $E_t^G N_{t+1}$. The resulting coefficients can then be equated and solved for the π coefficients. There are two possible values for π_{N1}, one less than 1 and one greater than $1/\sigma$. We choose the stable value since otherwise aggregate inventories would grow at a rate greater than $1/\sigma$. The transversality condition derived above prevents each firm from following such a path for accumulation of inventories; hence the choice of the stable root is the only choice consistent with the optimizing strategies of the firms.

Rather than treating R_{t+i}^j and N_{t+i}^j as the choice variables in (A1), we could have chosen D_{t+i}^j and N_{t+i}^j as the choice variables, in which case the same firm behavior would have been indicated, but it would have been clearer that firms choose their relative price to pick an expected level of sales that equates expected marginal revenue to expected marginal cost of production even though sales and production are not equal. The second first-order condition requires equality between the marginal cost of production today plus the expected marginal inventory holding costs and the discounted expected marginal cost of producing in the future.

Appendix 8B The Quasi-Reduced-Form Coefficients

$\pi_{R0} = \text{constant}$

$\pi_{R1} = (\Delta_2/\Delta_1)(\pi_{N1} - 1), \qquad \pi_{R1} < 0$

$\pi_{R2} = (J^2 B_4/\Delta_1) + (\Delta_2/\Delta_1)\pi_{N3}, \qquad \pi_{R2} > 0$

$\pi_{R3} = (\Delta_2/\Delta_1)\pi_{N2} + (\Delta_3/\Delta_1), \qquad \pi_{R3} > 0$

$\pi_{N0} = \text{constant}$

$\pi_{N1} = (1/2)[A - (A^2 - 4/\sigma)^{1/2}], \qquad 0 < \pi_{N1} < 1$

$\pi_{N2} = J(\beta_1 + J^2\beta_4)/(\pi_{N1} - A)\sigma(J\gamma_1 + \gamma_2)(\beta_1 + J^2\beta_3\beta_4), \qquad \pi_{N2} < 0$

$\pi_{N3} = J^2\beta_3\beta_4/(\pi_{N1} - A)\sigma(\beta_1 + J^2\beta_3\beta_4), \qquad \pi_{N3} < 0$

$\pi_{N4} = -\beta_3/\{\beta_3 + [\sigma(1 - \pi_{N1})(\beta_1 + J^2\beta_3\beta_4)/\Delta_1] + \sigma u\},$

$\quad -1 < \pi_{N4} < \pi_{N3} < 0$

$A = 1 + (1/\sigma) + \mu\Delta_1/(\beta_1 + J^2\beta_3\beta_4)$

$\Delta_1 = \beta_1 + J^2\beta_1\beta_4\gamma_1 + J\beta_1\beta_4\gamma_2 + J^2\beta_4$

$\Delta_2 = \beta_2 + J^2\beta_3\beta_4\gamma_1 + J\beta_3\beta_4\gamma_2$

$\Delta_3 = \beta_3 + J^2\beta_3\beta_4\gamma_1 + J\beta_3\beta_4\gamma_2$

$\mu = (\delta_1 J + \delta_2)$

$\pi_{Y0} = \text{constant}$

$\pi_{Y1} = [(\beta_1 + J^2\beta_3\beta_4)/\Delta_1](\pi_{N1} - 1) \qquad \pi_{Y1} < 0$

$\pi_{Y2} = [-J^2\beta_1\beta_4 + (\beta_1 + J^2\beta_3\beta_4)\pi_{N3}]/\Delta_1 \qquad \pi_{Y2} < 0$

$\pi_{Y3} = (J^2\beta_3\beta_4/\Delta_1)(1 - \pi_{N1}) \qquad 0 < \pi_{N3}$

$\pi_{Y4} = \beta_3(1 + \pi_{N4}) \qquad 0 < \pi_{N3} < \pi_{N4}$

$\pi_{X1} = \kappa_1\pi_{R1} + \kappa_2\pi_{Y1} \qquad \pi_{X1} < 0$

$\pi_{X2} = \kappa_1\pi_{R2} + \kappa_2\pi_{Y2}$

$\pi_{X3} = \kappa_1\pi_{R3} + \kappa_2\pi_{Y3} - \kappa_2(n_a/n)\pi_{Y4}$

$\pi_{X4} = \kappa_1(n_a/n)\pi_{Y4}$

Appendix 8C The Reduced-Form Coefficients

This appendix records the actual values of the reduced form coefficients, the λ coefficients, whose algebraic signs are given in table 8.3. For a typical variable, $Q_t = N_t$, Y_t, $\bar{R}_t$, s_t, or $\bar{h}_t$, the reduced form equation is the following:

$$Q_t = \lambda_{QN} N_{t-1} + \lambda_{Qk} k_t + \lambda_{Qm} m_{t-1} + \lambda_{Qv} v_t + \lambda_{Qw} w_t + \lambda_{Qz} z_t. \tag{C1}$$

In each case the λ coefficients are written as the response of the variable under full information plus a term in brackets $\{\cdot\}$ that is the deviation of the response due to incomplete information in the goods market.

Coefficients of N_t Equation

$$\lambda_{NN} = \pi_{N1} \qquad 0 < \lambda_{NN} < 1$$

$$\lambda_{Nk} = \pi_{N2} \qquad \lambda_{Nk} < 0$$

$$\lambda_{Nm} = 0$$

$$\lambda_{Nv} = \{(\pi_{N3} - \pi_{N4})(\lambda_{sN} \pi_{N4} \sigma_w^2 \sigma_z^2 / \Delta)\}, \qquad \lambda_{Nv} < 0$$

$$\lambda_{Nw} = \pi_{N3} - \{(\pi_{N3} - \pi_{N4})(\sigma_v^2 \sigma_z^2 / \Delta)\}, \qquad \lambda_{Nw} < 0$$

$$\lambda_{Nz} = \{(\pi_{N3} - \pi_{N4})(\alpha_3 + \lambda_{sN} \pi_{N4})(\sigma_v^2 \sigma_w^2 / \Delta)\},$$

Coefficients of Y_t Equation

$$\lambda_{YN} = \pi_{Y1}, \qquad \lambda_{YN} < 0$$

$$\lambda_{Yk} = \pi_{Y2}, \qquad \lambda_{Yk} < 0$$

$$\lambda_{Ym} = 0$$

$$\lambda_{Yv} = \{(\pi_{Y3} - \pi_{Y3})(\lambda_{sN} \pi_{N4} \sigma_w^2 \sigma_z^2 / \Delta)\}, \qquad 0 < \lambda_{Yv}$$

$$\lambda_{Yw} = \pi_{Y3} - \{(\pi_{Y3} - \pi_{Y4})(\sigma_v^2 \sigma_z^2 / \Delta)\}, \qquad 0 < \lambda_{Yw}$$

$$\lambda_{Yz} = \{(\pi_{Y3} - \pi_{Y4})(\alpha_3 + \lambda_{sN} \pi_{N4})(\sigma_v^2 \sigma_w^2 / \Delta)\}$$

Coefficients of $\bar{R}_t$ Equation

$$\lambda_{RN} = \pi_{R1}, \qquad \lambda_{RN} < 0$$

$$\lambda_{Rk} = \pi_{R2}, \qquad 0 < \lambda_{Rk}$$

$$\lambda_{Rm} = 0$$

$$\lambda_{Rv} = \{\pi_{R3}\lambda_{sN}\pi_{N4}\sigma_w^2\sigma_z^2/\Delta\}, \qquad \lambda_{Rv} < 0$$

$$\lambda_{Rw} = \pi_{R3} - \{\pi_{R3}\sigma_v^2\sigma_z^2/\Delta\} \qquad 0 < \lambda_{Rw}$$

$$\lambda_{Rz} = \{\pi_{R3}(\alpha_3 + \lambda_{sN}\pi_{N4})\sigma_v^2\sigma_w^2/\Delta\}$$

Coefficients of s_t Equation

$$\lambda_{sN} = [-(\theta/(1 - \theta))\pi_{R1} - \alpha_2(\kappa_1\pi_{R1} + \kappa_2\pi_{Y1})]/[1 + \alpha_1(1 - \pi_{N1})],$$

$$0 < \lambda_{sN}$$

$$\lambda_{sk} = [-(\theta/(1 - \theta))\pi_{R2} - \alpha_2(\kappa_1\pi_{R2} + \kappa_2\pi_{Y2}) + \alpha_1\lambda_{sN}\pi_{N2}]/(1 + \alpha_1)$$

$$\lambda_{sv} = 1 + \{\lambda_{sm} + 1\Theta_s\lambda_{sN}\pi_{N4}\sigma_w^2\sigma_z^2/\Delta(1 + \alpha_1)\}$$

$$\lambda_{sw} = [-(\alpha_2/\rho_2) - \alpha_2\pi_{x3} + \alpha_1\lambda_{sN}\pi_{N3} - (\theta/(1 - \theta))\pi_{R3}]/(1 - \alpha_1)$$

$$- \{\Theta_s\sigma_v^2\sigma_z^2/\Delta(1 + \alpha_1)\}$$

$$\lambda_{sz} = -[1/(1 + \alpha_1)] + \{\Theta_s(\alpha_3 + \lambda_{sN}\pi_{N4})\sigma_v^2\sigma_w^2/\Delta(1 + \alpha_1)\}$$

$$\Theta_s = [-(\theta/(1 - \theta))\pi_{R3} + \alpha_1\lambda_{sN}(\pi_{N3} - \pi_{N4}) - \alpha_2(\pi_{x3} - \pi_{x4})]$$

Coefficients of $\bar{h}_t$ Equation

$$\lambda_{hN} = [\pi_{R1}(1 + \alpha_1(1 - \pi_{N1})/(1 - \theta)]$$

$$- \alpha_2(\kappa_1\pi_{R1} + \kappa_2\pi_{Y1})]/[1 + \alpha_1(1 - \pi_{N1})]$$

$$\lambda_{hk} = [((1 + \alpha_1 - \theta)/(1 - \theta))\pi_{R2} - \alpha_2(\kappa_1\pi_{R2} + \kappa_2\pi_{Y2})$$

$$+ \alpha_1\lambda_{sN}\pi_{N2}]/(1 + \alpha_1)$$

$$\lambda_{hm} = 1$$

$$\lambda_{hv} = 1 + \{\theta_h(\lambda_{sN}\pi_{N4}\sigma_w^2\sigma_z^2/\Delta(1 + \alpha_1)]$$

$$\lambda_{hw} = \left[-(\alpha_2 | \rho_2) - \alpha_2 \pi_{X3} + \alpha_1 \lambda_{sN} \pi_{N3} + ((1 + \alpha_1 - \theta)/(1 - \theta)) \pi_{R3} \right]$$
$$- \{ \theta_h \sigma_v^2 \sigma_z^2 / \Delta(1 + \alpha_1) \}$$

$$\lambda_{hz} = \left[1/(1 + \alpha_1) \right] + \{ \theta_h (\alpha_3 + \lambda_{sN} \pi_{N4}) \sigma_v^2 \sigma_w^2 / \Delta(1 + \alpha_1) \}$$

$$\theta_h = \left[((1 + \alpha_1 - \theta)/(1 - \theta)) \pi_{R3} + \alpha_1 \lambda_{sN} (\pi_{N3} - \pi_{N4}) - \alpha_2 (\pi_{X3} - \pi_{X4}) \right]$$

Notes

1. Flood and Hodrick (1983b) describes the empirical regularities and discusses in detail the sense in which the model is consistent with them. A controversial aspect of the model is that real effects of monetary shocks depend only on the perceived rather than the unexpected shock. An unexpected shock is unpredictable based on past information, while an unperceived shock cannot be inferred from current information. This distinction separates the island models based on the work of Lucas (1972, 1973) and Barro (1976, 1980) from the wage indexing models based on the work of Gray (1976) and Fischer (1977).

2. Barro (1980), King (1982), and Grossman and Weiss (1982) also emphasize the information content of asset prices in their closed-economy models of the business cycle. Bhandari (1982) and Kimbrough (1983) stress these influences in open-economy frameworks.

3. The length of the period is not determined endogenously. Presumably it is defined by the length of time over which firms must hold their prices fixed. As such the assumption that this length of time coincides with the length of time over which people hold a given portfolio is an arbitrary analytical convenience. Both decisions are properly viewed as falling within the realm of economics, but developing tractable paradigms based on equilibria in which some decisions are made for a longer period of time than other decisions has proved difficult. Models with overlapping wage contracts such as Taylor (1979), Dornbusch (1982), and Bhandari (1982) only postulate the degree of overlap.

4. In this chapter we treat foreign demand as nonstochastic; in Flood and Hodrick (1983b) stochastic foreign demand is allowed. We discuss the aggregation leading to (2) in section 2.

5. In the model we postulate that firms take aggregate and economy-wide average decisions as invariant to their own behavior. Implicitly we treat the number of firms as very large, and our model is well defined in the limit as $J \to \infty$, which provides a formal justification for our behavioral assumption.

6. The stochastic disturbance is intended to capture noncyclical fluctuations in the costs of production produced by changes in the relative prices of raw materials, energy, and other real phenomena that are not included in the model. It is also the dual of the technological change disturbance used frequently in the literature.

7. The formulation of inventory costs allows negative inventories, which we interpret as a backlog of unfilled orders, as do Blinder and Fischer (1981), Blinder (1982), and Eichenbaum (1983).

8. Our specification abstracts from possibly important aspects of the economy associated with time-varying discount rates.

9. Eichenbaum (1983) analyzed an environment very similar to this one. He demonstrated the equivalence of the form of the decision rules at the industry level for three different industry structures: a J-plant monopolist, J perfect competitors, and J Nash competitors. Without knowledge of the number J, the aggregation of the decision rules we derive will be robust to alternative firm-level decision rules.

10. An alternative way of presenting the firm's maximization problem begins with the dynamic programming problem and works backward to the solution for the optimal prices. The two approaches are equivalent for quadratic optimization problems.

11. Recent empirical work, such as Hansen and Hodrick (1983), indicates that uncovered interest parity is only an approximation. In using this approximation, we are asserting that the errors made here are of no greater order of magnitude than the errors made in our other approximations.

12. We assume that the income effects of money demand do not dominate the direct relative price effects. Appendix 8.C indicates that the effect of a fall in output and the increase in the relative price could increase expected expenditure, increasing money demand and decreasing both the nominal domestic price and the exchange rate. Without further restrictions on the parameters, we cannot rule out this response.

13. If the demand for money were also sensitive to the anticipated change in the nominal price of the home good, another channel would arise that would contribute toward overshooting since the relative price causes h_t to be temporally lower than its steady state.

14. Flood and Garber (1983) analyze a fixed exchange rate regime that may collapse. Here we ignore such a possiblility.

15. We now assume that the political forces that lead to the previous exogenous domestic credit policy no longer dominate monetary policy, which frees it to be an instrument available for stabilization of real output.

References

Barro, R. 1976. "Rational Expectations and the Role of Monetary Policy." *Journal of Monetary Economics* 2 (January): 1–32.

Barro, R. 1980. "A Capital Market in an Equilibrium Business Cycle Model." *Econometrica* 48 (September): 1393–1417.

Bhandari, J. 1982. "Informational Efficiency and the Open Economy." *Journal of Money Credit and Banking* 14, no. 4 (November): 457–478.

Bhandari, J. 1983. "Staggered Wage Setting and Exchange Rate Policy in an Economy with Capital Assets." *Journal of International Money and Finance* 1, no. 3 (December): 275–292.

Blinder, A. 1982. "Inventories and Sticky Prices: More on the Microfoundations of Macroeconomics." *American Economic Review* 72 (June): 334–348.

Blinder, A., and S. Fischer. 1981. "Inventories, Rational Expectations, and the Business Cycle." *Journal of Monetary Economics* 8 (November): 277–304.

Clower, R. W. 1967. "A Reconsideration of the Microfoundations of Monetry Theory." *Western Economic Journal* 6 (January): 1–19.

Dornbusch, R. 1976. "Expectations and Exchange Rate Dynamics." *Journal of Political Economy* 84 (December): 1161–1176.

Dornbusch, R. 1982. "PPP Exchange Rate Rules and Macroeconomic Stability." *Journal of Political Economy* 90, 1 (February): 58–65.

Eichenbaum, M. 1983. "A Rational Expectations Equilibrium Model of Inventories of Finished Goods and Employment." *Journal of Monetary Economics* 12 (August): 259–278.

Fischer, S. 1977. "Long-term Contracts, Rational Expectations and the Optimal Money Supply Rule." *Journal of Political Economy* 85 (February): 191–205.

Flood, R. P., and P. M. Garber, 1983, "Collapsing Exchange Rate Regimes: Some Linear Examples." Working Paper, Northwestern University, forthcoming *Journal of International Economics*.

Flood, R. P., and R. J. Hodrick. 1983a. "Exchange Rate and Price Dynamics with Asymmetric Information." Working Paper 65-82-83 G.S.I.A. Carnegie-Mellon University.

Flood, R. P., and R. J. Hodrick. 1983b. "Optimal Price and Inventory Adjustment in an Open-Economy Model of the Business Cycle." National Bureau of Economic Research Working Paper 1089.

Gray, J. 1976. "Wage Indexation: A Macroeconomic Approach." *Journal of Monetary Economics* 2 (April): 221–236.

Grossman, S., and L. Weiss. 1982. "Heterogeneous Information and the Theory of the Business Cycle." *Journal of Political Economy* 19, no. 4 (August): 699–727.

Hansen, L., and R. Hodrick. 1983. "Risk Averse Speculation in the Forward Exchange Market: An Econometric Analysis of Linear Models." In J. Frenkel, ed., *Exchange Rates and International Macroeconmics*. Chicago: University of Chicago Press. 113–142.

Kimbrough, Kent., 1983. "The Information Content of the Exchange Rate and the Stability of Real Output under Alternative Exchange-Rate Regimes." *Journal of International Money and Finance* 2, no. 1 (April): 27–38.

King, R. "Monetary Policy and the Information Content of Prices." *Journal of Political Economy* 90 (April): 247–279.

Lucas, R. 1973. "Expectations and the Neutrality of Money," *Journal of Economic Theory* 4 (June): 103–124.

Lucas, R. 1973. "Some International Evidence on Output-Inflation Tradeoffs." *American Economic Review* 63 (June): 326–334.

Lucas, R. 1980. "Equilibrium in a Pure Currency Economy." In *Models of Monetary Economics*, edited by J. Kareken and N. Wallace. Minneapolis: Federal Reserve Bank.

Mussa, M. 1982. "A Model of Exchange Rate Dynamics." *Journal of Political Economy* 90 (February): 74–104.

Sargent, T. 1979, *Macroeconomic Theory*, Academic Press, New York.

Taylor, John B. 1979. "Stagged Wage Setting in a Macro Model." *American Economic Review Papers and Proceeding* 69 (May): 108–113.

Weiss, Lawrence. 1980. "The Role for Active Monetary Policy in a Rational Expectations Model." *Journal of Political Economy* 88, no. 2 (April): 221–233.

9 International Capital Mobility and the Coordination of Monetary Rules

Nicholas Carlozzi and John B. Taylor

International capital mobility is cited frequently by economists as a serious constraint on domestic monetary policy. Since highly mobile capital forces a close linkage among interest rates in different countries, it appears that any one country's interest rate cannot be manipulated independently in order to achieve an efficient domestic macroeconomic performance. Although the classic Mundell-Fleming models with flexible exchange rates show that perfect capital mobility need not reduce the effectiveness of monetary policy, recent research on exchange rate over-shooting, on the direct inflationary effects of exchange rate depreciation, and on the beggar-thy-neighbor contractionary repercussions of domestic monetary expansion seems to have reinforced the conventional reasoning that macroeconomic goals are difficult to achieve under such circumstances. In reviewing the literature, Tobin (1978) concluded that capital mobility is such a hindrance to efficient macroeconomic performance that we should "throw some sand in the wheels of our excessively efficient international money markets." By making the international capital market less efficient, domestic macroeconomic performance might become more efficient.

The purpose of this chapter is to develop a quantitative framework for evaluating macroeconomic policy rules in a world of flexible exchange rates and perfect capital mobility. We begin by defining a criterion for measuring macroeconomic performance. In early fixed-price demand-oriented models, the natural criterion for macroeconomic performance was real output stability; policy would be effective or ineffective depending on whether it could be used to stimulate, and thereby stabilize, real output. However, the resurgence of aggregate supply issues and renewed emphasis on the simultaneous determination of prices and output have created the need for a broader measure of macroeconomic performance, one that includes both price and output stability. The static Phillips curve policy trade-off—in which macroeconomic performance can be measured in terms of the level of inflation and output—could serve as such a measure of macroeconomic efficiency were it not for widely documented shifts of this trade-off. An alternative performance measure, in which macroeconomic performance is measured in terms of fluctuations in inflation and output, is used in this chapter.[1]

The framework for policy evaluation involves the application of this performance measure to a two-country model in which financial capital is perfectly mobile, exchange rates are flexible, and expectations are rational. Aggregate supply is modeled using a staggered price setting approach in which there are recurrent supply or price shocks in each country. We assume that all shocks to the model are due to such price shocks, abstracting entirely from demand shocks. It is assumed that the two countries are linked by aggregate spending spillovers, relative price effects, and markup pricing arrangements. Each country is assumed to follow a monetary policy rule that can be characterized by how strongly the money supply responds to price shocks. The model is solved and analyzed through deterministic and stochastic simulation techniques that enforce the rational expectations restrictions. Using these techniques we evaluate how the choice of a monetary policy rule in one country affects the macroeconomic performance of the other country. This provides a way to assess the importance of capital mobility for macroeconomic interdependence.

The results of this evaluation suggest that international capital mobility is not necessarily an impediment to efficient domestic macroeconomic performance. For certain values of the parameters of our model and for certain monetary policy rules, changes in the expected appreciation or depreciation of the exchange rate along with differentials between real interest rates in the two countries can permit macroeconomic performance in one country to be relatively independent of the policy rule chosen by the other country. The results do not hold universally, however. Interdependence can become stronger with alternative parameter or policy configurations. Our results therefore suggest a need for econometric work to determine the size of certain crucial parameters.

In section 1 we review the aggregate supply side of the model and show how policy can be evaluated in terms of output and price variability using a rudimentary quantity theory model of aggregate demand. In section 2 we discuss a more detailed model of aggregate demand, which includes interest rate effects, and we examine monetary policy in a closed economy version of this model. In order to achieve macroeconomic efficiency in the closed economy, policymakers must offset the effects of fluctuations in the expected inflation rate. It is shown that a real interest rate rule automatically provides this offset. Section 3 describes the full two-country model and examines the interaction between the macroeconomic policies of each country.

1. Aggregate Supply

The aggregate supply side of the model is derived from staggered wage-setting assumptions as modified to incorporate the price linkages important in open economy applications.[2] The staggered wage setting approach has the advantage of incorporating forward-looking (rational expectations) behavior while allowing for realistic short-run rigidities that lead to a trade-off between output and price stability. These rigidities also guarantee the effectiveness of monetary policy in stabilizing real output, despite the existence of rational expectations. Nevertheless an increase in the rate of money growth is neutral over the long run, increasing the rate of inflation but not output; that is, the long-run Phillips curve is vertical.

In general we assume that wages are set for n periods and that $1/n$ of all workers have their wages determined at the start of each period. The equations of the supply side for a single open economy (the home economy) can then be written:

$$x_t = \frac{\delta}{n} \sum_{i=0}^{n-1} \hat{w}_{t+i} + \frac{1-\delta}{n} \sum_{i=0}^{n-1} \hat{p}_{t+i} + \frac{\gamma}{n} \sum_{i=0}^{n-1} \hat{y}_{t+i} + \varepsilon_t, \tag{1}$$

$$w_t = \frac{1}{n} \sum_{i=0}^{n-1} x_{t-i}, \tag{2}$$

$$p_t = \theta w_t + (1-\theta)(e_t + p_t^*), \tag{3}$$

where p_t is the log of the price level, y_t is the log of real GNP relative to trend, w_t is the log of the average wage, x_t is the log of the contract wage set in period t to last three periods, e_t is the log of the exchange rate, and ε_t is a supply shock. The hats on the variables indicate expectations based on information available through period t. The asterisks identify variables external to the home country (the rest of the world). For example, p_t^* in equation (3) is the average price level in the rest of the world.

Equation (1) is the wage determination equation; it reflects the tendency for contract wages to be bid up if aggregate wages or prices are expected to rise or if aggregate demand, as represented by y_t, is expected to rise.[3] The distributed leads in equation (1) extend for n periods because contracts last n periods. The weights on these distributed leads are equal because workers are assumed to average future price, wage, and demand conditions over the n future periods of the contract. Parameter δ represents the relative importance of prices versus wages. In order to preserve the long-run neutrality of money growth, the weights on prices and wages together must sum to one, as indicated in the notation of equation (1). Parameter γ measures the sensitivity of wage adjustment to demand pressures. Equation (2) defines the aggregate wage in terms of contract wages negotiated in the current and previous periods.

Equation (3) is the price equation; it states that prices are set as a markup on wage costs, w_t, and the costs of imported inputs denominated in domestic currency units, $(e_t + p_t^*)$. The effects of exchange rates and foreign prices on domestic price determination, as represented in (3), are an important feature of the supply side of the model. It is through this channel that foreign price shocks or exchange rate depreciations (increases in e) have inflationary consequences. An alternative way to model such external price linkages would be to assume that wages are directly indexed to consumer prices that include the domestic price of imported goods. This alternative would give somewhat different dynamic responses of wages and prices to foreign price shocks or exchange rate changes. However, except for the extreme case of perfect, instantaneous indexing, the effects on the output-inflation trade-off would be similar to those obtained in this chapter.

At this point it is useful to review briefly how this aggregate supply framework (with the closed economy assumption $\theta = 1$) can be joined with a rudimentary treatment of aggregate demand to generate a macropolicy trade-off between output and price stability.[4] Consider the simple quantity equation $y_t + p_t = m_t$, where m_t is the log of the money supply, and suppose that monetary policy is driven by the rule $m_t = \alpha p_t$, in which α is the accommodation parameter. An aggregate demand relationship between p_t and y_t can be derived by substituting the money supply rule into the quantity equation, resulting in $y_t = -(1 - \alpha)p_t$. Substituting this aggregate demand relationship into (1) and substituting equations (2) and (3) into (1) results in a two-sided difference equation in x_t, involving both leads and lags. The leads from this equation can be eliminated to generate a stochastic difference equation in x_t. The shock ε_t is the disturbance in this relation. From (3), one can then obtain an autoregressive moving average, ARMA $(n - 1, n - 1)$, representation for p_t in which the parameters depend on the policy parameter α and the structural parameters δ

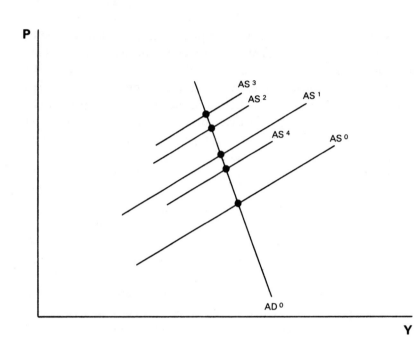

Figure 9.1
Steep aggregate demand curve

and y. The behavior of y_t follows directly from the aggregate demand relation. The variances of both p_t and y_t can then be calculated from these relationships. The properties of the variances are such that the variance of p_t increases and the variance of y_t decreases as α rises. This traces out a trade-off curve; a more accommodative policy (higher α) results in more output stability and less price stability.

The mechanics of this trade-off and its dependence on α can be explained graphically. Figure 9.1 illustrates an aggregate supply curve corresponding to the difference equation for p_t. The supply curve shifts with lagged movements in p and the shock term ε_t. The α parameter determines the slope of the aggregate demand curve, also shown in figure 9.1.

The slope of this curve determines how large the output effects of a supply shock will be. A steep aggregate demand curve (α near 1) results in very small output fluctuations, given the size of supply shocks. However, α close to 1 also causes a given shock to the aggregate supply curve to persist for a long time. A flat aggregate demand curve, as illustrated in figure 9.2, increases output fluctuations while reducing price fluctuations.

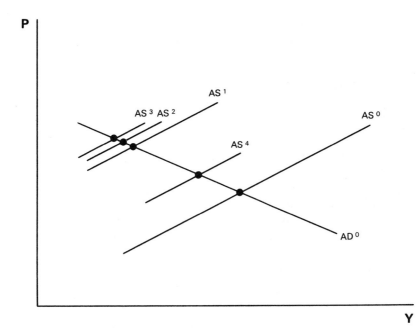

Figure 9.2
Flat aggregate demand curve

2. Aggregate Demand, Interest Rates, and Policy Rules

A more explicit model of aggregate demand than the simple quantity equation is necessary in order to capture the impact of capital mobility on the output-price stability trade-off. Our approach to the demand side is conventional and corresponds closely with that of the Mundell-Fleming models. We distinguish between the effects of the real and the nominal interest rate. The real interest rate is assumed to affect expenditures on investment and consumer durable goods, while the nominal interest rate is assumed to affect the demand for money. Inflationary expectations, which determine the differential between the real and the nominal rate of interest, are formed rationally. We also allow nominal interest rates to differ at home and abroad to allow for the expected rate of exchange rate appreciation, a modification of the Mundell-Fleming model explored by Dornbusch (1976) and others.

The aggregate demand equations for the home country can be written as:

$$y_t = -dr_t + f(e_t + p_t^* - p_t) + gy_t^* \tag{4}$$

$$m_t - p_t = -bi_t + ay_t \tag{5}$$

$$r_t = i_t - \hat{\pi}_t \tag{6}$$

where $\pi_t = p_{t+1} - p_t$ is the rate of inflation, r_t is the real interest rate, i_t is the nominal interest rate, and m_t is the log of the money supply. Equation (4) is an "IS"-type equation in which total demand depends on the real interest rate, terms of trade, and foreign demand (parameters d, f, g, b, and a are positive). Inclusion of the terms of trade in this way permits short-run deviations from purchasing power parity. The elasticity is positive because exports are stimulated and imports are reduced by a higher relative price of foreign goods. Equation (5) is the money demand equation, and equation (6) defines the real rate of interest. Because our analysis will not consider demand side shocks, we have omitted shift terms from these equations. All variables are measured as proportional deviations from secular trend and therefore have a zero mean.

In a simple quantity model of aggregate demand, the natural way to write the monetary reaction function is in terms of the money supply, as was done in section 1. There are obvious alternatives to money supply rules when interest rates play an explicit role in demand determination. Interest rate rules in particular, either a nominal interest rate rule:

$$i_t = \alpha_i p_t, \tag{7}$$

or a real interest rate rule,

$$r_t = \alpha_r p_t, \tag{8}$$

are possible characterizations of monetary policy. Note that (7) and (8) as well as the money supply rule ($m_t = \alpha p_t$) considered in the previous section can be interpreted as prices rule such as those recently discussed as alternatives to monetarist policies. They state that the interest rate should be increased whenever prices rise above target. In this model the price target is normalized to zero.

Before turning to the case of a two-country model with capital mobility, it is useful to consider the analysis of a closed economy.[5] To close the economy we set $f = g = 0$ and $\theta = 1$. A reduced form aggregate demand curve (in $p - y$ space) can be derived by substituting the interest rate and money response rules into (4) and (5). This results in the following alternative aggregate demand equations:

$$y_t = -d\alpha_i p_t + d\hat{\pi}_t, \tag{9}$$

$$y_t = -d\alpha_r p_t, \tag{10}$$

$$y_t = -h(1 - \alpha)p_t + hb\hat{\pi}_t, \tag{11}$$

for the nominal interest rate rule, real interest rate rule, and money rule, respectively, where $h = (a + b/d)^{-1}$.

As is clear from these equations, the rules differ in two ways: in how they effect the slope of the aggregate demand curve and in how they offset the effect of the expected inflation rate on aggregate demand. Both the nominal interest rate rule and the money rule result in aggregate demand equations in which the expected inflation rate has an impact. This is a disadvantage of these rules since it results in another source of instability. This instability could be avoided by using a money supply rule in which the money supply responded to changes in the expected inflation rate. In other words the money supply rule could be written as $m_t = \alpha p_t + \beta\hat{\pi}_t$. If the response of the money supply to expected inflation were exactly equal to the interest rate coefficient in the money demand equation—that is, if $\beta = -b$—then the effect of a change in the expected rate of inflation would be perfectly offset. The primary advantage of the real interest rate rule is that it automatically offsets the effects of shifts in expected inflation on aggregate demand.

The dynamic response of the economy to supply shocks with and without the inflation offset appears in figures 9.3 and 9.4. (The parameters used to generate this and following simulations are reported in table 9.1.) The disturbance generating these responses is a one-period shock to the contract wage equation. As a result of this shock, output declines and prices increase over the short run before returning to their initial levels. The mechanics of wage contracting lead to a maximum decline in real output during the third period following the disturbance, simultaneous with the peak in the real interest rate. The inflation offset reduces the magnitude of these output and interest rate effects while increasing price and nominal interest rate adjustments. In figure 9.4 the behavior of the money supply illustrates the intervention necessary in order to offset changes in inflationary expectations.

The importance of offsetting variations in the expected inflation rate can be illustrated graphically. Suppose that a monetarist policy is adopted

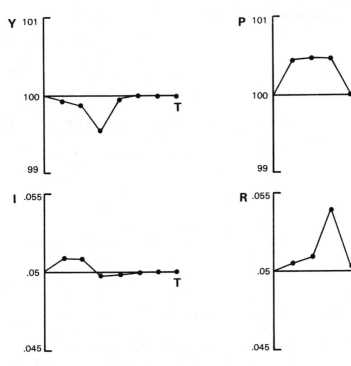

Figure 9.3
Price shock without inflation offset

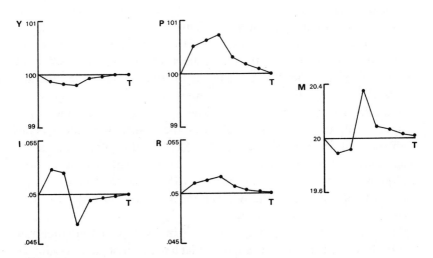

Figure 9.4
Price shock with inflation offset

Table 9.1
Parameter values used in model simulations

Parameter	Value
δ	0.5
γ	1.0
θ	0.8 (0.7)
n	3.0
d	1.2
f	0.1 (0.3)
g	0.1 (0.3)
b	4.0
a	1.0

Note: The home and foreign economies are equal in size and are symmetrically parameterized. The alternative parameter values shown in parentheses are used in the moderate interaction simulations of the two-country model reported in section 3. Parameter d is the semielasticity of aggregate demand with respect to the real rate of return. At the equilibrium level of the real rate, the interest elasticity of aggregate demand is approximately equal to -0.06. Parameter b is the semielasticity of money demand with respect to the nominal rate of return. At the equilibrium level of this rate, the interest elasticity of aggregate demand equals -0.2. This is a rough average of the estimates reported by Goldfeld (1973) and Simpson et al. (1979).

with $\alpha = 0$ and without any attempt to offset expected inflation. If a supply shock shifts the aggregate supply curve upward, as shown in figure 9.5, then output initially will fall and prices will rise. Because the price effects take time to work through the system of staggered contracts (in the diagram it is assumed that contracts last three periods, $n = 3$), there is a period of time in which the expected rate of inflation rises. Without a policy offset to this increase, the aggregate demand curve will shift to the right, partially reducing the contractionary effect of the shock. Because the price level eventually returns to its previous level (or trend path), subsequently there is a period of declining inflationary expectations. This decline results in an increase in the real rate of interest and causes the aggregate demand curve to shift back to the left. The shift to the left in turn causes a large decline in output before the economy returns to full employment. The responses of prices and output are shown by the intersections of the various supply and demand diagrams in figure 9.5. The dynamic response patterns corresponding to those price-output intersections in figure 9.5 are shown in figure 9.3. Note that there is a large increase in the real rate of interest in period 3, the same period in which the price level peaks and price declines are anticipated in future periods.

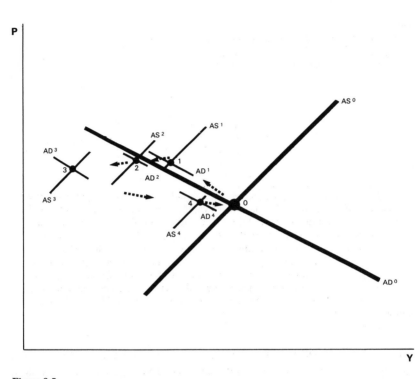

Figure 9.5
Price shock without inflation offset

This rise in real interest rates causes output to fall sharply in the same period, as is shown in the diagram.[6]

The pattern of nominal and real interest rate movements is much different when there is an attempt to offset the effects of the expected inflation rate on aggregate demand. In figure 9.6 we show the impact of the same aggregate supply shock when the money stock is increased or decreased to offset perfectly the effect of shifts in the expected inflation rate on aggregate demand. In this simulation $\beta = -b$. The dynamic response patterns for this alternative policy rule are shown in figure 9.4. Note the smooth patterns of real interest rate movements compared with the wide swings in figure 9.3. For this smooth movement in real interest rates, there is a corresponding irregular pattern for nominal rates. Recall that the aggregate supply shock first increases and subsequently decreases the expected rate of inflation. If real interest rates are to move smoothly,

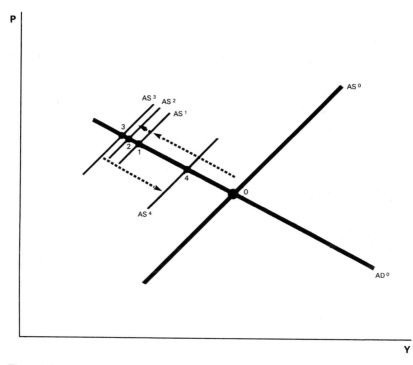

Figure 9.6
Price shock with inflation offset

then there must be an increase in nominal rates in the first few periods after a supply shock, followed by a fall in nominal rates below normal before returning to their original level. The pattern of the money supply is also irregular. The money supply is reduced below normal in the first few periods and subsequently rises above normal.

In terms of failing to offset the expected rate of inflation, nominal interest rate targeting is always worse than money stock targeting. With an interest rate target, the expected inflation-induced shifts in the IS curve translate into larger output fluctuations than with a money supply target. Using the algebra of equations (9) and (11), this can be seen by comparing the coefficients of expected inflation ($d > hb$).

As one should expect in a situation without demand shocks, there are certain equivalence relationships between the various types of price rules. The response of a money supply rule to prices will have exactly the same effects as an interest rate rule (ignoring the problem of offsetting expected inflation) if $\alpha_r = (h/d)(1 - \alpha)$. For example, a monetarist rule ($\alpha = 0$) results in a positively responding interest rate rule with a response coefficient equal to h/d. An interest rate rule that is completely nonresponsive ($\alpha_r = 0$) corresponds to a fully accommodative money supply rule ($\alpha = 1$).

A nominal GNP rule could also be contemplated within this framework. A nominal GNP rule takes the form $y_t + p_t = \alpha_n p_t$ where α_n is the response of nominal GNP to price disturbances. Although nominal GNP rules are usually discussed as if nominal GNP (or its growth rate) were unresponsive to prices ($\alpha_n = 0$), this results in very nonaccommodative policy. Clearly a given nominal GNP rule is equivalent to a real interest rate rule if $\alpha_r = (\alpha_n - 1)/d$.[7]

The previous analysis indicates that real interest rate rules (or more generally monetary rules that offset the effects of expected inflation on aggregate demand) ought to work better than money stock or nominal interest rate rules. In order to illustrate this, we have computed combinations in output and price stability for the closed economy version of the model using stochastic simulation techniques. These output-price stability points are computed under the assumption that independent and identically distributed random variables ε_t continually shock equation (3). By stochastically simulating the model for alternative values of the policy rules, the average fluctuations of output and prices can be computed for these different rules—measured in terms of the standard deviations of output and prices.

The results of this exercise are shown in figure 9.7. The triangles indicate output-price stability points corresponding to different monetary policy rules. All of the points indicated by triangles correspond to policies in which changes in the expected rate of inflation are offset. Points on the upper left-hand segment of the diagram correspond to accommodative policies—that is, policies in which the real interest rate rises only slightly in response to price movements above normal. Points on the lower right-hand segment of the diagram correspond to less accommodative policies. For these points real interest rates are increased by a larger amount in response to price shocks. The scatter of the points is due to the uncertainty associated with the stochastic simulations and could be eliminated by increasing the size of the samples.[8] Despite the scatter a downward sloping trade-off is evident. Note that the fixed money supply rule and the interest rate rule are well inside the scatter, supporting our earlier argument that such policies are inefficient.

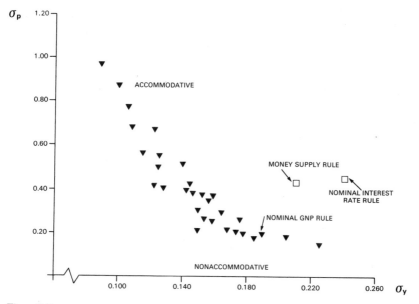

Figure 9.7
Price versus output stability in a closed economy with price shocks

Before proceeding with the two-country analysis, it is useful to consider the dynamic response of the closed economy to a classic macroeconomic policy shock: an unanticipated permanent increase in the level of the money supply. The macroeconomic responses to a 1 percent increase in money are shown in figure 9.8. There is a positive real output effect that diminishes exponentially to zero in the long run. Prices rise slowly at first but eventually by the same amount as the increase in money. Both the real and the nominal interest rate eventually decline, but the decline in the nominal rate is comparatively small. The nominal interest rate returns to the initial level more quickly than the real rate. Throughout the simulation the expected rate of inflation holds the real interest rate below the nominal rate, making the impact of monetary policy on real interest rates larger than its impact on the nominal rate. The plots in figure 9.8 pertain to the closed economy parameter values listed in table 9.1. For other parameter values we have experimented with (a small γ, for example), the nominal interest rate falls by a larger amount. The decline in the real rate is always larger than the decline in the nominal rate, however.

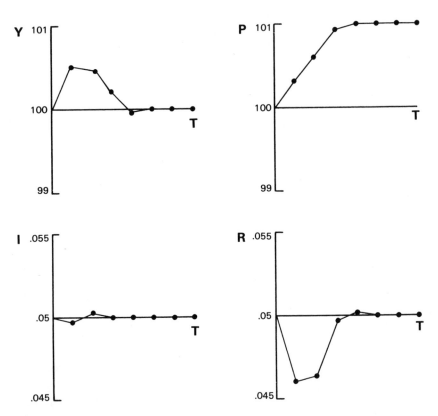

Figure 9.8
Money shock in closed economy

3. Monetary Policy in a Two-Country Model with Capital Mobility

We now consider the effects of capital mobility on macroeconomic performance in a two-country flexible exchange rate world. We have already summarized in equations (1) through (6) the basic elements of aggregate supply and aggregate demand for a single open economy. (We now emphasize that $\theta \neq 1$ and that neither f nor g equals zero.) To close the system we need to add a corresponding model for the rest of the world and to provide a link between capital markets in the home country and the rest of the world. We assume that international capital mobility can be approximated by the assumption of perfect capital mobility—that is, perfect substitutability between domestic and foreign interest earning assets plus instantaneous adjustment of capital flows. Algebraically the perfect capital mobility assumption can be written as:

$$i_t = i_t^* + \hat{e}_{t+1} - e_t.\tag{12}$$

In other words the domestic interest rate is equal to the rest of the world interest rate plus the expected rate of depreciation of the home currency.

The aggregate demand and aggregate supply equations for the rest of the world are given by:

$$x_t^* = \frac{\delta^*}{n} \sum_{i=0}^{n-1} \hat{w}_{t+i}^* + \frac{1 - \delta^*}{n} \sum_{i=0}^{n-1} \hat{p}_{t+i}^* + \frac{\gamma^*}{n} \sum_{i=0}^{n-1} \hat{y}_{t+i}^* + \varepsilon_t^*,\tag{13}$$

$$w_t^* = \frac{1}{n} \sum_{i=0}^{n-1} x_{t-i}^*,\tag{14}$$

$$p_t^* = \theta^* w_t^* + (1 - \theta^*)(p_t - e_t),\tag{15}$$

$$y_t^* = -d^* r_t^* - f^*(p_t^* + e_t - p_t) + g^* y_t,\tag{16}$$

$$m_t^* - p_t^* = -b^* i_t^* + a^* y_t^*,\tag{17}$$

$$r_t^* = i_t^* - \hat{\pi}_t^*.\tag{18}$$

The rest of the world equations (13) through (18), when combined with the capital mobility equation (12) and home country equations (1) through (6), form the complete model. How the model is solved depends on the exchange rate regime. With flexible exchange rates each country's money supply (m and m^*) can be set either exogenously or by a policy rule. With fixed exchange rates the money supply in only one country can be set, either exogenously or by a policy rule, while the other country's money supply is determined by the fixed exchange rate objective. No sterilization, in the usual sense of the word, is possible with perfect capital mobility. We will focus on flexible exchange rates.[9]

The dynamic response of the flexible exchange rate model to an unanticipated permanent increase in the home country money supply is shown in figure 9.9. These responses are calculated using the parameter values in table 9.1 that suggest a low degree of interaction between the two countries. The effects on prices and output in the home country are much like those in the closed economy model shown in figure 9.8. The increase in prices is slightly more rapid and the effect on output slightly smaller. Both real and nominal interest rates decline, with the real interest rate

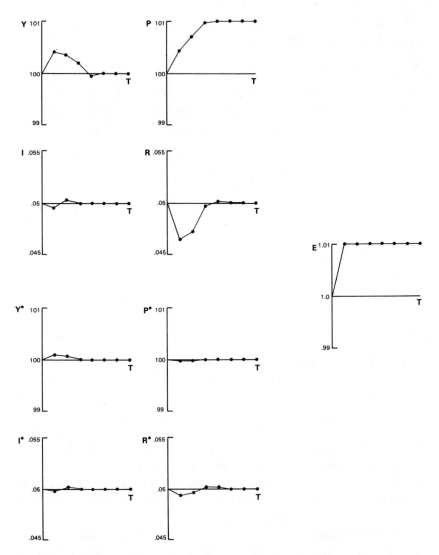

Figure 9.9
Money shock in two-country model

declining more than the nominal interest rate. The exchange rate in the home country depreciates in the first period by the same percentage as the increase in the home money supply. Hence, to a first approximation, the exchange rate immediately jumps to its new long-run equilibrium value. There is some overshooting, analogous to that studied by Dornbusch (1976), but this is very small in comparison with the size of the jump to the region of the new equilibrium rate. Despite perfect capital mobility, monetary policy in the home economy of this two-country model has many similarities with monetary policy in the closed economy model. A decline in real interest rates temporarily stimulates output and leads to a rise in prices. In addition the exchange rate depreciates, raising the real exchange rate to stimulate demand further and adding to the rise in the domestic price level.

The impact of the increase in the home money supply on foreign output is positive but fairly small. This contrasts with the Mundell-Fleming result that an expansionary monetary policy at home causes contraction in demand in the rest of the world due to the appreciation of the exchange rate.[10] According to this model the impact effects of monetary policy have the same sign at home and abroad. The reason is found in the price linkage or markup equations. The appreciation of the exchange rate in the rest of the world tends to reduce the foreign price level through its effect on import costs. This lower price level translates into an increase in real money balances in the rest of the world, despite the fixed nominal money supply. This increase in real money balances can stimulate demand and can offset the negative effects of the appreciation, unlike the Mundell-Fleming model where the fixed price level prevents the real money stock from increasing.

Given our focus on capital mobility, it is interesting to study the impact of the home monetary expansion on foreign interest rates. Because the exchange rate jumps almost exactly to the new long-run equilibrium value and then stays with very little overshooting at that value, there is only a very small expected appreciation of the home currency after the first period. Hence domestic and foreign nominal interest rates cannot diverge from each other by much. But recall that the nominal interest rate in the home country declined by only a small amount. Most of the stimulative effects of the monetary expansion came from the decline in real interest rates as caused by the increase in the expected inflation rate. Because monetary policy works in this model primarily by reducing the real interest rate and because it is nominal rather than real interest rates that are linked in this model by capital flows, it is possible for monetary policy to have powerful domestic effects.

We now go on to examine the output-price stability trade-off and how the world economy responds to supply shocks under alternative policy rules. From the analysis of section 2 it is clear that macroeconomic inefficiencies will result from a monetary policy rule that does not offset the impact of changes in the expected inflation rate on aggregate demand. So that we can assess whether capital mobility impinges on macroeconomic efficiency, we therefore focus on monetary rules for which such an inflation offset automatically occurs. Equivalently we limit our analysis to real interest rate rules. Since there are now two countries, we need to specify two such interest rate rules. Let these be:

$$r_t = \alpha_r p_t, \tag{19}$$

$$r_t^* = \alpha_r^* p_t^*. \tag{20}$$

The dynamic response of the model to a supply shock in the home country when $\alpha_r = \alpha_r^* = 0.2$ is shown in the charts in figure 9.10. What is perhaps most striking about this simulation is the small effect of the supply shock on the rest of the world. The rise in prices caused by the supply shock brings forth an increase in real interest rates in the home country, as called for in (19), but almost no change in the interest rate in the rest of the world. Unlike the case of an unanticipated increase in the money supply, the exchange rate is expected to change by significant amounts following a supply shock. These expected movements in the exchange rate permit a divergence between nominal interest rates in the two countries. In the early periods of the simulation, the exchange rate depreciates and is expected to depreciate, permitting the interest rate to rise at home relative to abroad. This rise is necessary if real interest rates are to rise. Later the exchange rate appreciates back to the long-run equilibrium value, and the nominal interest rate falls at home relative to abroad (as it should, because by this time the decline in the expected rate of inflation has its own negative effects on real interest rates).

These results suggest that the output-price performance generated by such supply shocks might be surprisingly unaffected by policy choice abroad despite perfect capital mobility. To test this proposition, we stochastically simulate the two-country model under parameterizations of

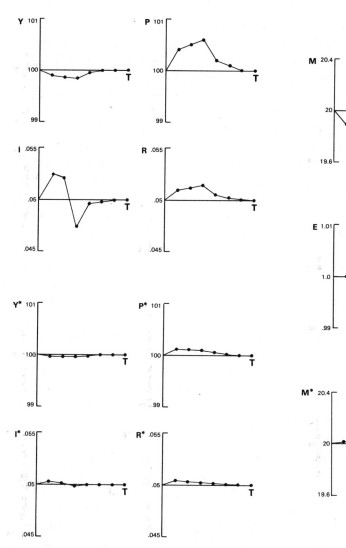

Figure 9.10
Price shock (with offset) in two-country model

equations (19) and (20) corresponding to different values of α_r and α_r^*. These calculations are made under the assumption that supply shocks continually occur in both countries, that these shocks are unanticipated and temporary, and that they are uncorrelated between the countries. In other words, ε_t and ε_t^* are serially and contemporaneously uncorrelated random variables. Only a limited number of policy rule parameterizations have been examined in order to save on computation costs.[11] Variances calculated for α and α_r^* equal to 0.2 and 0.6 are reported in figures 9.11 and 9.12. In figure 9.11 we have computed the variances of output and prices assuming a low degree of direct interaction between the countries. In figure 9.12 the interaction is moderate.[12]

Figures 9.11 and 9.12 indicate in what sense there is relatively little interaction between the policy rules in the two countries. For example, as the home country moves from a relatively nonaccommodative interest rate rule to a more accommodative interest rate rule, its output variability declines and its price variability increases. But the effect of this move on the other country's variability measure is very small. There is some indication that the rest of the world benefits from a more accommodative policy at home (its performance improves), but the effect is second order.

This relative independence is illustrated by figure 9.13, in which the standard deviations of output and prices under the moderate interaction parameterization are plotted for α_r ranging from 0.05 (accommodative) to 0.90 (nonaccommodative). These stability pairs are plotted first under the assumption that foreign policy is nonaccommodative ($\alpha_r^* = 0.6$) and second under the assumption that foreign policy is relatively accommodative ($\alpha_r^* = 0.2$). Figure 9.13 suggests a slight positive feedback between the policy choices of these two nations. When the home nation is interested in pursuing an accommodative domestic policy, it can achieve more efficient macroeconomic performance if the foreign nation also adopts an accommodative policy. And when domestic policymakers prefer a nonaccommodative response rule, macroeconomic performance is enhanced if a similar policy is chosen abroad. The results reported in figure 9.13 indicate, however, that the magnitude of this interaction is small.

4. Concluding Remarks

Our purpose has been to develop and test a quantitative framework for evaluating macroeconomic performance in a world of perfect capital

$\alpha_r^* = 0.6$ $\alpha_r^* = 0.2$

	0.188 0.147	0.423 0.111
$\alpha_r = 0.6$	0.188 0.147	0.181 0.144
	0.181 0.144	0.425 0.112
$\alpha_r = 0.2$	0.423 0.111	0.425 0.112

Key:

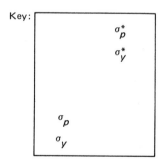

Figure 9.11

Two-country trade-offs: Low interaction——*Note:* The equal size, identical structure, and symmetric parameterization of the two countries ensure that this trade-off matrix is symmetric. This symmetry is taken into account in reporting the results for the two countries. The average of the standard deviations for the two countries is reported for similar policies.

$\alpha_r^* = 0.6$ $\alpha_r^* = 0.2$

| | 0.158 | | 0.344 |
| | 0.155 | | 0.122 |

$\alpha_r = 0.6$

| 0.158 | | 0.156 | |
| 0.155 | | 0.150 | |

| | 0.156 | | 0.326 |
| | 0.150 | | 0.111 |

$\alpha_r = 0.2$

| 0.344 | | 0.326 | |
| 0.122 | | 0.111 | |

Key:

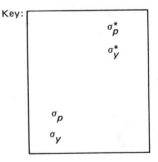

σ_p^*

σ_y^*

σ_p

σ_y

Figure 9.12
Two-country trade-offs: Moderate interaction——*Note:* The same reporting conventions
are followed as in figure 9.11.

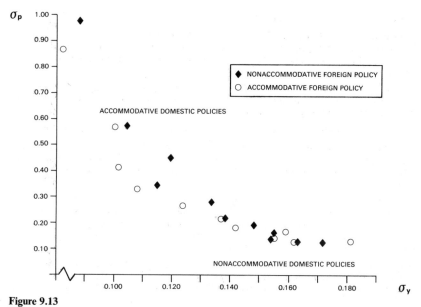

Figure 9.13
Price versus output stability in two-country model with price shocks

mobility. The framework is based on a simulation procedure for a two-country rational expectations model with price (or supply) shocks.

The simulation results suggest that if exchange rates are flexible, capital mobility does not necessarily place constraints on domestic macroeconomic performance and does not necessarily prevent individual countries from choosing their own monetary rules without interfering with other countries in significant ways. This conclusion is dependent on the particular model structure and parameter configuration we chose to investigate. Further research is required to determine the robustness of such results to widely different parameter and model configurations and to obtain econometric estimates of the crucial parameters in different countries.[13]

Notes

This research has been supported in part by a grant from the National Science Foundation. We wish to thank Matthew Canzoneri, Ray Fair, Brian Horrigan, David Papell, and Edmund Phelps for useful comments and assistance. The views expressed in this chapter are those of the authors and do not represent the official positions of the Federal Reserve Bank of Philadelphia or the Federal Reserve System.

1. See Taylor (1980), for example.

2. Bhandari (1982), Calvo (1983), Dornbusch (1982), Rehm (1982), and Taylor (1982) have used staggered wage-setting models of aggregate supply in an open economy framework. See Mussa (1982) and Liederman (1982) for alternative sticky-price approaches to aggregate supply in open economy models.

3. Because prices are partly influenced by foreign import prices, it is important to include both wages and prices in the contract determination equation in order to capture all of the dynamic effects of a foreign price disturbance.

4. This paragraph and the next provide a brief overview of the results in Taylor (1980).

5. Rehm (1982) has provided an extensive set of deterministic simulations to illustrate the dynamic properties of a closed economy model like this one and has also examined the case of a small, open economy. Calvo (1983) has studied a small, open economy model using continuous time techniques.

6. The dynamic response patterns shown in figure 9.3 were computed numerically for the parameter values shown in table 9.1 using the extended path algorithm described in Fair and Taylor (1983). The patterns show the response of the closed economy model to a one-unit shock to ε_t in the first period of the simulations. This corresponds to a temporary unanticipated contract wage shock, which we refer to simply as a supply shock in the text.

7. The simulation results reported in the text take advantage of this correspondence among response rules. The interest rate and nominal GNP response rule simulations are generated using a money response rule parameterized to yield the appropriate aggregate demand relations.

8. The stochastic simulation results are based on single runs of 500 periods for each parameter configuration. In order to ensure stationarity, the standard deviations are computed using the last 450 observations of each of these runs.

9. This model also could be used to investigate the choice of exchange rate regimes (fixed versus flexible) using the same stochastic simulation approach. See Carlozzi (1982) for this type of application using a different model.

10. See Dornbusch (1980: 201) for a discussion.

11. Johnson (1982) has computed two-country output-inflation trade-offs of this type in a model without capital mobility and with explicit exchange rate management and has explored alternative equilibrium concepts in the choice of rules in the two countries.

12. The parameter values for the low and moderate interaction simulations of the two-country model are reported in table 9.1.

13. Structural estimates can be obtained using the econometric procedures employed by Rehm (1982) to estimate small open economy models for Germany and the U.S.

References

Bhandari, J. S. 1982. "Staggered Wage Setting and Exchange Rate Policy in an Economy with Capital Assets." *Journal of International Money and Finance* 1:175–192.

Calvo, G. A. 1983. "Staggered Contracts and Exchange Rate Policy." In J. Frenkel, ed., *Exchange Rates and International Macroeconomics*. University of Chicago Press for National Bureau of Economic Research.

Carlozzi, N. 1982. "Economic Disturbances and Exchange Regime Choice." Working Paper 82–8. Federal Reserve Bank of Philadelphia.

Dornbusch, R. 1976. "Expectations and Exchange Rate Dynamics." *Journal of Political Economy* 84:1161–1176.

Dornbusch, R. 1980. *Open Economy Macroeconomics.* New York: Basic Books.

Dornbusch, R. 1982. "PPP Exchange Rate Rules and Macroeconomic Stability," *Journal of Political Economy* 90:158–165.

Fair, R., and Taylor, J. B. 1983. "Solution and Maximum Likelihood Estimation of Dynamic Nonlinear Rational Expectations Models." *Econometrica* 51:1169–1185.

Goldfeld, Stephen M. 1973. "The Demand for Money Revisited." *Brookings Papers on Economic Activity* 3:577–638.

Fleming, M. J. 1962. "Domestic Financial Policies under Fixed and under Floating Exchange Rates." *International Monetary Fund Staff Papers* 9:369–379.

Johnson, R. A. 1982. "Monetary Stabilization and Interdependence in a Two-Country Model." Unpublished paper. Princeton University.

Liederman, L. 1982. "Monetary Accommodation and the Variability of Output Prices, and Exchange Rates." *Carnegie Rochester Conference Series on Public Policy* 16:47–86.

Mundell R. 1961. "Flexible Exchange Rates and Employment Policy." *Canadian Journal of Economics and Political Science* 27:509–517.

Mundell, R. 1963. "Capital Mobility and Stabilization Policy under Fixed and Flexible Exchange Rates." *Canadian Journal of Economics and Political Science* 29:475–487.

Mussa, M. 1982. "A Model of Exchange Rate Dynamics." *Journal of Political Economy* 90:74–104.

Rehm, D. E. 1982. "Staggered Contracts, Capital Flows and Macroeconomic Stability in the Open Economy." Ph.D. dissertation, Columbia University.

Simpson, Thomas D., et al. 1979. "A Proposal for Redefining the Monetary Aggregates." *Federal Reserve Bulletin* 65:13–42.

Taylor, John B. 1980. "Aggregate Dynamics and Staggered Contracts." *Journal of Political Economy* 88:1–23.

Taylor, John B. 1982. "Macroeconomic Tradeoffs in an International Economy with Rational Expectations." In W. Hildenbrand, ed., *Advances in Economic Theory.* Cambridge: At the Press.

Tobin, J. 1978. "A Proposal for International Monetary Reform." *Eastern Economic Journal* 4:153–159.

10 Monetary and Exchange Rate Targets in an Optimal Control Setting

M. J. Artis and E. Karakitsos

1. Introduction

As the cumulative experience of monetary targeting in a number of developed economies has brought home some unpleasant lessons, the emphasis of practical policy formulation has shifted toward the exchange rate as an alternative or as a supplementary target.

This chapter seeks to make a contribution toward the resolution of some of the issues that arise in this context. In particular it attempts to compare alternative policy regimes on the basis of a robustness criterion: that is, to evaluate the performance of alternative regimes by examining the response of the economy to shocks of various kinds. This criterion was popularized by Poole's influential work (Poole 1970) and was used recently in the present context by Artis and Currie (1981).

The results hitherto obtained, however—with the exception of Currie and Karakitsos (1981)—have been confined, for reasons of analytical tractability, to those that can be derived from relatively small algebraic models with little or no dynamics and simple implicit objective functions. In the present study these restrictions are relaxed. First, the models used—those of the National Institute of Economic and Social Research (NIESR) and the London Business School (LBS)—are estimated econometric models with presumably realistic parameter values and complex dynamics. Second, the criterion function on which comparison is made is extended to include, besides price stability (which dominated the comparisons made in Artis and Currie), both unemployment and the current account of the balance of payments. Third, by considering alternative models of different specification, the analysis is extended to incorporate an additional source of uncertainty, that represented by doubts about which model specification comes nearer the truth. Finally the analysis is extended to include two alternative versions of the exchange rate target, the nominal or the real exchange rate (competitiveness).

The chapter is focused, for reasons explained in more detail in section 3 and appendix 10A, on comparisons of a pure monetary targets regime with augmented regimes, in which the monetary target is complemented by a nominal or real exchange rate target and on the response of the system to shocks of specified kinds under these alternative regimes. There are several ways in which an intermediate variable target may be enforced, with different results, for the various ultimate objectives of policy. Here three instruments are specified: the treasury bill rate, the rate of government spending (in real terms), and the standard rate of income tax, and the intermediate targets are achieved or approached in the context of optimizing an objective function that includes as arguments the ultimate targets of policy. Thus, given the initial choice of instruments, the economy always moves along its efficient frontier.

In the next section the two models employed in this study are briefly discussed; in section 3 the objective function is spelled out; in section 4 we present the main results derived from a specific set of shocks. The final section contains some conclusions and compares them with the approach and results obtained in Currie and Karakitsos (1981). There are three appendixes. The first deals with the deterministic optimal simulations (against which the shocked simulations are compared in section 4), the second examines the role of the public sector borrowing requirement (PSBR) as an intermediate variable, and the third consists of two tables that provided a schematic account of the two models in mathematical form.

2. The Two Models

The two models employed in this study are the forecasting models of the NIESR and the LBS (used here with forecast data bases for the period 1981:4–1986:3). Full listings of these models are available (NIESR 1979; LBS 1981), but it would be tedious to describe the models equation by equation. Instead we seek to compare and contrast the two in terms of the descriptions they give of the principal sectors of the economy, emphasizing those features of the models that seem especially important for the results we report in section 4. A good account of these same two models has already appeared in Arestis and Karakitsos (1982), whose treatment is largely followed here. Like them we illustrate the verbal account with reference to summary mathematical versions of each of the two models: these appear in tables 10C.1 (NIESR) and 10C.2 (LBS). Some recent simulation evidence that illustrates the comparative properties of the two models appears in Artis (1982).

Both models are of recognizable Keynesian stock in that they approach the determination of output by way of modeling and aggregating the components of demand. The supply side is represented through pricing equations, but these are not related to output decisions as such. A feature of the LBS model is its association with international monetarism in the specification of its pricing, exchange rate, and monetary sectors and the nexus joining them. Monetary variables also appear in the determination of demand components in the LBS model. In these respects the NIESR model is the more traditionally Keynesian of the two, especially in the version employed here, whose wage equation specification makes no reference to the pressure of demand.

Referring now to tables 10C.1 and 10C.2 equations (1) through (5) in the former and (1)′ through (5)′ in the latter depict the determination of consumption and investment in the NIESR and LBS models, respectively. As the single largest component of demand, the consumption equation is crucial. The NIESR specification offers real disposable income, bank lending, and inflation as determinants, the LBS model substituting real money balances for bank lending in an otherwise similar general specification; monetary feedback to consumption seems much greater as estimated in the LBS model, however. Investment expenditures are governed by a flexible accelerator relationship in both models, and each in addition incorporates terms in profitability and bank lending, supplemented by a real wealth term in the LBS model; both incorporate an interest rate term (nominal, NIESR; real, LBS), though conventional interest rate effects are rather small and, in any case, in the models as a whole are partly offset by the effects flowing from the corresponding refinancing requirement.[1]

The equations determining exports and imports, the current and capital account and export prices are set out as equations (6) through (10) and (6)′ through (10)′ of tables 10C.1 and 10C.2. In both cases the general specification of export and import volumes is identical; the determining factors are an activity variable (world trade for exports, GDP for imports) and relative prices. Export prices in both models are determined as a function of domestic and overseas prices. There is no explicit modeling of capital flows in the NIESR model, and the exchange rate is determined in a single equation that enforces purchasing power parity as an equilibrium condition but allows deviations to occur in response to changes in the U.K.–U.S. interest rate differential and the performance of the current account (acting as proxy for confidence). The LBS model contains a modeling of the capital account. Its exchange rate determination hypothesis reflects its global monetarist orientation, and its pricing, monetary, and exchange rate sectors are best taken together (equations (12)' through (16)' of table 10C.2).

The monetary approach to the exchange rate defines a relationship between domestic and overseas prices that approximates purchasing power parity and, given the implied nexus between domestic and foreign prices and the exchange rate, proceeds to determine the latter by determining the ratio of prices, using the quantity theory of money to do so. Thus relative money supplies (U.K. and world), given relative incomes, determine relative prices and hence the exchange rate.[2] Hence events that affect the money market ensue in the exchange rates moving to remove the resultant excess supply or demand for money.

Both models present the money supply as an endogenous variable, in fact essentially as the residual item in the banks' balance sheets, given the determination of the asset items in those balance sheets, the public sector deficit, and external financing. The NIESR model affords more detailed disaggregation of the monetary sector, although the money supply as such has no direct feedback into the real side of the economy (but bank lending influences both consumption and investment).

The domestic pricing equations of both models depend on wage costs and foreign prices. The wage equations are contrasting: the LBS model employs an augmented Phillips curve specification, and the NIESR model uses a real wage approach, which contains no reference to the pressure of demand. Finally although labor demand in the NIESR model is entirely determined by output, the LBS model specifies labor demand to depend entirely on the real wage. Labor supply is exogenous in each one.

Although large parts of the two models are specified in a similar way, there is sufficient difference in other sectors to provide the models with substantially different responses to identical stimuli (see Artis 1982). These differences in model properties are reflected in the results we report in section 4.

3. Objective Function

All of the runs reported here are the result of optimizing an objective function. We distinguish between different policy regimes according to the content of the objective function, which is specified to contain not only a set of ultimate objective variables (here, unemployment, inflation, the balance of payments) together with instrument variables (government, current spending, the standard rate of tax, and the treasury bill rate), but also a set, dependent on the regime, of intermediate variables. The total set of such variables comprises: the money supply (£M3), the public sector borrowing requirement (PSBR), the nominal (effective) exchange rate, and the real exchange rate or competitiveness.[3] The regimes we examine are distinguished by the subset of these variables that appear in the objective function. Thus we compare a regime of monetary targets with a regime in which monetary targets are augmented by the nominal exchange rate and a further alternative in which monetary targets are augmented by competitiveness (the real exchange rate). In the pure monetary target regime the intermediate variables include only the PSBR and the money supply. In the monetary target cum nominal exchange rate regime, the list of intermediate variables includes, in addition, the exchange rate, and in the monetary target cum/competitiveness regime, the intermediate variables incorporated in the objective function are the PSBR, money supply, and competitiveness.

It might be questioned why the comparisons are limited to a set of regimes in each one of which the money supply is one of the targets and more generally why the comparison of different policy regimes is carried out in this manner. The reason why the money supply appears in the objective function throughout is simple: it was found that one of the models in the comparison (the NIESR model) gave nonsensical results in optimization runs that excluded the money supply. However, the comparisons that are made between simple and augmented monetary target regimes are relevant to current policy debate where the issue seems to be more one of how to combine intermediate variable targets than it is of exclusive choice of one or the other target, so this constraint on the choice of regimes to be compared was not felt to be particularly onerous.[4]

The more general issue raised by our approach concerns the propriety of including in the objective function the values of intermediate variables. The theory of indicator variables, such as it is, suggests a logic of policy presentation that makes it sensible to describe and sometimes to formulate policy in terms of such variables. They are highly visible to economic agents, play a role in the transmission mechanism, and, being subject to some government control or influence, display for other agents a summary reading of government policy. Hence governments may wish to formulate policy in terms of such variables, and this in itself is good enough reason for them to appear in the objective function governing policy reactions.[5] There is another reason why such variables should appear in the objective function: economic models are known to be underspecified in some degree or another and hence can easily give absurd results in optimization runs. Bray (1982) instances the case of indirect taxes, reductions in which lead in the model he employs (the NIESR model) to reductions in both inflation and unemployment; naive optimization is thus likely to imply the complete removal of such taxes (possibly even their replacement by subsidies). One way of dealing with underspecification in the model would be to introduce penalty weights on the infringement of certain values of the variables in question; rather better is to incorporate in the objective function an intermediate variable that then has the function of checking absurd results. In the indirect tax case, for example, incorporating the PSBR might help prevent the extreme outcome from occurring. This general case for incorporating intermediate variables in the objective function is explored further in Bray (1982).

A formal representation of the main issues will clarify matters. The policy optimization problem in a deterministic context may be characterized as $\min J(Y_1, Y_2, U) | F(Y_1, Y_2, U) = 0$ where $Y_1 = [y_{11}, \ldots, y_{1T}]$, for $1 < t < T$ and y_{1t} denotes a vector of ultimate target variables endogenous to the model, y_{2t} a vector of intermediate target variables, and U_t a vector of instrument variables, and the minimization is to be carried out subject to the equations of the model $F(Y_1, Y_2, U) = 0$. The function J is the quadratic $\frac{1}{2}\sum_i q_i(x_1 - x_i^d)^2$, where the x_i, x_i^d are the actual and desired values of the target variables and the q_i a set of weighting factors. Table 10.1 gives the values of these, for a group of three ultimate variables, four intermediate variables, and three instrument variables, of which the first differences are also included. To give an indication of what these values mean, the column "equal priority change" is included, which shows that for example, a 1 percentage point reduction in inflation is rated as of equal priority to a reduction in unemployment of 130,000. These equal priority changes (R_i) are derived by noting that in the region of the minimum, no feasible combination of changes in the x_i could change the value of J; in other words, where P_i is the priority attached to Δx_i, $\Delta J = \sum P_i \Delta x_i = 0$ or using the definition of J, $\Delta J = \sum_i q_i(x_i - x_i^d) \Delta x_i = 0$. The equal priority change $R_i = Ph/Pi = \Delta x_i/\Delta x_n$ is thus given by $q_n(x_n - x_n^d)/q_i(x_i - x_i^d)$ where n denotes the objective variable chosen as numeraire;

Table 10.1
Detailed specification of quadratic objective function for LBS and NIESR models

Variables	Units	Desired value x_i^d	Equal priority change R_i^a	Weight q_i NIESR	Weight q_i LBS
Ultimate targets					
$\dot{P}$	% p.a.	0	1	4	1
U	000s	500	130	0.1×10^{-3}	0.27×10^{-4}
CA	£m, per quarter	0	280	0.5×10^{-4}	0.37×10^{-4}
Intermediate targets					
$PSBR$	£m, per quarter	1,000	650	0.8×10^{-4}	0.15×10^{-4}
$\dot{M}$	% p.a.	3	6.5	1	1
ER	% p.a. (EER)	0	5	10	1
$COMP$	Index value	1	0.06	1,000	1,000
Instruments					
G	£m, per quarter, constant prices	10,000	400	0.2×10^{-4}	0.4×10^{-5}
T	% point	20	3.2	1	3,400
r	% point	3	6.5	0.5	0.15×10^{-4}
Damping terms					
ΔG		0		0.2×10^{-4}	0.4×10^{-5}
Δr		0		1 in 2d quarter 1,000 in other quarters	0.15×10^{-2}
ΔT		0			3,400 in 2d quarter; 0.34 × 10 in other quarters

Note: The function is $J = \frac{1}{2}\sum q_i(x_i - x_i^d)^2$;
a. $R_i = \dfrac{q_n(x_n - x_n^d)}{q_i(x_i - x_i^d)}$ where n is the numeraire.

clearly R_i is dependent on the actual values of x_i, x_n as well as the desired trajectories and the weights. The x_i differed as between the common assumptions forecast data bases of the two models, and the weights were consequently adjusted so as to maintain the same priorities (P_i, and hence R_i) for each.

We now turn to the results obtained as a result of applying this objective function, its content varying with the regime as described, to the two models.

4. Results

The optimal deterministic runs for each policy regime are set out in appendix A and discussed there. Our principal interest is in the response of the system, given the objective function, to shocks. The relevant results, then, are the differences between the instrument settings and target variables between the shocked and the base deterministic optimal run, and it is in these terms that the data in tables 10.2 through 10.5 are presented.

Four particular shocks have been considered: a world price shock, a world price shock combined with a world trade shock, an aggregate demand shock, and an aggregate supply shock. We have not been able to consider two other sources of shocks (money market and international capital market), for which theoretical considerations indicate that exchange rate targets are expected to perform better than monetary targets. In the case of a money market shock it was difficult to devise one that would have been common to both models. An international capital market shock could not be considered at all in the case of the LBS model (because the world interest rate does not enter any behavioral equations in the version of that model we employ), and in the case of the NIESR model the effects of a 2 percent change in the U.S. interest rate turned out to be quite negligible. We now turn to a consideration of the results for each case.

World Price Shock

In the case of the NIESR model this is a permanent shock increase of 5 percent in a number of world price indexes: world wholesale prices, the world price of manufactures, the price of imported goods excluding oil, the price of imported services, and the price of imported and exported oil. In the case of the LBS model it is again a permanent shock increase of 5 percent in the world export price of manufactures in foreign currency and the world price of oil.

The results are shown in table 10.2. The table shows the deviations from the optimal deterministic base run in all the objective and instrument variables (units as in table 10.1), under the three alternative regimes, first in the NIESR model (top half of the table) and then in the LBS model (lower half). In some instances the ranking of performance would differ according as to which objective—for example, inflation or unemployment—was emphasized, but such evenhandedness would be inappropriate here since our objective function has already specified the weighting factors with which the changes in objective variables should be combined, so we choose to characterize overall performance in terms of the joint contribution to the deterioration of the cost function of the group of three ultimate objective variables. Table 10.6 provides an overall summary based on this criterion. In these terms in the case of a world price shock, both models agree that a regime of monetary targets outperforms those of monetary and nominal exchange rate targets and monetary targets and competitiveness. In fact in terms of quantitative importance the regime of monetary targets in the LBS model is by far superior to the other two regimes, whereas in the NIESR model the difference is not so striking.

In the NIESR model the world price shock, when policy is optimally revised, results in a small increase in unemployment and inflation and a small deterioration in the current account under any regime, while both fiscal and monetary policies turn out to be contractionary. The contractionary policy is required not so much to reduce inflation (for it is shown in appendix A that in the NIESR model demand management has almost no effect in reducing inflation) as to prevent a substantial deterioration in the current account. The inevitable result is that unemployment rises slightly.

In the LBS model the world price shock, when policy is optimally revised, produces a completely different picture: inflation falls, unemployment is increased, and the current account slightly deteriorates. The optimal policy is also very different from that of the NIESR model. While monetary policy is contractionary in both models, fiscal policy is expansionary in the LBS model (which explains the fall in unemployment). The different situation in the two models is the result of the different effect of world prices on the exchange rate. In the NIESR model there is only a moderate appreciation in the exchange rate (not enough to prevent an

Table 10.2
Optimal response under MT, $MT + ER$, and $MT + COMP$ to a world price shock (5% in world prices), NIESR and LBS models

Regime	Monetary targets (MT)						Monetary and exchange rate targets (nominal) ($MT + ER$)						Monetary and exchange rate targets (competitiveness) ($MT + COMP$)					
	Year 1	Year 2	Year 3	Year 4	Year 5	Average	Year 1	Year 2	Year 3	Year 4	Year 5	Average	Year 1	Year 2	Year 3	Year 4	Year 5	Average
NIESR																		
U	6	1	0	4	5	4	1	4	3	7	7	4	11	8	2	15	21	11
$\dot{P}$	0.2	0.5	0.5	0.4	0.4	0.4	0.2	0.5	0.5	0.4	0.4	0.4	0.1	0.5	0.5	0.5	0.3	0.4
CA	−75	−31	−3	−26	−57	−38	−86	−21	0	−21	−58	−37	−55	−21	0	2	−17	−18
Y	0.0	0.0	0.0	0.0	0.0	0.0	0.1	0.0	−0.1	−0.1	0.0	0.0	−0.1	0.0	0.0	−0.1	−0.1	−0.1
$\dot{M}$	0.0	−0.2	0.0	0.0	0.0	0.0	0.3	−0.5	−0.3	−0.1	0.0	−0.1	−0.5	−0.8	−0.2	0.0	0.0	−0.3
$PSBR$	−37	−33	−1	−2	3	−14	−26	−49	−4	10	30	−8	−46	−57	12	−38	−45	−35
ER	2.1	1.2	1.0	0.6	0.2	1.0	2.1	1.3	1.0	0.5	0.2	1.0	2.3	1.2	0.9	0.5	0.3	1.0
$COMP$	−0.6	−0.6	−0.4	−0.3	−0.3	−0.4	−0.6	−0.6	−0.4	−0.3	−0.3	−0.4	−0.5	−0.7	−0.4	−0.3	−0.2	−0.4
G	−38	−38	−43	−62	−72	−51	−25	−44	−42	−63	−70	−49	−44	−45	−30	−85	−110	−63
T	0.0	0.0	0.0	−0.1	−0.1	0.0	0.0	0.1	0.1	−0.1	−0.1	0.0	0.1	0.2	0.2	−0.1	−0.3	0.0
r	0.3	0.1	0.2	0.3	0.3	0.2	0.3	0.3	0.3	0.3	0.4	0.3	0.6	0.3	0.3	0.3	0.4	0.4
LBS																		
U	−51	−93	−96	−97	−119	−91	−29	−14	−39	−51	−57	−38	−27	−35	−29	−34	−39	−33
$\dot{P}$	0.1	−0.3	−0.7	−0.5	−0.3	−0.3	0.1	0.0	−0.3	−0.1	0.0	−0.1	0.1	−0.2	−0.5	−0.3	−0.1	−0.2
CA	−49	31	5	−2	−21	−7	−60	42	49	57	75	33	−49	52	57	70	81	42
Y	0.3	0.7	0.8	1.0	1.1	0.8	0.3	0.4	0.7	0.9	0.9	0.6	0.2	0.5	0.6	0.7	0.8	0.6
$\dot{M}$	−0.3	−0.3	−0.3	−0.3	−0.1	−0.3	0.1	0.4	0.2	0.1	0.1	0.2	−0.1	0.1	0.0	0.0	0.0	0.0
$PSBR$	13	4	−10	6	76	18	100	67	6	−19	−12	28	42	32	−40	−57	−37	−12
ER	0.7	2.0	2.5	2.9	3.1	2.2	0.3	0.6	0.5	0.5	0.4	0.5	0.4	1.2	1.2	1.3	1.3	1.1
$COMP$	−2.6	−1.0	−0.6	−0.5	−0.5	−1.0	−2.9	−1.6	−1.3	−1.2	−1.2	−1.6	−2.7	−1.3	−1.1	−0.9	−1.0	−1.4
G	89	133	142	154	196	143	43	6	43	60	68	44	45	37	34	34	50	39
T	4.3	7.8	7.5	7.8	7.5	7.0	5.3	10.5	9.7	7.2	5.3	7.7	5.2	9.5	8.0	6.0	4.5	6.7
r	0.6	0.7	0.7	0.7	0.6	0.7	0.2	0.0	−0.1	−0.2	0.0	0.0	0.3	0.1	−0.1	−0.3	−0.1	0.0

increase in inflation) whereas in the LBS the appreciation is substantial (and rising through time), resulting in a fall in inflation. Thus it is not a paradox that fiscal policy is expansionary in the LBS and contractionary in the NIESR model.

World Trade and Price Shock

Here, in addition to the world price shock that we have already considered, we included a permanent shock decrease of 5 percent in world trade. In the case of the NIESR model the shocks were introduced into world trade in manufactures and total world trade. In the LBS model the shock was introduced through the world index of industrial production.

In terms of the overall effect on ultimate targets, the best policy regime in the NIESR model is monetary targets, whereas in the LBS it is monetary targets combined with competitiveness. In the former model the combined effect of a world trade shock and a world price shock, when policy is allowed to respond, is an increase in both inflation and unemployment and a deterioration in the current account (table 10.3). The optimal policy is again contractionary (both fiscal and monetary policy tighten), and the reason is once more the deterioration in the current account. The slight increase in the rate of interest is also consistent with keeping the exchange rate higher to contain inflation. The appreciation in the exchange rate, though, is not enough to offset imported inflation.

In the LBS model unemployment rises and the current account deteriorates—as indeed occurs in the NIESR model—but inflation is falling rather than rising. The rapid appreciation in the exchange rate more than offsets imported inflation, and thus inflation is reduced in the LBS model. One important difference between the world price shock alone and the combined shock of world trade and world price in the LBS model is that in the former shock, fiscal policy is expansionary while in the latter it is contractionary. This is because in the case of the combined effect, the current account deteriorates substantially (because of the fall in world trade) and thus calls for a contractionary fiscal policy. In the case of the world price shock alone, there is almost no effect on the current account, and thus fiscal policy expands to reduce unemployment.

Aggregate Demand Shock

This represents a permanent increase in the savings ratio. In both cases—NIESR and LBS—the shock is introduced through the error term of the

Table 10.3
Optimal response under MT, $MT + ER$, and $MT + COMP$ to external shocks (-5% in world trade and 5% in world prices), NIESR and LBS models

Regime	Monetary targets (MT)						Monetary and exchange rate targets (nominal) ($MT + ER$)						Monetary and exchange rate targets competitiveness ($MT + COMP$)					
	Year 1	Year 2	Year 3	Year 4	Year 5	Average	Year 1	Year 2	Year 3	Year 4	Year 5	Average	Year 1	Year 2	Year 3	Year 4	Year 5	Average
NIESR																		
U	48	80	124	131	123	101	48	96	116	137	141	108	62	95	124	136	138	111
P	0.3	0.6	0.5	0.4	0.5	0.5	0.3	0.6	0.5	0.5	0.3	0.5	0.3	0.6	0.5	0.5	0.4	0.5
CA	−274	−196	−122	−183	−246	−204	−266	−168	−148	−158	−199	−187	−232	−175	−130	−170	−205	−182
Y	−0.6	−0.8	−1.0	−0.9	−0.8	−0.8	−0.7	−1.0	−0.9	−0.9	−0.9	−0.9	−0.8	−0.9	−1.0	−0.9	−0.8	−0.9
$\dot{M}$	0.9	0.7	0.3	0.2	0.1	0.4	0.6	−0.1	0.1	0.1	0.0	0.1	0.3	0.0	0.2	0.2	0.1	0.1
$PSBR$	−63	−4	−26	11	43	−8	−52	−85	24	19	41	−11	−100	−44	−6	4	2	−29
ER	1.7	1.2	1.0	0.4	−0.1	0.8	1.8	1.2	0.9	0.4	0.1	0.9	1.8	1.0	0.8	0.3	−0.1	0.8
$COMP$	−0.9	−0.5	−0.2	−0.3	−0.3	−0.4	−0.8	−0.5	−0.3	−0.3	−0.2	−0.4	−0.8	−0.6	−0.3	−0.3	−0.2	−0.4
G	−115	−131	−209	−191	−164	−162	−108	−164	−163	−204	−214	−171	−150	−156	−186	−197	−204	−179
T	0.0	0.0	0.0	0.2	0.4	0.1	0.1	0.3	0.3	0.1	−0.1	0.1	0.0	0.1	0.2	0.2	0.2	0.1
r	0.1	0.1	0.2	0.5	0.5	0.3	0.5	0.3	0.4	0.5	0.7	0.5	0.5	0.3	0.4	0.5	0.6	0.5
LBS																		
U	10	14	72	80	13	38	2	−2	67	84	10	32	−2	37	147	169	90	88
P	−0.4	−1.3	−1.7	−1.8	−2.1	−1.5	−0.4	−1.4	−1.8	−1.7	−2.0	−1.5	−0.5	−1.3	−1.5	−1.6	−2.1	−1.4
CA	−282	−214	−235	−207	−268	−214	−284	−221	−244	−224	−293	−253	−304	−226	−173	−94	−145	−189
Y	−0.4	−0.4	−0.3	−0.1	0.4	−0.2	−0.4	−0.3	−0.3	−0.1	0.4	−0.2	−0.3	−0.5	−0.6	−0.6	−0.1	−0.4
$\dot{M}$	0.4	0.6	0.2	−0.3	−0.3	0.1	0.3	0.5	0.2	−0.1	−0.1	0.1	0.6	0.7	0.1	−0.4	−0.5	0.1
$PSRB$	12	0	−35	−6	72	9	13	4	−27	13	122	25	125	78	−273	−286	−170	−105
ER	3.7	3.4	4.1	5.9	7.9	5.0	3.8	3.7	4.4	6.0	7.9	5.1	3.6	3.0	3.4	5.0	7.2	4.5
$COMP$	−0.4	−0.4	−0.3	−0.1	0.4	−0.2	−0.6	−0.6	−0.5	−0.1	0.1	−0.4	−0.8	−1.0	−0.8	−0.2	0.3	−0.5
G	2	−12	−120	−132	−55	−63	17	13	−111	−134	−44	−52	9	−43	−237	−275	−201	−149
T	4.2	7.2	6.2	6.0	6.0	6.0	4.3	7.3	6.2	6.2	5.8	6.0	5.0	9.2	7.5	5.0	3.3	6.0
r	−0.7	−0.9	−0.6	0.3	0.4	−0.3	−0.6	−0.7	−0.6	0.2	0.2	−0.3	−0.4	0.3	−1.1	−1.1	0.3	−0.7

consumption equation. The shock is of the impulse variety, but given the autoregressive nature of the consumption equation in both models, the shock is in effect a permanent one and represents a 5 percent autonomous reduction in consumers' expenditure.

The results for both models appear in table 10.4. In terms of overall performance (table 10.6) both models agree that a regime of monetary and nominal exchange rate targets is superior to either a regime of monetary targets or to a regime of monetary targets and competitiveness. As with the previous shocks, though, the two models provide a completely different picture. In the NIESR model unemployment tends to rise; it reaches a peak in the second year and then gradually tapers off. The effect on inflation is negligible. The current account improves substantially in the first year (because the recession implies fewer imports), but it then quickly moves into a deficit. Optimal monetary policy reacts by cutting interest rates, and by the time the recession (in terms of Y) has come to an end, the rate of interest has been restored to its preshock level. Fiscal policy, though, does not react according to theoretical considerations, and it appears as if it is adding to the recession rather than alleviating it, by cutting public expenditure and increasing taxes, at least for the first three years; albeit this perverse reaction dies away through time. This point is examined further in appendix B. The main conclusion is that this adverse behavior of fiscal policy is due to the short-term commitment to control the PSBR.

In the LBS model the situation is very different. At least under the nominal regimes (MT and $MT + ET$) unemployment seems to be falling rather than rising. In the first year of the shock it increases but then substantially falls. This behavior accords with prior theoretical considerations. The fall in consumer demand leads to a small recession (-0.9 in Y), but real government expenditure rises although the income tax rate is raised at the same time so that the PSBR target is met. It is important, though, to note that the PSBR is allowed (under monetary and nominal exchange rate targets) to rise in the first year, as would be expected.

Inflation in the LBS model tends to fall, whereas it is negligible in the NIESR model. This is mainly a reflection of the way monetary policy is used. In the NIESR model it is directed toward fighting unemployment, whereas in the LBS model it aims at inflation. As with the other shocks, the behavior of the exchange rate is crucial for inflation, and this has a further feedback effect on the exchange rate. Thus when the exchange rate

Table 10.4
Optimal response under MT, $MT + ER$, and $MT + COMP$ to a demand shock (-5% in consumers' expenditure), NIESR and LBS models

Regime	Monetary targets (MT)						Monetary and exchange rate targets (nominal) ($MT + ER$)						Monetary and exchange rate targets (competitiveness) ($MT + COMP$)					
	Year 1	Year 2	Year 3	Year 4	Year 5	Average	Year 1	Year 2	Year 3	Year 4	Year 5	Average	Year 1	Year 2	Year 3	Year 4	Year 5	Average
NIESR																		
U	110	143	92	47	26	83	108	134	96	33	10	76	104	125	97	41	9	75
P	0.0	−0.2	0.1	0.0	−0.2	0.0	0.0	−0.2	0.0	0.0	0.0	0.0	0.1	−0.2	0.1	−0.1	−0.1	0.0
CA	615	252	25	−15	−15	172	604	234	33	−58	−47	153	596	219	49	−36	−53	155
Y	−2.1	−0.8	0.1	0.2	0.1	−0.5	−2.0	−0.7	0.0	0.3	0.2	−0.4	−2.0	−0.6	−0.1	0.0	0.2	−0.4
$\dot{M}$	−1.9	−0.5	−0.4	−0.4	−0.2	−0.7	−1.3	0.5	0.0	0.0	−0.2	−0.2	−1.5	0.3	0.0	−0.1	−0.2	−0.3
$PSBR$	349	97	110	−35	−29	98	343	141	71	4	−6	111	346	165	65	−33	−3	108
ER	1.2	0.2	−0.4	−0.2	0.1	0.2	1.0	0.3	−0.3	−0.2	0.1	0.2	1.0	0.1	−0.4	−0.3	−0.1	0.1
$COMP$	0.7	−0.2	−0.3	0.0	0.0	0.0	0.6	−0.1	−0.3	−0.1	0.0	0.0	0.6	−0.1	−0.2	−0.1	0.0	0.0
G	−47	−23	13	−11	−20	−18	−55	−18	−25	15	10	−15	−37	15	−25	−2	21	−6
T	0.7	1.3	0.8	0.0	−0.4	0.5	0.5	0.8	0.4	0.0	−0.3	0.3	0.7	1.1	0.5	0.0	−0.1	0.4
r	−1.3	−0.2	0.3	0.3	0.3	−0.1	−1.8	−0.5	0.0	0.2	0.2	−0.4	−1.7	−0.4	0.0	0.2	0.3	−0.3
LBS																		
U	44	−48	−39	−60	−80	−37	36	−62	−50	−67	−84	−45	−19	44	62	59	65	42
P	0.6	−0.2	−0.7	−0.3	−0.1	−0.1	0.6	−0.3	−0.8	−0.3	−0.1	−0.3	0.5	0.0	−0.2	0.2	0.3	0.2
CA	168	34	−50	−54	−75	4	168	25	−64	−65	−84	−4	102	36	43	84	102	73
Y	−0.9	0.1	0.1	0.2	0.3	0.0	−0.9	0.2	0.3	0.3	0.3	0.0	−0.6	0.0	−0.2	−0.2	−0.3	−0.3
$\dot{M}$	0.0	−0.1	−0.2	−0.2	0.0	−0.1	−0.1	−0.1	−0.3	−0.2	0.0	0.0	0.6	0.2	0.0	0.1	0.2	0.2
$PSBR$	26	−2	−18	6	86	20	28	−5	−18	11	83	19	375	116	−123	−103	−17	50
ER	−1.3	0.1	0.5	0.9	1.1	0.3	−1.1	0.4	0.8	1.1	1.3	0.5	−1.4	−0.9	−1.1	−1.3	−1.5	−1.2
$COMP$	−0.5	0.3	0.2	0.2	0.2	0.1	−0.4	0.4	0.3	0.3	0.3	0.2	−0.6	−0.2	−0.3	−0.4	−0.4	−0.4
G	−17	64	66	98	135	69	−2	86	84	113	144	85	59	−67	−108	−110	−118	−69
T	4.5	7.5	7.0	7.7	7.3	6.8	4.5	7.7	7.2	7.7	7.3	7.0	4.7	8.7	7.5	5.3	3.5	6.0
r	0.1	0.2	0.4	0.4	0.3	0.3	0.3	0.3	0.5	0.5	0.4	0.4	0.9	0.5	−0.1	−0.3	0.1	0.2

falls in the first year (under monetary and nominal exchange rate targets), inflation rises. In the other four years when the exchange rate appreciates, inflation falls.

The behavior of the current account is similar in both models (under monetary and nominal exchange rate targets), first improving (mainly because of reduced imports) and then deteriorating. The quantitative difference is the result of the severity of the recession under revised optimal policy (-2 percent in the NIESR model and -0.9 percent in the LBS).

Aggregate Supply Shock

This shock is a 5 percent increase in wages and salaries per employee (for the whole economy). In both models the shock is introduced by the error term of the wage equation, and, as with the aggregate demand shock, although it is of the impulse variety, because of the autoregressive nature of the equation in both models the shock is a permanent one in effect.

The results are presented in table 10.5 for all policy regimes and for both models. In terms of the cost contribution of all ultimate targets (table 10.6), it is evident that a regime of monetary targets is not supported by either model. In the NIESR model the optimal regime is a combination of monetary targets with competitiveness. In the LBS model it is a combination of monetary and nominal exchange rate targets.

As with the other shocks, the detailed picture that emerges from the two models is quite different. In the NIESR model (under a regime of monetary targets and competitiveness) unemployment rises, reaches a peak in the third year, and then subsides. Inflation also rises, reaches a peak in the second year, disappears in the fourth year, and falls in the fifth year below its preshock level. The current account first deteriorates and then improves. The optimally revised policy consists of a contractionary fiscal as well as monetary policy.

In the LBS model (under monetary and nominal exchange rate targets) unemployment reaches its maximum fall in the first year, and then the effect gradually dies out. This is strikingly different from the NIESR model where unemployment rises rather than falls. The explanation of this phenomenon is to be found in the way fiscal policy is revised in the two models under a wage increase. In the NIESR model fiscal policy is contractionary; in the LBS model it is expansionary in the first two years and only afterward becomes contractionary. To test whether the policy is stabilizing, we examined the effects of the same wage shock when instru-

Table 10.5
Optimal response under MT, $MT + ER$, and $MT + COMP$ to a supply shock (5% in wages), NIESR and LBS models

Regime	Monetary targets (MT)						Monetary and exchange rate targets (nominal) ($MT + ER$)						Monetary and exchange rate targets (competitiveness) ($MT + COMP$)					
	Year 1	Year 2	Year 3	Year 4	Year 5	Average	Year 1	Year 2	Year 3	Year 4	Year 5	Average	Year 1	Year 2	Year 3	Year 4	Year 5	Average
NIESR																		
U	16	60	114	157	175	104	25	84	125	122	96	90	26	76	121	120	95	58
$\dot{P}$	1.2	3.2	0.9	-0.1	-0.9	0.9	1.2	3.0	1.0	0.0	-0.5	0.9	1.1	3.1	1.0	0.0	-0.5	0.9
CA	-118	-86	76	159	208	35	-145	-68	72	41	-34	-27	-135	-90	77	35	-33	-29
$\dot{Y}$	-0.1	-0.5	-0.9	-1.0	-0.9	-0.7	-0.2	-0.7	-0.9	-0.6	-0.3	-0.5	-0.2	-0.6	-0.9	-0.6	-0.3	-0.5
$\dot{M}$	0.6	1.1	-0.5	-0.1	-1.5	-0.2	0.3	-1.1	-0.7	0.0	0.1	-0.3	0.0	-1.2	-0.6	-0.1	0.2	-0.4
$PSBR$	-129	-108	37	-48	-122	-74	-122	-84	24	1	-34	-43	-130	-54	25	20	-9	-30
ER	-0.7	-2.3	-2.7	-2.9	-2.1	-2.1	-0.4	-2.3	-2.9	-3.2	-3.1	-2.4	-0.3	-2.4	-2.8	-3.3	-3.1	-2.4
$COMP$	-0.4	-0.2	0.4	0.6	1.0	0.3	-0.2	-0.4	0.2	0.4	0.5	0.1	-0.1	-0.5	0.3	0.3	0.5	0.1
G	-57	-176	-248	-300	-318	-220	-83	-218	-255	-180	-95	-166	-81	-189	-243	-172	-94	-156
T	-0.6	-0.6	0.2	0.1	-0.4	-0.3	-0.8	-0.9	0.3	1.1	1.3	0.2	-0.7	-0.7	0.5	1.1	1.2	0.3
r	0.3	0.8	0.9	0.8	1.6	0.9	1.0	1.1	0.8	0.7	0.5	0.8	1.2	1.1	0.9	0.7	0.5	0.9
LBS																		
U	-49	-43	2	8	-10	-19	-94	-41	-4	10	3	-25	-62	8	37	44	43	14
$\dot{P}$	1.4	0.2	-0.5	-0.4	-0.2	-0.1	1.3	0.1	-0.4	-0.3	-0.2	0.1	1.3	0.3	-1.1	-0.2	-0.2	0.2
CA	75	23	-16	-37	-42	1	35	-12	-23	-27	-23	-10	52	24	37	38	59	42
$\dot{Y}$	0.1	-0.1	-0.2	-0.2	-0.1	-0.1	0.3	0.1	-0.1	-0.2	-0.2	0.0	0.2	-0.2	-0.4	-0.4	-0.4	-0.2
$\dot{M}$	0.0	0.0	0.1	0.1	0.1	0.0	0.2	-0.2	-0.1	0.0	0.1	0.0	0.3	0.2	0.1	0.1	0.0	0.2
$PSBR$	53	11	-3	4	37	20	272	78	-72	-124	-112	9	174	-3	-85	-150	-242	-61
ER	0.0	-0.4	-0.8	-0.9	-0.7	-0.6	0.1	-0.3	-0.6	-0.7	-0.6	-0.4	-0.2	-1.1	-1.7	-1.9	-1.8	-1.4
$COMP$	0.5	0.3	-0.1	-0.1	-0.1	0.1	0.5	0.3	0.1	0.1	0.0	0.2	0.4	-0.1	-0.3	-0.3	-0.3	-0.1
G	91	78	14	11	35	46	152	73	33	13	17	57	98	0	-38	-54	-81	-51
T	4.5	7.7	6.8	7.0	6.7	6.5	5.7	11.0	10.2	7.5	5.5	8.0	5.2	9.5	8.0	5.8	4.4	6.5
r	0.3	0.1	0.0	0.0	0.1	0.1	1.3	0.8	0.2	-0.2	-0.1	0.4	0.3	-0.1	-0.5	-0.9	-0.5	-0.3

Table 10.6
Rank of regime performance

Type of shock	Regime	Monetary targets (MT)	Monetary and exchange rate targets (nominal) (MT + ER)	Monetary and exchange rate targets (competitiveness) (MT + COMP)
Demand	NIESR	3	1	2
	LBS	2	1	3
Supply	NIESR	3	2	1
	LBS	2	1	3
World price	NIESR	1	2	3
	LBS	1	3	2
World price and world trade	NIESR	1	2	3
	LBS	2	2	1

Note: 1, 2, and 3 indicate first, second, and third. The performance is judged by $PC_{UT} - DC_{UT}/DC_{UT}$ where PC_{UT} = the cost contribution of ultimate targets $(U, \dot{P}\ CA)$ in the objective function under the shock and DC_{UT} = the deterministic cost contribution of ultimate targets.

ments are not allowed to respond (policy is not revised). It turns out that when policy is revised optimally, both inflation and unemployment fall more than when policy is kept unchanged, and furthermore, although the current account deteriorates in both cases, the deterioration is less when policy is revised.

Table 10.6 summarizes the results, ranking the policy regimes according to the overall effect on ultimate variables experienced under the different shocks. In the case of the NIESR model, the simple monetary targets regime performs best in two out of four cases and in the case of the LBS model in only one out of four cases. For five of the total of eight cases, a combination of monetary targets with the exchange rate (nominal or real) outperforms a simple monetary targets regime.

5. Conclusions

In this study we set out to compare monetary and exchange rate targets or, more accurately, pure and exchange rate-augmented monetary targets in the context of optimal policy responses to stochastic disturbances. The analysis was conducted for a set of four shocks (aggregate demand, supply, world prices, and a combined world trade and prices disturbance) on two different models of the economy. The size of shocks chosen was essentially arbitrary, and no effort was made to mimic the variances, let alone the covariances, of shocks of the kind considered. Moreover some disturbances of empirical and policy significance had to be omitted from consideration by reason of the way the models are constructed. There is also the problem that intermediate target strategies have no announcement or expectational effects in the models employed (in partial mitigation, the issue here is of a comparison of alternative regimes, the expectational effects of which may be very similar, thus canceling on comparison). Therefore there is a plentiful agenda for further work. Despite these qualifications, however, the results obtained do appear significant in that a pure monetary targets regime is outperformed by the alternative considered in a majority of cases. Moreover the most notable omissions from the class of disturbances considered—money demand[6] and capital flow shocks—are both ones where a priori considerations point to a strong preference for exchange rate targets.

Such a preference, moreover, was the outcome of the earlier study by Currie and Karakitsos (1981). It is worth stressing that this outcome was the result of a rather different kind of approach to the problem. In Currie and Karakitsos, an earlier version of the NIESR model was used than the one employed here; it contained an augmented Phillips curve specification of the wage equation, providing significantly different overall model properties (see Henry, Karakitsos, and Savage 1982). These enabled a direct comparison to be made of exchange rates and monetary targets (in contrast to the position we faced in this study), but this was done on the basis of comparing the trajectories of ultimate variables and their response to shocks with monetary growth or the exchange rate set to deliver the same terminal inflation rate. These important differences suggest that the two studies should be viewed as complementary rather than as duplications, which lends further weight to the degree of agreement to be found in their results.[7]

Appendix 10A The Deterministic Optimal Policy Runs

In the text we have concentrated on the robustness issue in comparing regime performances and hence have chosen to emphasize the results obtained in stochastic optimal policy simulation. Nevertheless the deterministic simulations are of interest and so are reported here.

Like the results quoted in the text, the simulations all refer to a five-year period corresponding to a data base for 1981:4–1986:3 derived from the November 1981 forecast in the case of the NIESR model and from the October 1981 forecast in the case of the LBS. In each case the simulations are calculated against a base common assumptions forecast, which was identical for the two models in respect of the set of instrument variables employed here (treasury bill rate was set at 12 percent, real government expenditure at £6100 million, and the standard rate of tax at 30 percent), though no attempt was made to standardize the two base runs in respect of other exogenous variables.

The results presented in tables 10.A1 and 10.A2 are given for all variables, except Y, ER, and $COMP$, as arithmetic differences between each optimal run and the common assumptions or do-nothing case of the corresponding model. For the other three variables the optimal values are given as percentages of the corresponding do-nothing case. The runs cover a total of twenty quarters, but for the sake of economy in presentation, only the average of every successive four quarters is presented together with the overall twenty-quarter average.

Each of the optimal runs reported here is based on an objective function which incorporates intermediate target variables. But before discussing them it is worth indicating what happened when the NIESR model was subjected to an optimizing run with only ultimate objective variables appearing in the objective function. The results of this run showed that an attempt to reduce inflation and unemployment and balance the current account using fiscal and monetary policy can be achieved at a small cost in the NIESR model. In particular unemployment is monotonically reduced, and within five years it is 1.6 million lower compared with the do-nothing case. Inflation rises initially, reaches a peak after two years (1.5 percent higher than in the do-nothing case), and then declines, becoming almost equal to the inflation rate of the do-nothing case. The current account, though, continuously deteriorates and by the end of the fifth year is £4500 million lower than in the do-nothing case. This is achieved by continuously increasing government expenditure (which by the end of five years is £3000 million per quarter higher than in the do-nothing case), cutting the standard tax rate to 20 percent, and lowering interest rates to levels barely above zero (on occasions they even become negative). More-

Table 10A.1
NIESR model: Deterministic optimal policy

Variables	Monetary targets						Monetary and exchange rate targets (nominal): M priority reduced					
	Year 1	Year 2	Year 3	Year 4	Year 5	Average	Year 1	Year 2	Year 3	Year 4	Year 5	Average
U	−3	−49	−148	−306	−456	−192	−78	−209	−324	−503	−626	−348
P	0.0	0.1	0.5	0.3	0.7	0.3	0.2	0.5	0.3	0.0	0.6	0.3
CA	36	−187	−373	−816	−1289	−526	−260	−506	−697	−1446	−1488	−819
Y	−0.1	0.4	1.3	2.3	3.2	1.4	0.9	2.0	2.5	3.3	3.7	2.5
$\dot{M}$	−1.5	−3.2	2.9	5.0	7.1	2.1	3.2	11.7	14.5	12.1	11.1	10.5
$PSBR$	35	293	689	1260	1609	777	175	381	534	1153	1579	765
ER	0.8	−1.2	−1.4	−2.0	−3.7	−1.5	−1.9	−2.6	−2.0	−1.9	−3.1	−2.3
$COMP$	0.4	−1.0	−0.5	−0.8	−1.6	−0.7	−1.1	−1.1	−0.4	−0.5	−1.2	−0.9
G	36	198	437	801	1086	512	183	422	559	964	1219	669
T	0.6	1.0	0.7	1.5	2.5	1.2	0.1	−0.2	−0.9	−0.3	1.8	0.2
r	2.0	−0.1	−0.9	−1.0	−4.6	−0.9	−3.7	−6.6	−7.2	−6.4	−8.4	−6.5

Variables	Monetary and exchange rate targets (competitiveness)						Monetary and exchange rate targets (nominal)					
	Year 1	Year 2	Year 3	Year 4	Year 5	Average	Year 1	Year 2	Year 3	Year 4	Year 5	Average
U	−8	−56	−150	−318	−475	−201	−20	−61	−152	−321	−469	−204
$\dot{P}$	0.0	0.1	0.4	0.2	0.8	0.3	0.0	0.1	0.4	0.2	0.8	0.3
CA	16	−197	−376	−847	−1344	−550	−11	−207	−378	−856	−1294	−549
Y	0.0	0.5	1.3	2.4	3.3	1.5	0.1	0.5	1.3	2.4	3.2	1.5
$\dot{M}$	−1.0	−2.5	3.2	5.1	7.3	2.4	−0.7	−2.2	3.3	5.0	7.3	2.6
$PSBR$	44	318	674	1295	1658	798	90	316	661	1305	1644	803
ER	0.6	−1.1	−1.4	−2.0	−3.9	−1.6	0.5	−1.1	−1.4	−2.0	−3.5	−1.5
$COMP$	0.3	−0.9	−0.5	−0.8	−1.4	−0.7	0.3	−0.9	−0.5	−0.8	−1.5	−0.7
G	42	203	423	828	1133	526	72	207	419	829	1112	528
T	0.4	0.7	0.5	1.6	2.7	1.2	0.4	0.7	0.5	1.5	2.6	1.1
r	1.6	−0.3	−1.0	−1.1	−4.9	−1.1	1.4	−0.5	−1.1	−1.3	−4.3	−1.1

Note: Variable values are given as deviations of the optimal values from a common assumption simulation. In the case of Y, ER, and $COMP$ the values are given as percentage of the common assumption simulation. In all other cases the values are arithmetic differences.

Table 10A.2
LBS model: Deterministic optimal policy

Variables	Monetary targets						Exchange rate targets (nominal)					
	Year 1	Year 2	Year 3	Year 4	Year 5	Average	Year 1	Year 2	Year 3	Year 4	Year 5	Average
U	-198	-853	-972	-1017	-996	-807	-500	-755	-982	-985	-942	-833
$\dot{P}$	0.0	-1.9	-2.1	0.9	2.8	0.0	-0.5	-1.2	-0.2	1.3	2.9	0.5
CA	-105	-643	-1218	-1402	-1459	-965	-412	-640	-1004	-1302	-1627	-997
Y	0.8	3.8	4.8	5.1	5.1	3.9	2.3	3.3	4.5	4.9	5.2	4.0
M	-0.8	-0.4	1.1	2.8	5.9	1.7	1.2	-0.9	1.4	4.3	10.4	3.3
$PSBR$	-140	469	946	1463	1927	933	17	-272	904	2085	2679	1083
ER	1.7	6.5	7.0	4.5	-3.1	3.7	1.9	4.1	4.3	0.4	-8.1	0.5
$COMP$	1.0	2.3	1.1	-0.6	-3.5	0.0	0.6	1.1	0.5	-1.8	-6.5	-1.2
G	447	1322	1614	1789	1809	1396	807	1273	1705	1768	1680	1447
T	3.8	6.8	6.8	7.0	6.7	6.2	5.2	9.8	8.3	5.2	2.7	6.2
r	0.7	2.3	3.4	4.3	-0.7	2.0	-0.5	-1.4	1.6	2.2	-3.0	-0.2

Variables	Monetary and exchange rate targets (competitiveness)						Monetary and exchange rate targets (nominal)					
	Year 1	Year 2	Year 3	Year 4	Year 5	Average	Year 1	Year 2	Year 3	Year 4	Year 5	Average
U	-419	-710	-1039	-1086	-977	-845	-484	-782	-1061	-1033	-863	-844
$\dot{P}$	-0.4	-0.9	0.2	1.9	3.9	0.9	-0.5	-1.7	-0.9	0.6	2.6	0.0
CA	-351	-652	-1127	-1407	-1366	-981	-316	-643	-1102	-1369	-1414	-969
Y	1.9	3.1	4.7	5.5	5.2	4.1	2.0	3.4	4.7	4.9	4.4	3.9
M	1.0	0.9	3.3	4.8	7.8	3.6	-0.4	-1.0	1.1	3.2	6.7	1.9
$PSBR$	-108	-330	1082	2044	2322	1002	-80	-417	795	1639	2100	808
ER	1.5	2.3	0.9	-3.5	-10.8	-1.9	3.1	6.1	7.0	4.0	-3.0	3.4
$COMP$	0.4	0.1	-1.1	-3.2	-6.6	-2.1	1.3	2.0	1.3	-0.8	-4.3	-0.1
G	696	1184	1769	1910	1740	1460	801	1309	1834	1832	1662	1488
T	5.0	9.3	8.0	4.6	3.2	6.5	5.7	10.7	9.7	7.2	5.2	7.7
r	-13.	-3.6	-0.9	1.8	-2.5	-1.3	1.4	-1.3	1.5	2.6	-1.6	0.5

Note: Variable values are given as deviations of the optimal values from a common assumption simulation. In the case of Y, ER, and $COMP$ the values are given as percentage of the common assumption simulation. In all other cases the values are arithmetic differences. Each year value is the average of four quarters.

over, the behavior of *PSBR* and $\dot{M}$ in this run is particularly disturbing. The rate of growth of £M3 reaches a peak within the second year at 46 percent, while the *PSBR* monotonically increases, reaching a maximum at the end of five years, at £8000 million per quarter higher than in the do-nothing case.

Evidently the optimization exercise forces the model into an area where its gives unacceptable results. Nonextremists, we hope, would argue that if the growth rate of the supply of money were to rise to 46 percent per year, the *PSBR* were to rise to £36,000 million per year, and interest rates were to drop to as low as 2 to 3 percent, inflation would not simply be an average 0.5 percent higher and the exchange rate only 4 percent lower than in the do-nothing case. If we are to take the results of this model seriously, we have to insure ourselves against the possibility it may not be very close to the real world (that is, insure against model uncertainty). This we can easily achieve within an optimization framework by including in the objective function the intermediate targets of *PSBR* and $\dot{M}$.

The explanation of this behavior of the NIESR model lies in the theoretical underpinnings of its structure. Inflation is mainly of the cost-push variety, and in this version of the model wage inflation is not influenced by demand pressures. This implies that it is almost impossible to reduce inflation by demand management. On the other hand one can use demand management to reduce unemployment without creating any inflation. In this case the inflation-unemployment trade-off almost disappears. An infinite expansion of the economy is prohibited by the deficit in the current account. Thus the important trade-off is between unemployment and the current account rather than between unemployment and inflation.[8]

The reason why in this optimization run interest rates fall dramatically is that the stock of money (£M3) is an output variable; it does not enter any behavioral equation. This in itself is not a problem; many economists would argue that this is how it should be. The real problem is that there are no strong effects emanating from the monetary sector and feeding into the real sector (see table 10C.1). This, combined with the lack of a strong demand-pull inflation, leads to the conclusion that interest rates ought to become as low as possible to promote the unemployment objective.

With this discussion as a background, we can examine the performance of the alternative policy regimes of monetary targets, monetary and exchange rate targets (nominal), and monetary targets and competitiveness at a deterministic level within the NIESR model (table 10A.1). For the reasons discussed a direct comparison between monetary targets alone and exchange rate targets alone is not very meaningful in this model (see, though, Currie and Karakitsos 1981). However, a measure of the relative performance of the two policy regimes can still be obtained by comparing the regime of monetary targets with the regime of monetary and exchange rate targets when the priority of monetary targets is reduced, and in table 10A.1 we report the results of an experiment in which the priority on the monetary target was reduced by 50 percent. A performance measure of the rival policy regimes is the percentage improvement in cost contribution of all ultimate targets (inflation, unemployment, and current account) over the corresponding cost contribution of the do-nothing case.[9]

A common feature in all four cases is the reduction in unemployment, a slight increase in inflation, and a deterioration in the current account. In all cases the optimal policy is a combination of expansionary government expenditure with an increased income tax rate and lower interest rates. Increased taxation is the result of wanting to keep the *PSBR* under control (by including it in the objective function). The slightly better performance of monetary and exchange rate targets over monetary targets is explained by the relatively more expansionary fiscal policy, which raises the *PSBR* to a somewhat higher level, and the somewhat lower interest rates, which permit a small rise in the money supply relative to monetary targets. When the $\dot{M}$ priority is reduced, interest rates are allowed to fall significantly, substantially stimulating the economy.

Table 10A.2 provides a comparison of all four rival policy regimes for the LBS model. Here a direct comparison of monetary versus exchange rate targets is possible because in the LBS model the money supply directly enters many behavioral equations (consumption, exchange rate; see table 10C.2). This does not imply that the LBS model is a better-specified model than the NIESR because in many instances there is no sound theoretical reason for inclusion of the money supply in some relationships. Whatever the theoretical controversy, the fact remains that in the LBS model, there is a significant inflation-unemployment trade-off, whether one is attempting to squeeze inflation out of the system or reduce unemployment. This, combined with the effect that the stock of money has on important variables of the model, prohibits interest rates from falling to very low levels.

The percentage contribution of all ultimate targets over the corresponding cost contribution of the do-nothing case for each policy regime is 48 percent in the case of monetary targets, 47.8 percent in the case of exchange rate targets, 44.4 percent in the case of monetary targets and competitiveness, and 52.3 percent in the case of monetary and exchange rate targets (nominal). These results illustrate the superiority of monetary and (nominal) exchange rate targets over the other three alternative regimes. This seems to be an important result inasmuch as monetary and nominal exchange rate targets along with monetary targets and competitiveness came out to be the superior policy regimes in the NIESR model. Although there is nothing to choose (on a deterministic level) between monetary and nominal exchange rate targets on the one hand and monetary targets and competitiveness on the other, in the NIESR model there seems to be a good reason for the preference of the former regime on the grounds of model uncertainty.

A common feature in all four policy regimes in the LBS model is a substantial reduction in unemployment, a very small (on average) increase in inflation (although there are signs of accelerating inflation at the end of five years) with a continuous deterioration in the current account. Although the same pattern seems to emerge from the NIESR model, there are important quantitative differences between the two models. In the LBS model unemployment is reduced on average by more than 800,000 with no average increase in inflation (at least in two policy regimes) and an average deterioration of less than £100 million in the current account. In the NIESR model unemployment is reduced on average by only 200,000 inflation is higher by only 0.3 of 1 percentage point, and the current account deteriorates by something more than £500 million.

Fiscal policy in both models turns out to be expansionary, with increased real government expenditure and higher tax rates, a result in both cases of targeting the *PSBR*. It is also very important that the degree of fiscal expansion as measured by the *PSBR* is almost the same in the two models.[10] What seems to be of enormous difference in the two models is the role of monetary policy. In the NIESR model, interest rates tend to fall whatever the policy regime. In the LBS model, especially under monetary targets, interest rates tend to rise. The reason for this different behavior of interest rates is that in the NIESR model, interest rates play an extremely Keynesian role, affecting only private residential investment (which is a small proportion of total expenditure) and the exchange rate through capital movements, whereas in the LBS model, the monetary sector is built along the lines of what has come to be known in the literature as international monetarism. An increase in the rate of interest reduces the demand for money (the velocity is increased), prices have to rise to equilibrate the money market (through the quantity theory of money), and the exchange rate falls (through the purchasing power parity theorem). On the other hand an increase in income leads to a rise in the demand for money, prices have to fall to equilibrate the money market, and the exchange rate rises. The supply of money, being an endogenous variable, is mainly affected by the *PSBR*.

Under monetary targets (in the LBS model) expansionary fiscal policy tends to raise the *PSBR* and income and so reduces unemployment, but at the same time the current account worsens. The demand for money tends to increase due to rising income but tends to fall due to rising interest rates. The supply of money initially falls but soon starts rising because of an accelerating increase in *PSBR*. Hence the initial excess demand for money that puts a downward pressure on prices is soon reversed, leading to rising inflation. The situation is aggravated through the simultaneity of prices and the exchange rate. When inflation is falling, the exchange rate tends to appreciate, and this feedback to prices makes inflation even lower. But as soon as inflation starts rising (because of developments in the money market), there is a big effect on the exchange rate with a feedback effect on inflation, thus producing signs of accelerating inflation.

In conclusion, the deterministic runs show that a regime of monetary and nominal exchange rate targets is preferable to either a regime of monetary targets or to a regime of monetary targets and competitiveness. This conclusion seems to be supported by both models—the NIESR and the LBS. Furthermore a regime of intermediate targets when combined with policies that simultaneously aim at ultimate targets produce results that, judged in terms of ultimate targets, indicate the same quantitative pattern (a reduction in unemployment with very small increase in inflation and a deterioration in the current account). There seems to be a consensus on how fiscal policy ought to be used in the two models, although the same cannot be said for monetary policy.

Appendix 10B The *PSBR* as a Target Variable

Traditional Keynesian theory argues that whenever there is a shock that reduces aggregate demand, the optimal response ought to be an increase in government expenditure or a reduction in the standard tax rate, or both. If monetary policy is to be used to offset the fall in aggregate demand, then interest rates ought to be cut. Implicit in this argument is that there is only one target: unemployment. In the case where unemployment is only one among many conflicting objectives (as in our specification of the objective function), it is more difficult to make a prejudgment as to the right direction of the optimal response. Resort to the corresponding deterministic optimal run may provide a useful insight. In the case of the regime of monetary targets (NIESR model) the deterministic run indicates that the unemployment target is of overriding concern. This implies that in the face of a shock that reduces aggregate demand, the initial response ought to be to offset this fall. We have already observed, however, that the optimal response to a demand shock in the NIESR model under monetary targets does not accord with this theoretical presumption. Instead what we observe is a cut in public expenditure and a rise in the standard tax rate. Nevertheless interest rates are allowed to fall, as is to be expected from theoretical considerations.

If we were to judge the stance of fiscal policy by the *PSBR*, however, we would have concluded that fiscal policy had been stabilizing. The fact that unemployment rises by 110,000 in the first year would have been interpreted as the inevitable price to pay because of the unexpected fall in demand. However, it has long been recognized that the nominal *PSBR* may be a misleading indicator of the stance of fiscal policy (see, for example, Shaw 1979) and that targeting the *PSBR* is likely to be destabilizing, at least in the case of demand shocks, where the impact effect of such shocks on output and hence on tax revenues and the *PSBR* must lead to adjustments in fiscal instruments that amplify the impact effect if the *PSBR* target is to be maintained.

To test the hypothesis that targeting the nominal *PSBR* in the short run is destabilizing, we repeated the run with the same demand shock under monetary targets in the NIESR model but with the priority on the *PSBR* reduced. The results are given in table 10B.1; for comparison purposes we have reproduced the relevant part from table 10.4. Together they confirm the destabilizing character of nominal *PSBR* targets, for when the priority on maintaining this target is reduced, government expenditure is seen to rise in the first year where previously it was cut, and although the income tax rate again rises, the increase is smaller than it was when a high priority was attributed to the *PSBR* target (the small rise is in accordance with not completely abolishing the *PSBR* targets). Although the *PSBR* is positive in the first year in both cases, it is much larger in the case when the *PSBR*

Table 10B.1
NIESR model: Optimal response to a demand shock (-5% in consumer's expenditure), varying the *PSBR* priority

Variables	Monetary targets (*MT*)						Monetary targets: *PSBR* priority reduced (*MTP*)					
	Year 1	Year 2	Year 3	Year 4	Year 5	Average	Year 1	Year 2	Year 3	Year 4	Year 5	Average
U	110	143	92	47	26	83	6	74	63	26	10	36
$\dot{P}$	0.0	−0.2	0.1	0.0	−0.2	0.0	0.1	−0.1	0.0	0.0	0.0	0.0
CA	615	252	25	−15	−15	172	373	131	−36	−61	−36	74
Y	−2.1	−0.8	0.1	0.2	0.1	−0.5	−1.1	−0.3	0.2	0.2	0.1	−0.2
$\dot{M}$	−1.9	−0.5	−0.4	−0.4	−0.2	−0.7	−1.2	0.2	0.1	0.0	0.0	−0.2
$PSBR$	349	97	110	−35	−29	98	891	355	86	−58	−25	250
ER	1.2	0.2	−0.4	−0.2	0.1	0.2	0.5	0.1	−0.3	−0.1	0.0	0.0
$COMP$	0.7	−0.2	−0.3	0.0	0.0	0.0	0.3	0.0	−0.2	0.0	0.0	0.0
G	−47	−23	13	−11	−20	−18	246	79	−12	−22	−16	55
T	0.7	1.3	0.8	0.0	−0.4	0.5	0.2	0.4	0.2	0.0	0.0	0.2
r	−1.3	−0.2	0.3	0.3	0.3	−0.1	−1.4	−0.4	0.1	0.2	0.2	−0.3

priority is reduced, illustrating the misleading nature of the *PSBR* as a measure of the stance of fiscal policy. As a result unemployment rises only by 6,000 in the first year when the *PSBR* priority is reduced, while it rises by 110,000 in the other case.

It must be stressed, though, that this result does not hold true for all types of shock, whether positive or negative. It is equally important to emphasize that the destabilizing property of targeting the *PSBR* arises also from the fact that the policymaker pursues a short-term *PSBR* target. In the example considered, the policymaker is assumed to respond to any short-lived shocks, and therefore all targets in the objective function automatically become short-term targets. In the deterministic runs, on the other hand, the targets are traded off over a long horizon and thus can be interpreted as long-term objectives. In addition the nature of the deterministic runs makes the objectives long-term ones because short-term shocks are ignored (the policy is not revised) on the ground that these shocks are expected to cancel out. Furthermore this does not imply that the deterministic optimal policy ought to be applied for the next five years whatever the new developments in the economy. New information about the actual state of the endogenous variables and the assumed values of the exogenous variables will certainly be incorporated, and thus the new deterministic optimal policy will be revised (sequential open loop policy).

Appendix 10C The NIESR and LBS Models

Tables 10C.1 and 10C.2 provide a schematic account of the two models employed. In the interest of brevity of presentation and in order to provide a readily comprehensible description of the models, we have taken liberties in aggregating the model equations themselves and have deliberately abstracted from both the dynamic structure of the equations and from numerical presentation of their steady state values. The aim is to provide a rigorous account in which the interconnections are clear. For a full listing, readers are referred to NIESR (1979) and LBS (1981).

Glossary of Variables

Y = real national income
C = real consumption

I = real investment including stock building

G = real government expenditure

X = real exports

Q = real imports

Y^d = real disposable income

P = price level

$\dot{P}$ = inflation rate

BLP = bank lending to the private sector

BLG = bank lending to the government

T = taxes

CU = capacity utilization

R = market interest rate

π = index of profitability

WT = index of world trade

PX = prices of exports

P_w = world prices

ER = effective exchange rate

CA = current account

$\sum CA$ = accumulated sum of CA

R_w = world interest rate

B = bonds outstanding

CR = currency held by the public

FO = overseas financing

M = money supply (M3 variety)

$\dot{M}$ = sterling M3 four quarter percentage change

DS = sight deposits

TD = time deposits

V = wealth of the private sector

$\dot{W}$ = wage inflation

W = wage level

U = unemployment

L = labor supply

E = employment

r = interest rate on government debt

FC = net foreign currency position

$\Delta(FC)$ = capital flows

ER^e = expected exchange rate

Y_w = real world income

$\bar{Y}$ = normal or natural level of output

L^d = demand for labor

$PSBR$ = public sector borrowing requirement, £ million per year

Table 10C.1 NIESR Model

(1) $Y = C + I + G + X - Q$

(2) $C = C(Y^d, BLP/P, \dot{P}), C_1 > 0, C_2 > 0, C_3 < 0$

(3) $Y^d = Y - T$

(4) $T = t \cdot (P \cdot Y)$

(5) $I = I[\Delta Y \cdot CU], BLP/P, R, \pi]I_1 > 0, I_2 > 0, I_3 < 0, I_4 < 0$

(6) $X = X\left(WT, \dfrac{(PX)(ER)}{P_w}\right), X_1 > 0, X_2 < 0$

(7) $Q = Q\left(Y, \dfrac{P_w}{(P)(ER)}\right), Q_1 > 0, Q_2 < 0$

(8) $(PX) = PX\left(P, \dfrac{P_w}{ER}\right), PX_1 > 0, PX_2 > 0$

(9) $(CA) = X \cdot (PX) - Q\left(\dfrac{P_w}{ER}\right)$

(10) $(ER) = (ER)\left[(R - R_w), \left(\dfrac{CA}{P}\right), \left(\dfrac{P_w}{P}\right)\right], ER_1 > 0, ER_2 > 0,$

$\qquad ER_3 > 0$

(11) $\Delta(BLG) = G - T - \Delta B - \Delta(CR) - \Delta(FO)$

(12) $\Delta M = \Delta(CR) + \Delta(SD) + \Delta(TD)$

(13) $\dfrac{CR}{P} = C(Y), CR' > 0$

(14) $\dfrac{SD}{P} = SD(R, Y), SD_1 < 0, SD_2 > 0$

(15) $\Delta B = B(R, r, \Delta V), B_1 < 0, B_2 > 0, B_3 > 0$

(16) $\Delta V = rB + Y - C - I - T = \Delta M + \Delta B$

(17) $\Delta(TD) = \Delta(BLG) + \Delta(BLP) - \Delta(SD)$

(18) $\Delta\left(\dfrac{BLP}{P}\right) = BLP\left(\dfrac{\Delta V}{P}, Y, R\right), BLP_1 < 0, BLP_2 > 0, BLP_3 < 0$

(19) $R = R(r)$, $R' > 0$

(20) $\dot{P} = P\left(\dot{W}, \dfrac{P_w}{(ER)}\right)$, $P_1 > 0$, $P_2 > 0$

(21) $\dot{W} = W\left[\dot{P}, \left(1 - \dfrac{T}{W}\right)\right]$, $W_1 > 0$, $W_2 < 0$

(22) $U = L - E$

(23) $E = E(Y)$, $F' > 0$

Table 10C.2 LBS Model

(1)′ $Y = C + I + G + X - Q$

(2)′ $C = C(Y^d, M/P, \dot{P})$, $C_1 > 0$, $C_2 > 0$, $C_3 < 0$

(3)′ $Y^d = Y - T$

(4)′ $T = t \cdot (P \cdot Y)$

(5)′ $I = I[\Delta Y, BLP/P, V/P, (P - \dot{P}), \pi]$, $I_1 > 0$, $I_2 > 0$, $I_3 > 0$,

$\qquad I_4 < 0$, $I_5 > 0$

(6)′ $X = X\left(WT, \dfrac{(PX)(ER)}{P_w}\right)$, $X_1 > 0$, $X_2 < 0$

(7)′ $Q = Q\left(Y, \dfrac{P_w}{(P)(ER)}\right)$, $Q_1 > 0$, $Q_2 < 0$

(8)′ $(PX) = PX\left(P, \dfrac{P_w}{ER}\right)$, $PX_1 > 0$, $PX_2 > 0$

(9)′ $(CA) = X \cdot (PX) - Q \cdot \left(\dfrac{P_w}{ER}\right)$

(10)′ $\Delta(FC) = (FC) - (FC)_{-1} = -(CA)$

(11)′ $(FC) = FC[ER^e - ER), (R - R_w)]$, $FC_1 < 0$, $FC_2 > 0$

(12)′ $(ER) = ER\left[\left(\dfrac{M_w}{M}\right), \left(\dfrac{Y}{Y_w}\right), \left(\dfrac{B_w}{R}\right), \left(\sum CA\right)\right]$, $ER_M < 0$, $ER_Y > 0$,

$\qquad ER_R < 0$, $ER_{\Sigma CA} > 0$

(13)′ $\Delta M = G - T - \Delta B - (FO) + \Delta(BLP)$

(14)′ $R = R(r)$, $R' > 0$

(15)′ $\Delta V = rB + Y - C - I - T = \Delta M + \Delta B$

(16)′ $\dot{P} = P\left(\dot{W}, \dfrac{P_w}{ER}\right)$, $P_1 > 0$, $P_2 > 0$

(17)′ $\dot{W} = W[\dot{P}, (Y - \bar{Y})]$, $W_1 > 0$, $W_2 > 0$

$$(18)' \quad U = L - L^d$$

$$(19)' \quad L^d = L\left(\frac{\dot{W}}{\dot{P}}\right), \ L' < 0$$

Notes

1. Thus, for example, a rise in the rate of interest leads to refinance of outstanding national debt at higher coupons and so to an increase in property income and added consumption. This weighs against the deflationary impact of the higher interest rates on investment spending.

2. The demand for money might allow for the influence of interest rates as in $(12)'$, with the additional implication that a rise in domestic rates causes a depreciation of the currency since it reduces the demand for money. However, although the rate of interest is included in $(12)'$, for the sake of completeness, the corresponding term was missing from the version of the model we employed.

3. Defined as Px/Pw. e where Px = U.K. export prices of manufactures, Pw = world price of manufactures, and e is the effective exchange rate in £ per \$.

4. See the *Financial Statement and Budget Report* 1982–83.

5. An important additional reason for thinking that indicator variables are significant is the belief that the credible announcement of policy targets for such variables itself exerts favorable effects on behavior. But this kind of effect is not comprehended by either of the models employed here.

6. If monetary targets meant monetary base targets, then money supply (high-powered money multiplier) shocks should be considered as well.

7. There were several other, less important, differences. For example, in the Currie-Karakitsos paper, only two instruments (government spending and the treasury bill rate) were employed, the time horizon was limited to 4, as opposed to 5, years, and the initial conditions were different (corresponding to the time period 1975:4–1978:3 rather than to the period 1981:4 to 1986:3 used here).

8. For a comparison of the policy implications of this type of wage equation with a conventional Phillips curve in the NIESR model, see Henry, Karakitsos, and Savage (1982).

9. The cost contribution of ultimate targets is: 12,141 in the do-nothing case; 9985 in the monetary targets case; 8862 under monetary and exchange rate targets ($\dot{M}$ priority reduced); 9904 under monetary and exchange rate targets; and 9911 under monetary targets and competitiveness.

10. Whether the stance of fiscal policy ought to be measured by nominal or real *PSBR* or even cyclically adjusted real *PSBR* is a matter of considerable controversy.

References

Arestis, P., and Karakitsos, E. 1982. "An Evaluation of Two Large-Scale UK Models within an Optimal Control Framework: The Crowding-Out Issue." *PROPE Discussion Papers* 49, Imperial College (March).

Artis, M. J. 1982. "Why do Forecasts Differ?" Paper presented to the Bank of England Academic Panel, February.

Artis, M. J., and Currie, D. A. 1981. "Monetary Targets and the Exchange Rate: A Case for Conditional Targets." *Oxford Economic Papers* (July).

Bray, Jeremy. 1982. *Production, Purpose and Structure*, London: Francis Pinter.

Currie, D., and Karakitsos, E. 1981. "Monetary and Exchange Rate Targets in the NIESR Model: A Stochastic Control Evaluation." *Queen Mary College Discussion Papers* 78 (October).

Henry, S. G. B., Karakitsos, E., and Savage, D. 1982. "On the Derivation of the 'Efficient' Phillips Curve." *Manchester School* (June).

London Business School. 1981. "The London Business School Quarterly Econometric Model of the United Kingdom Economy." *Centre for Economic Forecasting* (October).

National Institute of Economic and Social Research. 1979. "Listing of the Interim NIESR Model IV." Discussion Paper 28. London. National Institute of Economic and Social Research.

Poole, W. 1970. "Optimal Choice of Monetary Policy Instruments in a Single Stochastic Macro Model." *Quarterly Journal of Economics* (June).

Shaw, G. K. 1979. "The Measurement of Fiscal Influence." In S. T. Cook and P. M. Jackson, eds., *Current Issues in Fiscal Policy*. Oxford: Martin Robertson.

11 Wage Contracting, Exchange Rate Volatility, and Exchange Intervention Policy

Matthew B. Canzoneri and John M. Underwood

1. Introduction and Summary

A frictionless model of the economy, with wages and prices moving each period to clear the labor and goods markets, is generally considered to be inconsistent with certain stylized facts about the real world. In such a model employment and output adjust immediately to any economic disturbance; there is no persistence of effects, no business cycle. Also money is neutral in such an economy, and if monetary disturbances are the primary source of exchange rate and price level movements, the model is incapable of explaining the apparent fact that exchange rates are more volatile than prices. Dornbusch's (1976) approach to this problem was to postulate that the goods market clears more slowly than the money market. Representing price stickiness by a Phillips curve and assuming that the money market clears instantaneously, he derived his celebrated overshooting result for the exchange rate.

In this chapter we attribute the slow adjustment in the real side of the economy to wage contracting.[1] We consider both the neoclassical contracting model of Gray (1976), Fischer (1977a), and Canzoneri (1980) and the neo-Keynesian model of Taylor (1980). This approach has a number of advantages. We do not have to assume that prices are fixed in the short run, so the question of the relative variability of prices and exchange rates has more meaning. We can identify the degree of inertia imposed on the real side of the economy with either the average length of contracts or the sensitivity of wages to expected demand conditions, and we can vary the degree of inertia to assess the effect of slower adjustment on persistence and the relative variability of prices and exchange rates. More important, and also more controversial, we can give these positive results a normative interpretation. We can, for example, suggest which agents are helped or hurt by exchange rate overshooting. We can also suggest which agents would be helped or hurt by an intervention policy that curbed the exchange rate overshooting.

Some monetarists assert that price and exchange rate fluctuations are due primarily to monetary disturbances. It turns out that most of our results depend crucially on the validity of this assertion. Our basic conclusions may be summarized as follows:

1. If goods market disturbances, rather than monetary disturbances, are the primary source of price and exchange rate fluctuations, then a frictionless model of the economy may not be inconsistent with the observation that exchange rates are more volatile than prices. This real world fact may not be a paradox that needs to be explained.

2. If on the other hand the monetarist assertion is correct, then a frictionless economy cannot explain the observed volatility of exchange rates relative to prices, but both contracting models can. In addition increasing the degree of inertia embodied in the contracts increases the volatility of exchange rates relative to prices.

3. Taylor's contracting model implies more persistence than Gray's and is more closely related to Dornbusch's fixed-price model.

4. The existence of wage contracting presumably benefits labor market participants and may also benefit portfolio managers by stabilizing the real interest rate, especially if goods market disturbances are an important source of price and exchange rate variation. If, however, the monetarist assertion is correct, then the conversion of some one-period contracts to two-period contracts will hurt both portfolio managers and the labor market participants under existing contracts by destabilizing both the real interest rate and employment.

5. An intervention policy that leans against the wind to stabilize nominal or real exchange rate fluctuations will benefit both labor market participants and portfolio managers if the monetarist assertion is correct. If instead goods market disturbances are the primary source of price and exchange rate fluctuations, then such a policy may benefit portfolio managers at the expense of labor market participants by stabilizing the real interest rate but destabilizing employment.

2. The Positive Implications of Wage Contracting

First we show how monetary and goods market disturbances affect the exchange rate and price level in the flexible wage economy that we take as a benchmark. Then we impose two different forms of contracting on the labor market and examine their implications for the volatility of exchange rate and price level movements. In particular we want to see whether either form of contracting helps to explain our stylized facts by increasing exchange rate volatility and/or decreasing price level volatility and by imparting more persistence to the effects of disturbances. The economy operates quite differently under these two forms of contracting; in fact they really constitute two different views of the supply side of the economy. Thus we are also interested in identifying the particular features in the economy that are important if a given form of contracting is to help explain the stylized facts.

A Flexible Wage Model: The Benchmark Case

Our basic framework is similar to Dornbusch's (1976). We consider a single country that produces a differentiated product but whose bonds are perfect substitutes for foreign bonds. Demand for the country's product is given by

$$y_t = \bar{y} - \delta(p_t - e_t - p_t^*) + u_t + \tilde{z}_t \tag{1}$$

where y, p, e, and p^* are the logs of output, its home currency price, the exchange rate, and the foreign currency price of foreign output, and u and $\tilde{z}$ are disturbance terms.[2] Supply of the product is fixed at its full employment or natural rate, $\bar{y}$:

$$y_t = \bar{y}. \tag{2}$$

This is a consequence of the flexible wage assumption; the nominal wage moves each period to clear the labor market.[3]

Incipient capital movements ensure that

$$r_t = r_t^* + e_{t+1|t} - e_t \tag{3}$$

where r and r^* are the nominal rates of return on domestic and foreign bonds and $e_{t+1|t} - e_t$ is the expected rate of depreciation of the domestic currency. Expectations are assumed to be rational; $e_{t+1|t}$ is the expected value of next period's exchange rate based on complete current and lagged information. Home country residents hold the entire domestic money stock; money demand is given by

$$m_t - p_t = -\lambda r_t + y_t - \tilde{v}_t \tag{4}$$

where m is the log of the domestic money stock, and $\tilde{v}$ is a velocity disturbance.[4]

We want to model both temporary and permanent monetary and goods market disturbances. A "$\sim$" over a disturbance indicates that it is serially uncorrelated and normally distributed. $\tilde{v}$ is a temporary monetary disturbance, and $\tilde{z}$ is a temporary goods market disturbance; m and u are assumed to follow a random walk,

$$m_t = m_{t-1} + \tilde{m}_t \text{ and } u_t = u_{t-1} + \tilde{u}_t, \tag{5}$$

so $\tilde{m}$ and $\tilde{u}$ are permanent monetary and goods market disturbances.

For simplicity we set p_t^* and r_t^* equal to zero; then we have this solution to the flexible wage model:

$$p_t = \sum_0^\infty \tilde{m}_{t-i} + [1/(1 + \lambda)]\tilde{v}_t + [\lambda/\delta(1 + \lambda)]\tilde{z}_t, \tag{6}$$

$$e_t = \sum_0^\infty \tilde{m}_{t-i} + [1/(1 + \lambda)]\tilde{v}_t - (1/\delta)\sum_0^\infty \tilde{u}_{t-i} - [1/\delta(1 + \lambda)]\tilde{z}_t.$$

Solution techniques are discussed in appendix 11A.

Money is neutral in this frictionless economy. A permanent increase in the money supply produces permanent and proportionate increases in the price level and the exchange rate; it has no effect on the expected rate of depreciation, $e_{t+1|t} - e_t$. By contrast a temporary increase (which is equivalent to a positive $\tilde{v}_t$) produces an expected rate of appreciation and therefore has less than proportionate effects on the price level and the exchange rate. A permanent increase in demand for the home good is immediately offset by a permanent increase in the terms of trade, which is achieved by a permanent appreciation of the exchange rate; there is, however, no change in the expected rate of appreciation or in the price level. A temporary increase produces an expected rate of depreciation and a temporary increase in the terms of trade that is absorbed by both the price level and the exchange rate.

The important thing to note is that in our benchmark case, monetary disturbances, whether permanent or temporary, have an equal impact on the exchange rate and the price level. This result is inconsistent with our stylized fact that exchange rates are more volatile than prices, and it is the paradox that the sticky price models of Dornbusch (1976) and others were built to explain.

It is also interesting to note, however, that goods market disturbances may have more impact on exchange rates than on prices. Permanent disturbances are totally absorbed by the exchange rate, and temporary disturbances have a larger impact on the exchange rate than the price level if the interest semielasticity of money demand is small ($\lambda < 1$). If price and exchange rate movements are determined primarily by goods market disturbances, then our flexible wage model probably is not inconsistent with our stylized fact.

In summary our benchmark flexible wage economy is inconsistent with the stylized fact that exchange rates are more volatile than prices if the monetarist view prevails and exchange rate movements are primarily monetary phenomena. If instead exchange rate movements result from goods market disturbances, then we may have no paradox to explain.

The flexible wage model is definitely inconsistent with our second stylized fact concerning persistence. The effects of both monetary and goods market disturbances are immediate and complete within the period in which they occur. The system requires no further adjustment.

A Neoclassical Contracting Model

Fischer (1977a), Gray (1976), and Canzoneri (1980) have developed contracting models in which the nominal wage must be specified in a labor contract before markets meet and production occurs. In a popular version of these models there is a supply of labor derived from utility maximization and a demand for labor derived from profit maximization, and wage setters choose the wage expected to clear the market.

If labor supply is perfectly inelastic and if there are no productivity disturbances, then the market clearing real wage is a time-invariant constant, $\overline{w - p}$.[5] The labor contract specifies nominal wage rates, so the wage setters must first predict the price levels that will prevail during the contract period and then set the wage rates accordingly. For example, the contract wage for period $t + i$ will be

$$w_{t+i} = \overline{w - p} + p_{t+i|t} \tag{8}$$

in a contract negotiated at the end of period t; wage setters expect this wage to clear the market in period $t + i$.

The real wage that actually obtains in period $t + i$ will not be the market clearing one unless the wage setters predict the price level perfectly; that is,

$$w_{t+i} - p_{t+i} = \overline{w - p} - (p_{t+i} - p_{t+i|t}). \tag{9}$$

With probability one, the plans of both suppliers and demanders of labor cannot be realized so the contract also specifies (perhaps implicitly) an employment rule that relates employment in period $t + i$ to the real wage that actually obtains in period $t + i$. We follow the authors referred to above in assuming that the employment rule is identical to the profit-maximizing firm's demand curve, but there are other possibilities.[6] The output supply curve in period $t + i$ for firms under this contract is

$$y_{t+i} = \bar{y} + \theta(p_{t+i} - p_{t+i|t}) \tag{10}$$

and the slope of this curve, θ, depends positively on the marginal productivity of labor.[7]

The aggregate supply curve we use in place of equation (2) is

$$y_t = \bar{y} + (1 - \phi)\theta(p_t - p_{t|t-1}) + \phi[0.5\theta(p_t - p_{t|t-1}) + 0.5\theta(p_t - p_{t|t-2})]. \tag{11}$$

We assume that some firms are covered by contracts that last only one period while others are covered by contracts lasting two periods; ϕ is the fraction of firms covered by two-period contracts. If ϕ is equal to zero, all of the contracts are renegotiated at the end of each period, and output fluctuates about its natural rate with one-period price prediction errors. If ϕ is greater than zero, all of the one-period contracts and half of the two-period contracts are being renegotiated at the end of each period; the other half of the two-period contracts are going into their second and final period. The second term on the right-hand side of (11) comes from the one-period contracts; the third is due to the two-period contracts.

By increasing ϕ from zero to one, we can increase the inertia in the labor market and assess its implications for the volatility of price and exchange rate movements and for the persistence of effects.[8] We could also include contracts that lasted more than two periods, but the implications of such an extension will be obvious.

We consider first the case in which ϕ is equal to zero; all contracts last just one period. In this case we have the solution to the neoclassical contracting model, $\phi = 0$:

$$p_t = \pi_1 \tilde{m}_t + \Sigma_1^\infty \tilde{m}_{t-i} + \pi_3 \tilde{v}_t + \pi_4 \tilde{z}_t \tag{12}$$

$$e_t = \varepsilon_1 \tilde{m}_t + \Sigma_1^\infty \tilde{m}_{t-i} + \varepsilon_3 \tilde{v}_t - (1/\delta)\Sigma_0^\infty \tilde{u}_{t-i} - \varepsilon_4 \tilde{z}_t \tag{13}$$

where

$$\pi_1 = \frac{(1 - \rho)(1 + \lambda)}{(1 - \rho)(1 + \lambda) + \theta} \qquad \varepsilon_1 = [1 + (\theta/\delta)]\pi_1$$

$$\pi_3 = \frac{(1 - \rho)}{(1 - \rho)(1 + \lambda) + \theta} \qquad \varepsilon_3 = [1 + (\theta/\delta)]\pi_3$$

$$\pi_4 = [\rho/(1 - \rho)]\pi_3 \qquad \varepsilon_4 = (1/\delta) - [1 + (\theta/\delta)]\pi_4 > 0$$

and

$$\rho = \lambda/(\lambda + \delta) < 1.$$

The derivation of this solution is discussed in appendix 11A.

The first point to note is that contracting decreases the impact of monetary disturbances on the price level and, if $\delta < 1$, increases the impact of monetary disturbances on the exchange rate.[9] In this way contracting can explain the stylized fact that exchange rates are more volatile than prices. Contracting does little, however, to help explain our stylized fact in the case of goods market disturbances. Permanent goods market disturbances are still totally absorbed by the exchange rate, and contracting mutes the impact of temporary disturbances on both the price level and the exchange rate.[10]

These results for monetary disturbances can be explained in terms of overshooting of the exchange rate and undershooting of the price level. Figure 11.1 shows how a permanent increase in the money supply at time t_0 affects the price level and the exchange rate over time. (The analysis of temporary monetary disturbances is analogous.) In the flexible wage model, the full effect of $\tilde{m}_{t_0}$ on p_t and e_t is immediate and permanent, as represented by the solid line in figure 11.1. With one-period contracts, however, the price level will undershoot in the first period; this is represented by a dashed line in figure 11.1. The rising price level and falling real wage increase output and therefore money demand; consequently a less-than-proportionate increase in the price level is needed to equilibrate the money market. The exchange rate will overshoot, as shown by the dotted line in figure 11.1, if δ is less than one. The less-than-proportionate increase in the price level leaves an increase in the real supply of money that must be accommodated by an increase in demand. The increase in output raises transactions demand, and if this is not sufficient to fill the gap, the interest rate falls. It is clear from the interest parity equation, equation (3), that this requires the exchange rate to overshoot and create the expectation of an appreciation; otherwise risk-neutral portfolio managers would not hold domestic bonds. The condition on δ, which we assume to hold, keeps the output effect on money demand from

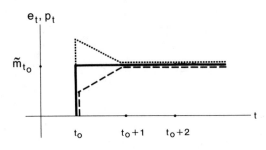

Figure 11.1
Effect of a permanent increase in the money supply on the price level and exchange rates:
$\phi = 0$

reversing this result by limiting the effect of the fall in the terms of trade on demand for the domestic good.[11]

From (11) and (12) output is given by

$$y_t = \bar{y} + \theta\pi_1\tilde{m}_t + \theta\pi_3\tilde{v}_t + \theta\pi_4\tilde{z}_t. \tag{14}$$

The impact of monetary disturbances on output and the amount of exchange rate overshooting and price level undershooting all depend on the size of θ.[12] A bigger θ implies a more elastic supply of output. Thus in response to an unanticipated increase in the money supply, the increase in output does more to equilibrate the money market, and the price level does less; in terms of figure 11.1, the price level undershoots more. And with a bigger supply effect, the terms of trade must fall further to equilibrate the goods market; the exchange rate overshoots more to produce this terms of trade effect.

So θ is an important parameter in this explanation of output, price, and exchange rate fluctuations in response to monetary disturbances. A large θ is implied by a high marginal productivity of labor and a relatively wage-elastic employment rule.[13]

One-period contracts do allow deviations in output from its full employment level, but they do not explain the persistence in these deviations that we have taken as our second stylized fact. Similarly it is clear from equations (12) and (13) that the price level and the exchange rate adjust fully to any disturbance after only one period.

With $\phi > 0$, some contracts last two periods, and we have this solution to the neoclassical contracting model, $\phi > 0$:

$$p_t = \pi_1 \tilde{m}_t + \pi_2 \tilde{m}_{t-1} + \Sigma_2^\infty \tilde{m}_{t-i} + \pi_3 \tilde{v}_t + \pi_4 \tilde{z}_t \tag{15}$$

$$e_t = \varepsilon_1 \tilde{m}_t + \varepsilon_2 \tilde{m}_{t-1} + \Sigma_2^\infty \tilde{m}_{t-i} + \varepsilon_3 \tilde{v}_t - (1/\delta)\Sigma_0^\infty \tilde{u}_{t-i} - \varepsilon_4 \tilde{z}_t \tag{16}$$

where

$$\pi_1 = \frac{(1-\rho)^2(1+\lambda)^2 + 0.5\phi\theta(1-\rho) + 0.5\phi\theta\rho(1-\rho)(1+\lambda)}{(1-\rho)^2(1+\lambda)^2 + \theta(1-\rho)(1+\lambda) + 0.5\phi\theta(1-\rho)(1+\lambda) + 0.5\phi\theta^2}$$

$$\pi_2 = \frac{(1-\rho)(1+\lambda)}{(1-\rho)(1+\lambda) + 0.5\phi\theta} \qquad \varepsilon_2 = [1 + 0.5\phi(\theta/\delta)]\pi_2$$

and π_3, π_4, ε_3, and ε_4 are as defined in (12) and (13).

With two-period contracts it takes two periods for the price level and the exchange rate to adjust to a permanent monetary disturbance. A permanent disturbance that occurs in the first period of a two-period contract will also cause a price prediction error in the second period of the contract.[14] This implies a positive correlation in the deviations from full employment for firms covered by two-period contracts:

$$y_t = \bar{y} + \theta(\pi_1 \tilde{m}_t + \pi_3 \tilde{v}_t + \pi_4 \tilde{z}_t) + 0.5\phi\theta\pi_2 \tilde{m}_{t-1}. \tag{17}$$

Output cycles about its natural rate.

The size of ϕ, the proportion of contracts lasting two periods, also affects the magnitude of the immediate impact of a permanent monetary disturbance on the price level, the exchange rate, and output. Figure 11.2 shows how price level undershooting and exchange rate overshooting are affected.[15] (The solid lines reproduce the results for the case $\phi = 0$; the dashed and dotted lines obtain if $\phi > 0$.) The overshooting of the exchange rate increases. It also turns out that the immediate impact on output and the real exchange rate, $e - p$, is magnified.[16] So the increase in exchange rate overshooting outweighs the decrease in price level undershooting, and the existence of two-period contracts helps explain the fact that exchange rates are more volatile than prices.

The reason for these results is that portfolio managers see the permanent monetary disturbance and understand that it will also affect the future output of firms with contracts that carry over to the next period. This recognition affects their exchange rate predictions and thus their current demands for money and bonds. For example, for a positive disturbance, the existence of two-period contracts decreases the expected rate of appreciation of the home currency and lowers the current demand for it; this

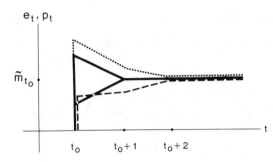

Figure 11.2
Effect of a permanent increase in the money supply on the price level and exchange rate:
$\phi > 0$

then increases the impact on the current price level, output, and exchange
rate.

Summarizing, neoclassical contracting helps explain the stylized fact
that exchange rates are more volatile than prices in the presence of monetary disturbances. Increasing the length of some of the contracts goes
even further in explaining the fact in the presence of permanent monetary
disturbances. This form of contracting does little to help explain the
stylized fact in the presence of goods market disturbances, but then goods
market disturbances probably had more impact on exchange rates than on
prices in the flexible wage model; there was no paradox to be explained.
Neoclassical contracting also can help explain persistence. The economy
is fully adjusted to a permanent monetary disturbance only after the last
existing contract is renegotiated. Persistance, however, may be better
explained by the neo-Keynesian contracting model discussed in the next
section; there temporary and permanent disturbances are passed from
one contract to the next successively through time.

Neo-Keynesian Contracting Model

Taylor (1979, 1980) has developed a contracting model that is less neoclassical in nature and more closely related to Dornbusch's (1976) sticky
price model. In Taylor's model wages are set (with some modification
for demand conditions) to preserve the relative wage structure over contracts. Contracting is once again staggered, with, say, half of the contracts
being renegotiated each period. This is an important feature in Taylor's
model because it allows the effects of a disturbance to be passed from

one contract to the next; that is, disturbances affecting existing contracts are passed on to new contracts by the attempts of wage setters to preserve the relative wage structure over all contracts. The staggering of contracts is the source of the strong persistence of effects in Taylor's model. Price in Taylor's model is a constant markup over the average wage, and employment is determined by the demand for output. These features give the model a neo-Keynesian flavor despite its incorporation of rational expectations formation.[17]

More specifically the demand side of the economy—equations (1), (3), and (4)—is retained (though we will drop the permanent goods market disturbance, $\tilde{u}_t$, for simplicity of exposition), and the supply side is replaced by

$$x_t = 0.5(x_{t-1} + x_{t+1|t-1}) + 0.5\gamma[(m-p)_{t|t-1} + (m-p)_{t+1|t-1}] + \tilde{x}_t, \quad (18)$$

$$p_t = w_t = 0.5(x_t + x_{t-1}). \tag{19}$$

All contracts specify a fixed nominal wage for two periods; half of the contracts are renegotiated at the beginning of each period. x_t is the log of the wage specified in a contract negotiated at the beginning of period t. The first term in the wage-setting equation (18) reflects the fact that wage setters try to maintain their own wage relative to the wages that will exist in other contracts during the two periods covered by the contract. The second term says that expected demand pressures, as measured by expected real balances, are also take into account;[18] γ measures the importance of demand conditions in the negotiations, and it is an important parameter in Taylor's contracting model. $\tilde{x}_t$ is a disturbance in the wage-setting process; we assume initially that it is independent of $\tilde{m}_t$, $\tilde{v}_t$, and $\tilde{z}_t$ even though this implies (perhaps unrealistically) that current actual demand conditions play no role in the wage-setting process. Equation (19) is the price-setting equation; w_t is the average wage across contracts at time t.

Using these equations, we derive the solution to the neo-Keynesian contracting model:[19]

$$x_t = \alpha x_{t-1} + (1-\alpha)m_{t-1} + \tilde{x}_t \tag{20}$$

$$p_t = \alpha p_{t-1} + 0.5(1-\alpha)(m_t - m_{t-1}) + 0.5(\tilde{x}_t + \tilde{x}_{t-1}) \tag{21}$$

$$e_t = \beta_1 x_{t-1} + \beta_2 m_{t-1} - \beta_3 \tilde{x}_t + \beta_4 \tilde{m}_t + \beta_5 \tilde{v}_t - \beta_6 \tilde{z}_t \tag{22}$$

where

$$\alpha = (1 + 0.5\gamma - \sqrt{2\gamma})/(1 - 0.5\gamma),$$

$$\beta_1 = 0.5(1 - \delta)(1 + \alpha)/[\delta + \lambda(1 - \alpha)] \qquad \beta_2 = 1 + \beta_1,$$

$$\beta_3 = [0.5(1 - \delta) + \lambda\beta_1]/(\delta + \lambda) \qquad \beta_4 = 1 + \lambda\beta_2,$$

$$\beta_5 = 1/(\delta + \lambda) \qquad\qquad\qquad\qquad \beta_6 = 1/(\delta + \lambda).$$

The absolute value of α is less than one for all positive values of γ. so the wage-price process is stable. A positive wage disturbance increases expected future prices and lowers expected future real balances; this has a moderating effect on next period's contract wage. The larger is γ, the smaller is α and the stronger is the moderating influence.[20]

Permanent monetary disturbances and temporary wage disturbances generate persistent effects on all variables in the model, effects that last even after all of the existing contracts have been renegotiated. Any disturbance that gets into the wage-setting process will have persistent effects. Permanent disturbances get in because they affect expected future real balances. Temporary monetary and goods market disturbances would get in if they were correlated with $\tilde{x}_t$—that is, if current actual demand conditions affected the wage-setting process.

To illustrate how permanent monetary disturbances pass through the economy, we have solved equations (20), (21), (22), and (1) for their moving average representations under the assumption that all other disturbances are equal to zero:[21]

$$x_t = \Sigma_{i=1}^{\infty} w_i \tilde{m}_{t-i} \qquad \text{where} \quad w_i = 1 - \alpha^i \qquad\qquad (23)$$

$$p_t = \Sigma_{i=1}^{\infty} \pi_i \tilde{m}_{t-i} \qquad \text{where} \quad \pi_1 = 0.5(1 - \alpha) \qquad\qquad (24)$$

$$\pi_i = 1 - 0.5\alpha^{i-1}(1 + \alpha) \qquad i \geq 2,$$

$$e_t = \Sigma_{i=0}^{\infty} \varepsilon_i \tilde{m}_{t-i} \qquad \text{where} \quad \varepsilon_0 = \beta_4 > \varepsilon_1 \qquad\qquad (25)$$

$$\varepsilon_i = 1 + \beta_1 \alpha^{i-1} \qquad i \geq 1,$$

$$y_t = \bar{y} + \Sigma_{i=0}^{\infty} \eta_i \tilde{m}_{t-i} \quad \text{where} \quad \eta_0 = \delta\beta_4 > \eta_1 \qquad\qquad (26)$$

$$\eta_i = \delta[0.5(1 + \alpha) + \beta_1]\alpha^{i-1} \qquad i \geq 1.$$

Permanent monetary disturbances are neutral in the long run; that is, w_{∞}, π_{∞}, and ε_{∞} are all equal to one, and η_{∞} is equal to zero. However, it takes an infinite amount of time for a given disturbance to work its way through the system.

Hence the present model produces overshooting patterns for the exchange rate that are very similar to Dornbusch's. In response to a positive disturbance, the exchange rate overshoots its long-run value, and the price level undershoots; after one period both begin a smooth exponential decay to their long-run values. The real exchange rate and output similarly go positive and then decay back to their natural rates. Smaller values of γ imply larger values of α, more overshooting of the exchange rate and output, and a slower decay to the long-run values.

3. Normative Implications of Wage Contracting and Monetary Policy

In this chapter we have ascribed the slow adjustment in the goods market and the consequent overshooting of the exchange rate to wage contracting. The neoclassical contracting model discussed in section 2 suggests certain measures of volatility in exchange rates and prices that may be relevant from a normative point of view,[22] and these measures are not necessarily the ones that were focused on in the last section; there we were engaged in explaining certain stylized facts that are of interest to observing economists.

Here we begin by identifying the measures of volatility that would seem to be relevant to the wage setters and the portfolio managers in our economy. Then we examine the implications of wage contracting and monetary policy for these normative measures of volatility. We consider two kinds of policy. One offsets the cycling of employment and output brought on by long-term contracting; the other smooths the exchange rate overshooting. Not surprisingly we find some trade-offs between the interests of wage setters and portfolio managers. Once again the results depend crucially on whether economic fluctuations are caused by monetary disturbances or by goods market disturbances.

Normative Measures of Volatility

The agents in our simple economy make decisions on the basis of their expectations of future prices and exchange rates. Wage setters are worried about price prediction errors and the deviations from full employment that they cause. Portfolio managers are worried about the variability of real interest rates.[23]

We realize that we are on precarious ground here. We have modeled only certain kinds of agents with certain kinds of problems. There are undoubtedly other agents in the real world for whom the size of prediction errors is not the only relevant measure of volatility. Some firms, for example, may have to incur adjustment or inventory costs for even perfectly foreseen fluctuations in demand. What is more, our labor contracts were not derived explicitly from a utility-maximizing framework, and their form may not be invariant in some of the policy experiments we want to perform.[24] Similarly our specification of the asset sector may not provide a robust explanation of portfolio managers' behavior. The specific results we derive are incomplete at best and should be viewed accordingly; however, we think that they provide an interesting and important complement to the positive implications of wage contracting discussed in the last section.

Wage setters in our model are worried about their price prediction errors. Those covered by one-period contracts are interested only in one-period price prediction errors; those covered by two-period contracts are interested in both one- and two-period price prediction errors. Serial correlation in disturbances, lags in the economic structure, and monetary policy can all cause the two to differ. Portfolio managers worry about unanticipated changes in the real interest rate,

$$[i_t - (pi_{t+1} - pi_t)] - [i_t - (pi_{t+1|t} - pi_t)] = -(pi_{t+1|t} - pi_t + 1) \qquad (27)$$

where $pi_t = (1 - \omega)p_t + \omega(e_t + p_t^*)$, pi is a price index and ω is the share of foreign goods in portfolio managers' market basket. So portfolio managers are interested in the one-period price index prediction error,[25]

$$pi_t - pi_{t|t-1} = \omega(e_t - e_{t|t-1}) + (1 - \omega)(p_t - p_{t|t-1}) \qquad (28)$$

which depends on both price and exchange rate prediction errors.

Wage Contracting and Agents' Normative Measures of Volatility

The one-period price and exchange rate prediction errors that are relevant to portfolio managers can be calculated from equations (15) and (16):

$$p_t - p_{t|t-1} = \pi_1 \tilde{m}_t + \pi_3 \tilde{v}_t + \pi_4 \tilde{z}_t, \qquad (29)$$

$$e_t - e_{t|t-1} = \varepsilon_1 \tilde{m}_t - (1/\delta)\tilde{u}_t + \varepsilon_3 \tilde{v}_t - \varepsilon_4 \tilde{z}_t. \qquad (30)$$

We showed in section 2 that wage contracting causes the exchange rate and price level to overshoot and undershoot, respectively, their flexible wage values in response to both permanent and temporary monetary disturbances.[26] The price level's undershooting will help portfolio managers, but the exchange rate's overshooting will hurt them. On balance wage contracting will be beneficial to portfolio managers if $(1 - \omega)$, the share of the domestic good in their market basket, is large enough. Increasing ϕ, the proportion of contracts that last two periods, will hurt portfolio managers because it increases the exchange rate overshooting and decreases the price level undershooting in response to permanent monetary disturbances.[27]

Wage contracting does not matter to portfolio managers in the case of permanent goods market disturbances; they are always absorbed by the exchange rate. Temporary goods market disturbances, however, have less impact on both the price level and the exchange rate with wage contracting. It is difficult to assess the implications of this for portfolio managers since a positive price prediction error tends to cancel the negative exchange rate prediction error in the price index prediction error.[28] However, we might expect that wage contracting benefits portfolio managers in the case of goods market disturbances.

For wage setters covered by one-period contracts, the relevant measure of volatility is the size of the one-period price prediction error (29). For wage setters covered by two-period contracts, the relevant measure may be taken to be

$$0.5(p_t - p_{t|t-1}) + 0.5(p_{t+1} - p_{t+1|t-1}) = 0.5\pi_1(\tilde{m}_{t+1} + \tilde{m}_t) + 0.5\pi_2\tilde{m}_t$$
$$+ 0.5\pi_3(\tilde{v}_{t+1} + \tilde{v}_t) \qquad (31)$$
$$+ 0.5\pi_4(\tilde{z}_{t+1} + \tilde{z}_t),$$

the average price prediction error over the life of the contract.

Wage setters must benefit from wage contracting; otherwise they would not do it. The interesting question here is how contractors under existing one- and two-period contracts are affected by an increase in ϕ, that is, by the conversion of other one-period contracts to two-period contracts. We showed in section 2 that increasing ϕ magnified the immediate impact of permanent monetary disturbances on prices but muted the lagged effect; that is, $d\pi_1/d\phi$ is positive, but $d\pi_2/d\phi$ is negative.[29] So an increase in ϕ makes one-period contractors, and probably two-period contractors as well, worse off.

Summarizing, the existence of wage contracting will probably benefit both wage setters and portfolio managers, especially if goods market disturbances are an important source of price and exchange rate fluctuations. However, an increase in ϕ, the conversion of some one-period contracts to two-period contracts, will hurt both portfolio managers and wage setters under existing contracts if monetary disturbances are an important source of price and exchange rate fluctuations.

Wage Contracting and Monetary Policy

Wage contracting slows adjustment in the labor market, and this introduces persistence and exchange rate overshooting. A lagged feedback rule for monetary policy can take the persistence out of deviations in employment and output about their natural rates, and an exchange intervention policy can smooth exchange rate fluctuations. In this section we examine the effects of these two policies on the various agents in our economy. We also examine the effects of a policy that stabilizes the real exchange rate. Once again the results depend on whether monetary or goods market disturbances are the primary causes of price and exchange rate fluctuations.

Countercyclical Policies   Let the money supply process be represented by

$$m_t = m_{t-1} + \tilde{m}_t + h_t \tag{32}$$

where h_t represents policy. It should be obvious that the lagged feedback rule,

$$h_t = -m_{t-1} = -\Sigma_1^\infty \tilde{m}_{t-i} \tag{33}$$

offsets all expected effects due to permanent monetary disturbances. If it were imposed, equations (15), (16), and (17) would reduce to

$$p_t = \pi_3(\tilde{m}_t + \tilde{v}_t) + \pi_4 \tilde{z}_t, \tag{34}$$

$$e_t = \varepsilon_3(\tilde{m}_t + \tilde{v}_t) - (1/\delta)\Sigma_0^\infty \tilde{u}_{t-i} - \varepsilon_4 \tilde{z}_t \tag{35}$$

$$y_t = y + \theta[\pi_3(\tilde{m}_t + \tilde{v}_t) + \pi_4 \tilde{z}_t]. \tag{36}$$

It is clear from (36) that the cyclical effects in output and employment have been eliminated, even though two-period contracts still exist.[30]

The lagged feedback policy (33) reduces two-period price prediction errors to one-period price prediction errors:

$$p_t - p_{t|t-2} = p_t - p_{t|t-1} = \pi_3(\tilde{m}_t + \tilde{v}_t) + \pi_4 \tilde{z}_t. \tag{37}$$

It converts the permanent monetary disturbances into temporary ones. Hence there is no useful information embodied in one-period price predictions that is not already embodied in two-period price predictions. In addition one-period errors are smaller because temporary monetary disturbances have less impact on the price level than permanent ones; that is, π_3 is less than π_1.[31] So the feedback policy (33) benefits both one- and two-period wage contractors if permanent monetary disturbances are an important determinant of price fluctuations.

Portfolio managers are also better off in this case because

$$e_t - e_{t|t-1} = \varepsilon_3(\tilde{m}_t + \tilde{v}_t) - \varepsilon_4\tilde{z}_t - (1/\delta)\tilde{u}_t. \tag{38}$$

Temporary monetary disturbances also have less impact on the exchange rate, so both components of the price index prediction error (28) are reduced.[32]

Exchange Intervention Policy   A policy of the form

$$h_t = -m_{t-1} - ge_t \qquad g > 0 \tag{39}$$

can control the exchange rate's overshooting in addition to removing the cyclical effects on output and employment. If it is imposed (and assuming for simplicity that ϕ is equal to zero), then (34), (35), and (36) become

$$p_t = \pi_3(\tilde{m}_t + \tilde{v}_t) + \pi_4\tilde{z}_t + \pi_5\tilde{u}_t + \pi_6\Sigma_{i=1}^{\infty}\tilde{u}_{t-i}, \tag{40}$$

$$e_t = \varepsilon_3(\tilde{m}_t + \tilde{v}_t) - \varepsilon_4\tilde{z}_t - \varepsilon_5 u_t - \varepsilon_6\Sigma_{i=1}^{\infty}\tilde{u}_{t-i}, \tag{41}$$

where

$$\pi_3 = \delta\eta \qquad\qquad \varepsilon_3 = (\delta + \theta)\eta$$

$$\pi_4 = (\lambda + g)\eta \qquad\qquad \varepsilon_4 = (1 + \theta)\eta$$

$$\pi_5 = g(1 + \lambda + g)\eta/(1 + g) \qquad \varepsilon_5 = \{\delta(1 + \lambda + g)$$

$$+ \theta[\delta(1 + g) + \lambda]\}\eta/\delta(1 + g)$$

$$\pi_6 = g/\delta(1 + g) \qquad\qquad \varepsilon_6 = 1/\delta(1 + g)$$

and

$$\eta = 1/[\delta(1 + \lambda + g) + \theta(\delta + \lambda + g)].$$

For large values of g, all exchange rate fluctuations are eliminated.

The one-period price prediction errors of interest to wage setters are

$$p_t - p_{t|t-1} = \pi_3(\tilde{m}_t + \tilde{v}_t) + \pi_4 \tilde{z}_t + \pi_5 \tilde{u}_t. \tag{42}$$

If price fluctuations are caused by monetary disturbances, then wage setters would favor a strong intervention policy to smooth, or even eliminate, exchange rate fluctuations.[33] Monetary disturbances and monetary policy push the exchange rate and the price level in the same direction, so a monetary policy that stabilizes the exchange rate will also stabilize the price level and make it more predictable. Goods market disturbances on the other hand either move the exchange rate and the price level in opposite directions (in the case of temporary disturbances) or are totally absorbed by the exchange rate (in the case of permanent disturbances). In either case a monetary policy that stabilizes the exchange rate will destabilize the price level and make it less predictable.[34] Wage setters would prefer that monetary policy allow the exchange rate to fluctuate freely and absorb some of the impact of these disturbances.[35]

Portfolio managers are worried about the one-period exchange rate prediction error

$$e_t - e_{t|t-1} = \varepsilon_3(\tilde{m}_t + \tilde{v}_t) - \varepsilon_4 \tilde{z}_t - \varepsilon_5 \tilde{u}_t \tag{43}$$

in addition to the price prediction error (42), as both are components in their price index prediction error (28).

A strong intervention policy will always reduce exchange rate fluctuations and make the exchange rate more predictable. In the case of monetary disturbances, this will benefit both wage setters and portfolio managers. Monetary disturbances make the price level and the exchange rate fluctuate in the same direction, so there is no cancellation in (28). A strong intervention policy will make both fluctuate less and in this way decrease portfolio managers' price index prediction errors.

Unlike wage setters, however, portfolio managers probably will favor some intervention in the case of goods market disturbances. Goods market disturbances make the price level and the exchange rate fluctuate in opposite directions, so price and exchange rate prediction errors tend to cancel in (28). With no intervention at all, permanent goods market disturbances are absorbed totally by the exchange rate. Some intervention to stabilize the exchange rate will make part of the disturbance be absorbed by the price level. Thus with some intervention, a smaller exchange rate prediction error in (28) will be offset further by a price prediction error in the opposite direction. This will clearly benefit portfolio managers. The case for temporary disturbances is less clear since the effect is shared with no intervention. The more important is the foreign good in the portfolio managers' market basket, the more likely are they to benefit from some intervention in this case as well.

Results are much the same for the policy

$$h_t = -m_{t-1} - g(e_t - p_t) \qquad g > 0 \tag{44}$$

which is intended to stabilize the real exchange rate, $e_t - p_t$. If it, instead of (39), is imposed (and ϕ is again set equal to zero), then the solution becomes

$$p_t = \pi_3(\tilde{m}_t - \tilde{v}_t) + \pi_4 \tilde{z}_t + \pi_5 \tilde{u}_t + \pi_6 \Sigma_1^\infty \tilde{u}_{t-i} \tag{45}$$

$$e_t - p_t = \varepsilon_3(\tilde{m}_t + \tilde{v}_t) - \varepsilon_4 \tilde{z}_t - \varepsilon_5 \tilde{u}_t - \varepsilon_6 \Sigma_1^\infty \tilde{u}_{t-i} \tag{46}$$

where

$$\pi_3 = \delta\eta \qquad\qquad \varepsilon_3 = \theta\eta$$

$$\pi_4 = (\lambda + g)\eta \qquad \varepsilon_4 = (1 + \lambda + \theta)\eta$$

$$\pi_5 = g(1 + \lambda)\eta \qquad \varepsilon_5 = [1 - (g\theta/\delta)](1 + \lambda)\eta$$

$$\pi_6 = g/\delta \qquad\qquad \varepsilon_6 = 1/\delta$$

and

$$\eta = 1/[\delta(1 + \lambda) + \theta(\lambda + \delta + g)].$$

Large values of g stabilize the real exchange rate against all disturbances except permanent goods market disturbances. A permanent increase in the demand for goods must be accommodated by a permanent real depreciation, but the intervention policy (44) tries to keep this from happening. The results for the price level and the nominal exchange can be quite explosive.[36] This illustrates the danger of leaning against the wind when targets are not adjusted to reflect changes in long-run equilibrium values.

The one-period price prediction errors of interest to wage setters are

$$p_t - p_{t|t-1} = \pi_3(\tilde{m}_t + \tilde{v}_t) + \pi_4 \tilde{z}_t + \pi_5 \tilde{u}_t. \tag{47}$$

As before, if price fluctuations are caused by monetary disturbances, wage setters would favor a strong intervention policy, and if price fluctuations

are caused by goods market disturbances, they would not. Free market fluctuations in the real exchange rate tend to absorb goods market disturbances, but they also carry monetary disturbances from financial markets to the goods market. Portfolio managers are worried about the price index prediction error (28), which can also be written as

$$pi_t - pi_{t|t-1} = p_t - p_{t|t-1} + \omega[e_t - p_t - (e_{t|t-1} - p_{t|t-1})]$$
$$= (\pi_3 + \omega\varepsilon_3)(\tilde{m}_t + \tilde{v}_t) + (\pi_4 - \omega\varepsilon_4)\tilde{z}_t + (\pi_5 - \omega\varepsilon_5)\tilde{u}_t.$$

$$(48)$$

Once again portfolio managers would prefer a strong intervention policy if the monetarist assertion is correct; their preferences are more ambiguous if goods market disturbances are the predominant shocks.

Summarizing, if monetary disturbances are the primary cause of price and exchange rate fluctuations, then both portfolio managers and wage setters will favor a strong exchange intervention policy to control the exchange rate's overshooting. Such a policy will stabilize the price level, the exchange rate, and the price index; it will make both the price level and the real rate of interest more predictable. If, however, goods market disturbances are the primary source of price and exchange rate fluctuations, then the monetary authorities may have to choose between portfolio managers and wage setters. Intervention shifts the effects of these disturbances from the exchange rate to the price level, increasing price prediction errors but possibly making the real interest rate more predictable.

Appendix 11A Model Solutions

We solve the models given in the chapter by the method of undetermined coefficients. We postulate that the dependent variables of interest, the exchange rate and the home good price, are linear functions of current and lagged disturbances. For example, we might postulate that, given the flexible wage model,

$$e_t = \tilde{m}_t + m_{t+1} + \varepsilon_3\tilde{v}_t - \varepsilon_4\tilde{z}_t - \varepsilon_5\tilde{u}_t - \varepsilon_6 u_{t-1}.$$

$$(A1)$$

From the money market equilibrium condition we have

$$p_t = \lambda(e_{t+1|t} - e_t) + m_{t+1} + \tilde{m}_t + \tilde{v}_t.$$

$$(A2)$$

We note that

$$e_{t+1|t} - e_t = -\varepsilon_3\tilde{v}_t + \varepsilon_4\tilde{z}_t + (\varepsilon_5 - \varepsilon_6)\tilde{u}_t.$$

$$(A3)$$

From equation (1) in the text, the goods market equilibrium condition is

$$e_t = p_t - 1/\delta(u_{t-1} + \tilde{u}_t + \tilde{z}_t). \tag{A4}$$

Using (A2) and (A3) we can solve (A4) for e_t as a function of the exogenous shocks. We equate the coefficients in this solution to those in (A1) and solve for the ε's. The resulting values are those in text equation (7). Knowing the ε's, we can use (A2) and (A3) to solve for text equation (8).

The fixed wage model is solved in a similar manner. First assuming that $\phi = 0$, we postulate that

$$e_t = \varepsilon_1 \tilde{m}_t + m_{t-1} + \varepsilon_3 \tilde{v}_t - \varepsilon_4 \tilde{z}_t - \varepsilon_5 \tilde{u}_t - \varepsilon_6 u_{t-1}, \tag{A5}$$

$$p_t = \pi_1 \tilde{m}_t + m_{t-1} + \pi_3 \tilde{v}_t + \pi_4 \tilde{z}_t + \pi_5 \tilde{u}_t + \pi_6 u_{t-1}. \tag{A6}$$

We can then substitute for e_t, p_t, and $p_{t|t-1}$ in the goods market equilibrium condition, $\theta(p_t - p_{t|t-1}) - \delta(e_t - p_t) - u_{t-1} - \tilde{u}_t - \tilde{z}_t = 0$. We can then solve for the ε's in terms of the π's. (Since this equation must hold for all possible values of the shocks, the coefficient of each shock must equal zero.) We can rewrite the money market equilibrium condition, equation (4) in the main text, as $(1 + \theta)p_t = \lambda(e_{t+1|t} - e_t) + m_{t-1} + \tilde{m}_t + \tilde{v}_t + \theta p_{t|t-1}$.

We can solve for p_t substituting for $e_{t+1|t} - e_t$ and $p_{t|t-1}$ using (A5) and (A6) and writing the ε's in terms of the π's. We can equate the coefficients from this equation with those in (A6) and solve for the π's. The model with ϕ different from zero is solved in the same way.

The neo-Keynesian contracting model is solved in two steps. First we postulate a solution for x_t: $x_t = \alpha_1 x_{t-1} + \alpha_2 m_{t-1} + \alpha_3 \tilde{x}_t$. Using this equation and equations (18) and (19) from the main text, we can solve for the α's. We then postulate a solution for e_t: $e_t = -\beta_1 x_{t-1} + \beta_2 m_{t-1} - \beta_3 \tilde{x}_t + \beta_4 \tilde{m}_t + \beta_5 \tilde{v}_t - \beta_6 \tilde{z}_t$. We use this equation, together with the money market equilibrium condition, to solve for the β's.

Appendix 11B   Moving Average Representation of the Solution to the Neo-Keynesian Contracting Model with Wage Disturbances

The following equations show how disturbances to the wage-setting process affect wages, prices, the exchange rate, and output under the assumption that all other disturbances are zero.

$$x_t = \sum_{i=0}^{\infty} \alpha^i \tilde{x}_{t-i} \qquad e_t = -\beta_3 \tilde{x}_t - \beta_1 \sum_{i=1}^{\infty} \alpha^{i-1} \tilde{x}_{t-i}$$

$$p_t = 0.5\tilde{x}_t + 0.5(1+\alpha) \sum_{i=1}^{\infty} \alpha^{i-1} \tilde{x}_{t-i}$$

$$y_t = -\delta(\beta_3 + 0.5)\tilde{x}_t - \delta(\beta_1 + 0.5(1+\alpha)) \sum_{i=1}^{\infty} \alpha^{i-1} \tilde{x}_{t-i}$$

With $\gamma < 2$ (see note 20), $0 < \alpha < 1$, and the effect of a wage disturbance on wage setting dies out monotonically. The price of the home good rises for two periods and then drops monotonically. The exchange rate may appreciate and output may fall for two periods before decaying monotonically to their long-run values.

Notes

We would like to thank J. Bhandari and D. Henderson for helpful suggestions on an earlier draft. The views expressed here are our own; they do not necessarily represent the views of the Federal Reserve Board or any other member of its staff.

1. Dornbusch (1976) stimulated many others. Weber (1981) and Bhandari (1981), for example, replaced Dornbusch's Phillips curve with the two familiar versions of the Lucas supply hypothesis. Flood and Hodrick (1982) use information asymmetries to try to explain some of the same stylized facts.

2. Dornbusch's (1976) specification included the interest rate. We have left it out for simplicity.

3. More generally, full employment output will not be a time-invariant constant. It will fluctuate with the terms of trade and with productivity disturbances.

Salop (1974) initiated a host of papers investigating the implications of the fact that labor supply is a function of wages deflated by an index of prices while labor demand is a function of wages deflated by just the price of the domestic product; one implication is that full employment output depends on the terms of trade. Gray (1976) initiated a host of papers investigating the implications of productivity disturbances and indexing in contracting models. Flood and Marion (1982), Marston (1984), and Turnovsky (1982) are recent examples of both; this chapter is an example of neither.

We assume that labor supply is perfectly inelastic, avoiding the issues raised by Salop, and that there are no productivity disturbances, avoiding the issued raised by Gray.

4. The income elasticity of demand has been set equal to one so that the money supply is effectively deflated by the price of domestic output. More generally we would have $m_t - pi_t = -\lambda r_t + \eta(p_t + y_t - pi_t) - \tilde{v}_t$ where pi is an index of domestic and foreign good prices. Letting $\eta = 1$, this specification becomes (4) above.

5. See note 3.

6. Barro (1977) and Waldo (1981), following the spirit of the implicit contracts literature, suggest that colluding suppliers and demanders of labor will settle on some other rule. Barro (1977) is justly critical of this kind of contracting model because of its lack of utility-maximizing foundation, but see also Fischer's (1977b) response.

7. Assuming that the production function is Cobb-Douglas, the first-order condition for profit maximization (in logs) is $(\psi - 1)n_{t+i} = \overline{w - p} + p_{t+i|t} - p_{t+i} - \ln \psi$ where ψ is labor's share of output. Choosing units so that $n_{t+i|t} = 0$, $\ln \psi = \overline{w - p}$ and $n_{t+i} = [1/(1 - \psi)](p_{t+i} - p_{t+i|t})$ making $y_{t+i} = [\psi/(1 - \psi)](p_{t+i} - p_{t+i|t})$. Hence, $\theta = \psi/(1 - \psi)$ and $d\theta/d\psi = 1/(1 - \psi)^2 > 0$ for $0 < \psi < 1$.

8. See Gray (1978) and Canzoneri (1980) for a discussion of the determinants of ϕ.

9. Starting with permanent disturbances, π_1 is clearly less than 1, and $\varepsilon_1 = 1 + (1 - \delta)\theta\rho/\lambda[(1 - \rho)(1 + \lambda) + \theta]$ is greater than 1 if $\delta < 1$. Similarly, for temporary disturbances, $\pi_3 = [1/(1 + \lambda)] - \theta/(1 + \lambda)[(1 - \rho)(1 + \lambda) + \theta]$ is less than $1/(1 + \lambda)$, and $\varepsilon_3 = [1/(1 + \lambda)] + (1 - \delta)\theta(1 - \rho)/\delta(1 + \lambda)[(1 - \rho)(1 + \lambda) + \theta]$ is greater than $1/(1 + \lambda)$ if $\delta < 1$.

10. Contracting does make the condition for $\tilde{z}_t$ to have a greater impact on e_t than p_t less stringent. $\varepsilon_4 > \pi_4$ if $\lambda < 1 + \theta$. In the flexible wage model, the condition was $\lambda < 1$.

11. It may be interesting to note that Dornbusch (1976) would get precisely the same condition for overshooting in his fixed-price model if he too had specified a unitary income elasticity of money demand. A small δ keeps demand from increasing too much in equation (1) in response to the decrease in the terms of trade.

12. The coefficients for the monetary disturbances in equation (14) depend directly on θ; that is, $d(\theta\pi_1)/d\theta = (1 - \rho)^2(1 + \lambda)^2/[(1 - \rho)(1 + \lambda) + \theta]^2 > 0$ and $d(\theta\pi_3)/d\theta = (1 - \rho)^2(1 + \lambda)/[(1 - \rho)(1 + \lambda) + \theta]^2 > 0$. Exchange rate overshooting depends directly on θ, $d(\varepsilon_1 - 1)/d\theta = (1 - \delta)(\rho/\lambda)(1 - \rho)(1 + \lambda)/[(1 - \rho)(1 + \lambda) + \theta]^2 > 0$, as does price level undershooting, $d(1 - \pi_1)/d\theta = (1 - \rho)(1 + \lambda)/[(1 - \rho)(1 + \lambda) + \theta]^2 > 0$.

13. A relatively elastic employment rule is also consistent with another stylized fact. Real wages do not seem to follow a strongly countercyclical pattern. However, a formal empirical application of this model may benefit from the disaggregation suggested by Lucas, Sargent, and Wallace; see Canzoneri (1978) and the references in it.

The implicit contracts literature referred to in note 6 suggests instead that the employment rule should be relatively inelastic as wage setters try to smooth employment variation.

14. Permanent goods market disturbances would have the same effect if they were not totally absorbed by the exchange rate.

15. For permanent monetary disturbances, the increased impact on the price level is shown by

$$\frac{d\pi_1}{d\phi} = \frac{.5\theta(1 - \delta)\rho(1 - \rho)^2(1 + \lambda)[(1 - \rho)(1 + \lambda) + \theta]}{\{(1 - \rho)^2(1 + \lambda)^2 + \theta(1 - \rho)(1 + \lambda) + .5\phi\theta[(1 - \rho)(1 + \lambda) + \theta]\}^2}$$

which is positive for all ϕ. The increase in exchange rate overshooting is apparent from the fact that $d(\varepsilon_1 - 1)/d\phi = (1 + \theta/\delta)d\pi_1/d\phi$.

16. As shown in note 15, $d\pi_1/d\phi > 0$; so the immediate impact on output is bigger for larger ϕ. From equation (1), this means that the immediate impact on $e - p$ must also be bigger.

17. These latter features are not necessary. We could, as in the last section, specify an employment rule and let the price level move to clear the goods market. Taylor, however, wanted a model that deemphasized the cyclical role of real wages; see note 13.

18. Taylor (1979, 1980) uses $y_{t|t-1}$ and $y_{t+1|t-1}$ to measure expected demand pressure. In his model these measures reduce to expected real balances, but in ours they do not (except in special cases where $e_{t+1|t-1} - e_{t|t-1} = 0$). Our specification is necessary to retain the simplicity of Taylor's solution. In particular, if we had used $y_{t+1|t-1}$ and $y_{t|t-1}$, we would have had to solve the following cubic equation in α: $\alpha = 0.5(1 - 0.5\gamma)(\alpha^2 + 1) - 0.5\gamma\alpha + 0.25\gamma\rho(1 - \delta)(1 - \alpha^2)(\alpha + 1)$.

19. Derivation of this solution is discussed in appendix 11A.

20. We will assume γ is less than two. If γ is greater than two, the moderating effect of expected demand pressures is so great that α is negative.

21. The moving average representations for $\tilde{x}_t$ disturbances are given in appendix 11A.

22. The normative implications of the neo-Keynesian contracting model discussed in section 2 are less clear to us, so we restrict our attention here to the neoclassical model.

23. Equation (3) asserts that risk-neutral agents dominate the market, but that does not preclude the existence of risk-averse agents. More generally, similar results would be obtained in a model in which bonds were imperfect substitutes.

24. See note 6.

25. Here, as above, we have set p_t^* equal to zero. Labor suppliers would be more like portfolio managers in this if we had not assumed that labor supply is perfectly inelastic; see note 3. Labor demanders would remain interested in own-price prediction errors.

26. See note 9.

27. See note 15.

28. ε_4 falls less than π_4; see note 10. Thus it is possible that portfolio managers will be worse off if ω is large enough.

29. See note 15 and the definition of π_2 in equation (14).

30. Indeed one might expect the number of two-period contracts to grow as a result of this policy because, as shown below, the variance of two-period prediction errors is diminished; see Canzoneri (1980).

31. When $\phi = 0$, $\pi_1 = \pi_3(1 + \lambda) > \pi_3$. Since $d\pi_1/d\phi > 0$ (see note 6) and $d\pi_3/d\phi = 0$, $\pi_1 > \pi_3$ for all ϕ between zero and one.

32. $\varepsilon_1 = [1 + (\theta/\delta)]\pi_1 > [1 + (\theta/\delta)]\pi_3 = \varepsilon_3$ since $\pi_1 > \pi_3$.

33. $d\pi_3/dg$ is clearly negative, and $\pi_3 \to 0$ as $g \to \infty$.

34. $d\pi_4/dg = \delta(1 + \theta)n^2 > 0$, and for permanent disturbances $\pi_5 = 0$ if g is set equal to zero.

35. Wage setters would actually prefer a policy that destabilized exchange rates in the case of temporary goods market disturbances. Setting $g = -\lambda$ would make $\pi_4 = 0$, but it would also increase ε_4 to $\varepsilon_4 = (1 + \theta)/(\delta + \theta\delta) = 1/\delta$; with this policy, temporary goods market disturbances (rather than permanent ones) would be totally absorbed by the exchange rate. Turnovsky (1983) and Buiter and Eaton (1980) have found similar results.

36. That is, $\pi_6 \to \infty$ as $g \to \infty$; the corresponding coefficient for the nominal exchange rate is $-\varepsilon_6 + \pi_6$, and $\pi_6 - \varepsilon_6 = (g - 1)/\delta \to \infty$ as $g \to \infty$.

References

Barro, R. 1977. "Long-term Contracting, Sticky Prices, and Monetary Policy." *Journal of Monetary Economics* 3:305–316.

Bhandari, J. 1981. "A Stochastic Macroequilibrium Approach to a Floating Exchange Rate Economy with Interest-Bearing Assets." *Weltwirtschaftliches Archiv* 117:1–19.

Buiter, W. H., and J. Eaton. 1980. "Policy Decentralization and Exchange Rate Management in Interdependent Economies." National Bureau of Economic Research Working Paper 531 (August).

Canzoneri, M. 1978. "The Returns to Labor and the Cyclical Behavior of Real Wages: The Canadian Case." *Review of Economics and Statistics* 60: (February): 19–24.

Canzoneri, M. 1980. "Labor Contracts and Monetary Policy." *Journal of Monetary Economics* 6:241–255.

Dornbusch, R. 1976. "Expectations and Exchange Rate Dynamics." *Journal of Political Economy* 84:1161–1176.

Fischer, S. 1977a. "Long Term Contracts, Rational Expectations, and the Optimal Money Supply Rule." *Journal of Political Economy* 85 (February): 191–205.

Fischer, S. 1977b. "Long-term Contracting, Sticky Prices and Monetary Policy: A Comment." *Journal of Monetary Economics* 3:317–323.

Flood, R., and R. Hodrick. 1982. "Exchange-Rate and Price Dynamics with Asymmetric Information." Unpublished manuscript (June).

Flood, R., and N. Marion. 1982. "The Transmission of Disturbances under Alternative Exchange Rate Regimes with Optimal Indexing." *Quarterly Journal of Economics* 97:43–66.

Gray, J. 1976. "Wage Indexation: A Macroeconomic Approach." *Journal of Monetary Economics* 2:221–235.

Gray, J. 1978. "On Indexation and Contract Length." *Journal of Political Economy* (February): 1–18.

Marston, R. 1984. "Real Wages and the Terms of Trade: Alternative Indexation Rules for an Open Economy." *Journal of Money, Credit, and Banking* (August): 285–301.

Salop, J. 1974. "Devaluation and the Balance of Trade under Flexible Wages." In G. Horwich, and P. Samuelson, eds., *Trade Stability and Macroeconomics*. New York: Academic Press.

Taylor, J. 1979. "Staggered Wage Setting in a Macro Model." *American Economic Review* 69:108–113.

Taylor, J. 1980. "Aggregate Dynamics and Staggered Contracts." *Journal of Political Economy* 88:1–23.

Turnovsky, S. 1982. "Wage Indexation and Exchange Market Intervention in a Small Open Economy." Unpublished manuscript, University of Illinois (October).

Turnovsky, S. 1983. "Exchange Market Intervention in a Small Open Economy." In J. S. Bhandari and B. H. Putnam, eds., *Economic Interdependence and Flexible Exchange Rates*. Cambridge: MIT Press.

Waldo, D. 1981. "Sticky Nominal Wages and the Optimal Employment Rule." *Journal of Monetary Economics* (May): 339–354.

Weber, W. 1981. "Output Variability under Monetary Policy and Exchange Rate Rules." *Journal of Political Economy* 89 (August): 733–758.

12 Financial Disturbances and the Effects of an Exchange Rate Union

Richard C. Marston

Exchange rate unions, in which a group of countries fix their exchange rates to float jointly relative to the rest of the world, have become an important element in the current mixed exchange rate system. The most prominent of these unions is the European Monetary System, a union fixing exchange rates among European currencies.[1] The EMS, as well as unions elsewhere, represents a significant departure from exchange rate flexibility with effects on union countries that need to be explored.

The reasons for forming unions vary widely, but one common aim is to reduce exchange rate volatility itself, specifically by eliminating movements in the crucial cross-exchange rates between union currencies. Countries in exchange rate unions often conduct much of their trade with other countries in the union; in the absence of the union, financial disturbances originating outside the union can lead to major fluctuations in the cross-exchange rates governing this internal trade. In the EMS pressures in the mark-dollar market have disrupted cross-exchange rates between the mark and other EMS currencies such as the franc.[2] Proponents of exchange rate unions claim that the fixing of cross-exchange rates will minimize the disruptive effects of such disturbances.

In this chapter the desirability of an exchange rate union is analyzed within the context of a three-country model, the three countries representing two members of the union as well as a nonmember country (with the dollar as its currency).[3] One of the currencies of the union, the mark, is subject to disturbances involving portfolio shifts between mark and dollar assets. The exchange rate union fixes the cross-exchange rate between the mark and the other union currency, thereby preventing the disturbance from affecting this key exchange rate. In the first part of the chapter we ask if formation of the union helps to stabilize the effective exchange rate of each member country. The answer to that question depends not only on trade shares used to weight the effective exchange rate but also on the pattern of financial integration between each union member and the other two countries. In the second part we ask if formation of the union stabilizes key macroeconomic variables such as output and prices.

Section 1 develops a financial model for two types of exchange rate regimes, fully flexible exchange rates and an exchange rate union floating against the dollar. The financial model includes interest-bearing assets that are imperfect substitutes for one another. Financial integration is defined in terms of the relative holdings of each of these assets as well as the degree of substitutability among them. The chapter shows how financial integration facilitates intraunion adjustment, not through the long-term financing of deficits within the union, as in Ingram (1973), but through immediate market adjustments in the absence of a union. The financial model is used in this section to analyze the impact of a union on effective exchange rates in a setting in which wages and the prices of domestic goods are temporarily fixed.

In section 2 this financial model is combined with a model of the real sector to determine how the union might modify the effects of financial disturbances on output. In this section divergences of interest between the member countries become particularly evident. One country necessarily gains by forming a union, while the other country loses the benefit of the insulation provided by a flexible cross-exchange rate. Offsetting such differences, however, may be an overall gain from diversification for both countries in the union. This diversification gain is shown to occur when there are financial disturbances originating in both countries that are less than perfectly correlated.

1. Effects of a Union on Exchange Rate Volatility

Exchange rate unions must be analyzed in a model with at least three countries since it is the interplay between the stabilized and freely floating exchange rates that is of interest. Our three countries consist of two potential members of the exchange rate union, countries 1 and 2, as well as a third country representing the rest of the world. Each country has its own currency; country 1's currency is called the franc, country 2's the mark, and country 3's the dollar. The exchange rates for these currencies are as follows:

X_t^1: franc price of the dollar,
X_t^2: mark price of the dollar, and
X_t^{12}: franc price of the mark.

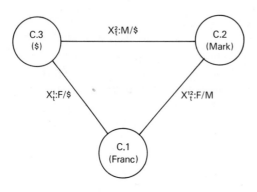

Figure 12.1
Relationship of currencies of countries 1, 2, and 3

Figure 12.1 illustrates how the three currencies are related. Triangular arbitrage ensures that the cross-exchange rate between the currencies of countries 1 and 2 is linked to the respective dollar exchange rates, $X_t^{12} = X_t^1 / X_t^2$. In an exchange rate union, this cross-exchange rate is fixed by foreign exchange intervention.

Each member country has two financial assets, money (M_t^i) and a home bond (H_t^i). Country 3 issues a dollar-denominated bond (F_t); the two member countries are assumed to be too small to influence the interest rate paid on this dollar bond (R_t^3). The public in each member country is assumed to hold four different assets: domestic money, bonds denominated in domestic currency (and issued by the domestic government), and bonds denominated in each of the other currencies, a range of assets permitting diversification of portfolios across the three currencies. (See table 12.1 for the balance sheets of the public and the monetary authorities of countries 1 and 2). Domestic money is issued by the monetary authority of that country, which in turn holds as assets domestic bonds and three types of foreign exchange reserves: dollar bonds and the bonds and money of the other potential member of the union.

The transactions demand for money plays a central role in determining prices and the exchange rate. The demand for money is assumed to depend positively on the ratio of nominal output ($P_t^i Y_t^i$) to nominal wealth (V_t^i), while the demand for home and foreign bonds depends negatively on this ratio. Holdings of each asset are expressed as a fraction of total

Table 12.1
Sectoral balance sheets

Country 1				Country 2			
Private sector		Monetary authority		Private sector		Monetary authority	
M_t^1	V_t^1	H_t^{1m}	M_t^m	M_t^2	V_t^2	H_t^{2n}	M_t^n
H_t^{11}		$X_t^{12}H_t^{2m}$	A_t^m	H_t^{22}		H_t^{1n}/X_t^{12}	A_t^n
$X_t^{12}H_t^{21}$		$X_t^1 F_t^m$		H_t^{12}/X_t^{12}		$X_t^2 F_t^n$	
$X_t^1 F_t^1$		$X_t^{12}M_t^{2m}$	M_t^{1n}	$X_t^2 F_t^2$		M_t^{1n}/X_t^{12}	M_t^{2m}

Note: The superscript m denotes the monetary authority of country 1, n the monetary authority of country 2. The public of country 1 holds its wealth (V_t^1) in the form of domestic money (M_t^1), domestic bonds (H_t^{11}), country 2's bonds $(H_t^{21}$, which enters the balance sheet at the exchange rate $X_t^{12})$, and foreign bonds $(F_t^1$, with exchange rate $X_t^1)$. The monetary authority of country 1 holds as assets home bonds (H_t^{1m}), dollar bonds $(X_t^1 F_t^m)$, as well as the bonds (H_t^{2m}) and money (M_t^{2m}) of country 2 with exchange rate X_t^{12}. Its liabilities consist of money held by the domestic public (M_t^m) and by the monetary authority of country 2 (M_t^{1n}), plus a balancing item (A_t^m), which offsets changes in exchange rates in the monetary authorities' balance sheets. The balance sheets of country 2 are explained analogously.

wealth, so that asset demands are homogeneous of degree one in $P_t^i Y_t^i$ and V_t^i.[4] (See table 12.2.)

The bonds of countries 1 and 2 pay interest rates of R_t^1 and R_t^2, respectively; the total expected return for the ith country investor includes the expected change in the exchange rate $Z^i = [E_t(X_{t+1}^i) - X_t^i]/X_t^i$, for $X_t^i = X_t^1, X_t^2, X_t^{12}$. The asset demands of the public are assumed to be gross substitutes; that is, asset demands are positively related to the own interest rate and negatively related to the returns on other assets. Each bond demand includes a stochastic element $(u_t^{hij}$, or $u_t^{fi})$, the properties of which will be specified below. The equilibrium conditions for the money and bond markets are set out in table 12.2.

Because of the inherent complexity of the three-country model, several additional assumptions are adopted to simplify the analysis:

1. Countries 1 and 2 are assumed to have identical behavior. The initial portfolios of the two countries are identical in the sense that the public of each country holds the same amount of its own domestic money and bonds, dollar bonds, and the bonds of the other country; one country's initial portfolio is thus the mirror image of the other country's portfolio.[5] The asset demands of the two countries, moreover, are equally

Table 12.2
Two-Country model of financial behavior

Country 1	Country 2

Asset Demands

Demand for money

Country 1:
$$M_t^1 = m^1\left(\frac{P_t^1 Y_t^1}{V_t^1}, R_t^1, R_t^2 + Z_t^{12}, R_t^3 + Z_t^1\right) V_t^1$$

Country 2:
$$M_t^2 = m^2\left(\frac{P_t^2 Y_t^2}{V_t^2}, R_t^2, R_t^1 - Z_t^{12}, R_t^3 + Z_t^2\right) V_t^2$$

Demand for franc bonds

Country 1:
$$H_t^{11} = h^{11}\left(\frac{P_t^1 Y_t^1}{V_t^1}, R_t^1, R_t^2 + Z_t^{12}, R_t^3 + Z_t^1\right) V_t^1 + u_t^{h11}$$

Country 2:
$$\frac{H_t^{12}}{X_t^{12}} = h^{12}\left(\frac{P_t^2 Y_t^2}{V_t^2}, R_t^2, R_t^1 - Z_t^{12}, R_t^3 + Z_t^2\right) V_t^2 + u_t^{h12}$$

Demand for mark bonds

Country 1:
$$X_t^{12} H_t^{21} = h^{21}\left(\frac{P_t^1 Y_t^1}{V_t^1}, R_t^1, R_t^2 + Z_t^{12}, R_t^3 + Z_t^1\right) V_t^1 + u_t^{h21}$$

Country 2:
$$H_t^{22} = h^{22}\left(\frac{P_t^2 Y_t^2}{V_t^2}, R_t^2, R_t^1 - Z_t^{12}, R_t^3 + Z_t^2\right) V_t^2 + u_t^{h22}$$

Demand for dollar bonds

Country 1:
$$X_t^1 F_t^1 = f^1\left(\frac{P_t^1 Y_t^1}{V_t^1}, R_t^1, R_t^2 + Z_t^{12}, R_t^3 + Z_t^1\right) V_t^1 + u_t^{f1}$$

Country 2:
$$X_t^2 F_t^2 = f^2\left(\frac{P_t^2 Y_t^2}{V_t^2}, R_t^2, R_t^1 - Z_t^{12}, R_t^3 + Z_t^2\right) V_t^2 + u_t^{f2}$$

Market equilibrium conditions: Money

Country 1:
$$M_t^1 = M_t^m = H_t^{1m} + X_t^1 F_t^m + X_t^{12}(H_t^{2m} + M_t^{2m}) - A_t^m - M_t^{1n}$$

Country 2:
$$M_t^2 = M_t^m = H_t^{2n} + X_t^2 F_t^m + (H_t^{1n} + M_t^{1n})/X_t^{12} - A_t^n - M_t^{2m}$$

Market equilibrium conditions: Bonds

Country 1:
$$H_t^{11} + H_t^{12} = \bar{H}_t^1 - H_t^{1m} - H_t^{1n}$$

Country 2:
$$H_t^{21} + H_t^{22} = \bar{H}_t^2 - H_t^{2m} - H_t^{2n}$$

Note: The asset demand functions are described in the text; for a description of the money supply expressions, see table 12.1. The bond equilibrium condition for country 1 states that the supply of bonds by the government $(\bar{H}_t^1)$ less holdings by the domestic monetary authority (H_t^{1m}) and the monetary authority of country 2 (H_t^{1n}) must equal the demands by the public of country 1 (H_t^{11}) and country 2 (H_t^{12}).

sensitive to changes in own interest returns, cross returns, output, or wealth. The initial levels of output are assumed to be equal in the two countries, as are the initial levels of wealth. This assumption of identical behavior rules out the effects of size or other asymmetries within the union, an interesting topic for later analysis.

2. The elasticity of the demand for money with respect to transactions is assumed to be unity. With the specification above, this assumption implies that a rise in nominal output with wealth constant will increase the demand for money proportionately, and a rise in wealth with output constant will leave unchanged the demand for money.[6] The demand for money is also assumed to be sensitive to a change in the home interest rate but not to changes in the interest rates on bonds denominated in other currencies; this assumption could be relaxed as long as the demand for money is less sensitive to foreign than to home interest rates.

3. The disturbances to be analyzed are all serially uncorrelated with mean zero. Assuming that expectations are rational, then $E_t X_{t+1}^i$, the expected value of the exchange rate for next period, must equal a stationary value, X_0^i. More complex types of disturbances would be interesting to study but would complicate the analysis significantly.

Behavior under Flexible Exchange Rates

To study the response of financial variables to stochastic disturbances, the asset demands are linearized around the equilibrium values of the exchange rates (X_0^i), interest rates (R_0^i), domestic prices, and output (P_0^i, Y_0^i). Each variable (with the exception of interest rates) is expressed as a percentage change from its stationary value, with a lower-case letter denoting the percentage change; each exchange rate, for example, is expressed as $x_t^i = (X_t^i - X_0^i)/X_0^i$. For convenience the initial values of all prices and exchange rates are set equal to unity.

The four equilibrium conditions in table 12.2 determine the interest rates and dollar exchange rates of countries 1 and 2 as functions of prices, output, the disturbances, and other variables. In the analysis the exchange rates will be of major interest. For this reason, the four equations are solved for the two exchange rates (x_t^i) as follows:

$$\begin{bmatrix} H_{X1}^1 & H_{X2}^1 \\ H_{X1}^2 & H_{X2}^2 \end{bmatrix} \begin{bmatrix} x_t^1 \\ x_t^2 \end{bmatrix} = \begin{bmatrix} -J^{11}(p_t^1 + y_t^1) - J^{12}(p_t^2 + y_t^2) - u_t^{h1} \\ -J^{21}(p_t^1 + y_t^1) - J^{22}(p_t^2 + y_t^2) - u_t^{h2} \end{bmatrix}, \qquad (1)$$

H_{Xj}^i and J^{ij} are excess demand coefficients, which summarize the effects of changes in exchange rates and transactions variables, respectively, on the excess demand for bond i. (The expressions for these coefficients are presented in the appendix.) The own coefficients are in both cases positive and the cross coefficients negative: $H_{X1}^1 = H_{X2}^2 > 0$, $J^{11} = J^{22} > 0$, $H_{X2}^1 = H_{X1}^2 < 0$, $J^{12} = J^{21} < 0$.[7] An increase in the franc price of the dollar, for example, leads to a rise in the demand for franc-denominated bonds for two reasons: a rise in X_t^1 leads to an increase in wealth measured in terms of francs; a rise in X_t^1 also leads to an expected appreciation of the franc (since the expected future value of the franc remains constant). Similarly an increase in the domestic price or output in country 1 leads to an increase in the demand for franc-denominated bonds because of the effect of higher transactions on the demand for money and hence on the interest rate in country 1. The cross-effects are explained analogously.

In this section we consider adjustments in the financial markets only. For this purpose we solve the two bond market equations for the effects of the financial disturbances, holding prices and output constant. We focus on the effects of a disturbance involving a shift from mark bonds to dollar bonds: $u_t^{h2} = -u_t^f < 0$, where $u_t^{h2} = u_t^{h21} + u_t^{h22} < 0$, $u_t^f = u_t^{f1} + u_t^{f2} > 0$. This is the type of disturbance that has led to undesirable variations in cross-exchange rates within Europe.[8] The three exchange rates react as follows:

$$x_t^1 = (H_{X2}^1 u_t^{h2})/A > 0,$$

$$x_t^2 = -(H_{X1}^1 u_t^{h2})/A > 0, \tag{2}$$

$$x_t^{12} = (H_{X1}^1 + H_{X2}^1)u_t^{h2}/A < 0,$$

where $A = H_{X1}^1 H_{X2}^2 - H_{X2}^1 H_{X1}^2 > 0$. Both the franc and the mark depreciate relative to the dollar, but the franc appreciates relative to the mark since $(H_{X1}^1 + H_{X2}^1) > 0$ (that is, the own effects dominate the cross-effects). How much the franc moves relative to the other two currencies is important in determining the net effect of the disturbance on country 1. Consider two cases.

1. Greater financial integration with the dollar market: Suppose country 1 has a higher degree of financial integration with country 3 than with country 2 in the sense that the demand for the franc is more sensitive to dollar returns and the holdings of dollar bonds are large relative to mark bonds.[9] Then the expression, $H_{X1}^1 + H_{X2}^1$, is large relative to the absolute value of the coefficient, H_{X2}^1. So the franc price of the mark moves more

than the franc price of the dollar. (Compare the expressions in (2).) In effect the relatively low degree of financial integration between countries 1 and 2 requires that the franc price of the mark bear the brunt of the adjustment while the franc price of the dollar changes relatively little.

2. Greater financial integration with the other union country: Alternatively, suppose country 1 is more highly integrated with country 2 financially. Then the excess demand coefficient, H_{X2}^1, is relatively large in absolute value. So the franc price of the dollar moves more than the franc price of the mark.

Thus the pattern of financial integration is a key ingredient in determining the impact of the financial disturbances.

Formation of the union does not necessarily stabilize the exchange rates for either member country if we consider effective exchange rates rather than just the cross-exchange rate between member currencies. To prepare for a comparison of the effective exchange rates in the two regimes, we now determine how these rates respond when all bilateral exchange rates are flexible. That will depend on the movements of the three bilateral rates but also on the pattern of trade among the three countries. If we define a_{1j} and a_{2j} for $j = 1, 2$, and 3 as the share of country j's good in country 1's and country 2's consumption, respectively, then the change in the effective exchange rates for the franc and mark can be expressed as:

$$s_t^1 = a_{12}x_t^{12} + a_{13}x_t^1,$$
$$s_t^2 = a_{21}(-x_t^{12}) + a_{23}x_t^2,$$

(3)

where by assumption $a_{12} = a_{21}$ and $a_{13} = a_{23}$. The change in the effective exchange rate for the franc, for example, is a weighted average of the changes in the franc price of the mark and the franc price of the dollar.

The effective exchange rate for the mark, s_t^2, definitely rises as a result of the disturbance since the mark depreciates relative to both the dollar and the franc (x_t^2 is positive and x_t^{12} negative). The effective rate for the franc, however, can rise or fall depending on the relative magnitude of x_t^1 and x_t^{12}, since the franc depreciates relative to the dollar and appreciates relative to the mark.

Behavior in an Exchange Rate Union

In an exchange rate union between countries 1 and 2, the monetary authorities intervene in the exchange market to keep fixed the franc price of the mark, $X_t^{12} = X_t^1/X_t^2$. The franc and the mark prices of the dollar then float together with the percentage changes in these rates given by $x_t^1 = x_t^2$. Suppose that the foreign exchange intervention is carried out by the monetary authority of country 1, which buys (or sells) country 2's currency and sells (or buys) country 1's currency to keep X_t^{12} fixed. (The results are the same if country 2 carries out this intervention.) The four asset equations described would then determine four variables: the interest rates on the franc and mark bonds, the dollar exchange rates for both currencies, which are tied together by intervention so that $x_t^1 = x_t^2$, and the holdings of country 2's currency by country 1's monetary authority, expressed as a deviation from a stationary value: $M_t^{2m} - M_0^{2m}$. The four equations can be solved for the dollar exchange rates as functions of prices, output, and the disturbances:

$$2(H_{X1}^1 + H_{X2}^1)x_t^i = -(J^{11} + J^{21})(p_t^1 + y_t^1) - (J^{12} + J^{22})(p_t^2 + y_t^2)$$
$$- (u_t^{h1} + u_t^{h2}). \tag{4}$$

In this equation, the expressions $H_{X1}^1 + H_{X2}^1$, $J^{11} + J^{21}$ and $J^{12} + J^{22}$ are all positive (the own effects predominate).

Once again we consider the effects of a mark-dollar disturbance ($u_t^{h2} < 0$) assuming that prices and output are constant. The franc and mark prices of the dollar change by:

$$x_t^i = -(H_{X1}^1 - H_{X2}^1)u_t^{h2}/2A > 0, \tag{5}$$

since $A = (H_{X1}^1 - H_{X2}^1)(H_{X1}^1 + H_{X2}^1)$. Given that $H_{X1}^1 > (H_{X1}^1 - H_{X2}^1)/2$, it is readily apparent from expressions (5) and (2) that formation of the union reduces the impact of the disturbance on the mark price of the dollar. That is because foreign exchange intervention associated with the union helps to disperse the effects of the disturbance to country 1's markets. For the same reason the union increases the impact of the disturbance on the franc price of the dollar. In fact the change in either dollar exchange rate in the union is just the average of the changes in the dollar rates in expression (2).

Comparison between Regimes

Under flexible rates, however, the franc-mark exchange rate also varies in response to this disturbance, so the net impact of the union on exchange rate variability is not at all apparent. So we compare the behavior of the effective exchange rates. We calculate the variances of the franc and mark effective exchange rates in both exchange rate regimes. For flexible exchange rates, the variances are:

$$\sigma_{s1}^2 = \left[\frac{a_{12}(H_{X1}^1 + H_{X2}^1) + a_{13}(H_{X2}^1)}{A}\right]^2 \sigma_{h2}^2, \tag{6}$$

$$\sigma_{s2}^2 = \left[\frac{-a_{21}(H_{X1}^1 + H_{X2}^1) - a_{23}H_{X1}^1}{A}\right]^2 \sigma_{h2}^2.$$

For the exchange rate union, they are:

$$\sigma_{s1}^2 = \sigma_{s2}^2 = \left[\frac{a_{13}(H_{X2}^1 - H_{X1}^1)}{2A}\right]^2 \sigma_{h2}^2. \tag{7}$$

The variances of the effective exchange rates depend partly on the consumption weights, a_{ij}. Also important are the excess demand coefficients, H_{Xj}^i, reflecting the relative degree of financial integration in countries 1 and 2.

Consider first the variance of the effective exchange rate of country 2, σ_{s2}^2. If there is a shift from the bonds of country 2 to dollar bonds under flexible rates, the mark depreciates relative to the dollar and the franc. Thus the mark's effective exchange rate must also depreciate. In the union, however, the mark depreciates only with respect to the dollar (with weight $a_{23} = a_{13}$). And the depreciation relative to the dollar is less than under flexible rates. Hence joining the union unambiguously stabilizes the effective exchange rate of the mark.

The effects of this financial disturbance on the effective exchange rate of the franc are not as clear-cut. Under flexible rates, in response to a shift out of mark bonds into dollar bonds, the franc appreciates relative to the mark and depreciates relative to the dollar. The response of the effective exchange rate for the franc is given by the condition:

$$s_t^1 \underset{<}{\overset{>}{=}} 0 \text{ as } \frac{a_{12}}{a_{13}} \underset{>}{\overset{<}{=}} \frac{-H_{X2}^1}{(H_{X1}^1 + H_{X2}^1)}. \tag{8}$$

The two sets of factors involved are the shares of country 2's and country 3's goods in country 1's consumption (a_{12} and a_{13}) and the response of the excess demand for country 1's bonds to changes in exchange rates. To examine the influence of financial factors, assume that the consumption shares are equal ($a_{12} = a_{13}$). If the demand for country 1's bonds is highly sensitive to the dollar exchange rate (the franc (mark) and dollar financial markets are relatively well integrated so that $(H_{X1}^1 + H_{X2}^1)$ is large relative to $(-H_{X2}^1)$), then the franc will vary mainly against the mark rather than the dollar. The effective exchange rate of the franc then will fall in response to this disturbance. The franc will rise in the opposite case where the member countries' financial markets are highly integrated with one another but not with the dollar market. The relative degree of financial integration between countries 1 and 2 therefore is a crucial factor in determining the movement of s_t^1.

There is an interesting intermediate case where under flexible rates the effective exchange rate of the franc is stable in the face of this disturbance. If the excess demand for H^1 satisfies the condition $-H_{X2}^1 = H_{X1}^1 + H_{X2}^1$, representing the case of no bias in the pattern of financial integration, then increases in the franc price of the dollar will offset declines in the franc price of the mark. Country 1's effective exchange rate, as well as its general price level, will be effectively insulated from this disturbance under flexible rates.

It is clear that in this intermediate case where the effective exchange rate is insulated from the disturbance that the switch to an exchange rate union will actually increase the variability of the franc. By joining the union, country 1 loses the benefits of a negative correlation between the dollar and the mark.

By comparing (6) and (7) we can determine if there are any circumstances in which the union reduces the variability of the effective exchange rate. Consider in turn the cases where s_t^1 rises or falls under flexible rates.

If s_t^1 rises under flexible rates, which can occur if the financial markets of the member countries are relatively well integrated, the franc must vary more in the union than in the flexible regime. s_t^1 rises when the depreciation of the dollar dominates the movement of the effective exchange rate of the franc (that is, the second term in σ_{s1}^2 dominates). But it was shown previously that introduction of the union increases the movement of the dollar relative to the franc so the variability of the effective exchange rate of the franc must be greater in the union.

If s_t^1 falls under flexible rates, it is possible for the union to reduce the variance of s_t^1. The condition for σ_{s1}^2 to be lower in the union is $a_{13}(H_{X1}^1 - H_{X2}^1)/2 < a_{12}(H_{X1}^1 + H_{X2}^1) + a_{13}H_{X2}^1$. s_t^1 falls (the right side of the inequality is positive) if the appreciation of the franc relative to the mark dominates the movement of the effective exchange rate (the term above involving a_{12} dominates). By joining the union, country 1 is able to fix this cross-rate and thereby substitute variability in the franc price of the dollar for variability in the franc price of the mark. As a result the effective exchange rate of the franc may be less variable in the union. As the inequality suggests, this result is more likely the higher the degree of integration between the financial markets of each member country and the dollar market compared with integration between the markets of the member countries and the more important is trade between member countries compared with trade between each member country and country 3.

The conclusion of this analysis is that an exchange rate union benefits one member country but not necessarily the other. The country that is susceptible to capital accounts disturbances must gain as a result of the union, partly because a union stabilizes the important cross-exchange rate between member currencies but also because the union helps to disperse the disturbance into the financial market of the other country. The other country may gain if trade within the union is especially important, but only if financial markets in the absence of the union fail to moderate movements in the cross-exchange rate. Otherwise a union will actually increase the variance of its effective exchange rate.

2. Effects of a Union on Output Variability

In the preceding section, we showed how the two countries in the union fared quite differently following a financial disturbance in one country's market. The analysis was confined to financial markets only; we now expand the analysis to include a real sector determining output and prices. We investigate how formation of the union modifies the impact of the mark-dollar disturbance on output in each member country. Then we analyze a more general type of disturbance originating in the financial markets of both countries and thereby illustrate a diversification effect brought about by the union.

Expanded Model

To determine output, we introduce the following aggregate supply equation for each country

$$y_t^1 = c(p_t^1 - w_t^{1\prime}),$$
$$y_t^2 = c(p_t^2 - w_t^{2\prime}). \tag{9}$$

where $w_t^{i'}$ is the nominal wage in country i fixed in a contract at time $t - 1$ and p_t^i is the current price of country i's output (both expressed as percentage changes from stationary values). This function is derived from a contract model of wage determination based on a Cobb-Douglas production function of the form: $Y_t^i = (L_t^i)^{(1-c')}(K_t^i)^{c'}$, and a labor supply equation of the form $L_t^i = (W_t^i/P_t^i)^n$. After expressing variables as percentage changes (with the capital stock fixed), the model of aggregate supply can be written:

$$y_t^i = (1 - c')l_t^i, \quad \text{output} \tag{9a}$$

$$l_t^i = -(w_t^i - p_t^i)/c', \quad \text{labor demand} \tag{9b}$$

$$l_t^i = n(w_t^i - p_t^i), \quad \text{labor supply} \tag{9c}$$

$$w_t^{i'} = E_{t-1}p_t^i. \quad \text{contract wage} \tag{9d}$$

The contract wage is fixed on the basis of prices expected at time $t - 1$, so unexpected changes in prices at time t give rise to variations in output.

To keep the analysis tractable, we close the model with simple purchasing power parity conditions to determine prices in each country:

$$p_t^1 = p_t^3 + x_t^1,$$

$$p_t^2 = p_t^3 + x_t^2, \tag{10}$$

$$p_t^1 = p_t^2 + x_t^{12}.$$

Assuming that the price of country 3's output is constant (so that $p_t^3 = 0$), the second of these conditions says that a rise in the mark-dollar rate leads to a proportionate rise in the price of country 2's good. The adjustment of p_t^2 then modifies the impact of the disturbance on country 1. This is seen clearly in the third of the PPP conditions. The price of country 2's good in francs, $p_t^2 + x_t^{12}$, responds not only to changes in the cross-exchange rate (as in section 1) but to the rise in p_t^2 as well. In fact, the rise in p_t^2 is large enough to more than offset the appreciation of the franc relative to the mark so that p_t^1 unambiguously rises.

Comparison of Regimes with a Mark-Dollar Disturbance

Once again we consider the effects of a disturbance involving a shift between mark and dollar securities. As before the disturbance leads to a depreciation of both the franc and the mark relative to the dollar and to an appreciation of the franc relative to the mark. We first solve the equations for the exchange rate (1), output (9), and prices (10) to obtain reduced form expressions for all three variables under flexible exchange rates. Since we are interested primarily in output, we present the expressions for y_t^1 and y_t^2 below:

$$y_t^1 = \frac{-cN^{12}}{N}(-u_t^{h2}) > 0,$$

$$y_t^2 = \frac{cN^{11}}{N}(-u_t^{h2}) > 0. \tag{11}$$

where $N^{11} = H_{X1}^1 + J^{11}(1 + c) > 0$, $N^{12} = H_{X2}^1 + J^{12}(1 + c) < 0$, and $N^{11}N^{22} - N^{12}N^{21} > 0$. In response to the disturbance, output rises in both countries, but output rises less in country 1 than in country 2. (It is easy to show that $N^{11} > -N^{12}$.)

Why does output rise unambiguously in country 1? Recall that when prices and output are constant, the franc price of the mark appreciates so that the effective exchange rate of the franc may actually fall. When prices and output are variable, however, the appreciation of the franc relative to the mark is always dominated by the rise in country 2's price so that the price of country 2's good in francs rises, $p_t^2 + x_t^{12} > 0$. Hence country 1's price must rise too, and so also must country 1's output.

In the exchange rate union, intervention modifies the impact of the disturbance much as in the case where prices and output were constant. Country 1 shares the effect of the disturbance equally with country 2 so the two dollar rates rise together. As a result output rises by the same amount in each country:

$$y_t^1 = y_t^2 = \frac{c(N^{11} - N^{12})}{2N}(-u_t^{h2}) > 0. \tag{12}$$

(This equation is obtained by substituting into equation (4) the expressions (9 and 10) for output and prices.) In fact it is evident from this equation that output in the union rises by the average of the changes in output in countries 1 and 2 under flexible rates. The variances of output are therefore related as follows:

$$\sigma_{y1}^2\big|_{\text{flexible}} < \sigma_{y1}^2 = \sigma_{y2}^2\big|_{\text{union}} < \sigma_{y2}^2\big|_{\text{flexible}}.$$

Country 2 unambiguously gains by joining the union since the variance of its output is reduced. Country 1, in contrast, unambiguously loses as a result of joining the union since the variance of its output rises. Unlike the conclusion in the preceding section where financial adjustments alone were considered, this conclusion is unambiguous because the increase in country 2's price dominates the favorable exchange rate appreciation of the franc relative to the mark. Country 1, in effect, no longer can benefit from the negative correlation between exchange rates.

The relative degree of financial integration helps to determine how much more output changes in the union than under flexible rates. Consider country 1's output. We can express the increase in output experienced by country 1 in the union as a percentage of output under flexible rates:

$$\frac{y_t^1|_{\text{union}} - y_t^1|_{\text{flexible}}}{y_t^1|_{\text{flexible}}} = \frac{(N^{11} + N^{12})}{-2N^{12}}. \tag{13}$$

Like the ratio $(H_{X1}^1 + H_{X2}^1)/(-H_{X2}^1)$ in the model of section 1, the ratio $(N^{11} + N^{12})/(-N^{12})$ reflects the relative degree of financial integration between countries 1 and 2.

If the financial markets of the member countries are well integrated only with the dollar market, this ratio is relatively large so the loss for country 1 in joining the union is correspondingly large. To understand why this is true, consider an extreme case where the financial markets of the member countries are tied only to the dollar market. In that case $N^{12} = 0$,[10] so country 1's output is completely insulated from the disturbance under flexible rates. Because there are no direct ties between the mark and franc bond markets, the rise in x_t^2 (depreciation of the mark) has no effect on x_t^1, so the cross-rate x_t^{12} must fall (franc appreciate relative to the mark) as much as x_t^2 rises. With that large an appreciation of the cross-rate, the rise in p_t^2 (which is proportional to x_t^2) is offset completely so p_t^1 (and hence y_t^1) are insulated from the disturbance. By joining the union, country 1 loses the insulation provided by the cross-exchange rate.

The more integrated are the financial markets of countries 1 and 2, on the other hand, the less difference the union makes to output variability. So while the relative degree of financial integration does not determine whether country 1 gains or loses from the union, it does determine how much country 1 loses (and country 2 gains). Notice that these results are quite different from those in section 1 where, in the case of relatively high integration with the dollar market, the union was advantageous to country 1. With output varying, higher integration with the dollar market makes the union even more undesirable for country 1.

Capital Account Disturbances in Both Countries

We have shown that the union increases the variability of output in country 1 when mark-dollar disturbances are important. The mark-dollar disturbance may be the prevalent form of financial disturbance in the EMS, but it is useful to consider a more general form of disturbance, which originates in the financial markets of both member countries. When capital account disturbances originate in the financial market of only one member country, an exchange rate union disperses the effects of the disturbances to the financial market of the other member country. If both countries experience capital account disturbances, in contrast, there may not seem to be any benefits from union for either country. Yet if the disturbances in each market are not perfectly correlated, both member countries can benefit from a union.

Assume that the disturbances represent shifts out of the bonds of the member countries and into dollar bonds, u_t^{h1}, $u_t^{h2} < 0$. The variances of these disturbances are assumed to be equal, $\sigma_{h1}^2 = \sigma_{h2}^2$, but the covariance between them, σ_{h12}, may be positive or negative. The variances of output in the two exchange rate regimes are as follows. For flexible exchange rates, they are:

$$\sigma_{y1}^2 = \frac{c^2}{N^2}[(N^{22})^2\sigma_{h1}^2 + (N^{12})^2\sigma_{h2}^2 - 2N^{12}N^{22}\sigma_{h12}],$$

$$\sigma_{y2}^2 = \frac{c^2}{N^2}[(N^{21})^2\sigma_{h1}^2 + (N^{11})^2\sigma_{h2}^2 - 2N^{21}N^{11}\sigma_{h12}].$$
(14)

For exchange rate unions, they are:

$$\sigma_{y1}^2 = \sigma_{y2}^2 = \frac{c^2}{N^2}\left[\frac{(N^{12})^2 + (N^{11})^2 - 2N^{12}N^{11}}{4}\right](\sigma_{h1}^2 + \sigma_{h2}^2 + 2\sigma_{h12}). \quad (15)$$

These equations are obtained by solving equations (9), (10), and either (1) or (4) depending on the regime, for output as a function of both disturbances and calculating the variances of the resulting expressions.

It is easy to show that

$$\sigma_{yi}^2|_{\text{flexible}} > \sigma_{yi}^2|_{\text{union}} \text{ as long as } \sigma_{h12} < \sigma_{hi}^2.$$

Both members benefit from the union by reducing the variances of their output as long as the disturbances are less than perfectly correlated. By joining the union, the two countries gain from a diversification effect by which one disturbance is offset against another. With a symmetrical rather than an asymmetrical pattern of disturbances, the exchange rate union is beneficial to both countries.

3. Conclusion

Exchange rate unions are attractive to many countries because they shield bilateral exchange rates from financial disturbances, which could otherwise disrupt trading relationships of importance to the member countries. In fixing these bilateral rates, however, countries implicitly elect to share the effects of disturbances that otherwise might impinge directly on only one country. As a result some countries may find themselves worse off in a union.

This chapter has focused on one disturbance, which has been particularly important in the EMS, a disturbance arising from portfolio shifts between dollar and mark securities. Under flexible exchange rates such a disturbance leads indirectly to fluctuations in the bilateral rates between the mark and other European currencies. Such changes in bilateral rates are undesirable in themselves, but the remedy offered by the union may be worse than the disease, at least for the country not directly affected by the disturbance. We showed that formation of the union helps to stabilize the effective exchange rate of the country directly affected by the disturbance but not necessarily the effective rate of the other country. The union stabilizes the latter rate only if the financial markets of the union members have a relatively low degree of integration in the absence of the union. We then extended the analysis to include a real sector and showed that the union reduces the variability of output for the country directly affected by the disturbance but necessarily raises the variability of output of the other country. The union in effect disperses the disturbance so that it is shared equally by both countries.

Finally we analyzed a different type of disturbance, which shows the union in a better light. This is a general disturbance involving shifts between dollar securities and those of each of the member countries. If the shifts are less than perfectly correlated, both countries benefit from a diversification effect in joining the union. The sharing of the disturbance in this case results in a lower variance of output for both countries.

Appendix 12A Explicit Solution of the Financial Model

When the equilibrium conditions for the money and bond markets of countries 1 and 2 as given in table 12.2 are linearized around their equilibrium values, the result is expression (1) in the text. The coefficients in this expression are given below with their assumed signs:[11]

$$H_{X1}^1 = \left(h^{11}(\cdot) - h_Y^{11} \frac{P_0^1 Y_0^1}{V_0^1} \right) (X_0^{12} H_0^{21} + X_0^1 F_0^1) + X_0^{12} V_0^2 h^{12}(\cdot)$$

$$- \left[h^{12}(\cdot) - h_Y^{12} \frac{P_0^2 Y_0^2}{V_0^2} \right] H_0^{12} - V_0^1 (h_2^{11} + h_3^{11}) + X_0^{12} V_0^2 h_1^{12} > 0.$$

$$H_{X2}^1 = - \left(h^{11}(\cdot) - h_Y^{11} \frac{P_0^1 Y_0^1}{V_0^1} \right) X_0^{12} H_0^{21} - X_0^{12} V_0^2 h^{12}(\cdot)$$

$$+ X_0^{12} \left[h^{12}(\cdot) - h_Y^{12} \frac{P_0^2 Y_0^2}{V_0^2} \right] \left[X_0^2 F_0^2 + \frac{H_0^{12}}{X_0^{12}} \right] + V_0^1 h_2^{11}$$

$$- X_0^{12} V_0^2 (h_1^{12} + h_3^{12}) < 0.[2]$$

$$J^{11} = - \frac{P_0^1 Y_0^1}{V_0^1} \left[V_0^1 m_Y^1 \frac{(V_0^1 h_1^{11} + X_0^{12} V_0^2 h_1^{12})}{V_0^1 m_1^1} - V_0^1 h_Y^{11} \right] > 0.$$

$$J^{12} = - \frac{P_0^2 Y_0^2}{V_0^2} \left[V_0^2 m_Y^2 \frac{(V_0^1 h_2^{11} + X_0^{12} V_0^2 h_2^{12})}{V_0^2 m_2^2} - X_0^{12} V_0^2 h_Y^{12} \right] < 0.$$

Because financial behavior in the two countries is assumed to be identical, $H_{X1}^1 = H_{X2}^2$, $H_{X2}^1 = H_{X1}^2$, $J^{11} = J^{22}$, and $J^{12} = J^{21}$.

Notes

I would like to thank my colleagues at the Institute for Advanced Studies in Vienna for their helpful comments on an earlier draft. Financial support from a German Marshall Fund Fellowship and a National Science Foundation grant (SES — 8006414) is gratefully acknowledged.

1. The terminology is potentially confusing. In this study, the term *exchange rate union* refers to an arrangement in which member countries of the union maintain fixed exchange rates between member currencies, but with each country retaining its own central bank with control over its national monetary policy. This limited type of union, which Corden (1972:3) calls a "pseudo-exchange-rate union," is to be distinguished from a "complete exchange rate union," or monetary union, with a single central bank and a union-wide currency.

2. Gaston Thorn, president of the European Commission, for example, has pointed to "large-scale flows of short-term speculative capital between the U.S. dollar and the German mark"

as a specific cause of strains within the EMS. "Dollar Sustains Rise on Europe's Markets," *International Herald-Tribune*, May 18, 1983.

3. Tower and Willett (1976) provide a comprehensive survey of the literature on optimum currency areas, which examines the conditions necessary for successful exchange rate or monetary unions; McKinnon (1963) and Mundell (1961) are two classic contributions to this literature. Some recent studies have used more formal models to analyze unions than previously. Canzoneri (1982) examines an exchange rate union as part of his study of foreign exchange intervention in two and three country settings, while Marston (1984) analyzes real and monetary disturbances in exchange rate unions but, unlike here, in a model where perfect asset substitutability is assumed.

4. Henderson (1977) has a similar formulation of transactions demand. For previous models of financial behavior with imperfect substitutability, see Branson (1977), Girton and Henderson (1977), and Herring and Marston (1977).

5. The assumption of identical behavior does not require that country 1 hold equal amounts of its initial wealth in country 1 and country 2 bonds, only that its initial holdings of country 1 (2) bonds be equal to country 2's initial holdings of country 2 (1) bonds.

6. This assumption is reasonable if money is dominated in the portfolio by interest-bearing assets and therefore is held primarily for transactions purposes.

7. All of the inequalities follow from the assumptions made earlier with the exception of that for H_{X2}^1, which requires additional assumptions detailed in appendix 12A.

8. Later we consider a more general type of financial disturbance affecting the bond markets of both member countries.

9. Since the two member countries are assumed to be identical, country 2 has a higher degree of financial integration with country 3 than with country 1.

10. All of the terms in N^{12} involve holdings of one member country's bonds by the other member country, so $N^{12} = 0$ when these cross-holdings are eliminated.

11. The derivatives of the money demand functions in table 12.2 are denoted by m_Y^i, m_1^i, m_2^i, m_3^i for the four arguments of those functions, respectively; a similar notation is used for the bond demand functions.

12. H_{X2}^1 is assumed to be negative. Sufficient conditions for H_{X2}^1 to be negative are (a) $h_1^{12} + h_3^{12} \geq 0$, an equal rise in R_t^1 and R_t^3 leads to a rise (or no change) in country 2's demand for country 1's bonds; and (b)

$$1 - \frac{h_y^{12}}{h^{12}(\cdot)} \frac{P_0^2 Y_0^2}{V_0^2} < \frac{V_0^2}{(X_0^2 F_0^2 + H_0^{12}/X_0^{12}}$$,

the wealth elasticity of country 2's demand for 1's bond is less than the ratio of total wealth to wealth held in foreign assets (a ratio greater than unity). H_{X2}^1 could be negative under much weaker conditions since the other terms in the expression above are negative.

References

Branson, William H. 1977. Asset markets and relative prices in exchange rate determination. *Sozialwissenschaftliche Annalen* 1.

Canzoneri, Matthew B. 1982. Exchange intervention policy in a multiple country world. *Journal of International Economics* 13:267–289.

Corden, W. M. 1972. *Monetary Integration*. Essays in International Finance 93. Princeton.

Girton, Lance, and Dale Henderson. 1977. Central bank operations in foreign and domestic assets under fixed and flexible exchange rates. In *The Effects of Exchange Rate Adjustments*, P. Clark et al., eds. Washington, D.C.: U.S. Treasury.

Henderson, Dale. 1977. Modelling the interdependence of national money and capital markets. *American Economic Review* 67:190–199.

Herring, Richard J., and Richard C. Marston. 1977. *National Monetary Policies and International Financial Markets*. Contributions to Economic Analysis 104. Amsterdam: North-Holland.

Ingram, James C. 1973. *The Case for European Monetary Integration*. Essays in International Finance 98. Princeton.

McKinnon, Ronald I. 1963. Optimum currency areas. *American Economic Review* 53:717–725.

Marston, Richard C. 1984. Exchange-rate unions as an alternative to flexible exchange rates. In *Exchange Rate Theory and Practice*, J. F. O. Bilson and R. C. Marston, eds. Cambridge: National Bureau of Economic Research.

Mundell, Robert A. 1961. A theory of optimum currency areas. *American Economic Review* 51:657–665.

Tower, Edward, and Thomas D. Willett. 1976. *The Theory of Optimum Currency Areas*. Special Papers in International Economics 11. Princeton.

List of Contributors

Michael J. Artis
Department of Economics
University of Manchester
Manchester, England

Jagdeep S. Bhandari
Department of Economics
West Virginia University

Stanley W. Black
Department of Economics
University of North Carolina

Willem H. Buiter
London School of Economics
London, England

Matthew B. Canzoneri
International Finance Section
Federal Reserve Board
Washington, D.C.

Nicholas Carlozzi
J. J. Lowrey and Co.
New York, New York

Robert Driskill
Department of Economics
Ohio State University

Jonathan Eaton
Department of Economics
University of Virginia

Robert P. Flood
Department of Economics
Northwestern University

Robert J. Hodrick
Kellogg School of Management
Northwestern University

E. Karakitsos
Department of Electrical
Engineering
Imperial College of Science and
Technology
London, England

Stephen A. McCafferty
Department of Economics
Ohio State University

Richard C. Marston
Department of Finance
University of Pennsylvania

Michael L. Mussa
Graduate School of Business
University of Chicago

Jerome L. Stein
Department of Economics
Brown University

John B. Taylor
Department of Economics
Stanford University

Stephen J. Turnovsky
Department of Economics
University of Illinois

John M. Underwood
International Finance Section
Federal Reserve Board
Washington, D.C.

Index